THE QUILTER'S CATALOG

THE QUILTER'S CATALOG

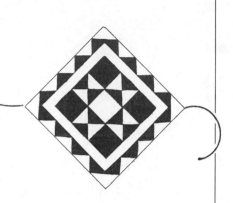

by
Vicki Brooks
and
Linda Stokes

Peter Greif,
General Editor

THE MAIN STREET PRESS • PITTSTOWN, NEW JERSEY

First edition 1987

Published by
The Main Street Press
William Case House
Pittstown, New Jersey 08867

Published simultaneously in Canada by
Methuen Publications
2330 Midland Avenue
Agincourt, Ontario M1S 1P7

Printed in the United States of America
10 9 8 7 6 5 4 3 2 1

Cover design by Robert Reed
Text design by Frank Mahood

Library of Congress Cataloging-in-Publication Data

Brooks, Vicki.
  The quilter's catalog.

  Bibliography: p.
  1. Quilting—United States—Equipment and supplies—
Directories. I. Stokes, Linda. II. Title.
TT835.B726 1987   746.9'7'02573   86-23657
ISBN 0-55562-004-3
ISBN 0-55562-003-5 (pbk.)

Table of Contents

Intro-
duction

The need for a comprehensive one-volume guide to quilting supplies, design sources, publications, services, shows, and collections has long been apparent. Because quilt making has grown so phenomenally as a leisure activity in the 1980s, it has been difficult to keep up with all the new products and programs which have accompanied this growth. And after two years of careful research and documentation, let us assure you that the task of compiling *The Quilter's Catalog* has not been easy! But it has been very challenging and rewarding to consider so much interesting material. We are confident that this book is as complete and as useful a source for the quilter as can be found.

The Quilter's Catalog does not contain advertising. Every item and service included has been chosen for its utility and its appropriateness. Thousands of questionnaires were mailed and telephone calls were made over many months to secure information on the most interesting and useful material. Early on, we made a decision to include only those firms and individuals who responded to our inquiries, who shared our own enthusiasm for quilts and quilting. If they did not respond to our requests, it is even more likely that they would not answer yours.

Central to the search for the best quilting materials and information are the many hundreds of local shops which provide almost daily service to the quilter. A good number of these businesses will fill orders by mail. Their names and addresses are included in an appendix at the end of this book. Without their help, it would have been impossible to provide as complete a picture of the quilting scene.

Manufacturers and craftsmen who offer special products and services were another important source of information for us. These firms can be of great help to quilters who live in areas far distant from a quilting shop, as their products are often available by mail directly to the consumer. If your favorite shop doesn't carry their products, therefore, you might want to write directly to the manufacturer for descriptive literature. As is the case with many quilt shop brochures and catalogs, some

of these companies request that you send a self-addressed, stamped envelope (SASE) with your inquiry. We have indicated where one is required—a #10 envelope is preferable in most cases.

In all discussions of products—whether tools, fabrics and batting, kits, or gift items—we have excluded prices (except for descriptive literature, books, and swatch samples). It was our decision to eliminate them because they are subject to change at the producer's whim. We hope you'll use the information listed to order as many brochures and catalogs as suit your fancy.

Completing special sections of *The Quilter's Catalog* — among them Good Reading, The World of Quilting, and Touring the Museums—required our particular attention. We believe you will find the chapter on books and periodicals the most up-to-date survey of quilting literature available. It does, of course, reflect those books and magazines we consider to be truly worthwhile. The World of Quilting presents information on organizations furthering the art of quilting. It, too, is selective, including only those groups who shared their interest in quilt making with us. Touring the Museums covers the rapidly growing movement by historical societies and fine arts institutions to preserve and document our quilting heritage. We hope that you will take the time to visit and support those collections in your area.

With this first *Quilter's Catalog* now complete, we want to encourage you to share your interests and discoveries with us. We recognize that our job has really only just begun. If there is a group, a new product, an interesting museum collection, an essential book that deserves a place in a future edition of *The Quilter's Catalog*, drop us a line in care of The Main Street Press.

No project of this scope is possible without the enthusiasm and support of many people. We would like to acknowledge the tireless efforts of our general editor, Peter Greif, in whipping thousands of pieces of material into shape. Frank Mahood and John Fox spent countless hours on the attractive design; Mariann Arnitz and Martin Greif, on editing reams of copy. We thank them all.

THE QUILTER'S CATALOG

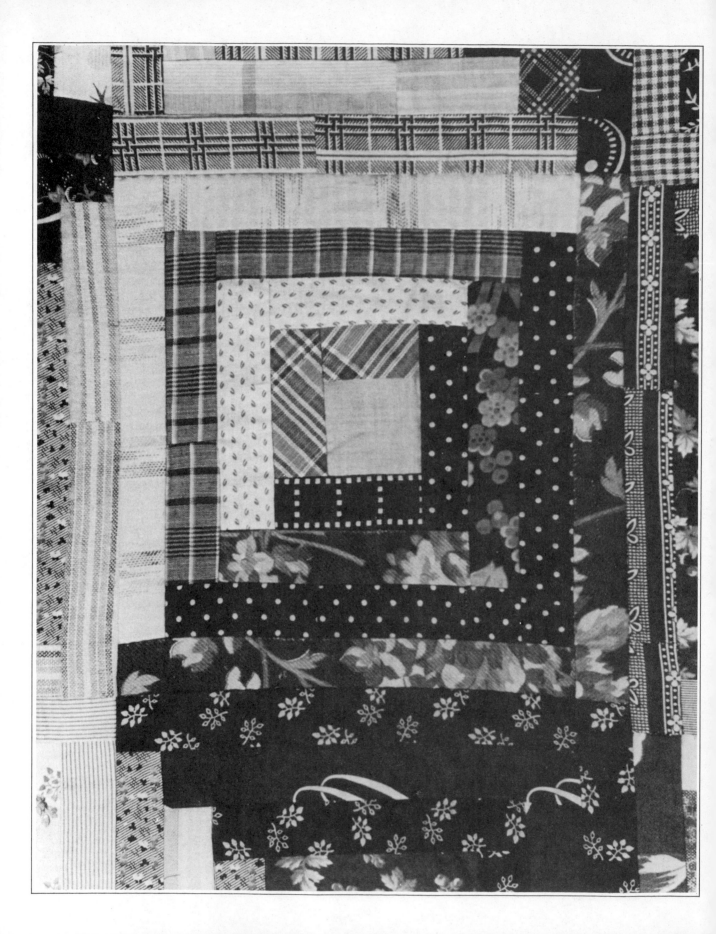

1. Starting with the Basics: Fabrics and Batting

As an avid quilter, you are probably always on the lookout for new fabrics to add to your scrap basket, whether you are currently involved in a project or are simply hoarding bits and pieces against the time when you will be able to begin a new one. You probably haunt your local fabric and quilt shops to check on new arrivals, but you may want to search farther afield. Listed here are many shops which, in addition to selling fabrics and batting on a retail basis to local customers, will mail orders promptly and efficiently. Most offer swatch collections of their current stock for a minimal charge. For even more convenience, some package pre-cut fabrics in a wide range of colors, prints, and sizes.

When ordering by mail, it is best to respond promptly after the receipt of the swatches. Dye lots tend to change from bolt to bolt, and manufacturers discontinue fabrics with little or no warning. Most shops will not accept returns of cut fabrics, so measure carefully, and make sure that you really like your selections. (You could swap leftovers with fellow quilters, or save them for your scrap basket.)

Many experienced quilters recommend the use of only natural fabrics—cotton, wool, linen, silk—for durability, ease of stitching, and color clarity. No matter what fabrics you are using, it always makes sense to prewash them before measuring and cutting to check colorfastness and avoid possible shrinkage.

When you are ready to put your quilt together, there are numerous types of batting available for filler, including polyester, wool, and cotton, all offered in many sizes. Many fabric and batting suppliers also stock muslin in suitable widths for backing the finished quilt.

THE BRASS GOOSE. Both at its retail shop and by mail, The Brass Goose specializes in cottons from such well-known manufacturers as Spring Mills, Wamsutta, and Concord. Several hundred separate prints and solids are generally available, but the company cautions that the quilter should order all fabric needed for a particular project at the same time since dye lots tend to change and patterns or colors can be discontinued by the manufacturer. Introductory packet of 250 swatches with catalog, $3. Quarterly update of twenty new fabrics, $4 per year.

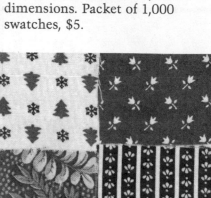

Brewer Fabric Shop
Twin City Plaza
Brewer, ME 04412
(207) 989-2564

pling bound to please even the most demanding quilter. In addition to Mountain Mist and Yours Truly batting in sizes ranging from a 12"-square pillow to a 120" by 120" quilt, the shop carries cotton batting in 81" by 96" and 81" by 108" dimensions. Packet of 1,000 swatches, $5.

The Brass Goose
328 S. Royal Ave.
Front Royal, VA 22630
(703) 636-6266

BREWER FABRIC SHOP. Among the 1,100 bolts of cotton fabric stocked at this Maine shop are selections from Concord, Ameritex, VIP, and Peter Pan. To aid in your selection, Brewer Fabric Shop will send a packet of more than 1,000 swatches—a sam-

BUFFALO BATT & FELT. Buffalo Batt & Felt manufactures polyester batting in a wide variety of sizes. Quilt batts are offered in twin, double, king/queen, and crib sizes, or can be ordered by the yard in 50" widths for odd-size projects. Pillow inserts come in 14", 16", and 18" squares. Dupont Quallofil pillow inserts, comparable to down in softness, are available in the same sizes and in larger 20" and 24" squares. The company will fill mail orders; its products are also available at quilt shops throughout North America. Brochure and swatches, $1.

Buffalo Batt & Felt
3307 Walden Ave.
Depew, NY 14043
(716) 688-7100

CABIN FEVER CALICOES. Pure cotton solids in over 200 colors of quilt-weight cloth are a specialty at Cabin Fever Calicoes. Devotees of Amish quilting will appreciate the company's prepackaged Amish Fabric Paks, available in three different color tones—greens and blues, reds and purples, or blacks and browns. Each pack can be ordered in quarter-yard, half-yard, or full-yard sizes. In addition, Cabin Fever Calicoes stocks unusual woven homespun in twenty-two different patterns. Homespun or cotton swatches are $2, a complete catalog, $1, and a catalog with selected swatches, $2.75.

Cabin Fever Calicoes
54 Range Rd.
Center Sandwich, NH 03227
(603) 284-6690

CALICO HOUSE. Featuring an extensive selection of cotton calico prints and solids, muslins, and batting, Calico House's retail shop is located in a rural Virginia village. If you don't happen to live within reach, the shop's owners, Polly and Bruce Hogshead, will be glad to send your order by mail. Brochure available at no charge.

Calico House
State Rt. 737
Rt. 4, Box 16
Scottsville, VA 24590
(804) 286-2979

THE CLOTH CUPBOARD. Unusual Japanese wood-block prints in subtle color combinations are a specialty at The Cloth Cupboard. The 100% cotton prints are 45″ wide. Bleached and unbleached muslin, also pure cotton, comes in hard-to-find widths of 90″ and 108″, making both ideal for quilt backs. More than two dozen large swatches of the Japanese prints are offered by The Cloth Cupboard for $2.50; descriptive literature is available for a self-addressed, stamped envelope.

The Cloth Cupboard
P.O. Box 2263
Boise, ID 83701
(208) 345-5567

COMMUNITY QUILTS. Over 100 solid-color cottons and 50 solid chintzes comprise the swatch collection available by mail from Community Quilts. The cottons are from 45″-wide bolts; the chintzes, from bolts which range from 45″ to 54″ wide. Swatches and a special mail-order newsletter, $2.

Community Quilts
7710 Woodmont Ave.
Bethesda, MD 20814
(301) 654-7763

COUNTRY HOUSE QUILTS. Country chintz and reproduction homespun, both in 48″ widths, are stocked in profusion at Country House Quilts. The supplier also carries Yours Truly and Fairfield batting in all sizes and shapes, and offers calicoes, denims, and linens in many prints and colors. Brochure with samples, $1.

Country House Quilts
170 S. Main
Zionsville, IN 46077
(317) 873-2828

COUNTRY HOUSE
QUILTS
873-2828
170 S. MAIN
ZIONSVILLE, IND.
46077

THE COTTON PATCH. As its name implies, The Cotton Patch specializes in 100% cotton fabrics. Its swatch assortment contains more than 350 pieces grouped by type, from cotton solids to large and small prints, stripes, and plaids. An unusual offering at The Cotton Patch is a special collection of eleven different Amish fabric kits. Each color grouping was coordinated by Roberta Horton for use in her book, *An Amish Adventure*, and includes five half-yard pieces of solid cotton with similar color tones. Choose from black, purple, gray, green, burgundy, and other hues. Catalog and fabric swatches, $3.

The Cotton Patch
1025 Brown Ave.
Lafayette, CA 94549
(415) 284-1177

FAIRFIELD PROCESSING CORP. A cotton and polyester blend makes Fairfield's Poly-fil Cotton Classic Batting ideal for quilters. The batting is blended in such a way that it resists bunching up; the 80% cotton blend facilitates smooth passage of your needle through the fabric. Fairfield's Poly-fil batting is available in a range of sizes

and fullnesses by the package or in rolls by the yard. Look for it at most quilt and fabric stores, or contact the company for a dealer near you.

Fairfield Processing Corp.
P.O. Box 1130
Danbury, CT 06813
(203) 744-2090

G STREET FABRICS. Any quilter looking for hard-to-find fabrics in the natural fibers—silk, cotton, wool, and linen—should investigate the wide assortment carried by G Street Fabrics. The firm offers Portfolio Sample Charts of linens, cotton prints, woolens, silks, and other fabrics for $10 per chart (the price is applicable towards your first order). An unusual custom sample service is also offered. If you provide information such as fabric type, colors, and amount of material needed (send design sketches or photos if you like, or swatches of complementary materials you are planning to use), G Street will send a set of sample swatches chosen according to your specifications. Fee for selection service, $1. Brochure available at no charge.

G Street Fabrics
11854 Rockville Pike
Rockville, MD 20852
(302) 231-8998

GUTCHEON PATCHWORKS. In addition to providing a wide range of pure cotton prints and solids carefully selected from other manufacturers' offerings, Gutcheon Patchworks offers its own American Classic line of fabric, specially designed with quilters

in mind. Plain cottons, cotton prints, and polished cottons are always available, all in 44/45″ widths. Gutcheon also stocks top quality muslin for backing, and Swiss Metrosene 100% cotton quilting thread for putting it all together. A swatch set is available for $2; Gutcheon sells

all of its fabrics by mail order and offers a bonus of two free yards of fabric for every ten yards ordered.

Gutcheon Patchworks, Inc.
P.O. Box 57, Prince St. Sta.
New York, NY 10012
(212) 505-0305

HEARTFELT. The quality wool batting manufactured by Heartfelt is tailor-made for quilters: it comes in 90″ widths, so there is no need to piece it, and it is specially "needlepunched" — a technique that prevents shifting and lumping. Wool's lightness and insulating qualities make it ideal for quilt batting; Heartfelt recommends that your fabrics be chosen from natural fibers such as cotton, linen, and silk, and that you use a thread count of no less than 180 threads per square inch. To assure longevity, your finished quilt should be aired frequently and dry cleaned

when needed. Brochure and batting sample, $2.

Heartfelt
R.F.D. 340
Vineyard Haven, MA 02568
(607) 693-1483

Heartfelt
3053 Shattuck Ave.
Berkeley, CA 94705
(415) 843-3013

HEARTFELT
100% WOOL BATTING™

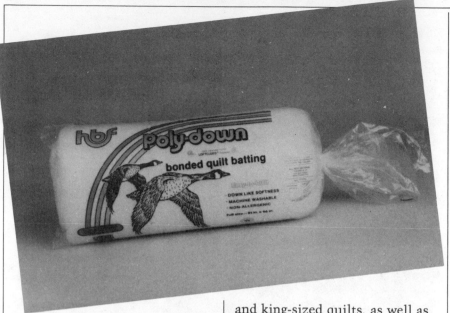

HOBBS BONDED FIBERS. The newest quilt batting offered by Hobbs is called Poly-Down. Made of Celanese Fortrel Loft-guard polyester, it is designed to retain air and to resist packing even after many washings. Hobbs sells Poly-Down by the yard and in pre-measured packages for twin, full, queen, and king-sized quilts, as well as in covered pillow inserts for smaller quilt projects. Poly-Down is sold in most quilt and fabric shops; brochure and sample available for SASE.

Hobbs Bonded Fibers
Craft Products Division
P.O. Box 151
Groesbeck, TX 76642
(817) 792-3223

INVERNESS FABRICS. Inverness specializes in first-quality 100% cotton prints and solids in 44/45″ widths. All are available by mail order (minimum cut is ½ yard; minimum order, one yard). White and natural muslin (90″ wide) is also offered, as is white or natural quilting thread in 250-yard spools. Inverness carries Mountain Mist batts in 81″ by 96″ sizes. Swatches and order form, $1.

Inverness Fabrics
1142 Quarry Rd.
Caledonia, NY 14423
(716) 538-6284

JOSEPH'S COAT. This New England shop specializes in unusual natural-fiber fabrics for quilts and creative clothing. If you specify the type of fabric you need, the staff of Joseph's Coat will personally select swatches for you. Specify cotton velveteens, cotton corduroys, Guatemalan ikat and stripes, Liberty and Italian pimas, solid polished cottons, or oriental wood-block prints. The charge is $1 for each type of fabric. A brochure about the store's many other offerings is available for no charge.

Joseph's Coat
26 Main St.
Peterborough, NH 03458
(603) 924-6683

MAPLE SPRINGS FARM. Robert and Sandra Rego, owners of Maple Springs Farm, offer wool batting from a truly primary source—their own flock of sheep. Batting for hand quilting comes in crib, twin, full, queen, and king sizes, each made in one large piece and rolled with tissue paper between layers for easy unfolding. Each order comes with care instructions. In addition, Maple Springs Farm has pillow-top wool filler in 12″, 14″, and 15″ squares. A catalog with many handy quilting tips, and a batting sample, are available for $1.

Maple Springs Farm
Dept. QC
1828 Hwy. PB
Verona, WI 53593
(608) 845-9482

MOUNTAIN MIST. Whether you are looking for polyester batting or prefer the more traditional look of pure cotton, Mountain Mist will undoubtedly have just what you need. The company has been producing 100% bleached cotton batting since 1846. Its polyester batting comes in standard sizes for all manner of quilt projects, and the Fatt Batt—over twice as thick as regular batting—is ideal for machine quilting of patterns such as Log Cabin and for projects such as crib quilts that may require repeated laundering. Mountain Mist products are widely available at quilt shops throughout North America or by mail. Catalog available at no charge.

Mountain Mist
The Stearns Technical Textiles
*　　Co.*
100 Williams St.
Cincinnati, OH 45215
(800) 543-7173

NORTON HOUSE. Norton House has recently expanded its selection of 100% cotton calicoes to more than 2,000 different prints and solids. For quilters lucky enough to live in the area, the shop boasts a large remnant table of fabrics—an ideal way to add to the scrap bag. If you're too far away, you'll appreciate being able to order special assortments of 4½″ or 6½″ square calico patches in your choice of varied color prints or specified color hues of blues, browns, greens, yellows, and pinks. Norton House has also put together packages of twenty-five cotton prints in ⅛-yard pieces; the package comes in assorted colors or in browns or blues. Mail order catalog, $1. Catalog with 350 swatches, $3.

Norton House
P.O. Box 578
1836 Country Store Village
Wilmington, VT 05363
(802) 464-7213

PATCHES. A mail-order fabric company specializing in cut squares of quality name-brand fabrics, Patches makes up sets of fifty cut squares in assorted patterns and colors and in sizes ranging from 4″ to 10″ squares. Calicoes, solids, velveteens, and corduroys are offered. Custom color selections are available in cut squares by special order; Patches will also custom-cut special colors, shapes, and sizes for you. Many of the cotton fabrics used in Patches' assortments are also available by the yard. Brochure available for SASE.

Patches
P.O. Box 140
Dalton, MA 01226
(413) 499-3043

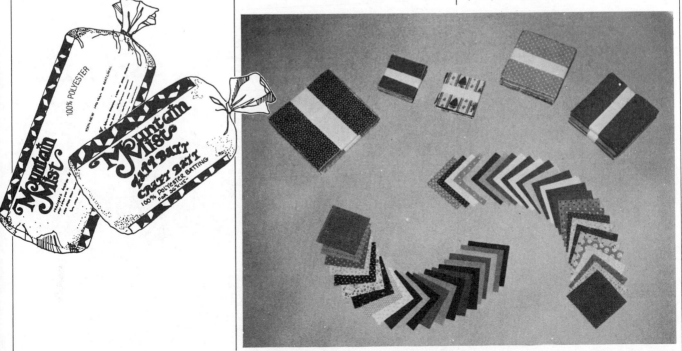

QUILT PATCH. The Quilt Patch carries over 500 bolts of 100% cotton calicoes and solids in its rural Pennsylvania shop. (Swatches are available if you wish to order by mail.) Several makes and grades of polyester batting for quilts and comforters are offered, including Fairfield and Mountain Mist; any size required can be cut from the large rolls kept on hand. Also featured are bleached and unbleached cotton muslins in several widths (including a 108″-wide cotton/polyester

PLUMHILL FARM. Plumhill Farm, a family-run enterprise with its own "modest" flock of sheep, offers wool quilt batting in two thicknesses and in crib, twin, double, queen, and king sizes, along with an unusually wide double size (80″ by 90″). The farm's batting is available only by mail; a brochure and samples are offered for $2, refundable with order.

Plumhill Farm
W9418 Woodside Rd.
Cambridge, WI 53523
(608) 423-4425

PUTNAM COMPANY. Manufacturers of Soft Shapes polyester batting in all popular quilt and craft sizes, the Putnam Company also makes pillow forms in a large selection of sizes and shapes including squares, rounds, rectangles, and hearts. Each form is filled with plump and resilient polyester fiber and is covered with a bleached white muslin case, so all you have to do is create the quilted cover for it. Putnam's products are offered at quilting and craft stores nationwide; or contact the company for the dealer nearest you.

Putnam Company, Inc.
P.O. Box 310
Walworth, WI 53184
(414) 275-2104

blend suitable for backing a large quilt). Catalog, $2.

The Quilt Patch
1897 Hanover Pike
Littlestown, PA 17340
(717) 359-5940

SEMINOLE SAMPLER. Quilters in search of solid-color cottons would do well to check the selection available at Seminole Sampler. More than 200 different cotton solids are carried (most of which are represented in the store's swatch packet). A special treat and an aid to busy quilters are the Seminole Sampler "parfaits"—a dazzling array of pre-cut fabric packets (½ yard per fabric) of color-co-ordinated cottons. There are thirty-five separate parfaits to choose from. And to make your quilting even easier, the shop staff will custom match your choices (you must send fabric sample) to the right mercerized cotton threads. Catalog, $2. Swatches, $2.65 per set.

Seminole Sampler
Savage Mill
Savage, MD 20763
(301) 792-8240

QUILTS & OTHER COMFORTS. More than 200 prints and solids, all first quality 100% cotton from major manufacturers, are in stock at any given time at Quilts & Other Comforts. Swatches of all current fabrics can be ordered for $1.50. A most attractive feature of the company's mail order catalog is its selection of fabric packets. The Super Charm Quilt Scrap Packet contains die-cut 5″ squares of 143 different prints in pairs— enough fabric for a 67″ by 85″ pieced quilt. Twelve separate fabric packets, each containing ten different printed fabrics in ¼-yard lengths, range from light pastels to multicolored bright tones. They can be mixed or matched to twelve different ¼-yard lengths of solid fabrics in either light or dark hues. Catalog, $1.25.

Quilts & Other Comforts
Box 394-3
6700 W. 44th Ave.
Wheatridge, CO 80034
(303) 420-4272

SILVER THIMBLE QUILT SHOP. The Silver Thimble carries more than 700 separate cotton calico prints and solids at any given time; of these, 300 to 400 are included in its swatch packet. If you have a hard time choosing just the right fabrics or haven't the time to measure and cut the countless shapes required for a pieced quilt, you may be interested in one of the shop's packs of fabric squares. Each pack contains 100 squares of assorted mini-prints and calicoes in a choice of 2″, 3″, 4″, 5″, and 6″ dimensions. Solid-color cotton squares (6″) come in packs of 100 or 50 assorted colors. Catalog, $1.50; swatches, $3.

The Silver Thimble Quilt Shop
Rt. 1, Lafayette Rd.
Hampton Falls, NH 03844
(603) 926-3378

TUMBLEWEED. Thousands of cotton calicoes are on hand at Tumbleweed. The shop updates its mail-order catalog several times a year, and its swatch collection is unusually complete. The proprietors note that, while most of their fabrics are pure cotton, a few polycotton blends are sometimes included for variety. No matter the fabric composition or size of your quilting project, you'll probably find the batting you need at Tumbleweed. The shop sells polyester batting by the yard in 47″, 97″, and 108″ widths and in thicknesses ranging from ¼″ to 3″. Catalog, $1.75.

Tumbleweed
99 Mt. Auburn St.
Cambridge, MA 02138
(617) 492-3279

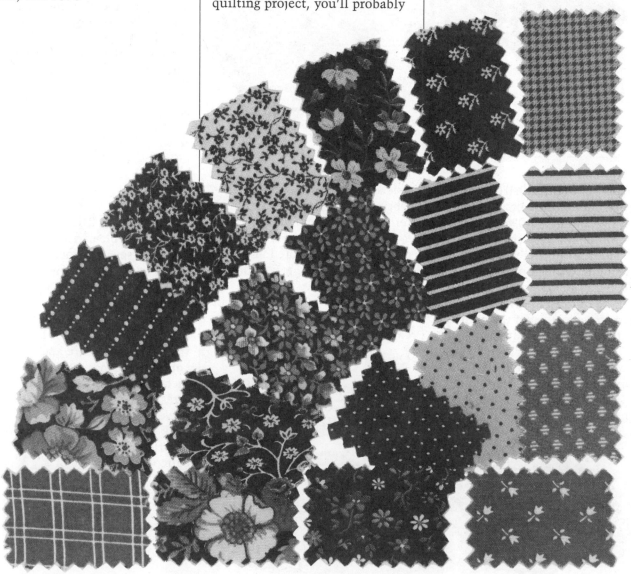

WOODSTOCK WOOL COMPANY.
One of the obvious advantages of wool batting is its warmth. There are less obvious but equally practical advantages for the quilter, according to the proprietors of Woodstock Wool Company. Wool batting is easy to work with—it doesn't lump or shift, or dull needles. Woodstock wool is scoured, picked, and carded with no abrasive chemical washes or treatments. The resulting batting is layered (usually to about ½" thickness). If you prefer thinner batting, simply start at one end and unroll a layer or two until you reach the desired thickness. Woodstock Wool's batting is offered in crib, twin, double, queen, and king sizes. Brochure and sample, $1.

Other Suppliers of Fabrics and Batting

Consult Directory of Suppliers for Addresses

Air Lite Synthetics Mfg., Inc., Pontiac, MI
Best Cottons & Calicoes, Gloucester, MA
Calico 'n Things, Marquette, MI
Chantilly Boutique, Austin, TX
Come Quilt with Me, Brooklyn, NY
Country Crafts & Fabrications, Folsom, CA
Cross Patch Quilting Center, Garrison, NY
Dorr Mill Store, Guild, NH
Hearthside Quilts, Shelburne, VT
Sandy Hunter, Inc., Hendersonville, NC

Needleart Guild, Grand Rapids, MI
Patience Corner Quilt Shop, Portsmouth, NH
Patterns by Jeaneau, Salt Lake City, UT
Quil Things, Acton, MA
The Quilt Patch, Marlboro, MA
Quilter's Peace, Garrison, NY
Quiltwork Patches, Corvallis, OR
Schoolhouse Collection, Canton, OH
Taylor Bedding, Taylor, TX
Treadleart, Lomita, CA
The Vermont Patchworks, Shrewsbury, VT
Yours Truly, Westminster, CA

2. The Tools of the Trade

The antique quilts so prized today for their beauty, design, and precise detailing are all the more remarkable when one considers the paucity of tools which early needleworkers had at their disposal. Eighteenth- and nineteenth-century quilters had to depend on their own skills and their eyes to make sure that fabrics were precisely measured, cut, and sewn. Each tiny stitch, from first joining of pieces to last flourish in the overall quilting design, had to be completed by hand.

Today's quilter, however, has many more sophisticated aids to call on: precision-cut stencils and templates in thousands of designs, special cutters which slice through layers of fabric effortlessly, accessories for machine quilting, erasable marking pens, rulers that are specially calibrated to include seam allowances, and more. Adventurous needleworkers can even design their own motifs and transfer them to template or stencil using appropriate tools; some quilt shops offer to take a customer's original designs and make such templates to order. Even eye strain is obsolete: special magnifying lamps enlarge the tiniest work areas, and automatic needle threaders make that once frustrating chore almost a pleasure. Many such tools are described in these pages.

Whether you are working on a large quilt or a pillow square, you'll find the right frame for the job. There are kits and plans for making your own, or ready-made ones. Some even fold for storage with the quilt in progress still attached. Your finished project can be displayed on a handsome rack; smaller pieces might be set off in graceful wood frames.

A selection of quilting notions made by Dritz Corporation.

AMERICAN QUILTER. Do-it-yourselfers will appreciate the useful stencil-cutting kit manufactured by The American Quilter. Intended for cutting, quilting, and painting stencils, the kit contains an electric stencil-cutting pen, two fine-point tips, one quilt tip, a 36″ by 11″ roll of Mylar plastic, and complete instructions. Quilters with artistic talent may want to create their own stencil designs, or trace existing patterns onto the plastic sheet in any arrangement to suit their individual preferences. The American Quilter's products, including stenciling patterns for appliqué and quilting, are available at quilt shops across North America or by mail. Brochure available for SASE.

The American Quilter
P.O. Box 7455
Menlo Park, CA 94026
(415) 854-2694

ARDCO TEMPLATES. Anthony R. DiChesere, inventor of ARDCO precision templates, has eliminated much of the guesswork and inaccuracy in marking and cutting quilt pieces. His window templates (precisely measured in many geometric shapes and sizes),

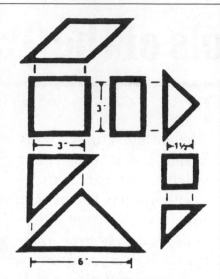

have the centers cut out. The template shape itself is measured to an exact quarter inch, permitting you to select any design or portion of a design and to trace it *ad infinitum* without fear that your fabric pieces will vary in size or seam allowance. In addition to various sizes of the classic square, diamond, hexagon, and triangle, there are more complicated shapes such as Dresden Plate, Tear Drop, and Cable. ARDCO templates are sold at retail shops across the country and by mail. Brochure available for SASE.

ARDCO Templates
Victory Tool & Die Co., Inc.
131 Colvin St.
Rochester, NY 14611
(716) 235-6756

CABIN FEVER CALICOES. One of the many quilter's aids featured in the extensive inventory at Cabin Fever Calicoes is a heavy-duty Olfa Rotary Cutter, one of many Olfa tools favored by needleworkers throughout North America. The rotary cutter slices easily through four or

more layers of fabric, making it indispensable for complicated projects such as those requiring strip piecing. Cabin Fever Calicoes also stocks replacement blades and Olfa's grid cutting mat, which helps to make cutting easier and more accurate. Catalog and seasonal brochures, $1.

Cabin Fever Calicoes
54 Range Rd.
Center Sandwich, NH 03227
(603) 284-6690

W. H. COLLINS. Among the many quilting aids manufactured by W. H. Collins is its Quilt and Sew Ruler, a clear plastic, flexible 18″ ruler that can make drafting any size patchwork or appliqué pattern a bit less difficult. The ruler features a zero centering hole; additional holes are placed every half inch for making circles and scallops. Other Collins products include an instant basting adhesive, called Glue Stick, to hold trim or appliqué firmly until permanently stitched; the glue is water soluble and non toxic. Collins's products are available at quilt and fabric shops across the country; contact the company if you can't find an outlet near you.

W. H. Collins Inc.
21 Leslie Ct.
Whippany, NJ 07981
(201) 887-4900

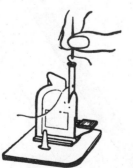

COME QUILT WITH ME. Pat Yamin, owner of Come Quilt With Me, has spent a number of years refining her mail-order catalog of quilting notions and other products. She chooses selected items from various manufacturers, items which have in common practicality and innovation. A case in point is this automatic needle threader, helpful in saving time, temper, and eyesight. Just drop your needle into the funnel, lay the thread across the groove, press a button, and you're through. The threader has a

support stand for thread and a built-in blade for easy thread cutting. Other items featured in the Come Quilt With Me catalog include quilters' pins, needles, cutters, templates, hoops, and stencils. Catalog, $2.50.

Come Quilt With Me
P.O. Box 1063
Brooklyn, NY 11210
(718) 377-3652

CONTEMPORARY QUILTS. Make a useful, inexpensive full-size (108" x 24") quilt frame using a kit from Contemporary Quilts and your own lumber and hardware. The kit includes cast-aluminum ratchet wheels and gears, complete plans and instructions, and a list of materials you'll need for assembly. The finished frame is easy to disassemble for storage, and the ratchet design firmly holds any size quilt, from crib to king. The kit is sold at retail shops and by mail. Brochure available.

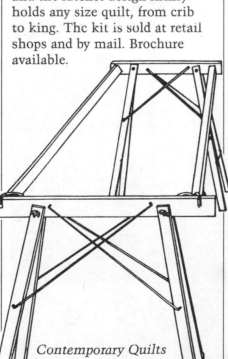

Contemporary Quilts
5305 Denwood Ave.
Memphis, TN 38119
(901) 683-8654

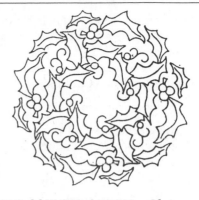

THE COUNTRY QUILTER. Claire Oehler, proprietor of The Country Quilter, updates her catalog twice a year to add special new quilting supplies and notions. Among the many items she carries is an extensive collection of plastic stencils by Quilting Creations and Stencil House. The unusual holly-wreath stencil shown here, a Gloria Hartley design, would be the perfect finishing touch for a Christmas quilt. The Country Quilter also features heavy plastic templates for such designs as Nine Patch, Stars, and Mariner's Compass. Catalog, $1.

The Country Quilter
Bonny Dr.
Somers, NY 10589
(914) 277-4958

DIANNA'S QUILTING SUPPLIES. Dianna Vale is a lecturer, author, designer, and quilter whose talents include the creation of original stencil designs that are available through her mail-order catalog. Among the

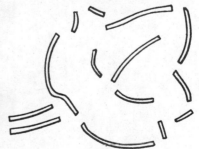

pre-cut stencils she offers is this single leaf pattern, which measures 3¼" by 3½". Others include feathers, tulips, pansies, rosebuds, and ivy. Catalog, $1.

Dianna's Quilting Supplies
1294 32nd Ave. NW
Salem, OR 97304
(503) 364-6355

Dazor lamps can be ordered directly from Downie Enterprises and are stocked at retail shops nationwide. Brochure available.

Downie Enterprises, Inc.
P.O. Box 9526
1208 Gordon St.
Charlotte, NC 28299
(704) 375-5095

DOWNIE ENTERPRISES. Even quilters with perfect vision can be subject to eye strain after hours of close work. To alleviate the problem, you might want to consider one of the Dazor Floating Arm Magnifier Lamps distributed by Downie Enter- prises. Offered in wheel-base or pedestal floor models and in a desk model, the lamp contains a powerful magnifier lens for sharp, clear enlargement of the work area, along with three 6-watt fluorescent tubes which emit cool, shadowless light.

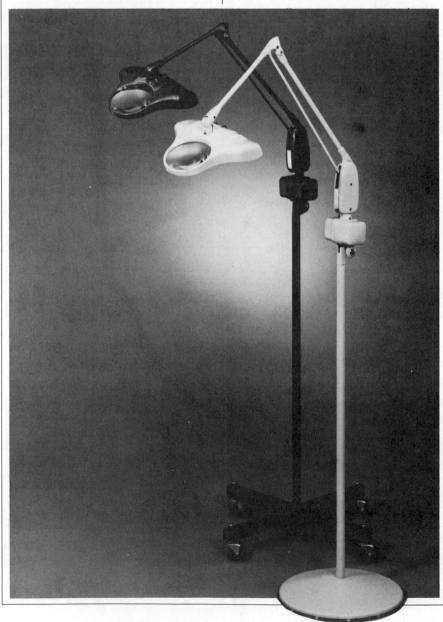

DRITZ. No matter what you need in the way of sewing no- tions, Dritz probably makes it. The Dritz name is a staple in fine fabric, needlework, and quilt shops throughout North America. Shown here are just two of the helpful tools available from this manufac- turer. Mark-B-Gone is a mark- ing pen (available in pink or blue) whose ink disappears ef- fortlessly in either hot or cold water, with or without deter- gent. The Tailor Tacker can be used to transfer quilt patterns from tracing paper to fabric. It comes complete with ten pieces of chalk in assorted colors for optimum visibility on any shade of fabric. Look for the Dritz display at your local quilt or fabric shop, or contact:

Dritz Corporation
P.O. Box 5028
Spartanburg, SC 29304
(803) 576-5050

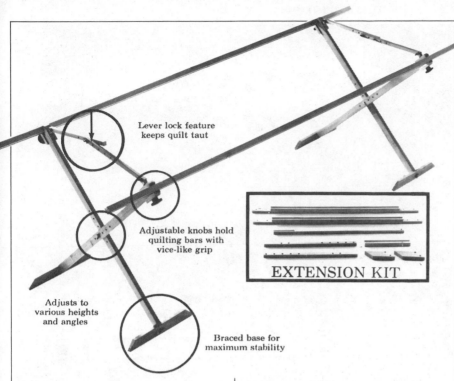

Lever lock feature keeps quilt taut

Adjustable knobs hold quilting bars with vice-like grip

Adjusts to various heights and angles

Braced base for maximum stability

EXTENSION KIT

Backstrom. Of special interest to quilters are Fiskars' 5" embroidery scissors and the 8" all-purpose scissors, available in left- or right-hand models. Both can be fitted with a combination scissors sheath and sharpener. Fiskars scissors are honed to cut even the most delicate or coarse fabrics smoothly and effortlessly. Look for the Fiskars display at your local quilt or fabric shop, or contact:

Fiskars
8711 W. Stewart Ave.
Wausau, WI 54401
(715) 842-2091

EDMUNDS. The Frank A. Edmunds company manufactures easy-to-assemble frame kits for a variety of projects. Shown is the company's maple quilting frame with stand. All wood parts are solid maple; the finished frame adjusts to any height and folds flat for storage. The primary kit makes a frame that will accommodate a quilt up to 87" wide; a separate ex-

tension kit can be purchased to expand the frame to a width of 116". Edmunds frame kits are available at your local quilt shop, or contact:

Frank A. Edmunds & Co., Inc.
6111 S. Sayre
Chicago, IL 60638
(800) 447-3516

In Illinois:
(312) 586-2772

FRAME MATE. An ideal accessory for lap quilting, the Frame Mate will hold 12" to 18" round hoops, 12" by 20" to 17" by 27" ovals, or an 18" square frame, freeing both hands to concentrate on needlework. Constructed of maple, it is light, portable, and easy to use. Adhesive-backed pile strips for one hoop or frame can be ordered with the Frame Mate, as can a 16" hoop. Brochure available.

The Frame Mate
P.O. Box 26964
Tempe, AZ 85282
(602) 838-8350

FISKARS. The lightweight, comfortable orange-handled scissors fashioned from surgical steel

that have become so popular in the United States were designed in 1960 by Finland's Olof

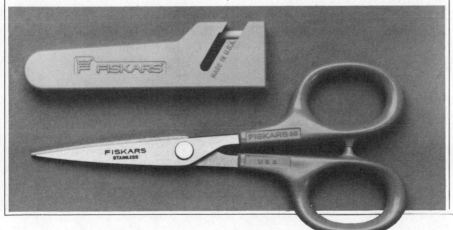

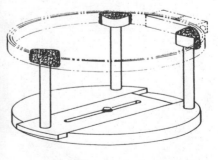

GEARY ASSOCIATES. More than three dozen sets of patchwork templates are offered by this Virginia firm. Ranging from simple designs such as Flower Basket and Pine Tree to the more complicated Feathered Star and Rose Window (shown), the template kits are pre-cut and accurately measured. Brochure available.

Geary Associates
5209 Portsmouth Rd.
Fairfax, VA 22032
(703) 273-7850

GIBBS. A manufacturer of needlework hoops for more than a century, Gibbs makes hoops in both round (8″, 10″, and 12″ diameter) and oval (12″ by 20″, 10″ by 15″, and 8″ by 12″)

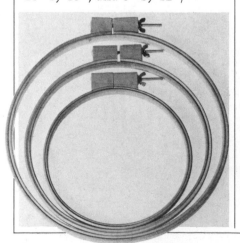

models. All hoops are made of hardwoods and are waxed and rounded to prevent snagging fine fabrics. Gibbs's quilting and rug-hooking frame (model #100) is crafted of solid oak and other hardwoods. The hoop can be easily adjusted to the most comfortable working position. Gibbs hoops and frames are available at quilt and fabric shops across the country; contact the company for an outlet near you.

The Gibbs Manufacturing Co.
606 6th St. NE
Canton, OH 44702
(216) 455-5344

GINGHER. No needleworker can afford to be without a good pair of pinking shears. Gingher's 7½″ shears are available in both right- and left-hand models and are guaranteed against defects in materials and workmanship. Gingher also makes quality sewing and embroidery scissors in many sizes for every task. Look for the Gingher display at your local quilt or fabric shop, or contact:

Gingher, Inc.
P.O. Box 8865
Greensboro, NC 27419
(800) 416-4437

nails. It has an opening to accommodate the nail; the metal surface protects sensitive fingers from pricks. Look for these thimbles at your local quilt or fabric shop, or contact:

High Country Quilts
4857A N. Academy Blvd.
Colorado Springs, CO 80907
(303) 598-1312

HABERHOUSE. One of the most unusual items in the Haberhouse catalog is the Wee Helper, a small needlework frame from PAB Designs that can be used on a table or on your lap to free both hands for more efficient stitching. You can stitch various sizes of fabric by placing the roller bars in different holes in the side pieces to give you from 2¾″ to 10½″ of open stitching space. Either 9″ or 12″ dowels are offered; an optional Conversion Package turns a 9″ frame into a 12″ frame with two roller bars and a brace bar. Catalog and price list, $1.50.

Haberhouse
1301 Brookwood Rd.
Shelby, NC 28150
(704) 482-1079

HIGH COUNTRY QUILTS. Two unusual thimble designs come from High Country Quilts. The Quilters Ridge Thimble features a ridge around the top to prevent the needle from slipping off. The Nimble Thimble is designed for stitchers with long

HINTERBERG DESIGN. Hinterberg Design's Homestead Quilting Frame features rock maple end frames, pine poles and trestle, and laminated birch ratchet wheels. It can be adjusted easily in height and tilts to any comfortable working angle. One of its most attractive features is that it can be quickly disassembled for storage, even with the quilt still attached to the poles. The QX-2000 is a portable but solid queen-size frame with all the convenience of the Homestead Frame. Extension kits are available for both frames. The 29″ Homestead

Quilting Hoop, constructed from hard maple, is also fully adjustable to almost any height and angle and will even rotate on its pedestal, facilitating the quilting of hard-to-reach areas. The Homestead hoop stand will also accommodate a quilt-as-you-go frame. All products may be ordered directly from the manufacturer. Brochures are available at no charge.

Hinterberg Design
467 North Main St.
West Bend, WI 53095
(800) 443-5800

In Wisconsin:
(414) 338-0337

HOUSE OF QUILTING. Designed to replace the traditional thimble, House of Quilting's unique hand-held tool will enable the quilter to make smaller stitches with greater ease and comfort. The company encourages mail orders.

House of Quilting
Rt. 3, P.O. Box 433
Fayetteville, NC 28306
(919) 868-3842

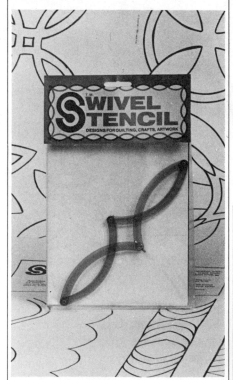

KALEIDOSCOPE V. This mail-order firm offers an ingenious design tool, the Swivel Stencil, that can make unlimited designs for borders, medallions, and shaped edges. Molded of transparent plastic, the stencil consists of four arcs riveted together at three joints and connected by a wing nut at the fourth. It can be maneuvered into many separate positions and then secured firmly with the wing nut. Brochure available for SASE.

Kaleidoscope V
P.O. Box 572
Newhall, CA 91322
(805) 259-5557

KLAUS B. RAU. Manufacturers of solid-oak quilting frames in sizes ranging from 30″ to 108″ in width, the Klaus B. Rau Company has also designed an ingenious stand called the Hoop Hand to facilitate lap quilting. Made of oak with a hand-rubbed finish, the Hoop Hand holds any size hoop. For right- or left-hand use, it can be adjusted to any angle, and fits comfortably under your legs, freeing both hands for needlework. Brochure available.

Klaus B. Rau Company
P.O. Box 1236
Coeur d'Alene, ID 83814
(208) 664-3942

MAPLE SPRINGS FARM. Among the many items available by mail from Maple Springs Farm are more than a dozen different computer-cut quilting stencils. Precisely cut from clear plastic, they can be used over and over again. The pre-cut slots are just the right width for either pencil or water-erasable marker. Shown is #450, a 12″-square floral pattern. Other quilters' aids selected for inclusion in Maple Springs' catalog include graphs, templates, rulers, and plans for various sizes of quilt frames. Catalog, $1.

Maple Springs Farm
Dept. QC
1828 Hwy. PB
Verona, WI 53593
(608) 845-9482

MARIE PRODUCTS. Manufacturers of American Heritage quilting hoops and stands crafted of solid hardwoods, Marie Products offers oval and round hoops, quilting frames, and sampler stands. Model 4550, shown here, will hold a quilt square as large as 24″ by 24″. Height, angle, and dimensions of the square can be adjusted as you choose. Marie Products are available at your local quilt or fabric shop, or contact:

Marie Products
P.O. Box 56000
Tucson, AZ 85703
(800) 421-4567

In Arizona:
(602) 888-9720

NEEDLEART GUILD. For more than fifty years, Needleart Guild has been supplying innovative quilting aids to needleworkers. Its latest mail-order catalog features countless stencil designs for large and small blocks, borders and corners, and continuous overall patterns. If you have a design of your own for which you need a stencil, supply Needleart Guild with an exact drawing; the firm can make up the stencil for you. Catalog, $1.50.

Needleart Guild
2729 Oakwood NE
Grand Rapids, MI 49505
(616) 361-1531

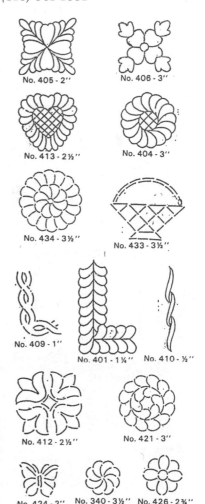

MARKS SCISSORS. Among the many different styles of scissors manufactured under the Marks trade name are these indispensable dressmaker shears. Offered in 7″ and 8″ lengths (the 8″ model is made in both right- and left-hand models), the shears are chrome plated and are available with optional enamel handles for extra comfort. Look for the Marks display at your local quilt or fabric shop, or contact:

Marks Scissors
℅ Zivi Hercules, Inc.
50 Kerry Pl.
Norwood, MA 02062
(617) 762-8310

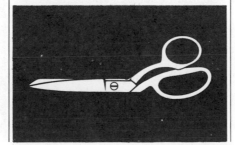

NEEDLEARTS INTERNATIONAL. Bonnie Benjamin, founder of this mail-order firm, specializes in providing exclusive stencil designs. Each design is reproduced on durable, translucent plastic and comes in from three to five graduated sizes, so that a quilter can choose just the right one for a particular project. Motifs include some with Oriental, Arabic, and Art Deco themes. Among Benjamin's most unusual offerings are stencils for Sashiko—an ancient Japanese needle-art form that translates well to quilt patterns. Catalog, $1 (refundable with order).

Needlearts International
P.O. Box 6447
Glendale, CA 91205
(213) 227-1535

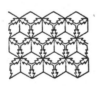

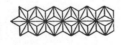

NORWOOD LOOMS. Norwood Looms offers a hand-crafted, solid-cherry quilting hoop in diameters measuring 18″, 26″, and 34″. The hoop comes with or without a sturdy, 32″-pedestal stand. Also available is a versatile quilt frame constructed from solid maple or cherry that will accommodate crib- to king-size frame arms and crossbars. The working surface can be adjusted and locked into any position and desired tension. Sold through selected dealers, the hoops and frames may be ordered directly from Norwood Looms if not available locally. Norwood offers a descriptive catalog for $1.

Norwood Looms
P.O. Box 167-B
Fremont, MI 49412
(616) 924-3901

OREGON RULE CO. Oregon Rule Co. manufactures and sells a comprehensive line of adhesive-backed Handy Rules. They are made of a metalized Mylar laminate with a bright brushed appearance, large numbers, and bold graduations combined to create an attractive and functional measuring tool. If you are

lucky enough to have a cutting table, you might want to affix a ruler permanently to the surface for easy and accurate reference. Look for Oregon Rules at your local quilt or fabric shop, or contact:

Oregon Rule Co.
P.O. Box 5072
Oregon City, OR 97045
(503) 657-8330

PRAIRIE FARM DESIGNS. If you are looking for pre-cut stencils in motifs perfect for an appliquéd crib quilt or baby pillow, Prairie Farm Designs may have what you need. Among its pre-cut plastic stencil kits are these two Amish children. Each measures

3" tall when completed. Other stencils include animal pull toys (cow, pig, goose, horse, rabbit, and bear), each 4" tall, and a 5" cat with a perky bow at its neck. Catalog available.

Prairie Farm Designs
578 S. Vine
Denver, CO 80209
(303) 778-7611

QUALITY LINE PRODUCTS. The Quilter's Frame, manufactured and distributed by Quality Line Products, comes in kit form and can be assembled for use as

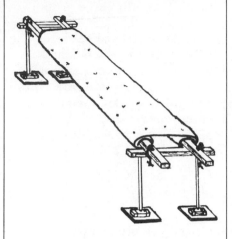

either a full-size frame (accommodating quilts up to 125" by 120") or a scroll frame, illustrated here. Made from knot-free pine, it comes complete with stands, C-clamps, and instructions for assembly. Brochure available.

Quality Line Products
320 N. 3rd W.
Hyrum, UT 84319
(801) 245-3994

THE QUILT PATCH. In both its retail shop and its catalog, this Massachusetts firm features an extensive line of fabrics, supplies, and notions. A case in point is this ingenious Chalk Wheel. It won't break or crumble like tailor's chalk, and

makes a fine, sharp line that's easy to rub off. The case holds a capsule of fine powdered chalk; refill capsules come in white or blue. Catalog available.

The Quilt Patch
208 Brigham St.
Marlboro, MA 01752
(617) 480-0194

THE QUILT PATCH. The large selection of stencils offered by this Pennsylvania shop and illustrated in its catalog gives quilters an opportunity to choose just the right design for any project. These stencils are precision-cut from heavy-duty Mylar plastic and range from geometric border designs to delicate florals such as the one illustrated. Its 11" by 11"

dimensions make it suitable for quilting entire blocks. Catalog, $2.

The Quilt Patch
1897 Hanover Pike
Littlestown, PA 17340
(717) 359-5940

QUILTER'S CORNER. Cath Heslin, owner of Quilter's Corner, is a quilter and designer whose idea for the Quilter's Quarter was based on her own experience with patchwork projects. The Quarter is a ¼″ measuring tool that eliminates the need to measure seam allowances. It is available in 8″, 12″, and 18″ lengths. Look for it at your local quilt or fabric shop, or contact:

Quilter's Corner, Inc.
P.O. Box 325
83 Main St.
Tappan, NY 10983
(914) 359-6866

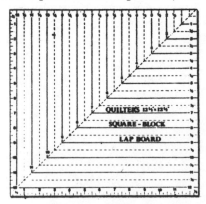

QUILTER'S RULE. Betty Gall, designer and owner of Quilter's Rule, has created several different measuring tools that quilters will find indispensable. Her Square Block Lap Board, for instance, is a marking and cutting guide for squares in any size from ½″ to 12½″. The Quilter's Rule is a 6½″ by 24″ measuring ruler. Other models include the Mini Rule (6″ by 6″) and two equilateral triangles, in 6″ and 12″ sizes. All are made of thick lucite with lines and numbers molded in the plastic for accuracy. Look for Quilter's Rules at your local quilt or fabric shop, or contact:

Quilter's Rule, Inc.
3201 Davie Blvd.
Ft. Lauderdale, FL 33312
(305) 587-5448

QUILTS & OTHER COMFORTS. If you take great pleasure in the actual quilting of a project, but dislike the time-consuming process of marking the pattern and removing the marks once you've finished stitching, you may want to try Quilt A-Peel.

Reusable self-adhesive templates adhere firmly to your material; simply quilt around the edges and peel off the template when you're through. Designs available include Twisting Vine, Dancing Tulips, Lovebirds, Ribbons & Flowers, and many others. The templates show clearly on light or dark colors, prints, or solids. They contain no oils and leave no residue, so they won't stain your quilt. Catalog, $1.25.

Quilts & Other Comforts
P.O. Box 394-3
6700 West 44th Ave.
Wheatridge, CO 80034
(303) 420-4272

QUILTWORK PATCHES. Among the many helpful notions described in the attractive Quiltwork Patches catalog are the thread locks and beeswax holder shown here. The thread locks

insert easily into spools to prevent loose threads and avert tangles. The beeswax holder changes all-purpose thread into quilting thread. (Beeswax refills

are sold separately.) Other items that quilters will find useful include needle cases, a needle threader with magnifier,

thimbles, pins, stencils, and many more. Catalog, $1.

Quiltwork Patches
P.O. Box 724-B
430 NW 6th St.
Corvalis, OR 97339
(503) 754-1475

RUFF CREEK WOODWORKS. Ruff Creek's unfinished, ready-to-assemble oak quilt rack is shipped with clear instructions for assembly and finishing. The completed rack will display up

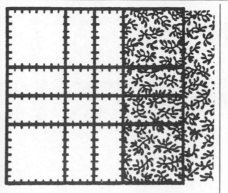

to five quilts in style. If you have a woodworker in the family, you might prefer to order Ruff Creek's full-size detailed plans and instructions to make your own rack in either a three-bar or five-bar model. Information available.

Ruff Creek Woodworks
P.O. Box 934
Rt. 19
Waynesburg, PA 15370
(412) 627-8044

SCHOOL FOR INQUIRING MYNDS.

Betty Jo Shiell, owner of this Florida firm, has put together four collections of plastic templates that will be useful additions to any quilter's tool box. From nineteen to thirty-six templates are included in each collection: choose Traditional Quilt Blocks, Eight-Pointed Star Quilt Blocks & Variations, Pieced-and-Appliquéd Blocks, or Miniature

and Christmas Patchwork. Mrs. Shiell also recommends the Quilter's Window, an exclusive design from Precision Patchwork. Shown here, it is a ruled, rigid 12" square of plastic that will help you to measure and cut strips and rectangles quickly and precisely. Order by mail, or look for these products at your local quilt or fabric shop. Brochure available.

School for Inquiring Mynds
241 E. Sixth Ave.
Tallahassee, FL 32303
(904) 222-7013

SHAKER SIMPLICITY.

The solid-maple quilt rack manufactured by Shaker Simplicity is based on

an authentic Shaker design. Its minimalism makes it an ideal display for a treasured quilt, as it won't distract from the art-istry and design of the quilt, but rather, will complement it. The rack measures 22" wide by 33" high. Its maple construction features mortise and tenon joinery and hand finishing; each rack is signed and dated by the maker. Brochure, $1.

Shaker Simplicity
Dept. MS86
4666 Quaker Trace Rd.
Eaton, OH 45320

THE SILVER THIMBLE.

One of the most useful items offered at The Silver Thimble Quilt Shop is this portable frame. Called the Quilt As You Go Hand Frame, it can be used for pillows and for patchwork quilts. Fully adjustable from 8" by 8" to 24" by 24", it is constructed of maple (or optional cherry) with a clear lacquer finish. The Silver Thimble's catalog lists a complete line of stencils, tools, and notions. Catalog, $1.50.

The Silver Thimble Quilt Shop
Rt. 1, Lafayette Rd.
Hampton Falls, NH 03844
(603) 926-3378

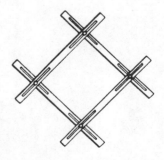

STENCILS AND STUFF. If you can't find the exact stencil design you want in this firm's mail-order catalog, chances are you'll have to make it yourself. Stencils and Stuff carries more than 500 pre-cut stencils manufactured by Quilting Creations by D.J. Each is composed of durable transparent plastic that can be easily washed and used over and over again. Border and corner designs, animals, birds, floral patterns, fruit, miniatures, and geometrics are included. Catalog, $2.

Stencils and Stuff
72 12th St., NW
Strasburg, OH 44680
(216) 878-5684

STENCIL EASE. Stencil an old-fashioned coverlet using the charming folk art designs for blocks and borders offered by Stencil Ease. The company's pre-cut stencils, brushes, fabric paints, and instruction booklets are available at local craft or quilt shops, or you may contact Stencil Ease directly for the name of the dealer nearest you.

Stencil Ease
P.O. Box 209
New Ipswich, NH 03071
(603) 878-3430

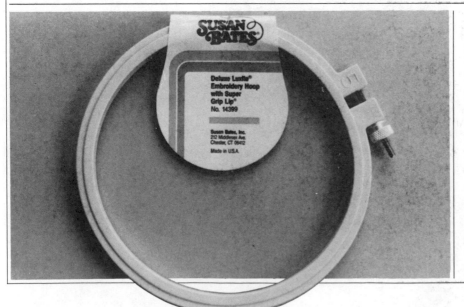

SUSAN BATES. Whether you need a wooden quilting hoop or a framing hoop, chances are that this manufacturer may have the size you require. Quilting hoops come in 14", 18", and 23" rounds and a generous 18" by 27" oval. Framing hoops measure from 4" to 12" in diameter. Other practical quilting supplies include needles in many types and sizes, needle threaders, and a handy 60" tape measure. All are available at local quilt or fabric stores, or contact:

Susan Bates Inc.
212 Middlesex Ave.
Chester, CT 06412
(203) 526-5381

SWISS-METROSENE. Whether you quilt by hand or by machine, you can't find a better thread than the 100% Egyptian long-fiber cotton manufactured by Swiss-Metrosene. It comes in thirty colors, from white and natural to spruce green and dark brown, and in 164-yard spools (white and natural are also packed in 500-yard spools). All Swiss-Metrosene thread is shrink proof and color fast and is cross-wound to prevent tangling. Look for the Swiss-Metrosene display at your local quilt or fabric shop, or contact:

Swiss-Metrosene Inc.
7780 Quincy St.
Willowbrook, IL 60521
(800) 323-7092

TREADLEART. As its name implies, Treadleart specializes in products and accessories for machine sewing and is an authorized dealer for several machine manufacturers. Among the many items in its catalog that will be of interest to quilters are special appliqué and walking feet to fit many different sewing machines. Catalog, $1.

Treadleart
25834 Narbonne Ave., Suite 1
Lomita, CA 90717
(213) 534-5122

TREASURES UNLIMITED. Through her mail-order catalog and at shows, Marjorie Geddes, owner of Treasures Unlimited, sells what she calls "heirloom quality tools and toys of stitchery." Among her offerings are some of the basic tools (scissors, thimbles, pin-cushions) necessary to all needlework. Basic in purpose, yes, but not in style or material. Treasures Unlimited offers gold, sterling-silver, and porcelain thimbles and pin-cushions; bone needle cases reminiscent of the Victorian era, and whimsical notions such as a pewter thimble and thread stand. In addition, Ms. Geddes periodically mails lists of antique tools she has available for sale and will conduct searches for collectors. Catalog, $2.50.

Treasures Unlimited
Dept. QC
5955 SW 179th Ave.
Beaverton, OR 97007
(503) 649-1041

YOURS TRULY. Among the many templates manufactured by Yours Truly are Dresden Plates, clamshells, circles, hearts, diamonds, triangles, and hexagons. Yours Truly stencils are composed of pre-cut Mylar plastic in dimensions of 5½" by 8¼" and 8¼" by 11". Motifs include Christmas patterns, borders, and garlands. Look for the Yours Truly display at your local quilt or fabric shop, or contact:

Yours Truly, Inc.
A Division of Burdett
Publications
5455 Garden Grove Blvd.
Westminster, CA 92683
(714) 891-7055

Other Suppliers of Tools

Consult Directory of Suppliers for Addresses

Barbie Beck, Fredericksburg, VA
The Brass Goose, Front Royal, VA
Brewer Fabric Shop, Brewer, ME
Brilliance, Redford, MI
Calico House, Scottsville, VA
Calico 'n Things, Marquette, MI
The Cloth Cupboard, Boise, ID
Community Quilts, Bethesda, MD
The Cotton Patch, Lafayette, CA
Country Crafts & Fabrications, Folsom, CA
Country House Quilts, Zionsville, IL
Patricia Cox, Minneapolis, MN
Creative Stitches, Honolulu, HI
Cross Patch Quilting Center, Garrison, NY
Dorr Mill Store, Guild, NH
EA of Hawaii, Kailua, HI
G Street Fabrics, Rockville, MD
Gutcheon Patchworks, New York, NY
Hapco Products Inc., Columbia, MO
Hearthside Quilts, Shelburne, VT

Hobby Time Helpers, Southwick, MA
Sandy Hunter, Inc., Hendersonville, NC
Joseph's Coat, Peterborough, NH
Kaye's Artistic Stitchery, West Branch, MI
Mountain Mist, Cincinnati, OH
Norton House, Wilmington, VT
Patience Corner Quilt Shop, Portsmouth, NH
Quil Things, Acton, MA
The Quilt Square, Meadville, PA
Quilter's Peace, Garrison, NY
Schoolhouse Collection, Canton, OH
Seminole Sampler, Ellicott City, MD
TJ's Quick Quilter, Kerrville, TX
Tumbleweed, Cambridge, MA
The Vermont Patchworks, Shrewsbury, VT
White Sewing Products Co., Cleveland, OH

3. Kits, Patterns, and Other Design Sources

Tried-and-true American patchwork patterns such as Double Wedding Ring, Dresden Plate, Log Cabin, Ohio Star, and Bear's Paw are still popular with the modern descendents of needleworkers who first pieced them a century or more ago. Yet avid quilters are always on the hunt for ideas that will help them interpret the classic quilt motifs in fresh, unusual ways. In addition, there are patterns based on Hawaiian motifs, Japanese Sashiko, Celtic stitchery, and other more exotic sources of inspiration. Whether your taste and sewing skill run to the simple or the complex, you'll find lots of ideas in the following pages.

If you're a novice, you might want to begin with a quilt kit before moving on to a more involved project that requires deftness with ruler and scissors as well as agility with a needle and thread. Most kits, whether for miniature or full-size quilts, include all pre-cut fabric pieces required, along with bias binding, muslin backing, quilting stencils, and clearly written instructions. Some quilt shops put together their own kits and will choose and cut fabrics to your order; others carry pre-packaged kits; and many stores subscribe to a pattern of the month service, insuring a never-ending source of new designs.

If you prefer to create your own quilts by combining various ready-made patterns in an arrangement uniquely your own, you can choose among hundreds of designs for appliqué, strip piecing, whitework, patchwork, and shadow trapunto. Some patterns combine several needlework skills (patchwork and cross stitch, for instance). You can even purchase a software program for your personal computer that will give you endless patchwork pattern variations at the push of a button. And if you are still looking for design ideas, consult Chapter 5 for reviews of the best available pattern books.

The finished projects in "Folk Animals 2," one of the charming pattern sets available from Donna Gallagher, Creative Needlearts.

AMERICAN QUILTER. If you want to coordinate your overall quilting design with your border motif, The American Quilter has just the thing. Its catalog features two quilting and stencil combination patterns—Country Tulips and Colonial Rose—with stencils suitable for either paint or appliqué. Other patterns the

COLONIAL ROSE

COUNTRY TULIPS

firm makes include both quilting and appliqué designs for clothing. The American Quilter's products are sold at local quilt shops and by mail. Brochure available for SASE.

The American Quilter
P.O. Box 7455
Menlo Park, CA 94026
(415) 854-2694

AMITY PUBLICATIONS. Suzy Lawson, a talented designer and one of the founders of Amity Publications, creates lively, amusing picture quilt patterns based on Amish themes. Her Amish Cats and Rats, shown here, is a playful variation of the Amish Ocean Waves pattern. The finished quilt, pieced, appliquéd, and quilted, will measure 45½" square. Other Lawson patterns include Amish Bars and Center Diamond, Buggy Ride, Teamwork, and Spinning Wheel. Each pattern includes a full-color illustration of the finished project, full-size pieces, instructions, a yardage and materials list, and a history or explanation of the design. Look for Amity patterns at your local quilt or fabric shop, or contact the firm directly. Catalog, $1.

Amity Publications
78688 Sears Rd.
Cottage Grove, OR 97424
(503) 942-7501

BETTY BOYINK. In addition to the excellent pattern books published by this firm, there are several pattern packets that will be of interest to quilters. Love Knots includes six traditional love knot blocks in 4", 6", 8", and 12" sizes, appliqué figures of a sunbonnet couple, complete directions for making wall, doll, crib, and full-size quilts using the patterns, and quilting details. Other packets currently offered are Diamond Starburst, Fantastic Quilt Collection (fans), Balloon Heart, and Pieced Alphabet. Brochure available. Betty Boyink patterns

tern pieces, and a color photo for inspiration. Catalog, $1.75; catalog and swatches, $3.

*Calico 'n' Things
P.O. Box 265
Marquette, MI 49855
(906) 228-7145*

IVA CAPPS. Amish Checkers is one of two appliqué and pieced quilt patterns created by Iva Capps. Included are instructions and full-size appliqué patterns for a 30″-square wall hanging.

and books are available at local quilt and fabric shops, or contact:

*Betty Boyink Publishing
818 Sheldon Rd.
Grand Haven, MI 49417
(616) 842-3304*

Capps's other current design, Lambs and Flowers, is a 40″-square wall hanging with four appliquéd lambs and pieced borders of flowers. Each lamb has separately stitched ears which are sewn into the appliqué. Catalog, $1.50.

*Iva Capps
3 Sylvan Ct.
Fredericksburg, VA 22405
(703) 371-6418*

CALICO 'N' THINGS. Among the many patterns and kits listed in this Michigan firm's mail-order catalog is a pattern for this award-winning quilt by Norma Graflund, which was completed c. 1984. Diamond Blending Star comes with complete step-by-step instructions, full-size pat-

CELTIC DESIGN CO. The expert quilter looking for a challenging new project will want to investigate the patterns offered by Philomena Wiechec of Celtic Design Co. Mrs. Wiechec hails from Ireland and has adapted the intricate interlocking motifs of her native land to bias appliqué quilting techniques. Among the Celtic patterns she has produced are border and clothing motifs and unusual medallions suitable for quilt blocks. Look for Mrs. Wiechec's patterns at your local quilt shop, or contact the company for a brochure.

Celtic Design Co.
834 W. Remington Dr.
Sunnyvale, CA 94087
(408) 735-8049

CENTRAL PRESS PUBLICATIONS. Two packages of designs published by Central Press, *New Expressive Quilting Designs: Originals for Quilts, Parts I and II*, present many charming block designs to beautify and accentuate the plain alternating squares of a patchwork or appliqué quilt. Dimensions range from approximately 4″ to 22″, and all designs are shown full size.

Central Press Publications
P.O. Box 172-Q
Canal Winchester, OH 43110

COTTONWOOD HEARTH. Debby Butts, owner of Cottonwood Hearth, has created a number of original appliqué designs

suitable for wall hangings, pillows, or quilt squares. Many of her motifs celebrate holiday themes, among them Easter

Friends, Halloween Hollow, Spirit of America, Bit o' Irish, and several Christmas designs. Her Dutch Flowers, shown here, is a more traditional pattern. The finished piece measures 14″ square. Each pattern includes a full-size design to be transferred to your own template or heavy paper, complete instructions, and a materials list. Brochure, 50¢.

Cottonwood Hearth
5958 SW 24th Terr.
Topeka, KS 66614
(913) 273-5958

PATRICIA COX. Patricia Cox develops one-of-a-kind quilting

designs and makes them available in pattern form. Among the many patchwork and appliqué patterns illustrated in her catalog is this exquisite Floral Fantasy, an intricate appliqué design offered in either king or double size. Catalog available.

Patricia Cox
6601 Normandale Rd.
Minneapolis, MN 55435
(612) 922-8083

COUNTRY APPLIQUES. Jan and Emil Kornfeind, proprietors of Country Appliques, produce an ever-increasing assortment of patterns suitable for machine or hand appliqué. Each pattern comes complete with full-size pieces, instructions, and a color illustration of the completed project. Shown is Country

Goose, a good project for a beginner, which is intended for a 14" hoop. Country Appliques patterns are available at your local quilt or fabric shop, or contact:

Country Appliques
P.O. Box 7109
Shawnee Mission, KS 66209
(913) 491-1237

Catalog, $1, available from:

Country Post
P.O. Box 1821
Kettering, OH 45429

COUNTRY QUILTER. Among the many patterns featured in the Country Quilter catalog are some unusual, nearly life-size designs in the Marshland series by Gloria Hartley. Each measures approximately 11" by 17"; use them individually, or together in a quilt or wall hanging. Shown here is #GH-105,

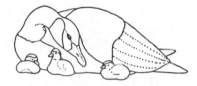

the Nesting Goose. Other geese are interpreted flying, swimming, feeding, and standing. Catalog, $1.

The Country Quilter
Bonny Dr.
Somers, NY 10589
(914) 277-4958

DESIGNS BY RD. Rosemary Fosner and Doris Y. Garrett have compiled three different floral designs and easy-to-understand instructions for marking, assembling, quilting, and finishing in a package called *Elegant Whole Cloth Quilt Designs.* For information, contact:

Designs by RD
260 Crestwood Circle
High Point, NC 27260

DIANNA'S QUILTING SUPPLIES. Dianna Vale is a talented artist who has put together a number of quilt design books chock-full of original quilting patterns. She has also created several appliqué patterns, among them Miss Milly, a charming little quilter designed for a 12" or 14" block.

Milly comes complete with full-size pattern pieces and a pattern for a miniature quilt. Catalog, $1.

Dianna's Quilting Supplies
1294 32nd Ave. NW
Salem, OR 97304
(503) 364-6355

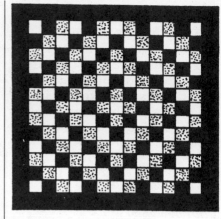

tions, fabric requirements, and quilting suggestions. The complete kit comes with specially selected wool shades in your choice of three color families, and a delicate calico backing fabric to complement the finished top. Brochures available.

Dorr Mill Store
P.O. Box 88
Hale St.
Guild, NH 03754
(603) 863-1197

DONNA GALLAGHER, CREATIVE NEEDLEARTS. Complete directions and full-size patterns for three patchwork animals, a quilted wall hanging, pillow, and weather-vane horse on stand are included in the Country Charm Folk Animals 2 packet from Donna Gallagher. A similar packet, Folk Animals 1, features patterns for a patchwork pig, cat, and duck, and a pieced duck in a hoop. These are just two of the many quilting patterns manufactured by this Ohio firm. Look for the Donna Gallagher display at your local quilt or fabric shop, or contact:

Donna Gallagher, Creative
* Needlearts, Inc.*
6060 Chickadee Pl.
Westerville, OH 43081
(614) 895-1017

EA OF HAWAII. Elizabeth Akana is an accomplished craftswoman, lecturer, and teacher who has created a full line of Hawaiian patterns for quilting and appliqué. Included are full-size patterns for pillows, crib quilts, wall hangings, and bed coverings. Two of the most popular island designs are Breadfruit and Plumeria. The

DORR MILL STORE. This New Hampshire retail and mail-order firm specializes in wool fabrics and yarns for a variety of needle crafts. It lists among its supplies more than 150 different shades of fabric and a variety of quilting kits and patterns for pillows, wall hangings, and bed coverings. Even the difficult Sunshine and Shadow quilt can be simplified utilizing a Dorr Mill kit. Instructions for the pattern include piecing direc-

Breadfruit motif symbolizes the tree whose fruit was an important part of the early Polynesian diet; Plumeria, one of the most popular of Hawaii's lei flowers, is also known as Frangipani. Catalog, $1; quarterly newsletter with helpful tips and a Hawaiian design pattern, $5 per year.

EA of Hawaii
Suite 360
150 Hamakua Dr.
Kailua, HI 96734
(808) 254-2767

HELEN M. ERICSON. In the late 1920s and early '30s, Scioto Danner of El Dorado, Kansas, sold quilts, tops, and patterns to local stores. This early business resulted in her publishing five booklets of patterns by the late 1960s, and Helen Ericson has now reprinted those original booklets and added many new patterns. Each booklet contains descriptions and illustrations; patterns are available separately. More than 200 different patterns are listed in Mrs. Ericson's brochure: to facilitate your ordering, she organizes them according to type: appliqué, pieced, combination pieced and appliqué, pieced stars, children's quilts, and all-over designs. Mrs. Ericson is shown holding a Feathered Star quilt; Horn of Plenty and Ladies' Dream are displayed behind her. Brochure, 25¢.

Helen M. Ericson
P.O. Box 650
Emporia, KS 66801
(316) 342-1033

Christmas offers patterns for an angel, Santa and Mrs. Santa, a snowman, a tree, and more. Each book is complete with instructions for finishing a variety of appliqué projects. Brochure, $1 plus SASE.

Ginger Designs
P.O. Box 3241
Newport Beach, CA 92663
(714) 631-6556

SALLY GOODSPEED. Sally Goodspeed has combed old newspapers and quilting journals, such as the 1929 *Woman's World Book of Patchwork*, for hundreds of lively appliqué and patchwork motifs which she then reproduces in pattern form. Among the most popular designs are these sunbonnet babies; a total of thirty separate

GINGER DESIGNS. Ginger Johnson has published several books of appliqué patterns suitable for either quilts or children's clothing. Her *Appliqués for Children* includes all of the colorful motifs that make up this charming crib quilt.

figures is available. Ms. Goodspeed's catalog contains many figurative and geometric patterns suitable for any number of quilting projects. Catalog, $2.25.

Sally Goodspeed
2318 N. Charles St.
Baltimore, MD 21218

GRAMMA'S GRAPHICS. Looking for a design idea for your next quilt project? If you'd like to create something uniquely your own, you might investigate Susan Johnson's Sun Print Kits.

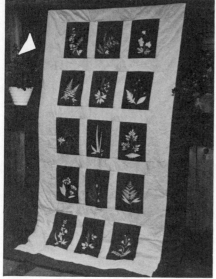

Mrs. Johnson, a quilter herself, has revived the art of blue-printing and applied it to her craft. The floral quilt illustrated was made by blueprinting pressed flowers, leaves, and ferns onto the quilt squares; all of the squares were completed in a single afternoon. You don't need any specialized skills in photography to employ the technique. Gramma's Graphics' Sun Print Kits include the necessary solution mix and complete instructions. You add the object or negative you wish

to print, the fabric, and other easily obtainable tools, along with some sunshine to develop your finished design. Brochure, $1 plus SASE.

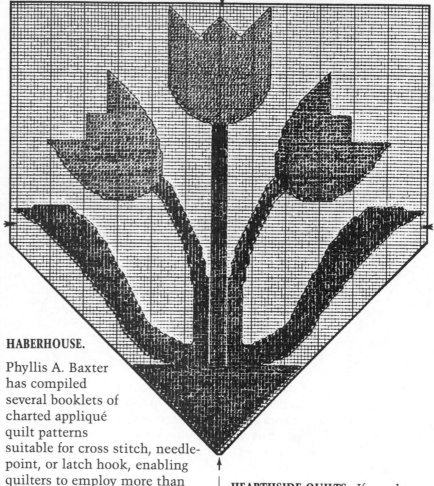

HABERHOUSE.

Phyllis A. Baxter has compiled several booklets of charted appliqué quilt patterns suitable for cross stitch, needle-point, or latch hook, enabling quilters to employ more than one method in the completion of a project. *Dutch Designs* includes directions and designs for a windmill, Dutch boy and girl, and several tulips. *Appliqué Quilt Patterns* contains a series of floral motifs. The designs can be worked in miniature (1″ equals 1′) or in full-size squares to be appliquéd to a quilt top or pillow. Catalog, $1.50.

Haberhouse
1301 Brookwood Rd.
Shelby, NC 28150
(704) 482-1079

Gramma's Graphics, Inc.
Dept. TQC
20 Birling Gap
Fairport, NY 14450
(716) 223-4309

HEARTHSIDE QUILTS. If you have decided to embark on your first quilt project, but are stymied by the details involved—the amount of material to buy, the measuring, and the cutting—Hearthside Quilts is for you. The firm's specialty is complete quilt kits; its full-color catalog has the most extensive selection of kits we've seen—from early classics such as Bear's Paw and Dresden Plate to more contemporary designs. Each kit is graded according to level of difficulty and includes die-cut

pattern pieces, thread, a quilting needle, batting, and muslin backing, along with complete instructions. (You can order just the quilt top, if you prefer.) All fabrics are 100% cotton; Hearthside Quilts offers a choice of color combinations, and most designs are available in many sizes, from crib to king. Catalog, $2.

Hearthside Quilts
P.O. Box 429M
Shelburne, VT 05482
(800) 451-3533

In Vermont:
(802) 985-8077

HOMESPUN QUILTS AND THINGS. Quilters who enjoy working in miniature will appreciate *Miniature Quilting Designs Out of Granny's Trunk*, a collection of 100 traditional designs by Liz Bartholomew. Motifs include cables, flowers, and other patterns. Many of the designs are very small and intricate, and therefore will require previous quilting experience. Other patterns would be appropriate for the small areas in full-size quilts. Eleven sheets of patterns are included.

Homespun Quilts and Things
3530 W. Mescal St.
Phoenix, AZ 85029

KATHY'S QUILTS. Kathy Munkelwitz has created several attractive contemporary designs and transferred them to patterns for machine or hand appliqué. Oriental Poppy, shown, makes a 14″ quilt block or a 23″ hoop. Iris and Kathy's Rose are of similar size. She also sells patterns for two crib quilts, Calico Ponies and Jolly Giraffe. Each comes with complete instructions. Brochure available for SASE.

Kathy's Quilts
Rt. 1
Isle, MN 56342
(612) 676-3359

THE MAIL POUCH. The Mail Pouch specializes in supplying appliqué patterns for quilt blocks, pillows, wall hangings,

and fabric art projects. Among its many offerings is a collection of seventeen designs called Little Patches, each 5″ square; the motifs include a contented fat cat and a single tulip in full bloom. Catalog, $3.

The Mail Pouch
P.O. Box 1373
Monrovia, CA 91016
(818) 579-9088

MANIFESTATIONS. Judy Houston has translated an art and retailing career into the design and marketing of patterns for quilting and appliqué. Shown is Azalea, one of the designs from Spring Flowers, a packet that includes full-size pattern pieces and instructions for that colorful bloom plus Camellia, Rose, Jonquil, Tulip, and Violet. Houston offers suggestions for appropriate colors and tips for machine or hand appliqué. Brochure available for SASE.

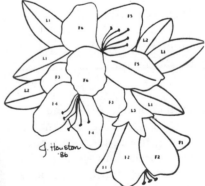

Manifestations
P.O. Box 850335
New Orleans, LA 70185
(504) 822-3009

MORNING CALL. Complete quilt patterns for full-size and wall quilts are the specialty at Morning Call. Each design contains complete instructions with diagrams and all necessary pattern pieces; most projects combine piecework and appliqué. Among the most charming designs is Wood Duck Morning, whose dozen colorful ducks combine to form a 37½'' by 34¾'' quilt. Brochure, $2. Morning Call Patterns are available at quilt and fabric shops, or contact:

Morning Call Patterns
P.O. Box 538
Wilmette, IL 60091
(312) 251-0247

MARGE MURPHY. All of the Heirloom Quilting Designs available from Marge Murphy were created and assembled by an experienced quilting teacher and maker of award-winning quilts. Marge Murphy designs are intended for use with the shadow trapunto technique. Yardage and notions requirements and complete instructions, from cutting to finishing, are included with the trapunto patterns, each of which is printed full size on heavy white paper. Among the

design packages offered are shells and sails, and borders and corners. Brochure available.

Marge Murphy
P.O. Box 6306
6624 April Bayou
Biloxi, MS 39532
(601) 392-3731

NEEDLEART GUILD. If you don't have the time or the temperament to begin and complete a full-size quilt, you might want to try a miniature quilt from the Needleart Guild's Amish Miniatures Collection. Finished quilts range from 10'' by 13'' to 17'' by 21''. Each will make a traditional Amish quilt in miniature. Choose Roman Stripes, Sunshine and Shadow, Amish Bars, Ohio Star, and many more. One of the most helpful touches is that each pattern comes complete with a clear plastic quilting stencil scaled exactly to match the miniature quilt dimensions. Assembly diagrams, full-size

pattern pieces, and a color photo of the finished quilt are also included. Catalog, $1.50.

*Needleart Guild
2729 Oakwood NE
Grand Rapids, MI 49505
(616) 361-1531*

NEEDLEARTS INTERNATIONAL. Specialists in the Japanese needlework technique of Sashiko, Needlearts International has created several patterns utilizing this unique art form. Shown is Ice Crystals,

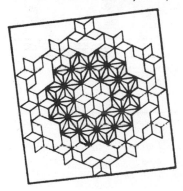

designed for a 14" or 16" round or square pillow, which would translate beautifully to a quilt block. The full-size pattern is packaged with suggestions for stitch placement, a materials list, and basic instructions in the Sashiko technique. Catalog available for SASE.

*Needlearts International
P.O. Box 6447
Glendale, CA 91205
(213) 227-1535*

OREGON TREASURES. One of the patterns created by Oregon Treasures is a variation on a classic theme—Log Cabin in the Round. Patterns are available to make a 38"-square wall hanging or a king- or queen-size quilt. Directions in-

clude fabric requirements and step-by-step instructions for cutting and sewing block and border strips. Other unusual pattern designs in the Oregon Treasures brochure include String of Jewels and Triangle Twist. Brochure available for SASE.

*Oregon Treasures
Rt. 2, P.O. Box 2892
Vale, OR 97918
(503) 473-2496*

OSAGE COUNTY QUILT FACTORY. Innovative patterns for appliqué, strip piecing, patchwork, and whitework are featured in Osage County Quilt Factory's colorful catalog. The tulip design shown features a 16" center and 31" borders; it can be used for either whitework or appliqué. There are patterns for picture quilts,

for pillows, for clothing, and for wall hangings. Owner/designer Virginia Robertson creates many of the motifs herself; they are manufactured in the firm's own factory, and come with complete instructions. Catalog, $1.

*The Osage County Quilt
   Factory
P.O. Box 490
400 Walnut
Overbrook, KS 66524
(913) 665-7500*

PATCHES & PATTERNS. Susan Powers, owner of Patches & Patterns, is a talented designer whose quilts have been featured in national magazines and in exhibitions. Five of her clever designs are now available by mail. Each includes full-size pattern pieces, fabric requirements, complete directions, and a color photograph of the finished project. Among the most unusual is this stained-glass butterflies wall hanging. Finished size is 52" by 52"; each block is 16" square. Brochure available.

*Patches & Patterns
P.O. Box 456-T
Georgetown, CT 06829
(203) 438-7155*

PATTERNS BY JEANEAU. White-work quilt patterns are the specialty at this mail-order firm. Its brochure illustrates nearly four dozen different patterns for crib quilts, full-size quilts, and tablecloths. Many of the patterns are available in several different sizes; all are printed on heavy white paper and include a photograph of the completed project and detailed instructions. Brochure, $1.

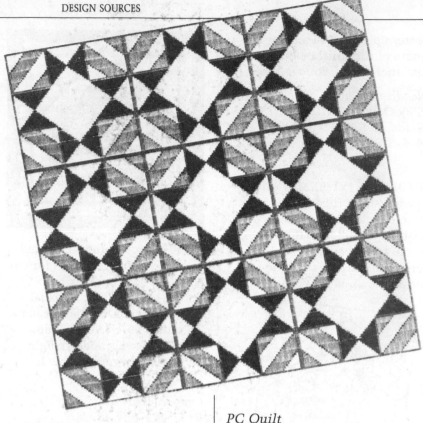

Patterns by Jeaneau
P.O. Box 17407
Salt Lake City, UT 84117
(801) 277-6620

PC QUILT. If you have access to an IBM personal computer or a compatible PC, you may want to have Nina Antze's software program. Quiltpc and Quiltjr are BASIC programs whose intent is to enable you to work with geometric quilt blocks to create your own quilt designs. A library of already-drawn blocks is included on either disk, and you can add your own designs to it, then combine them in endless combinations to produce unique patterns of your own. If you have a color monitor, of course, so much the better. If not, Antze's program will work on a monochromatic screen. Brochure available.

PC Quilt
7061 Lynch Rd.
Sebastopol, CA 95472
(707) 823-8494

PRAIRIE FARM DESIGNS. Among the patterns for quilting and appliqué created by Terry Fatout of Prairie Farm Designs is this charming Amish Threads wall hanging. It comes with instructions for a completed 18″ by 20″ appliquéd piece and for a complementary 7″ Amish doll. Teddy Family includes patterns and instructions for an 18″ appliquéd hoop design, 16″ ruffled pillow, and 9″ by 12″ Mama Bear pillow; the Wee Gardeners pattern is for a 38″ by 46″ appliquéd and pieced quilt, complete with flowers and picket fence. Catalog available.

Prairie Farm Designs
578 S. Vine
Denver, CO 80209
(303) 778-7611

THE QUILT PATCH. Three of the most popular quilt designs are offered in kit form by The Quilt Patch. Dresden Plate, Log Cabin, and Ohio Star come in either complete kits or in tops only to make any size quilt from crib to king, a wall hanging, or a 16"-square pillow. A complete kit includes pieces precisely cut from 100% cotton calico solids and prints, Fairfield batting, cotton/polyester backing, binding, a #8 needle, and thread. Catalog, $2.

The Quilt Patch
1897 Hanover Pike
Littlestown, PA 17340
(717) 359-5940

THE QUILT SQUARE. If you enjoy piecing and quilting, but find measuring and cutting the fabric tiresome and time-consuming, consider one of the complete kits available from The Quilt Square. Classic patterns include Windmill and Fox and Geese, and more unusual designs such as Card Trick, il-

lustrated here. Each kit includes pre-cut fabric in a choice of color combinations; muslin backing; and coordinated bias binding. If you prefer to work on a project that will more exactly complement your color scheme,

The Quilt Square offers three custom kits (Ohio Star, Nine Patch, and Monkey Wrench) that can be assembled to your order. Send a swatch of wallpaper, drapery fabric, or upholstery, and the firm will select and cut coordinating fabrics. Each custom kit includes accurately cut pieces, quilting stencil, muslin backing, borders, and instructions. Brochure, $2.

The Quilt Square
752 N. Main St.
Meadville, PA 16335
(814) 333-4383

QUILTER'S CORNER. Cath Heslin, proprietor of the Quilter's Corner retail shop, has designed four contemporary wall quilts that are available in pattern form. Each pattern includes a complete materials list and instructions. Motifs include America (shown), Ohio Amish Star, Lancaster Diamond, and The Quilter's Block. Heslin's patterns are available at local quilt and fabric shops, or contact:

Quilter's Corner
83 Main St.
Tappan, NY 10983
(914) 359-6866

QUILTER'S PEACE. Beginning quilters can be overwhelmed by the sheer size of a project. One answer might be to start with one of the miniature patterns in the Quilter's Peace Amish Collection. Detailed instructions for making six basic designs typical of traditional Amish quilts in miniature (6" to 9" square) are included. The finished blocks are suitable for framing, or for combining in pillow tops or as decorative embellishment on clothing. Many patterns for full-size quilts can also be ordered from Quilter's Peace. Catalog, $2.

Quilter's Peace, Inc.
P.O. Box 349
Albany Post Rd.
Garrison, NY 10524
(914) 424-4066

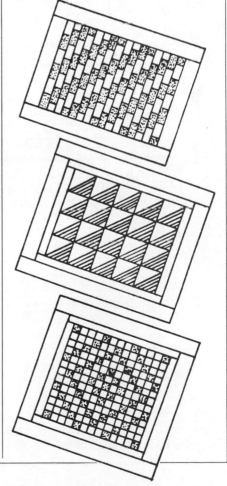

QUILTS & OTHER COMFORTS. Ode to Mother Goose, designed by Marla Gibbs Stefanelli, is one of a series of designer quilt pat-terns featured in the Quilts & Other Comforts catalog. All of the company's patterns for both traditional and contemporary quilt projects are full size, ready to use, with easy-to-follow instructions for machine or hand piecing and appliqué. Kits are offered for a number of the patterns to save you time, measuring, and cutting. Catalog, $1.25.

Quilts & Other Comforts
P.O. Box 394-3
6700 W. 44th Ave.
Wheatridge, CO 80034
(303) 420-4272

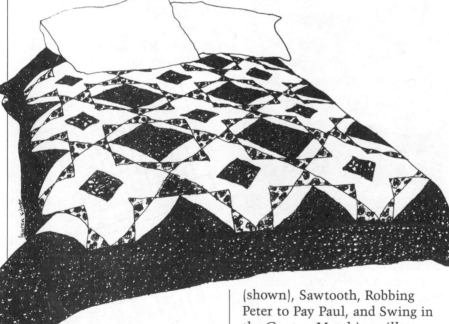

QUILTWORK PATCHES. Complete quilt kits from this full-service shop include pre-cut cotton patches for the top, borders to frame both the top and the back, a muslin quilt back cut to size, and polyester batting. Each kit comes with thorough and clearly written instructions. Among the kits currently offered are Hester's Garden (shown), Sawtooth, Robbing Peter to Pay Paul, and Swing in the Center. Matching pillow kits are available. If you prefer to cut your own fabric, consider one of the many patterns in the Quiltwork Patches catalog. Each pattern comes with full-size pieces, complete instructions for any size from crib to king, precalculated fabric requirements, and hand and machine directions for piecing, appliqué, and quilting. Catalog, $1.

Quiltwork Patches
P.O. Box 724-B
430 NW 6th St.
Corvallis, OR 97339
(503) 754-1475

RAINBOW QUILTS. Needleworkers who find quilting to be the most satisfying and challenging aspect of a project will appreciate the quilt blocks manufactured and sold by Rainbow Quilts. Patterns in cross stitch and outline are stamped on quality white fabric in 18″ blocks. You may order blocks by the dozen or in 20- or 30-block sets. Choose blocks alone, blocks with color scheme and floss, or a complete quilt top—blocks, floss, sashing, and borders. Devotees of appliqué will want to consider Rainbow Quilts' Hawaiian quilt blocks—seven different appliqués stamped and ready to cut out and affix to a 24″ square. Each design is done on a color that makes a striking contrast to its block. Individual blocks can be ordered; or you might choose a complete pillow kit, which includes block, appliqué, batting, backing, and quilting thread. Catalog, $1.50.

Rainbow Quilts
143 NE Fourth Ave.
Delray Beach, FL 33444
(305) 278-8988

MARY K. RYAN DESIGN. Experienced quilters will appreciate the clear instructions

and full-size pieces included in two timeless patterns from Mary K. Ryan. Both Mariner's Compass (shown) and Feathered Star are intricate, beautiful designs which, when properly executed, result in heirloom-quality quilts. Each pattern will make a wall quilt or can be used as a central medallion or a quilt block. For further information, contact:

Mary K. Ryan Design
Grandview Terr.
Rutland, VT 05701
(802) 773-6563

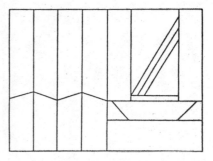

clothing or, in multiples, border a quilt. This original pattern by Kaye includes designs for a boat block and an ocean/sky block, each measuring 4½″ by 5¾″. The Seminole Sampler catalog includes many other patterns for patchwork and appliqué. Catalog, $2 (refundable with order).

Seminole Sampler
P.O. Box 658
Ellicott City, MD 21043
(301) 465-6266

SCHOOLHOUSE COLLECTION. The staff at this Ohio quilt shop has put together a number of kits that will be of interest to the many quilters whose leisure time is limited. Among the kits they make available through the mail is a classic Double Wed-

ding Ring. Others include Dresden Plate, Hexagon Star, Schoolhouse, and Teddy Bear. For information, contact:

Schoolhouse Collection Ltd.
4315 Hills & Dales Rd.
Canton, OH 44708
(216) 477-4767

BARBARA WILLIAMS. This comical baseball player would be a perfect decoration on the wall of a Little Leaguer's room. It is one of a number of original full-size patterns designed and sold by Barbara Williams and measures a generous 12″ by 20″. Or choose a rock singer, a monk, a Santa Claus, a cowboy, an Indian, or a 1920s flapper. Williams also has created patterns for several contemporary album quilts. Catalog, $2.

Barbara Williams
2642 Phaeton Dr.
Oroville, CA 95966

SEMINOLE SAMPLER. Equipped with just a rotary cutter and a

ruler, you can make a strip-pieced sailboat to decorate

WONDERART. Under the Wonderart name, Needlecraft Corporation of America manufactures ten different cross-stitch designs suitable for quilt blocks. Each design is printed on 50% cotton, 50% polyester fabric; quilting lines are included. The 18''-square blocks come in packages of six, with instructions and a list of thread requirements. Violets is shown here; other motifs include Snowflowers, Tea Rose, Daisies, Americana, and Spring Blossoms. Look for the Wonderart display at your local quilt or fabric shop, or contact:

Needlecraft Corp. of America, Inc.
North Industrial Blvd.
Calhoun, GA 30701
(404) 629-5232

BONNIE LYNN YOUNG. Bonnie Lynn Young designs and sells patterns for miniature quilts and folk dolls; her preference is for country motifs. Shown here are Young's Shaker doll (11½'' tall), pinwheel quilt, and heart quilt. Brochure, $1.

Bonnie Lynn Young
314 S. Clinton Ave.
Lindenhurst, NY 11757
(516) 226-7885

Other Suppliers of Kits and Patterns

Consult Directory of Suppliers for Addresses

The Brass Goose, Front Royal, VA
Brewer Fabric Shop, Brewer, ME
Cabin Fever Calicoes, Center
   Sandwich, NH
Calico House, Scottsville, VA
The Cloth Cupboard, Boise, ID
Community Quilts, Bethesda, MD
Country Crafts & Fabrications,
   Folsom, CA
Country House Quilts, Zionsville,
   IN
Creative Stitches, Honolulu, HI
Cross Patch Quilting Center,
   Garrison, NY
Dakota Factory Outlet, Webster, SD
G Street Fabrics, Rockville, MD
Heritage Quilting Designs, Cedar
   Rapids, IA
Hobby Time Helpers, Southwick,
   MA
Honey Bee Patterns, Jenison, MI

Joseph's Coat, Peterborough, NH
Kaleidoscope V, Newhall, CA
Maple Springs Farm, Verona, WI
Norton House, Wilmington, VT
Patches, Dalton, MA
Patience Corner Quilt Shop,
   Portsmouth, NH
The Pattern Factory, Puyallup, WA
Deanna Powell, Melbourne, FL
Quality Line Products, Hyrum, UT
The Quilt Patch, Marlboro, MA
Quilter's Rule, Ft. Lauderdale, FL
School for Inquiring Mynds,
   Tallahassee, FL
The Schoolhouse Collection Ltd.,
   Canton, OH
Silver Thimble Quilt Shop,
   Hampton Falls, NH
Treadleart, Lomita, CA
Tumbleweed, Cambridge, MA
Yours Truly, Westminster, CA

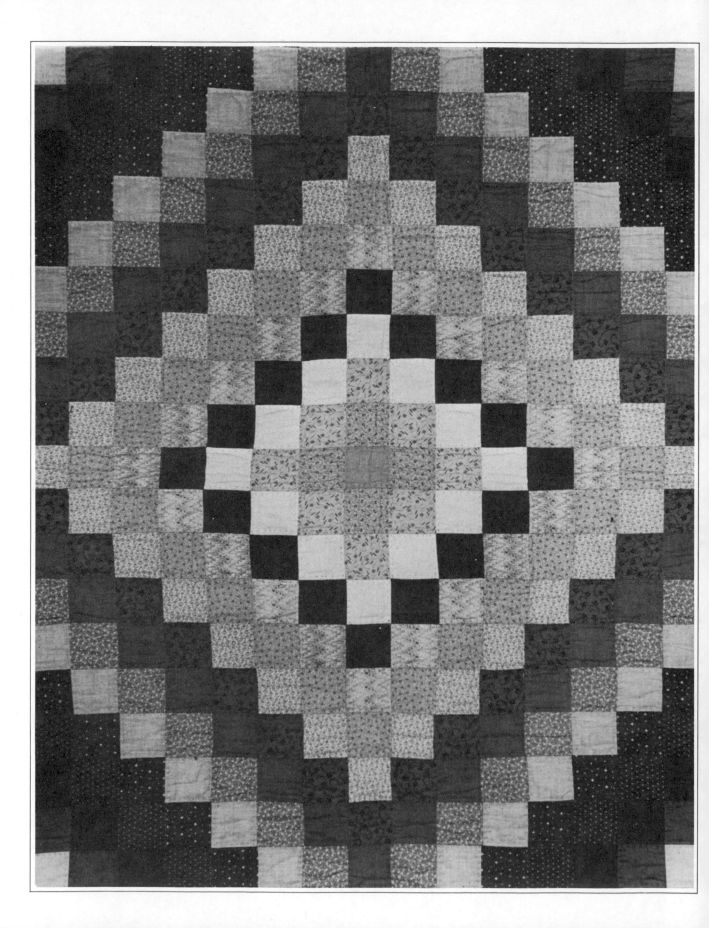

4. Finishing, Restoration, and Appraisal Services

"It took me more than twenty years, nearly twenty-five, I reckon. . . . My whole life is in that quilt. It scares me sometimes when I look at it. All my joys and sorrows are stitched into those little pieces. . . . I tremble sometimes when I remember what that quilt knows about me."—*The Standard Book of Quilt Making and Collecting*, by Marguerite Ickis.

How often we as students of the art of quilt making have read and pondered these words. Our understanding of them is almost instinctive, for they express not only the thoughts and feelings of an anonymous quilter of a bygone era, but also our own. The message transcends time and place and is as familiar to any individual as it is to the collective body of quilt artisans.

Today, quilt makers and quilt collectors alike recognize that quilts, both antique and contemporary, embody a unique aspect of the human spirit. They are as worthy of our appreciation and careful preservation for that reason as they are for their material, historic, or artistic value. The services rendered by a growing circle of professional restoration and conservation experts and quilt appraisers enable quilters and collectors to document and protect their quilts in a knowledgeable and scientific manner. It is a shared responsibility to preserve the art of the quilt for this and future generations to enjoy.

In this chapter are listed individuals and groups throughout the United States who provide restoration, conservation, and appraisal services and supplies for antique quilts and less venerable, but no less treasured, contemporary bedcoverings. Contact may be made either by letter of inquiry, or, where noted, by telephone.

Occasionally, both beginners and seasoned quilters require the expertise and time-saving services professionals have to offer. Hand quilting, pattern drafting, and quilt-top marking are among the finishing services listed here.

New England

Appraisal Services

JUDI BOISSON
89 Main St.
Westport, CT 06880
(203) 226-4100

CRANBERRY QUILTERS
161 Bay Rd.
S. Hamilton, MA 01982
(617) 468-3871

PHYLLIS HADERS
158 Water St.
Stonington, CT 06378
(203) 535-4403

MT. VERNON ANTIQUES
P.O. Box 66
Rockport, MA 01966
(617) 546-2434

Restoration and Conservation Services

DEBORAH BEDE
20 Old Concord Rd.
Henniker, NH 03243
(603) 428-3353

Recommended by the New Hampshire Historical Society

CRANBERRY QUILTERS
161 Bay Rd.
S. Hamilton, MA 01982
(617) 468-3871

Offers restoration services on antique quilts.

LINDA EPPICH ETOFFE
45 Devon Ct.
E. Greenwich, RI 02818
(401) 884-7342

PAULA GULBICKI
231 Melrose St.
Auburndale, MA 02166
(617) 965-1609

NEW ENGLAND QUILT TRADITION
123 Church St.
Guilford, CT 06437
(203) 453-4135

Offers restoration services for antique quilts.

SUSAN POWERS
Patches & Patterns
P.O. Box 456
Georgetown, CT 06029
(203) 438-7155

Provides restoration services for antique quilts.

THE TEXTILE CONSERVATION CENTER
Museum of American Textile History
800 Massachusetts Ave.
North Andover, MA 01845
(617) 686-0191

Work performed by the TCC staff includes collection surveys, on-site and laboratory examinations, stabilizations, washing, mounting, fumigation procedures, and emergency first aid. Estimates regarding cost and procedure are submitted to the client for approval before any work is undertaken. Lectures and workshops on textiles are available to groups and institutions.

Finishing Services

LADYBUG QUILTING SHOP
612 Rt. 6A, Main St.
Dennis, MA 02638
(617) 385-2662

Provides professional quilting services.

SUSAN POWERS
P.O. Box 456
Georgetown, CT 06029
(203) 438-7155

Quilts and finishes antique quilt tops.

THE VERMONT PATCHWORKS
P.O. Box 229
Shrewsbury, VT 05738
(802) 492-3590

Offers a pattern drafting service: for the basic fee of $5, a full-size paper pattern in the desired block size is drafted from the customer's sketch or photo. Plastic templates are available for an additional charge.

The Mid-Atlantic Region

Appraisal Services

JUDI BOISSON
28-C Job's Lane
Southampton, NY 11968
(516) 283-5466
or
Studio 3F, 4 E. 82nd St.
New York, NY 10028
(212) 719-5188
(212) 734-5844

BRIDGEHAMPTON QUILT GALLERY
Main St.
Bridgehampton, NY 11932
(516) 537-0333

HAZEL CARTER
1604 Palm Springs Dr.
Vienna, VA 22180
(703) 938-3246

COUNTRY PATCHWORK
1603 Carlisle Rd.
Camp Hill, PA 17011
(717) 761-2586

M. FINKEL & DAUGHTER
936 Pine St.
Philadelphia, PA 19107
(215) 627-7797

LAURA FISHER ANTIQUE QUILTS &
    AMERICANA
1050 Second Ave., Gallery #57
New York, NY 10022
(212) 838-2596

TINA GRAVATT
Pied Piper Gallery
537 E. Girard Ave.
Philadelphia, PA 19125
(215) 432-9669

JANOS AND ROSS, INC.
110 East End Ave.
New York, NY 10028
(212) 988-0407

Offers appraisals on antique
quilts, specializing in Amish
designs. Mail-order appraisals
are available for $15 per quilt
(provide clear photographs and a
self-addressed, stamped
envelope).

PATRICIA CHAPIN O'DONNELL
315 Lafayette Ave.
Swarthmore, PA 19081
(215) 543-5720

Ms. O'Donnell's appraisal serv-
ices are recommended by the
Chester County Historical
Society of Pennsylvania.

STELLA RUBIN ANTIQUES
12300 Glen Rd.
Potomac, MD 20854
(301) 948-4187

THOS. K. WOODARD AMERICAN
    ANTIQUES & QUILTS
835 Madison Ave.
New York, NY 10021
(212) 988-2906

Restoration and Conservation Services

C.J. BROWN
P.O. Box 226
Staten Island, NY 10308
(718) 967-4755

Provides minor repair and
restoration services, including
evaluating and cleaning of all-
cotton quilts when deemed
appropriate.

CALICO PATCH QUILT SHOPPE
5158 Peach St.
Erie, PA 16509
(814) 864-2978

Offers complete restoration
services and sells a top-quality
restoration kit.

THE COTTON PATCH
5417 Main St.
Williamsville, NY 14221
(716) 634-4544

Offers limited repair services for
old quilts.

MARGARET FIKIORIS, TEXTILE
    CONSERVATOR
Henry Francis Du Pont Winter-
    thur Museum
Winterthur, DE 19735
(302) 656-8591

LAURA FISHER ANTIQUE QUILTS &
    AMERICANA
1050 Second Ave., Gallery #57
New York, NY 10022
(212) 838-2596

PIE GALINAT
230 W. 10th St.
New York, NY 10014
(212) 741-3259

GRANDMOTHER'S PATCHES
Eagle Village Shops
Rt. 100, P.O. Box 398
Uwchland, PA 19480
(215) 458-5382

Provides simple restoration
services on the premises. Quilts
requiring extensive restoration
procedures are referred to a local
professional restorer.

TINA GRAVATT
Pied Piper Gallery
537 E. Girard Ave.
Philadelphia, PA 19125
(215) 432-9669

THE JAMAR TEXTILE RESTORATION
    STUDIO
250 Riverside Dr.
New York, NY 10025
(212) 866-6426

Offers complete restoration and
repair services for 18th-, 19th-,
and 20th-century textiles.
Owner Tracy Jamar has extensive experience in repairing
damaged and age-worn quilts;
other services available are re-
binding, preparing quilts for
mounting and display, and ad-
vising on the care and cleaning
of antique textiles. For further
information, send a self-
addressed, stamped envelope
with your inquiry.

DENA KATZENBERG
Baltimore Museum
Museum Drive
Baltimore, MD 21218
(301) 396-7101

MARGARET T. ORDONEZ
University of Maryland
Symons Hall, Room 1200
College Park, MD 20742
(301) 454-3311

VIRGINIA PLEDGER
1738 Royden Trail
Annapolis, MD 21401
(301) 849-3351

BETSY PROKAP
Quilt Care
Valhalla, NY 10595
(914) 946-3358

Offers major repair and restoration services.

QUILT PATCH
3932 Old Lee Hwy.
Fairfax, VA 22030
(703) 273-6937

HELENE VON ROSENSTIEL, INC.
382 11th St.
Brooklyn, NY 11215
(718) 788-7909

A full-service costume and textile conservation and restoration center which offers cleaning, repairing, and mounting procedures for quilts. Mail-order conservation supplies are also available through the firm. Brochure available.

ELLY SEABOLD
Gallery of Graphic Arts
1601 York Ave.
New York, NY 10028
(212) 988-4731

BARBARA SMEAD
Classics in Cotton
2747 Carter Farm Ct.
Alexandria, VA 22306
(703) 360-3107

TALAS
213 W. 35th St.
New York, NY 10001-1996
(212) 736-7744

Provides quality products for all aspects of art conservation and archival treatment. Quilters may purchase such products as Orvus Paste, silk crepeline, muslin, silk and cotton thread, cotton gloves, and acid-free tissue paper and storage boxes by mail or at the Talas showroom. Catalog, $5.

TEXTILE CONSERVATION ASSOCIATES
1420 Dartmouth Dr.
Bethlehem, PA 18017
(215) 865-9916

THE TEXTILE CONSERVATION WORKSHOP, INC.
Main St.
S. Salem, NY 10590
(914) 763-5805

Finishing Services

CALICO PATCH QUILT SHOPPE
5158 Peach St.
Erie, PA 16509
(814) 864-2978

Offers professional quilting services at reasonable prices.

THE COTTON PATCH
5417 Main St.
Williamsville, NY 14221
(716) 634-4544

Employs professional quilters who will mark, quilt, and bind quilt tops.

CREATIVE QUILTING WORKSHOP
415 High St.
Bethlehem, PA 18018
(215) 868-0376

Provides professional quilting information.

JOHN FREEMAN
P.O. Box 430
Norristown, PA 19404
(215) 539-3010

Serves as a consultant to individuals and groups who are seeking contemporary, traditional-style quilts for decorating purposes.

TINA GRAVATT
Pied Piper Gallery
537 E. Girard Ave.
Philadelphia, PA 19125
(215) 423-9669

Offers professional quilting services.

JOE & MARY KOVAL
550 Lutz School Rd.
Indiana, PA 15701
(412) 465-7370

Offer hand-quilting services for antique quilt tops.

LIGONIER QUILT SHOP
305 E. Main St.
Ligonier, PA 15658
(412) 238-6359

Provides professional quilting information.

SUE'S QUILT CUTTING SERVICE
126 Edgewood Rd.
Ossining, NY 10562
(914) 762-3524

This service will cut, from the customer's own fabric, any of over 100 different patchwork and appliqué patterns. Prices vary according to quilt size.

VILLAGE QUILT SHOP, INC.
1328 Grandin Rd. SW
Roanoke, VA 24015
(703) 343-3311

Provides professional quilting information.

The Midwest

Appraisal Services

BARLOND SEWING CENTER
295 E. Columbia
Battle Creek, MI 49015
(616) 962-9588

DARWIN BEARLEY
98 Beck Ave.
Akron, OH 44302
(216) 376-4965

Recommended by the Western

Reserve Historical Society of Ohio.

CARROW & McNERNEY COUNTRY ANTIQUES
P.O. Box 125
Winnetka, IL 60093
(312) 441-7137
(312) 446-7516

MARY ELLYN & GORDON JENSEN
2017 E. 13th St.
Davenport, IA 52803
(319) 322-4905

SANDRA MITCHELL
739 Mohawk
Columbus, OH 43206
(614) 443-6222

OH, SUZANNA
6 S. Broadway
Lebanon, OH 45036
(513) 932-8246

PATCHES QUILT SHOP
337 S. Main
St. Charles, MO 63301
(314) 946-6004

Restoration and Conservation Services

AMERICAN INSTITUTE FOR CONSERVATION
Zoe Annis Perkins, Textiles
  Group
533 Woodard Dr.
St. Louis, MO 63122
(314) 721-0067

VIRGINIA GUNN
819 Quinby Ave.
Wooster, OH 44691
(216) 262-8581

Recommended by the Hunter Museum of Art, Chattanooga, Tennessee.

KATE HENERY
1202 Fourth Ave.
Alton, IA 51003

Recommended by the Hunter Museum of Art, Chattanooga, Tennessee.

MARY ELLYN & GORDON JENSEN
2017 E. 13th St.
Davenport, IA 52803
(319) 322-4905

Offer custom cleaning services for soiled or stained all-cotton quilts. Estimates given prior to cleaning.

HELEN KELLEY
2215 Stinson Blvd.
Minneapolis, MN 55418
(612) 789-8207

Recommended by the Hunter Museum of Art, Chattanooga, Tennessee.

HAROLD E. MAILAND
Textile Conservation Service
3001 N. New Jerscy St., #105
Indianapolis, IN 46205

Recommended by the Cincinnati Art Museum, Cincinnati, Ohio.

MINNESOTA QUILTERS
Gail Sweeney
2504 114th St.
Burnsville, MN 55337

Recommended by the Minnesota Historical Society, St. Paul, Minncsota.

OHIO HISTORICAL SOCIETY
1895 Velma Ave.
Columbus, OH 43211
(614) 466-1500

Offers professional advice on the care, display, and dating of old quilts.

THE SAMPLER
314 Water St.
Excelsior, MN 55331
(612) 474-4794

Offers limited restoration/conservation services.

SUE ELLEN WHITE
144 Amity Dr.
Waterloo, IA 50701

Recommended by the Hunter Musem of Art, Chattanooga, Tennessee.

Finishing Services

BARLOND SEWING CENTER
295 E. Columbia
Battle Creek, MI 49015
(616) 962-9588

Provides professional quilting information.

HEARTHSIDE QUILTER'S NOOK
10731 W. Forest Home Ave.
Hales Corners, WI 53130
(414) 425-2474

Provides professional quilting information.

CHRIS KLEPPE
110 N. 80th St.
Milwaukee, WI 53213
(414) 476-3420

Offers a reasonably priced precision drafting service. A full-size pattern for any non-copyrighted patchwork or appliqué pattern up to 18″ square can be accurately reproduced. Individual pattern pieces with seam allowances are also available.

MAPLE SPRINGS FARM
1828 Hwy. PB
Verona, WI 53593
(608) 845-9482

Washes and recards old wool and adds new wool to original batts.

NEEDLE IN THE HAYSTACK
2307 E. 10th St.
Anderson, IN 46012
(317) 644-7700

Provides professional quilting information.

QUILT MARKINGS, ETC.
Shirley Hutabarat
630 N. Fountain
Wichita, KS 67220
(316) 681-0906
and
Stephanie Evans
4860 N. Harding
Wichita, KS 67220
(316) 744-3088

Specializes in marking quilting designs for white-on-white or whole cloth quilt tops of all sizes. Other services include marking wall hangings, pillows, clothing, tablecloths, and patchwork quilts as well as custom design of quilt patterns according to customer specifications.

THE SAMPLER
314 Water St.
Excelsior, MN 55331
(612) 474-4794

Provides a finishing service for old quilt tops as well as professional custom quilting services for new ones.

STITCHIN POST-YARN BOUTIQUE
14227 Old State Rd.
Middlefield, OH 44062
(216) 632-1787

Provides custom quilting services.

STITCH ON NEEDLEWORK SHOP, INC.
926 Massachusetts St.
Lawrence, KS 66044
(913) 842-1101

Provides professional quilting information.

SUGAR RIVER FARMS, INC.
P.O. Box 663
New Glarus, WI 53574
(608) 527-5157

Washes, recards, and adds new wool to old wool quilt batts.

The Southeast

Appraisal Services

KATY CHRISTOPHERSON
2211 Cherokee Pkwy.
Louisville, KY 40204
(502) 451-4679

Recommended by the Hunter Museum of Art, Chattanooga, Tennessee.

MAREE DOWDEY
1200 Hancock
Columbia, SC 29205
(803) 787-7861

Recommended by the McKissick Museum, Columbia, South Carolina.

MILDRED LOCKE
P.O. Box 157
Bell Buckle, TN 37020

Recommended by the Hunter Museum of Art, Chattanooga, Tennessee.

QUILTWORKS, INC.
5891 SW 73rd St.
S. Miami, FL 33143
(305) 666-0166

BETS RAMSEY
P.O. Box 4146
Chattanooga, TN 37405
(615) 265-4300

Recommended by the Hunter

Museum of Art, Chattanooga, Tennessee.

TOLL HOUSE QUILTS
3900 Taft Hwy.
Signal Mountain, TN 37377
(615) 886-5977

MERIKAY WALDVOGEL
1501 Whitower Rd.
Knoxville, TN 37919
(615) 691-8117

Recommended by the Hunter Museum of Art, Chattanooga, Tennessee.

SHELLY ZEGART QUILTS
12 Z River Hill Rd.
Louisville, KY 40207
(502) 897-7506

Restoration and Conservation Services

KATY CHRISTOPHERSON
2211 Cherokee
Louisville, KY 40204
(502) 451-4679

Recommended by the Hunter Musem of Art, Chattanooga, Tennessee.

MAREE DOWDEY
1200 Hancock
Columbia, SC 29205
(803) 787-7861

Recommended by the McKissick Museum, Columbia, South Carolina.

SUE DREW
3933 Croydon Rd.
Montgomery, AL 36109
(205) 277-4976

Recommended by the Birmingham Museum of Art, Birmingham, Alabama.

MARY KATHERINE JARRELL
5825-D Hunting Ridge Ln.
Charlotte, NC 28212

Recommended by the Hunter Museum of Art, Chattanooga, Tennessee.

EVA EARLE KENT
2315 Kimberlin Heights Dr.
Knoxville, TN 37920
(615) 573-0769

Recommended by the Hunter Museum of Art, Chattanooga, Tennessee.

MILDRED LOCKE
P.O. Box 151
Bell Buckle, TN 37020

Recommended by the Hunter Museum of Art, Chattanooga, Tennessee.

QUILTWORKS, INC.
5891 SW 73rd St.
S. Miami, FL 33143
(305) 666-0166

Sells restoration/conservation supplies and offers consultations on preservation methods.

BETS RAMSEY
P.O. Box 4146
Chattanooga, TN 37405
(615) 265-4300

Recommended by the Hunter Museum of Art, Chattanooga, Tennessee.

The Southwest

Appraisal Services

BUCKBOARD ANTIQUES & QUILTS
1411 N. May
Oklahoma City, OK 73107
(405) 943-7020

BECKY SUDSBURY
c/o M.E.S.D.A.
P.O. Box 10310
Winston-Salem, NC 27108
(919) 722-6148

TOLL HOUSE QUILTS
3900 Taft Hwy.
Signal Mountain, TN 37377
(615) 886-5977

Provides complete repair, conservation, and re-binding services and sells acid-free materials for proper quilt storage.

SHELLY ZEGART QUILTS
12Z River Hill Road
Louisville, KY 40207
(502) 897-7566

Finishing Services

TOLL HOUSE QUILTS
3900 Taft Hwy.
Signal Mountain, TN 37377
(615) 886-5977

Employs a small group of professional quilters who quilt antique tops with authentic materials and designs.

WANDA'S QUILTING
7310 Manatee Ave.
W. Bradenton, FL 33529
(813) 794-2405

Provides professional quilting information.

MARY GRUNBAUM
3213 Knox St.
Dallas, TX 75205
(214) 528-1321

Recommended by the Dallas Historical Society.

PINE COUNTRY QUILTS
The Carriage House
413 N. San Francisco
Flagstaff, AZ 86001
(602) 779-2194

BRYCE REVELEY
Gentle Arts Complete Antique Textile Service
936 Arabella St.
P.O. Box 15832
New Orleans, LA 70115
(504) 895-5628

THE SALT BOX
2310 Fagot St.
Metairie, LA 70001
(504) 837-0539

Restoration and Conservation Services

CATHERINE ANTHONY
10925 Roaring Brook Ln.
Houston, TX 77024
(713) 465-9126

Recommended by the Hunter Museum of Art, Chattanooga, Tennessee.

BUCKBOARD ANTIQUES & QUILTS
1411 N. May
Oklahoma City, OK 73107
(405) 943-7020

Offers limited restoration services.

COUNTRY FAIR QUILT PATCH
1401 Lake Air Dr.
Waco, TX 76710
(817) 776-5710

Provides minor repairs on old quilts.

PINE COUNTRY QUILTS
The Carriage House
413 N. San Francisco
Flagstaff, AZ 86001
(602) 779-2194

BRYCE REVELEY
Gentle Arts Complete Antique
  Textile Service
936 Arabella St.
P.O. Box 15832
New Orleans, LA 70115
(504) 895-5628

Specializes in the cleaning,
restoration, conservation, and
mounting of antique quilts,
with an emphasis on crazy quilt
restoration and mounting.

THE SALT BOX
2310 Fagot St.
Metairie, LA 70001
(504) 837-0539

TEXAS CONSERVATION CENTER
The Panhandle-Plains Historical
  Museum
P.O. Box 967, W.T. Station
Canyon, TX 79016
(806) 655-7191

Offers a variety of treatments
for historic textiles, including
fumigation, wet, dry, and spot
cleaning, reintegration, color
matching, and material analysis
and fiber identification. Special
storage and display boxes and
support devices are available
through the Center. Estimates
are provided in advance.

Finishing Services

PINE COUNTRY QUILTS
The Carriage House
413 N. San Francisco
Flagstaff, AZ 86001
(602) 779-2194

Employs a team of professional
quilters who will quilt and bind
pre-pieced tops.

The Rocky Mountains

Appraisal Services

HIGH COUNTRY QUILTS
4857A N. Academy Blvd.
Colorado Springs, CO 80907
(303) 598-1312

THE HISSING GOOSE GALLERY
P.O. Box 597
Ketchum, ID 83340
(208) 726-3036

Restoration and Conservation Services

HIGH COUNTRY QUILTS
4857A N. Academy Blvd.
Colorado Springs, CO 80907
(303) 598-1312

**ROCKY MOUNTAIN REGIONAL
CONSERVATION CENTER**
2420 S. University
Denver, CO 80208
(303) 733-2712

Finishing Services

HIGH COUNTRY QUILTS
4857A N. Academy Blvd.
Colorado Springs, CO 80907
(303) 598-1312

Provides professional quilting
information.

The Far West

Appraisal Services

**THE MARGARET CAVIGGA QUILT
  COLLECTION**
8648 Melrose Ave.
Los Angeles, CA 90069
(213) 659-3020

CHARLOTTE EKBACK
49 Charles St.
Moorpark, CA 93021
(805) 529-0020

Recommended by the Hunter
Museum of Art, Chattanooga,
Tennessee.

JODI'S MERCANTILE
710 Sutter St.
Folsom, CA 95630
(916) 351-0804

PEACE AND PLENTY
7320 Melrose Ave.
Los Angeles, CA 90046
(213) 937-3339

Provides written appraisals for
antique quilts, including the
pattern name, quilt dimensions,
condition, approximate date,
family information if available,
and the retail or insurance
value. Fee, $25 per quilt.

QUILT WITH EASE
3122 Broadway at Pacific
Everett, WA 98201
(206) 258-1955
(206) 743-3344

MARGARET SCHUKER
230 Colt Rd.
Rancho Palos Verdes, CA 90279

Recommended by the Hunter

Museum of Art, Chattanooga, Tennessee.

DIANNA VALE
1294 32nd Ave. NW
Salem, OR 97304
(503) 364-6355

Restoration and Conservation Services

HAZEL HYNDS
2140 Valley Glen Ln.
Orange, CA 92667

Recommended by the Hunter Museum of Art, Chattanooga, Tennessee.

JODI'S MERCANTILE
710 Sutter St.
Folsom, CA 95630
(916) 351-0804

SANDRA METZLER
P.O. Box 1043
Willits, CA 95490

Recommended by the Hunter Museum of Art, Chattanooga, Tennessee.

QUILT WITH EASE
3122 Broadway at Pacific
Everett, WA 98201
(206) 258-1955
(206) 743-3344

NANCY ROWLEY
900 Kenroy Terr.
Wenatchee, WA 98801
(509) 884-8382

Recommended by the Hunter Museum of Art, Chattanooga, Tennessee.

SAWTOOTH QUILT SHOP
1560 Fourth St.
San Rafael, CA 94901
(415) 453-1711

Offers custom handwashing, repair, and restoration services.

MARGARET SCHUKER
2830 Colt Rd.
Rancho Palos Verdes, CA 90274

Recommended by the Huner Museum of Art, Chattanooga, Tennessee.

THE TEXTILE CONSERVATION WORKSHOP
3538 Digger Pine Ridge
Winters, CA 95694
(916) 795-4602

Proprietor Nancy Sloper Howard uses state-of-the-art equipment and techniques in conservation and restoration. Inquiries welcome; estimates given.

GEORGIA VASKO
443 Wyndgate Rd.
Sacramento, CA 95825

Recommended by the Hunter Museum of Art, Chattanooga, Tennessee.

VALDA WHITMAN
86 Marin View
Mill Valley, CA 94941

Finishing Services

THE MARGARET CAVIGGA QUILT COLLECTION
8648 Melrose Ave.
Los Angeles, CA 90069
(213) 659-3020

Provides professional quilting services for pre-pieced tops.

BETTY FERGUSON
1013 Marshall
Richland, WA 99352
(509) 946-0370

Offers a custom negative service which prepares negatives from the client's photographs for Cyanotype printing on fabric. Full tone or high contrast is available, sizes are 5″ by 7″ or 8″ by 10″.

JODI'S MERCANTILE
710 Sutter St.
Folsom, CA 95630
(916) 351-0804

Provides professional quilting information.

LOG CABIN CALICOES
184 E. Plumb Lane
Reno, NV 89502
(702) 825-7030

Provides professional quilting information.

QUILT WITH EASE
3122 Broadway at Pacific
Everett, WA 98201
(206) 258-1955

Provides professional quilting information.

SAWTOOTH QUILT SHOP
1560 Fourth St.
San Rafael, CA 94901
(415) 453-1711

Offers professional hand quilting and custom binding services.

DIANNA VALE
1294 32nd Ave. NW
Salem, OR 97304
(503) 364-6355

Offers a consultation service to help customers select fabrics, patterns, and quilting designs for their own projects.

A GALLERY OF
AMISH QUILTS
Design Diversity from a Plain People

Pure
FABRICATION

CALICO and BEYOND:
The Use of Patterned Fabric in Quilts

Heirloom Quilting Designs

AMERICAN
QUILTS AND

CRIB QUILTS
and Other Small Wonders
Including complete patterns and instructions
for making your own crib quilts

THE SCRAP LOOK
Designs, Fabrics, Colors and
Piecing Techniques for Creating Multi-Fabric Quilts
JINNY BEYER

Ohio Quilts:
A Living Tradition

THE COMPLETE BOOK OF
QUILTMAKING

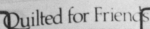

QUILTS

Quilted for Friends
DELAWARE VALLEY SIGNATURE QUILTS, 1840–1855

PICTURES
1001 PATTERNS FOR PIECING BY CAROL LaBRANCH

TEN
AFRO-AMERICAN
QUILTERS

An Exhibition
Organized by
Mississippi Department
of Archives and History

*Kentucky
Quilts
1800–1900*
The Kentucky Quilt Project

THE NEW CALIFORNIA QUILT

5. Good Reading

Books—like fabric, needles, and thread—are valuable tools in the art and craft of quilt making. Within their pages is a wealth of information and inspiration for both the beginner and the more experienced quilter. Practical instructional material, traditional and contemporary sources of design, and special techniques, as well as the artistic, historic, and sociological aspects of the quilt-making tradition, are just some of the subjects covered in today's publications. With so many interesting and informative books available it is little wonder, then, that many quilters' libraries are rivaled only by their fabric collections.

Listed and annotated in this chapter are our selections from the many quilting publications currently available, all chosen with a wide variety of interests, needs, and abilities in mind. Our brief comments are offered to help quilters choose those books which best suit their purposes.

Although the list is as up-to-date as possible, new books are constantly being written and many older publications often become unavailable without warning. Visiting the local library, book store, and quilt shop and watching for new book reviews in quilting periodicals such as those included in this chapter will enable you to remain well informed about current offerings.

We've chosen the best among current quilting periodicals, magazines which on a regular basis bring you news of all the latest techniques, products, and trends in quilting. You may want to subscribe to several, if you are not already doing so.

There are several purchasing alternatives open to the quilter who is searching for a particular book. Many of the titles listed here can be found at local book stores or quilt shops: these outlets are usually happy to place a special order if what you want is not in stock. A list of mail-order book dealers is included at the end of this chapter, as are the addresses of the book publishers, most of whom accept direct orders from the consumer.

A selection of quilt books offered at Community Quilts, Bethesda, Maryland.

How-To Books

This diverse category covers a wide range of subjects—from basic and advanced instructional material for traditional and innovative techniques to seldom discussed topics such as how to hold a quilt show. Instructions are thorough and are often presented in a step-by-step format. Any patterns which might accompany the text are used to support the instructional material.

AMERICAN PATCHWORK AND QUILTING by the editors of *Better Homes and Gardens*. As attractive to the eye and the imagination as it is informative, this encyclopedia of quilting covers every aspect of quiltmaking, collecting, displaying, and preservation. In addition to the numerous splendid color photographs of antique and contemporary quilts, there are well-illustrated, step-by-step directions that explain all the basic patchwork and appliqué techniques. Complete instructions and patterns for all the quilts and projects pictured are included; however, most of the patterns are printed on grids and will need to be enlarged to the correct scale. This is a beautiful gift worth giving to a friend or to yourself, one that will certainly appeal to all levels of quilting ability. 320 pages, $24.95. Published by Better Homes and Gardens Books, The Meredith Corporation.

AMERICAN QUILTS AND HOW TO MAKE THEM by Carter Houck and Myron Miller. Antique quilts never seem to lose their appeal despite the development of new ideas, patterns, and construction techniques constantly coming into the quilting forum. Here are full-size patterns for reproducing or adapting over fif-

ty heirloom quilt designs, such as Whig Rose, Crown, and Wandering Foot. Basic instructions, brief histories, and photographs of each quilt are included. The patterns shown will appeal to the intermediate and advanced quilter. 200 pages, $14.95. Published by Charles Scribner's Sons.

AN AMISH ADVENTURE by Roberta Horton. Ten well-organized, clearly written lessons help the quilter develop an Amish sense of color, beginning with basic color concepts and simple designs and gradually working towards complex color arrangements and patterns. Sixteen pages of color photographs and numerous diagrams illustrate the text and provide plenty of inspiration for your own projects. Drafting instructions are included for making your own Amish quilting stencils and full-size patchwork templates. For all levels of ability. 53 pages, $13.95, plus $1.50 postage. Published by C&T Publishing.

AMISH QUILT PATTERNS by Rachel T. Pellman. Quilters who admire the striking visual qualities of traditional Amish quilts, but who lack the confidence in reproducing them, will appreciate this clearly

detailed handbook. Along with color and fabric suggestions, there are also complete instructions and full-size templates for thirty different quilts. In addition, the author has assembled a collection of lovely quilting designs which echo the finest quilting stitches found in Amish masterpieces. The patterns shown can be accomplished by the beginner and the more advanced quilter. 128 pages, $10.95, plus 5% postage. Published by Good Books.

APPLIQUÉ ALBUM QUILTS by Sandra Sigal and Melanie Fabian. Machine and hand-stitching techniques are described in a concise, step-by-step manner for assembling a contemporary version of the appliqué album quilt. Closeup photographs that correspond with the instructions and full-size templates for sixteen different block designs are included for making either a large quilt, lap quilt, or pillow tops. Patterns and techniques are geared toward the intermediate quilter. 24 pages, $5.98. Published by Gick Publishing Inc.

THE ART AND TECHNIQUE OF CREATING MEDALLION QUILTS

INCLUDING A RICH COLLECTION OF HISTORIC AND CONTEMPORARY EXAMPLES

JINNY BEYER

THE ART AND TECHNIQUE OF CREATING MEDALLION QUILTS by
Jinny Beyer. Designer and teacher Jinny Beyer establishes guidelines—not strict rules—for the successful planning, drafting, and construction of medallion quilts. No patterns are given, but the encouragement for the quilter to develop and bring to life her own ideas *is* freely given. Numerous photographs of contemporary and antique medallion quilts, as well as an historical account of this genre, are included. Best suited to the intermediate and advanced quilter. 169 pages, $29.95, hardcover edition. Published by EPM Publications, Inc.

AUSTRALIAN PATCHWORK DESIGNS by Margaret Rolfe. Australian birds, flowers, and animals are the inspiration for sixty original patchwork and appliqué designs. All patterns are actual size and can be used for creating full-size quilts, pillow tops, and other projects. Complete instructions for hand and machine stitching and detailed illustrations will appeal to all levels of quilting

ability. 150 pages, $12.95, plus $1.50 postage. Published by Sterling Publishing Co., Inc.

THE BASICS OF QUILTED CLOTHING by Nancy Martin. Getting started in the craft of making attractive quilted garments will be enjoyable and rewarding with this information-packed text as your guide. Instructions for sewing jackets, vests, children's clothes, tote bags, and even men's neckties are well defined and illustrated. Written for the beginner to the intermediate levels of ability. 69 pages, $8.00, plus $1.50 postage. Published by That Patchwork Place.

BEARS, QUILTS, AND OTHER LITTLE LUVS by Millie Leathers. Ten small quilts and a variety of bears and other toys reflect the author's life-long appreciation for American folk art. Full-size patterns and detailed instructions make each project a joy to create and share. For the intermediate and advanced levels of ability. 64 pages, $16.50, plus $1.50 postage. Published by Millie Leathers.

BIAS, TWO METHODS AND BINDING by Diana Leone. Step-by-step directions for two methods of making bias strips are carefully explained and illustrated in this instruction sheet. Charts for determining the yield of bias from one yard of fabric, as well as expert tips for binding a quilt, are also given. For all levels of ability. 4 pages, $2.95, plus 15% postage. Published by Leone Publications.

THE BOSTON COMMONS QUILT by Blanche Young and Helen

Young. An updated and refined version of the traditional Boston Commons pattern is presented in the authors' usual expert and efficient style. Complete instructions and detailed illustrations, as well as full-size multiple templates and quilting designs printed on pull-out sheets, will help the beginner or the expert create a lovely quilt. 36 pages, $8.95, plus $1 postage. Published by Young Publications.

BRANCHING OUT—TREE QUILTS by Carolann Palmer. Bask in peaceful contentment under the protective arms of a tree quilt. Full-size templates for twenty-two original quilts inspired by traditional patterns, plus complete instructions and diagrams, make these and several other small projects a joy to stitch. For the intermediate and advanced quilter. 96 pages, $11.95, plus $1.50 postage. Published by That Patchwork Place.

CALICO AND BEYOND by Roberta Horton. If you are sometimes overwhelmed by all the printed fabrics in your collection—especially the unusual ones—and wonder how you might use them to their best advantage, then this workbook will certainly be helpful to you. A well-organized, straightforward text, accompanied by many diagrams, teaches the quilter how to achieve greater visual and textural interest in patterned quilts. Color photographs of various scrap quilt styles—from traditional, folk-type to Japanese and Afro-American quilts—will inspire and challenge the quilter to break away from the mundane and try something unusual and extraordinary. For beginning, in-

termediate, and advanced levels of ability. 53 pages, $14.95, plus $1.50 postage. Published by C&T Publishing.

CATHEDRAL WINDOW—A NEW VIEW by Mary Ryder Kline. Enjoy the challenge of stitching an entire quilt, or perhaps just a pin cushion, pillow top, or other small project, using the Cathedral Window pattern or one of its three relatives. Full-size templates and complete sewing details, as well as several project plans, are included. For the intermediate to advanced levels of ability. 55 pages, $6, plus $1.50 postage. Published by That Patchwork Place.

CHRISTMAS QUILTS by Marsha McCloskey. Celebrate Christmas with a special quilt that embodies the rich imagery and joyful spirit of this holiday. The antique and contemporary Christmas quilts featured in the colorful "gallery" will inspire the quilter to create her own beautiful version. Twenty patchwork and appliqué patterns derived from these examples are presented with full-size templates and scaled piecing

B-83

Christmas Quilts
by Marsha McCloskey

diagrams. Instructions are concise and include machine piecing and hand appliqué methods. For all levels of ability. 72 pages, $11.95, plus $1.50 postage. Published by That Patchwork Place.

THE COMPLETE BOOK OF MACHINE QUILTING by Robbie and Tony Fanning. For those who prefer the time-saving benefits of machine piecing and quilting, this is one of the most informative and complete handbooks available. With an ordinary home sewing machine, attractive, good quality quilts and quilted gift items can be made. Instructions are thorough and are illustrated with many diagrams and photographs. Written for all levels of ability. 334 pages, $16.95. Published by Chilton Book Company.

THE CONTEMPORARY SAMPLER by Katie Pasquini. Here is a contemporary approach to sampler quiltmaking that uses traditional patchwork patterns in unusual and visually exciting ways. Over 130 block designs and their patterns have been grouped into six basic design categories and three skill levels. Also included are helpful diagrams and easy step-by-step instructions. For the beginner as well as the intermediate and advanced quilter. 76 pages, $9.95, plus $1.50 postage. Published by Sudz Publishing.

CRAZY QUILT PATCHWORK by Dixie Haywood. A contemporary interpretation of the Crazy quilt technique described in an easy yet thorough manner. Patterns for nineteen small and large projects—from clutch bags to full-size quilts—are included.

For all levels of ability. 80 pages, $4.95, plus 85¢ postage. Published by Dover Publications, Inc.

CREATING MEMORY QUILTS by Madonna Auxier Ferguson. Delicate watercolors and line drawings, interwoven with fifty-three patchwork and appliqué patterns, illustrate the author's fondest memories of childhood in the country. Full-size templates for traditional blocks such as Dutchman's Puzzle, Grandmother's Favorite, and

Red Cross are given in 4″, 8″, and 12″ sizes. Instructions and templates for creating several full-size quilts such as Geese on Parade and Brick Wall are also included. Quilters of all levels of skill will enjoy the patterns, poems, and drawings. 80 pages, $14.50, plus $1.50 postage. Published by Betty Boyink.

CREATIVE QUILTMAKING IN THE MANDALA TRADITION by Jean Eitel. The ancient mandala, rich in mystical symbolism, translates beautifully into the quilting medium. Advice for planning a design and selecting appropriate symbols will enable the quilter to achieve dramatic results. Eighteen full-size appliqué and patchwork patterns, both traditional and original, and twelve beautiful quilting designs, plus a gallery of color photographs, accompany the text. For the intermediate and expert quilter. 176 pages, $16.95. Published by Chilton Book Company.

CREATURE COMFORTS by Marie Shirer and Barbara Brackman. Learn to design and stitch out-of-the-ordinary patchwork animals using the authors' expertly detailed techniques, beautiful illustrations, and easy-to-follow text. Over one dozen projects are shown and include full-size templates and complete instructions. Conveniently spiral-bound. Requires intermediate to advanced skills. 134 pages, $16.95. Published by Wallace-Homestead Book Company.

THE CURVED TWO-PATCH SYSTEM by Joyce M. Schlotzhauer. An ingenious but amazingly simple technique for creating patch-

work flowers and leaves based on a square unit of two gently curved patches is so clearly detailed that even a beginner would not find it intimidating. Seventy block patterns, thirty-

six border designs, and thirteen full-size quilt layouts—all original—are included. For all levels of ability. 133 pages, $16.95. Published by EPM Publications.

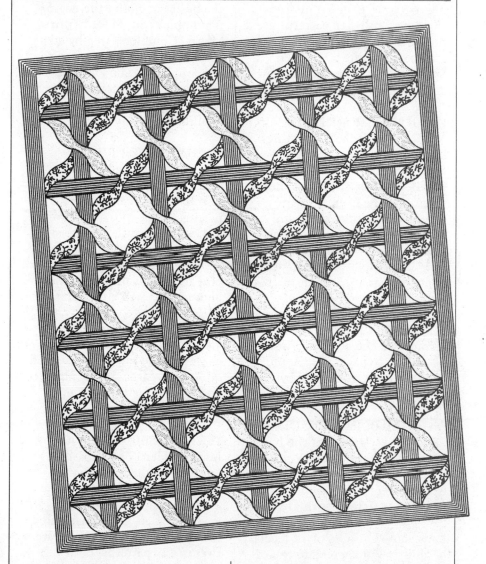

CURVES UNLIMITED by Joyce Schlotzhauer. This is a companion to *The Curved Two-Patch System* with slight modifications of the original technique that allow new and exciting design possibilities to emerge. Over 100 block patterns and fifty border designs, plus color

photographs and layouts for fourteen quilts will inspire the quilter to try her hand at one of these patterns, or perhaps urge her to create her own unique designs. Intermediate or advanced skills are necessary. 155 pages, $24.95. Published by EPM Publications.

DIAMOND PATCHWORK by Jeffrey Gutcheon. Contemporary quilt artists will find the author's methods for re-shaping traditional square patterns into diamonds an exciting and novel approach to quiltmaking. Color photographs, detailed instructions, and full-size patterns are included. For the intermediate and expert quilter. 72 pages, $9.95. Published by Gutcheon Patchworks, Inc.

FEATHERED STAR SAMPLER by Marsha McCloskey. The nine Feathered Star variations shown here certainly make an extraordinary sampler quilt, but they might also be used to create several other interesting quilt designs. With a little extra patience, along with the accurate, full-size templates, piecing sequence diagrams, and quick bias strip piecing method, the quilter will be encouraged to try this complex pattern. For intermediate and advanced levels of ability. 16 pages, $3.95, plus $1.50 postage. Published by That Patchwork Place.

FINE HAND QUILTING by Diana Leone. Every aspect of the hand quilting process—a subject which, surprisingly, has often been neglected or skimmed over—is explained with great care and detail in this valuable handbook. Quilters of all levels of ability will appreciate the expertise and finesse with which the author describes each technique. Helpful photographs accompany the text. 82 pages, $11.95, plus 15% postage. Published by Leone Publications.

FIRST STEPS IN QUILTING by Leslie Linsley. Beginners often find the thought of making a full-size quilt for their first attempt at quilting a bit overwhelming. Here, several easily managed projects, such as pillows, placemats, and children's accessories, will teach the basics and offer the beginner a quick reward for her first efforts. Complete, step-by-step instructions, full-size patterns, and ample diagrams will help the beginner get started. 144 pages, $15.95. Published by Doubleday & Co., Inc.

THE FLYING GEESE QUILT by Blanche Young and Helen Young. The Flying Geese pattern has long been a favorite for piecing scraps into a charming, folk-art-style quilt. Time-saving techniques, a multiple template system, complete instructions, plus numerous diagrams and photographs will guide the quilter every step of the way. Full-size posterboard templates are included. For the beginner as well as the more experienced quilter. 35 pages, $8.95, plus $1 postage. Published by Young Publications.

THE FRIENDSHIP QUILT BOOK by Mary Golden. The Crossroads Quilters Guild of Wenham, Massachusetts, describes how members successfully organized, designed, and constructed a friendship quilt. Featured are twenty 12″ patterns, both original and traditional, patchwork and appliqué, easy and complex, with detailed start-to-finish instructions, full-size templates, and helpful diagrams. A very useful guide for any group of friends contemplating a similar project. The patterns and ideas will appeal to beginners and advanced

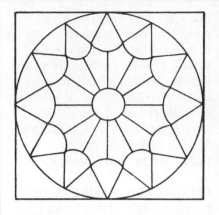

quilters alike. 152 pages, $14.95. Published by Yankee Books.

FROM THE PRAIRIE, A CHILD'S MEMORIES by Joan Vibert and Linda Brannock. Originally recorded in a diary in the year 1883, patterns for two doll quilts and two patchwork pin cushions are among the many country-style projects eight-year-old Sarah Jane describes for the reader. Requires only basic skills. 44 pages, $6.50, plus $2 postage. Published by Evening Star Farm, Inc.

A GARDEN OF QUILTS by Mary Elizabeth Johnson. Flower quilts, both appliqué and pieced, antique and new, bloom

in exquisite profusion across the pages of a book quilters will find to be a source of joy and inspiration. Full-size patterns and expert instructions offer the quilter an opportunity to reproduce any one of the forty quilts shown. Information for repairing antique quilts and drafting patterns from them is also included. For the intermediate to the advanced levels of ability. 158 pages, $19.95. Published by Oxmoor House.

AT GRAMDMA'S KNEE by Joan Vibert and Joyce Whittier. Special dolls need warm, cozy quilts, too. Full-size templates, plus complete instructions, piecing diagrams, and quilting suggestions accompany each of the twelve quilt patterns. A delightful book for grandmas, mothers, and children alike. Beginner to intermediate skills required. 42 pages, $6.50, plus $2 postage. Published by Evening Star Farm, Inc.

THE GREAT AMERICAN LOG CABIN by Carol Ann Wien. The many design possibilities of the Log Cabin pattern and its variations have continued to fascinate quilters for generations. Complete step-by-step instructions and full-size templates, plus helpful information on basic quiltmaking techniques, are included. For beginner to intermediate levels. 140 pages, $16.95. Published by E.P. Dutton, Inc.

HAWAIIAN QUILTING MADE EASY by Milly Singletary. Complete instructions and seven traditional block patterns will introduce the quilter to the unique beauty and artistry of Hawaiian quilts. Suitable for the beginner and intermediate levels of ability. 48 pages, $5, plus $1 postage. Published by Sunset Publications.

HOUSING PROJECTS by Nancy J. Martin. Capture the comforts of hearth and home in patchwork. Featured are ten different full-size House patterns with detailed instructions for completing fifteen quilts of various sizes. Also included are plans for small projects with a house theme, such as pillows, a table runner, or a pinafore. For beginner and intermediate levels of ability. 88 pages, $9.95, plus $1.50 postage. Published by That Patchwork Place.

HOW TO HOLD A QUILT SHOW—A PRACTICAL GUIDE by Ruth Culver. Holding a quilt show may be an exciting experience, but there are many practical and organizational considerations to be made before the show can be called a "success." Here is a guide that explains in logical and carefully detailed terms all the necessary steps from beginning to end. 176 pages, $17.95, plus $1.75 postage. Published by Culver Publications.

HOW TO MAKE A QUILT, 25 EASY LESSONS FOR BEGINNERS by Bonnie Leman. An easy-to-understand self-instruction manual or a useful guideline for teaching others the basics of patchwork and appliqué. 44 pages, $3.95, plus $1 postage. Published by Leman Publications, Inc.

INVESTMENTS by Diana Leone. Clear and concise construction and fitting techniques are found in this guide for making quilted vests for children and adults. Project plans for several different designs can be made from the master patterns included on separate fold-out sheets. For intermediate to advanced skill levels. 103 pages, $11.95, plus 15% postage. Published by Leone Publications.

THE JOY OF QUILTING by Laurie Swim. Twenty-five imaginative projects, ranging from the simple to the complex, are found in this bold, colorful new approach to pictorial appliqué quiltwork.

With skill and simplicity, the author explains how her designs can be copied on everything from place mats and clothing to wall hangings. Her techniques for designing original quilting projects are clearly those of an accomplished professional, yet she is able to explain those methods in a way that appeals to both beginning and experienced quilters. Full-color illustrations of original works accompany the text. 96 pages, $12.95, plus $1.75 postage. Published by The Main Street Press.

LAP QUILTING by Georgia Bonesteel. Completing not just one, but perhaps several full-size quilts can be a reasonable goal for even the busiest person simply by following the innovative, but easy to understand, instructions for machine piecing and portable lap quilting described here. Information from start to finish and full-size patterns for seventy traditional designs, are included. Will appeal to all levels of ability. 122 pages, $19.95. Published by Oxmoor House.

LAP QUILTING by Muriel Breckenridge. Lap quilting on a portable tapestry frame can be a convenient, yet accurate, alternative to traditional frame quilting. Basic piecing and appliqué directions, individual project plans, and assembly techniques for large and small quilted articles are plainly detailed. For the beginner as well as the more experienced quilter. 95 pages, $6.95. Published by Sterling Publishing Co., Inc.

LESSONS IN PAINLESS PATCHWORK by Betty Jo Shiell. This modest booklet is packed with useful information for learning, teaching, or improving basic quilting skills. Accurate full-size templates for over thirty traditional patchwork patterns, several quilting designs, and plenty of helpful diagrams add to the appeal of this publication. For the beginner and the intermediate quilter. 26 pages, $4.50. Published by The School for Inquiring Mynds.

LET'S MAKE A PATCHWORK QUILT USING A VARIETY OF SAMPLER BLOCKS by Jessie MacDonald and Marian H. Shafer. Beginners will find this to be a worthwhile source of information and patterns for a successful start in quiltmaking. Most of the thirty-seven patterns are full-size and progress from the beginner level to a more advanced level of skill. Numerous diagrams provide extra help along the way. 128 pages, $15.95. Published by Farm Journal, Inc; order from Doubleday & Co., Inc.

LITTLE PATCHWORK THINGS by Nancy Donahue. Those who love miniatures will appreciate the complete instructions and helpful diagrams for making doll-size quilts, clothing trims, and other small projects. Full-size templates for thirty-nine traditional patchwork patterns in the 3″ block size are included. For intermediate and advanced levels of ability. 104 pages, $7.50, plus $1.50 postage. Published by Dicmar Publishing.

LOG CABIN QUILTS by Bonnie Leman and Judy Martin. Everything you always wanted to know about making a Log Cabin quilt can be found here. Features include patterns and illustrations for thirty different Log Cabin variations, as well as complete instructions for hand and machine piecing, traditional hand quilting, tying and quilt-as-you-go methods. Will appeal to the beginner as well as the intermediate level quilter. 35 pages, $6.95, plus $1 postage. Published by Moon Over the Mountain Publishing Co.; order from Leman Publications.

THE LONE STAR by Blanche Young and Helen Young. Despite its appeal, the Lone Star has often been relegated to "some day" because of the extra time and patience needed to complete it successfully. Easy and efficient step-by-step instructions and detailed diagrams will guide the quilter through every phase until the Lone Star quilt becomes a reality. Full-size posterboard templates and quilting designs are printed on pull-out sheets. For intermediate and advanced levels of ability. 36 pages, $8.95, plus $1 postage. Published by Young Publications.

MACHINE APPLIQUÉ by Karen Bray. This manual for successful machine appliqué can be appreciated by beginners as well as the more experienced seamstress. Clearly written step-by-step directions, helpful illustrations, full-size patterns, and photographs of beautifully executed machine-appliquéd projects signify the author's expertise. 48 pages, $7, plus $1 postage. Published by Karen Bray.

Making Animal Quilts: Patterns and Projects

Willow Ann Soltow

MAKING ANIMAL QUILTS: PATTERNS AND PROJECTS by Willow Ann Soltow. Translating folk-art animal motifs into the quilting medium can be accomplished with ease and perfection whether the quilter chooses to follow any of the twenty basic appliqué projects exactly or whether she decides to create her own interesting variation. Complete start-to-finish instructions, numerous line drawings, and 200 full-size appliqué templates enable the quilter to stitch a charming crib quilt or wall hanging, or perhaps add a country look to clothing, book covers, or other small items. In addition, the author presents an informative discussion on the origin of familiar American animal motifs. 192 pages, $12.95, plus 5% postage. Published by Good Books.

MAKING AN OLD-FASHIONED PATCHWORK SAMPLER QUILT ON THE SEWING MACHINE by Andrea L. Shedletsky. Well-defined step-by-step instructions, detailed diagrams, and helpful charts will enable even the beginner to machine piece a quilt with ease

and success. Full-size templates for twenty-four traditional patchwork patterns are included. For all levels of ability. 48 pages, $3.95, plus 85¢ postage. Published by Dover Publications, Inc.

MAKING A TRADITIONAL APPLIQUÉ SAMPLER QUILT by Andrea L. Shedletsky. Twelve original designs inspired by traditional patterns offer an introduction to the art of appliqué. Actual-size templates, block diagrams, and thorough step-by-step directions accompany the author's advice for creating a special quilt. Beginner and intermediate skills required. 48 pages, $3.95, plus 85¢ postage. Published by Dover Publications, Inc.

MANDALA by Katie Pasquini. Creating a mandala quilt of your own design needn't be a forbidding enterprise. Discover how to develop and draft a basic design, and then how to enhance it with fill-in patterns. Instructions are included for making whole-cloth and pieced mandalas. No patterns are given—only methods and plenty of encouragement and inspiration. For intermediate and advanced levels of ability. 108 pages, $9.95, plus $1.50 postage. Published by Sudz Publishing.

MARILYN'S MACHINE-STITCHED SEW SIMPLE QUILTS: SPIRALING LOG CABIN DESIGN by Marilyn Greene. Fabric and tool requirements, cutting layouts and methods, as well as one-step sewing machine assembly techniques for nine Log Cabin quilt sizes are complete, well-organized, and easy to follow. Numerous illustrations are included so nothing is left to the

imagination. For all levels of ability. Spiral-bound for convenience. 62 pages, $10.75, postpaid. Published by Dav-a-lyn Enterprises.

MINI APPLIQUÉD HEARTS by Sondra Rudey. Clear, easy-to-understand start-to-finish instructions for making a charming heart motif doll quilt, wall hanging, or room accent are featured in this pattern sheet. 4 pages, $3.95, plus 15% postage. Published by Leone Publications.

A MINIATURE PATCHWORK CHRISTMAS by Evelyn Anderson and Margaret Schucker. Decorate the Christmas tree with miniature patchwork ornaments. All nineteen designs are traditional, but easy to piece, and include full-size patterns and complete instructions and diagrams. A great way for the beginner to take her first stitches. As an added bonus, there are plans for a Swedish dowel tree. Requires only beginning or intermediate skills. 64 pages, $6.50, plus $1 postage. Published by Donagil Publications.

MORE EARLY AMERICAN STENCILS IN COLOR by Alice B. Fjelstul and Patricia B. Schad. Stenciled quilts and coverlets occupy only a small corner in our quilting legacy, but the few surviving examples display a sense of color, design, and craftsmanship equal to their patchwork and appliqué counterparts. Reproduced here are dozens of floral, bird, and fruit motifs traced directly from early 19th-century coverlets. The instructions for stenciling on fabric and other surfaces are simple and direct. For all levels

of ability. 143 pages, $18.95. Published by E.P. Dutton.

MORE LAP QUILTING by Georgia Bonesteel. An up-date on *Lap Quilting* which presents new techniques and time-saving devices, as well as all the basic information needed for starting and finishing a traditional style quilt. Curved patchwork and appliqué designs are included in the collection of over sixty full-size patterns. For all levels of experience. 131 pages, $18.95. Published by Oxmoor House.

OF THEE I SING by Joan Vibert and Linda Brannock. Patterns and instructions for seven small patriotic quilts are found in the latest book in the popular Sarah Jane series. Beginner and intermediate skills required. 50 pages, $7.50, plus $2 postage. Published by Evening Star Farm, Inc.

PATCHWORK PATTERNS by Jinny Beyer. Drafting patterns for even the most complex geometric designs can be done simply and accurately by following the author's clever and systematic

approach to this troublesome task. Helpful diagrams and easy to understand instructions guide the quilter every step of the way. For all levels of ability. 200 pages, $15.95. Published by EPM Publications, Inc.

PATCHWORK QUILTING WITH WOOL by Jean Dubois. The wool quilt, a unique and seldom-explored chapter in the history of quiltmaking, offers a fascinating challenge to the contemporary quilter's skill and creativity. Traditional patterns and methods are easily adapted to wool as shown through the expert instructions and numerous drawings and photographs. Requires intermediate or advanced levels of skill. 179 pages, $5.95, plus 85¢ postage. Published by La Plata Press; order from Dover Publications, Inc.

PATCHWORK QUILTS FOR KIDS YOU LOVE by Linda Seward. Children love the warmth and comfort of a quilt that has been made especially for them. Over fifty block designs with child-oriented themes have been assembled in the pattern section. Complete start-to-finish instructions and full-size templates are included. For beginner and intermediate levels of ability. 192 pages, $9.95. Published by Sterling Publishing Co., Inc.

PATCHWORK SAMPLER LEGACY QUILT by Bonnie Leman and *Quilter's Newsletter* staff. Twelve patterns set into a sampler quilt will enable the quilter to advance her skills by teaching her to master complex piecing techniques. Complete instructions and full-size

templates in 8″ and 12″ block sizes are given for each design. Requires intermediate to advanced patchwork skills. 74 pages, $7.95, plus $1 postage. Published by Leman Publications.

THE PERFECT PATCHWORK PRIMER by Beth Gutcheon. Choosing the right fabrics, making accurate templates, piecing small patches into neat and attractive patterns, and quilting itself often pose many problems for the beginner. Here, a self-taught quilter offers her own easy-to-follow methods for creating "perfect patchwork." Although no full-size block patterns are included, there are instructions for drafting your own templates for traditional designs. Numerous illustrations and photographs accompany the text. Written especially for the beginner. 267 pages, $9.95, plus $1.50 postage. Published by David McKay Co., Inc; order from Gutcheon Patchworks.

PIECES OF THE PAST by Nancy J. Martin. Traditional quilts continue to enchant us with their often uncertain origin, their time-softened colors and prints, and their remarkable workmanship. With an historical account of American quilting and expert advice for selecting fabrics and patterns as your guide, creating traditional-style quilts will become a source of pride and pleasure. Beautiful color photographs of antique and contemporary traditional-style quilts, as well as full-size templates and piecing diagrams for fifty block designs, make this a noteworthy publication. Those with all levels of quilting experience will find interesting ideas here. 152 pages, $16.95, plus $1.50 postage. Published by That Patchwork Place.

PRIZE COUNTRY QUILTS by Mary Elizabeth Johnson. Color photographs, piecing diagrams, and full-size patterns accompany each of the fifty country-theme quilt blocks submitted to *Progressive Farmer's* second quilt block contest. In addition, there is a chapter to help the quilter create her own designs, as well as one on basic appliqué, embroidery, patchwork, and trapunto methods. For beginner to intermediate levels of ability. 230 pages, $19.95. Published by Oxmoor House.

PROJECTS FOR BLOCKS AND BORDERS by Marsha McCloskey. Twenty easy to piece 8'' blocks and several border patterns, plus six basic project plans, will help the beginner develop the confidence and skill needed for personalizing her work. The block patterns are both traditional and original, patchwork and appliqué, and are used to make a variety of small quilts, pillows, aprons, and other easily sewn items. Complete construction methods and full-size templates are included. Written especially for the beginner. 104 pages, $11.95, plus $1.50 postage. Published by That Patchwork Place.

THE QUICK AND EASY GIANT DAHLIA ON THE SEWING MACHINE by Susan A. Murwin and Suzzy C. Payne. Innovative, uncomplicated techniques for creating a beautiful Giant Dahlia quilt with pleasing results are presented in a step-by-step manner. Full-size pattern pieces for three different

sizes are provided. For all levels of ability. 80 pages, $3.50, plus 85¢ postage. Published by Dover Publications, Inc.

QUICK AND EASY PATCHWORK ON THE SEWING MACHINE by Susan A. Murwin and Suzzy C. Payne. Machine piecing can be an easy and time-saving alternative to hand piecing, but needn't sacrifice quality and beauty. Learn the authors' techniques through their clear instructions and diagrams. Full-size templates are given for twelve quilt patterns. For beginner to expert levels of experience. 80 pages, $3.50, plus 85¢ postage. Published by Dover Publications, Inc.

THE QUICK QUILTMAKING HANDBOOK by Barbara Johannah. Revolutionary, but simple, time-saving machine piecing techniques that do not overlook the importance of high quality workmanship or the warmth and appeal of traditional quilts are described here. Concise, step-by-step directions and detailed diagrams explain how to piece squares, triangles, diamonds, and other geometric shapes into quilts that can be used and enjoyed by all. For the beginner as well as the more experienced quilter. 128 pages, $8.95, plus $1 postage. Published by Pride of the Forest Press.

THE QUILT-AS-YOU-GO GUIDE by Nancy Donahue. Quilting-as-you-go offers many advantages to today's busy quiltmaker. The step-by-step methods described here are easily understood, even by the beginner, and are aimed at achieving top quality results. Helpful diagrams and charts support the instructional

material. No patterns are included. For all levels of ability. 52 pages, $6, plus $1.50 postage. Published by Dicmar Publishing.

THE QUILT DESIGN WORKBOOK by Beth and Jeffrey Gutcheon. Complete construction details for thirty-five contemporary, graphic quilt designs, each with a full-page sketch, illustrate how one design can achieve varied and exciting visual effects with different color arrangements. Basic quilt-making techniques and methods for developing original patterns are also discussed. The beginner as well as the more advance quilter can benefit from the information given here. 176 pages, $8.95, plus $1.50 postage. Published by The Alchemy Press; order from Gutcheon Patchworks.

QUILTED CLOTHING by Jean Ray Laury. Quilted clothing—from the elegant to the practical—can be designed and constructed with beautiful results using these competent instructions, diagrams, and attractive photographs as your guide and inspiration. Patterns and ideas for creating 100 different garments are included, but especially noteworthy are several pieces with ethnic influences, such as kimonos and Tibetan panel coats. For all levels of ability. 154 pages, $18.95. Published by Oxmoor House.

A QUILTER'S CHRISTMAS by Nancyann Johanson Twelker. Christmas tree ornaments, teddy bears, and festive wall quilts are just some of the ideas quilters and other needleworkers will enjoy making for home decorating or gift giving. Full-size patterns and clear instructions are provided for each project. Geared toward the intermediate needleworker. 76 pages, $8, plus $1.50 postage. Published by That Patchwork Place.

QUILT HOOPS by Yvonne L. Amico. Full-size patterns and complete step-by-step instructions are given for making seven different quilt hoop wall hangings. Numerous photographs and good directions make it easy to construct such designs as Mariner's Compass and Love Ring. Intermediate skills required. 25 pages, $4.98. Published by Gick Publishing.

QUILTING FOR BEGINNERS by Agnes Frank and Linda Stokes. This primer covers all the basic aspects of quiltmaking in a clearly illustrated, step-by-step fashion that will appeal to beginners of all ages. Each of the twenty projects is shown in full-color and is accompanied by piecing diagrams, full-size templates, and easy to follow directions. Block sizes range from 6″ to 48″ and may serve as

the basis for larger quilts or may be used simply as they are, as wall-hangings, pillows, decorative elements, or crib or doll quilts. Tips for tackling a bed-size quilt are appended. 144 pages, $14.95, plus $1.75 postage. Published by The Main Street Press.

QUILTING WITH STRIPS AND STRINGS by Helen Whitson Rose. Even slender fabric remnants can be sewn into a beautiful and functional patchwork quilt. Forty-six full-size patterns, including Cobweb, Milky Way, and Martha Washington's Log Cabin, accompany the author's instructions and diagrams. For beginner through advanced levels of ability. 64 pages, $3.50, plus 85¢ postage. Published by Dover Publications, Inc.

QUILTING: TECHNIQUE, DESIGN, AND APPLICATION by Eirian Short. An exciting exploration of the four types of quilting with enthusiastic inspiration for their practical and artistic use. Unusual techniques, such as gathered quilting, are also discussed. Especially important is a chapter on quilted clothing and accessories where ideas and scaled patterns for beautiful jackets, vests, pockets, and purses are lavishly illustrated. For the intermediate and advanced quilter. 164 pages, $24. Published by B.T. Batsford Ltd; order from David & Charles.

THE QUILTMAKER'S HANDBOOK: A GUIDE TO DESIGN AND CONSTRUCTION by Michael James. Noted teacher and designer Michael James has written an excellent handbook, describing in clear detail the basic elements of patchwork and ap-

pliqué. The quilter learns not only how to use traditional patterns, but also how to design original quilt patterns. Numerous photographs, although not always of the best quality, illustrate the techniques and display some contemporary quilt designs. No patterns are included. Written especially for the beginner or for the intermediate quilter who wants to polish up her skills. 147 pages, $12.95. Published by Prentice-Hall, Inc.

QUILTS OF AMERICA by Erica Wilson. This colorful portfolio presents the fifty-one prize-winning quilts from the Great Quilt Contest of 1975. Patterns and instructions for sixteen quilts have been selected by the author to demonstrate different styles and techniques. Basic quilting directions have also been included. For the intermediate to advanced quilter. 218 pages, $19.95. Published by Oxmoor House.

QUILTS BEAUTIFUL, THEIR STORIES AND HOW TO MAKE THEM by Grace Simpson. History, patterns, and basic and advanced quilting techniques—all these features and more are found in *Quilts Beautiful*. Thirty-nine patchwork and appliqué patterns, eighteen of which are the author's own designs, have full-size templates, fabric requirements, color suggestions, and piecing diagrams. Yellow Rose of Texas, Old Tippecanoe, and Priscilla Alden are some of the patterns included. A nice addition to the beginner's and the more advanced quilter's library. 164 pages, $18 postpaid. Published by Hunter Publishing

Co.; order from Thimbles 'n' Roses.

QUILTS IN THE CLASSROOM, by Mary Coyne Penders. Here is a practical and inspirational guide to help the prospective quilting instructor teach and organize her class successfully. 98 pages, $12.50 postpaid. Published by Quiltwork Publications.

"QUILTERS": LEGACY QUILT PATTERNS edited by Patricia Holly. Sixteen traditional patchwork patterns used in the legacy quilt created by Illinois Quilters, Inc., for the play *Quilters*, plus twelve small Amish quilt designs, are presented in an attractive format. Accurate, full-size templates, dimension charts, and interesting commentary add to the appeal of this organization's latest publication. Spiral-bound. Requires intermediate and advanced skills. 36 pages, $7 postpaid. Published by Illinois Quilters, Inc.

QUILTMAKER'S BIG BOOK OF PATTERN GRIDS by Catherine Anthony and Libby Lehman. Pre-printed grids for four, nine, five, and seven patch patterns will enable the quilter to draft geometric patchwork designs with ease and accuracy. Instructions are concise and easy to understand. A basic eight-pointed star grid and a curved line pattern are also included. For all levels of quilting experience. 32 pages, $14.95, plus 15% postage. Published by Leone Publications.

QUILTMAKER'S BIG BOOK OF 12″ BLOCK PATTERNS by Catherine Anthony and Libby Lehman. Thirty-one old-fashioned patchwork favorites are drafted full-scale in the popular 12″ size. A template list, piecing diagram, and a small black-and-white drawing are included for each pattern. Requires intermediate to advanced skills. 32 pages, $14.95, plus 15% postage. Published by Leonc Publications.

QUILTMAKER'S BIG BOOK OF 14″ BLOCK PATTERNS by Catherine Anthony and Libby Lehman. Accurate, full-scale drawings and pattern pieces for twenty-three complex patchwork designs will put an end to hours of frustrating pattern drafting. Each 14″ block has its own template chart, piecing diagram, and black-and-white simulated fabric drawing. Intermediate and expert patchwork skills are necessary. 32 pagcs, $14.95, plus 15% postage. Published by Leone Publications.

SCRAPS CAN BE BEAUTIFUL by Jan Halgrimson. Scrap quilt fanciers will be inspired by this collection of over 100 traditional patchwork patterns, such as Aunt Jerusha, Hens and Chickens, and Spool. Black-and-white sketches of each design will help the quiltcr assemble the full-size templates easily and accurately. Block sizes range from 8″ to 22″, with many patterns given in several convenient sizes. Spiral-bound. For all levels of skill. 106 pages, $9, plus $1.25 postage. Published by Weaver-Finch Publications.

SOD HOUSE TREASURES AND OTHER NEBRASKA QUILT PATTERNS by Jan Stehlik. Cottonwood, Nebraska Windmill, and Sunflower—these and thirty-four other designs, both original and traditional, evoke images of the beauty and spirit of Nebraska homesteads. Folklore and historical notes accompany each full-size patchwork and appliqué pattern. A delightful collection for quilters who appreciate country life and regional themes. Requires intermediate skills. 83 pages, $7.75, plus $1 postage. Published by Jan Stehlik.

SMALL AMISH QUILT PATTERNS by Rachel Thomas Pellman. A companion to Amish Crib Quilts which includes basic patchwork and quilting instructions, plus full-size templates and piecing diagrams, for thirty different Amish crib quilts. A collection of traditional Amish

quilting motifs can be easily removed from the book for tracing and constructing quilting stencils. For all levels of quilting experience. 128 pages, $10.95, plus 5% postage. Published by Good Books.

SPOKEN WITHOUT A WORD by Elly Sienkiewicz. In recent years, quilters have expressed a renewed and avid interest in Baltimore album quilts. Assembled here is a collection of twenty-three authentic and properly documented full-size block patterns, including Early American, paper-folded, and ornate Victorian designs. The author offers a brief historic perspective, as well as advice on pattern-making, fabric selection, and stitching. Especially interesting is the "lexicon of symbols" which defines the meanings of flowers, plants, and other symbols frequently found in Baltimore album quilts. For intermediate to advance levels of ability. 65 pages, $14.95, plus $2.35 postage. Published by Turtle Hill press; order from Cabin Fever Calicoes.

STATE CAPITALS QUILT BLOCKS by Barbara Bannister and Edna P. Ford. Stitch a patchwork quilt block that represents your state capital. Fifty rare patterns, all full-size, are accompanied by instructions and yardage requirements. For the intermediate and advanced quilter. 80 pages, $2.95, plus 85¢ postage. Published by Dover Publications, Inc.

SUNBONNET BABIES DOING CHORES and **SUNBONNET BABIES AT PLAY** by Poppy Morse. Full-size appliqué patterns and instructions for six adorable Sunbonnet babies engaged in a variety of childhood activities are included in each booklet. Requires intermediate skills. 12 pages each, $3.50 each, plus $1 postage each. Published by Loveland Pattern Co.; order from

Patchwork House Patterns, Loveland Pattern Co.

A TEXAS QUILTING PRIMER by Beverly Ann Orbelo. This collection of thirty-two pieced and apliquéd patterns is as diverse as the history and landscape of Texas itself. Featured are Battle of the Alamo, Cowboy Star, Yellow Rose of Texas, Texas Tears, and more—all with actual-size templates and brief but interesting historical notes. For all levels of ability. 45 pages, $5. Published by Corona Publishing Co.

TRADITIONAL PATCHWORK PATTERNS by Carol Belanger Grafton. Create a stunning traditional patchwork quilt such as Cut-Glass Dish, Rocky Glen, or Bleeding Heart. Full-size templates, instructions, and illustrations are given for each of the twelve patterns. Requires intermediate to advanced skills. 51 pages, $3.50, plus 85¢ postage. Published by Dover Publications, Inc.

TREES AND LEAVES FOR QUILTERS by Betty Boyink. Leaf and tree patterns—fifty-two in all, both

patchwork and appliqué, familiar and unusual—will inspire many lovely projects. All patterns have full-size templates for 4", 8", and 12" block sizes. For intermediate and advanced quilters. 58 pages, $9.50, plus $1.50 postage. Published by Betty Boyink Publishing.

THE UNITED STATES PATCHWORK PATTERN BOOK by Barbara Bannister and Edna P. Ford. Here are fifty unusual patterns from the States-of-the-Union series that every collector will want to add to her library. Full-size patterns and instructions are included. For the intermediate and advanced quilter. 80 pages, $2.95, plus 85¢ postage. Published by Dover Publications, Inc.

WISCONSIN WILD FLOWER QUILT by The Covered Bridge Quilters. Color suggestions and embroidery details accompany each of the twenty full-size wild flower appliqués designed by the Covered Bridge Quilters for their prize-winning quilt. Requires intermediate to advanced skills. 20 pages, $5, plus $1 postage. Published by The Covered Bridge Quilters.

Patchwork and Appliqué Pattern Collections

Pattern books provide quilters with the basic design elements for creating beautiful and unique works of art. Listed here are books whose primary purpose is simply patterns—both patchwork and appliqué, traditional and contemporary. Any instructions which might be included are usually rudimentary and should not be confused with more complete how-to instructional books.

AMERICAN HISTORY IN PATCH-WORK PATTERNS: THE CHARTER OAK by Ione Benck McIntyre. The author presents an interesting history of the Charter Oak pattern group, complete with documented sources, scaled drawings, and full-size templates for each of the ten authentic variations. In addition, there are also drawings and references for forty related Oak patterns. Pattern collectors and quilters alike will appreciate this collection. Most designs require intermediate to advanced quilting skills. 52 pages, $5.95, postpaid. Published by The Patchwork Press.

AMISH INSPIRATIONS, by Suzie Lawson. Center Diamond, Amish Bars, and Hole in the Barn Door are just some of the traditional Amish patchwork designs featured in this pattern collection. Each of the forty-six designs includes full-size templates, border measurements, and scale drawings of the completed quilt. In addition, there are thirty-eight especially lovely quilting motifs—all drawn actual size—to complement and enhance the patchwork. Brief, but helpful, information covers such areas as the selection of appropriate fabrics and colors and Amish quilting techniques. For the intermediate to advanced quilter. 136 pages, $10.95, plus $1.50 postage. Published by Amity Publications.

BALTIMORE BRIDE'S QUILT PATTERN BOOK by Rita Woloshuk. Twenty-five full-size appliqué patterns, derived from a quilt in the author's collection and signed and dated "Baltimore County 1847, Mary Ann West,"

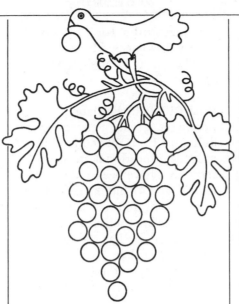

are found in this pattern book. A brief history of this quilt style, as well as rudimentary appliqué instructions, are also included. Printed on oversize, spiral-bound pages. Requires intermediate to advanced appliqué skills. 26 pages, $22.50. Published by Woloshuk Publications; order from Rita's Quiltn' Sewing Center.

BASKETS FOR QUILTERS by Betty Boyink. Here is a fine collection of twenty-one pieced and fourteen appliquéd basket patterns, complete with full-size templates for the 4", 8", and 12" block sizes. For the intermediate to advanced quilter. 50 pages, $9.50, plus $1.50 postage. Published by Betty Boyink Publications.

CHARLESTON MUSEUM QUILT PATTERNS by Nan Tournier and Karen King. Authentic reproductions of patchwork, appliqué, border quilting, and trapunto designs, taken from antique quilts in the Museum collection, are found in this modest pattern book. Requires intermediate to advanced

quilting skills. 12 pages, $5, plus $1 postage. Published by The Charleston Museum.

CHILD'S PLAY FOR QUILTERS by Betty Boyink. Wrap your child or grandchild in a quilt as special as he is. Over sixty patterns and ideas to choose from, to use as they appear or in an original design, including a patchwork alphabet, nursery rhyme characters, and traditional patterns with childhood appeal, are found here. Full-size templates are given for all patterns, with instructions and yardage requirements included for individual projects. For the beginner as well as the more advanced quilter. 58 pages, $9.50, plus $1.50 postage. Published by Betty Boyink Publications.

THE COLLECTOR'S DICTIONARY OF QUILT NAMES AND PATTERNS by Yvonne Khin. Searching for a particular quilt pattern or name can become a tiresome and frustrating task. Here is a one-stop reference guide to 2,400 quilt patterns, conveniently arranged according to shape and construction. Black and white illustrations of each design, plus multiple name listings, a glossary, a collecting guide, and an index, will aid in the identification process. For all quilters. 512 pages, $29.95, postpaid. Published by Acropolis Books, Ltd.

A CONSTELLATION FOR QUILTERS by Carol LaBranche. Here is a collection of over 600 patterns devoted solely to the quilter's favorite motif—the star. Drawings of four-pointed and multi-pointed stars, Feathered and Lone stars are precisely printed on grids for easy reproduction.

by Carol LaBranche, author of *Patchwork Pictures*

Special directions and drawings are provided for drafting such difficult designs as the five-pointed star, the hexagon/six-pointed star, and the LeMoyne star. Classic examples of these types, as well as others, are illustrated in full-color photographs. Requires intermediate and advanced skills. 144 pages, $14.95, plus $1.75 postage. Published by The Main Street Press.

COUNTRY CHILDREN by Patricia Cox. Any quilter who loves Sunbonnet Sue and Overall Bill will treasure Patricia Cox's versions of this old-fashioned favorite. Fifty-one girls and thirty-three boys, all different and all shown full-size, as well as color photographs of two quilts in this theme, are printed on spiral-bound pages. The designs require intermediate to expert skills. 85 pages, $13.50, postpaid. Published by One of a Kind Quilting Designs.

CRAZY QUILT STITCHES by Dorothy Bond. This small spiral-bound dictionary contains over 1,000 basic and ornate embroidery stitches for embellishing crazy quilts. For all levels of ability. 104 pages, $10, plus $1.50 postage. Published by Dorothy Bond.

DOLL QUILTS by Barbara Bannister. Create a charming doll quilt from this collection of over fifty traditional quilt patterns that have been reduced to 2'', 3'', and 4'' block sizes. Brief instructions and full-size templates are included. For the beginner as well as the more experienced quilter. 16 pages, $3.50, postpaid. Published by Barbara Bannister Needlecraft Books.

EARLY AMERICAN PATCHWORK PATTERNS by Carol Belanger Grafton. Create a patchwork quilt reminiscent of Early America from one of the twelve authentic designs in this collection. All patterns are full-size, with complete instructions. Try your hand at Steeplechase, Windmill, or any of the other handsome designs. 32 pages, $3.50, plus 85¢ postage. Published by Dover Publications, Inc.

EASY-TO-MAKE PATCHWORK QUILTS by Rita Weiss. Beginners, here is a pattern collection complied just for you. Pinwheels, Broken Dishes, and ten other old-fashioned favorites, each with full-size templates and construction details, will help you get started. 80 pages, $3.50, plus 85¢ postage. Published by Dover Publications, Inc.

AN ENCYCLOPEDIA OF PIECED QUILT PATTERNS, VOLS. 1-8 by Barbara Brackman. A comprehensive and well-documented reference guide to traditional patchwork patterns. Each volume contains hundreds of scale drawings for individual blocks within a certain family of patterns along with its name (or names) and its derivation. Several full-size patterns are also included in each volume. Printed on loose-leaf pages that can be easily placed in a binder. *Volume 1*, recently revised, contains One Patch, non-square blocks, multipatch, and strip quilt designs, plus a cumulative index to all eight volumes. *Volume 2* covers realistic patterns. *Volume 3* contains Four Patch patterns. *Volume 4* presents the Nine Patch category. *Volume 5* covers designs known as Square-in-a-Square. *Volume 6* deals with Maltese Cross and Nine X patterns. *Volume 7* offers numerous Wheel and Fan designs. *Volume 8* contains Star and miscellaneous patchwork patterns. This collection of patterns will prove to be a valuable companion to quilters of all levels of ability. Any of the volumes may be ordered individually or as a set. Prices are as follows and include postage: *Volume 1*, $6.50; *Volume 2*, $5.50; *Volume 3*, $6.50; *Volume 4*, $7.50; *Volume 5*, $6.50; *Volume 6*, $7.50; *Volume 7*, $7.50; *Volume 8*, $7.50; all eight volumes, $46. Published by Prairie Flower Publishing.

THE FARMER'S WIFE QUILT BOOK OF NEW PATTERNS AND DESIGNS, VOLS. 1-4, by Orine Johnson, reprinted by Barbara Bannister. Each volume contains approximately ten pieced and appliquéd patterns from the 1930s. Thumbnail sketches and full-size templates are provided for each design. $2.50 each, postpaid. Published by Barbara Bannister Needlecraft Books.

FAVORITE PATCHWORK PATTERNS by Henry Louis Pelletier. Twelve beautiful patchwork patterns, both traditional and contemporary, easy and complex, are found in one pattern collection. Complete instructions and full-size templates are included for designs such as Crazy Anne, Virginia, and Many-Pointed Star. For all levels of experience. 56 pages, $3.50, plus 85¢ postage. Published by Dover Publications, Inc.

FIRST, NINE AND ALWAYS by Millie Leathers. Several unique examples of the Nine Patch pattern are among the thirty-two antique quilts whose history and design are discussed. Attractive color photographs, full-size templates, and fabric requirements are provided for each, making this a worthwhile addition to the antique quilt lover's library. Intermediate to advanced skills required. 128 pages, $14.95, plus $1 postage. Published by American Quilter's Society.

500 FULL-SIZE PATCHWORK PATTERNS by Maggie Malone. Scale drawings for 500 different patchwork blocks, ranging in size from 8'' to 18'', are found in the first section of this source book. Each design has a coded list of pattern pieces which corresponds to the full-size templates provided in the second chapter. No piecing instructions are given. 168 pages, $9.95. Published by Sterling Publishing Co., Inc.

FLOWER GARDENS AND HEXAGONS FOR QUILTERS by Betty Boyink.

The variety of hexagon designs and pieced and appliquéd flower patterns present many possibilities to the quilter. Use them individually or combine several in new and exciting ways for a unique quilt. Full-size templates for 12'' blocks are given for each pattern. For intermediate to advanced levels of ability. 58 pages, $9.50, plus $1.50 postage. Published by Betty Boyink Publishing.

FOLK QUILTS AND HOW TO RECREATE THEM by Audrey and Douglas Wiss. Thirty charming and old-fashioned designs are included in this treasury of patchwork quilts made in rural and small-town America 50 to 125 years ago. Handsome full-color photographs and capsule histories of each quilt's origin, along with accurate, full-size templates, piecing diagrams, and brief instructions, make this a perennial favorite among quilters and folk art enthusiasts alike. For all levels of ability. 144 pages, $14.95, plus $1.75 postage. Published by The Main Street Press.

FRENCH BOUQUET, NANCY PAGE QUILT CLUB PATTERN reprinted by Barbara Bannister. Twenty-eight delightful floral appliqué patterns, each with full-size templates and instructions, will enable the quilter to reproduce a 1930s-style quilt. Requires intermediate to advanced skills. 32 pages, $7.50, postpaid. Published by Barbara Bannister Needlecraft Books.

GEOMETRIC PATCHWORK PATTERNS by Carol Belanger Grafton. Stonemason's Puzzle, Solomon's Temple, and Suspension Bridge are featured in a collection of twelve dazzling

geometric patchwork patterns. Full-size templates, instructions, and helpful charts, as well as an overall completed drawing, accompany each design. For the intermediate to expert quilter. 63 pages, $3.25, plus 85¢ postage. Published by Dover Publications, Inc.

GREAT SCRAP-BAG QUILTS by Jan Halgrimson. An exciting collection of traditional and unusual patchwork patterns suitable for scrap quilts is presented here. Among the 110 patterns are 15 Dresden Plate variations, as well as Puzzle Boxes, Nosegay, and Job's Tears. Accurate full-size templates and block diagrams are given for each design. Spiral-bound. For all levels of quilting experience. 108 pages, $9.50, plus $1.25 postage. Published by Weaver-Finch Publications.

HAWAIIAN QUILTING PATTERNS HDC-1 by Elizabeth Root. Wallhangings, pillow tops, or perhaps a sampler quilt might be made from any of the sixteen Hawaiian appliqué designs shown here. Full-size patterns

for 22'' blocks, quilting suggestions, and basic instructions are included. For intermediate to advanced levels of ability. 16 pages, $9, plus $1 postage. Published by Hawaiian Designing Collection.

HAWAIIAN QUILTING PATTERNS HDC-3 by Myrna Gross. Twenty Hawaiian designs, such as Orchid, Bird of Paradise, and Woodrose, are presented full size for appliquéing onto 22″ background squares. Basic instructions and quilting suggestions are also provided. For intermediate to advanced levels of experience. 20 pages, $10, plus $1 postage. Published by Hawaiian Designing Collection.

HAWAIIAN QUILT DESIGNS HDC-5 by Elizabeth Root. Four beautiful designs—Pineapple, Plumeria, Silversword, and Pikake—are printed full size on separate pull-out pages. Concise instructions, suggested quilting patterns, and optional borders are included for completing a 45″ medallion-style crib quilt or wall hanging. Requires intermediate to advanced appliqué skills. 4 pages, $10, plus $2 postage. Published by Hawaiian Designing Collection.

HEIRLOOM APPLIQUE by Pat Andreatta. The elegant beauty of each of the eighteen floral ap-

pliqué designs will inspire the quilter to create not one, but perhaps several heirloom quilts. The patterns are full size and are accompanied by basic appliqué instructions, as well as layout diagrams and yardage estimates for three different quilt plans. Spiral-bound on fold-out pages. Designed for intermediate and advanced quilters. 33 pages, $11.95, plus $1.50 postage. Published by Pat Andreatta.

HEIRLOOM QUILTS YOU CAN MAKE by Maggie Malone. Heirloom patchwork and appliqué quilts, now housed in museums and private collections, can become part of your own quilt collection. Full-size patterns, fabric requirements, and basic assembly diagrams for over thirty antique quilts will enable you to re-create one of these old-time designs. Photographs and a brief history of each quilt are included, as well as a special section of quilting motifs. For the intermediate to advanced quilter. 288 pages, $10.95. Published by Sterling Publishing Co., Inc.

KANSAS CITY STAR PATTERNS, VOLS. 1-11 reprinted by Barbara Bannister. Each volume of "Kansas City Star" patterns contains at least twenty old-fashioned patchwork designs. A must for serious collectors and quilters alike. Prices are as follows and include postage: *Volumes 1-6*, $3 each; *Volumes 7, 8, 11*, $4.50 each; *Volumes 9 and 10*, $6 each. Published by Barbara Bannister Needlecraft Books.

KENTUCKY MEDALLION APPLIQUÉ QUILT PATTERN BOOK edited by

Charlene Hooper. The fourteen elegant appliqué patterns found in the Kentucky Medallion quilt were stitched with care and devotion by several Kentucky quilters as a tribute to the art and craft of quiltmaking. Fabric requirements, construction details, and full-size templates will enable you to stitch your own heritage quilt. Requires intermediate and advanced skills. 28 pages, $8.50, plus $1.50 postage. Published by The Kentucky Heritage Quilt Society.

LADIES ART COMPANY CATALOG, 1928 reprinted by Barbara Bannister. Over 500 quilt patterns from the famous series begun in 1889 are found in this reprint edition. $3.95, postpaid. Published by Barbara Bannister Needlecraft Books.

MICHIGAN QUILTERS AND THEIR DESIGNS by Betty Boyink. Both traditional and original quilt patterns have been assembled in this collection of Michigan-oriented designs. All twenty-five patterns have full-size templates for 4″ and 12″ block sizes. Intermediate and advanced quilters who enjoy regional or theme quilts will appreciate this pattern book. 50 pages, $9.50, plus $1.50 postage. Published by Betty Boyink Publishing.

MINIATURE MAGIC by Gay Imbach. For the quilter who likes miniatures, here is a collection of over 150 traditional and original patchwork patterns for 3″, 4″, 5″, and 6″ block sizes. Also included are border patterns and appropriate quilting motifs. Photographs included. Requires intermediate and advanced skills. 96 pages, $12.95, plus 15% postage. Published by Imbach Publications.

NOVA SCOTIA PATCHWORK PATTERNS by Carter Houck. Twelve patchwork and appliqué patterns inspired by quilts from Nova Scotia museums and collections are accompanied by full-size templates and instructions. For all levels of experience. 64 pages, $3.95, plus 85¢ postage. Published by Dover Publications, Inc.

115 CLASSIC AMERICAN PATCHWORK QUILT PATTERNS by Maggie Malone. Burgoyne Surrounded, Delectable Mountains, and Lady of the Lake are just a few of the traditional patchwork patterns presented here. Each has been rated according to the level of skill necessary for piecing, so the beginner as well as the more experienced quilter will have several designs from which to choose. Full-size templates, charts for the total number of individual pieces needed per block, and yardage requirements for a complete quilt are included. 207 pages, $9.95. Published by Sterling Publishing Co., Inc.

101 PATCHWORK PATTERNS by Ruby McKim. Certainly a classic among patchwork pattern collections, whose appeal has not been lost over the decades. Fascinating bits of quilting lore are pieced between the instructional material and the full-size patterns. Jacob's Ladder, Lafayette Orange Peel, and Fruit Basket are just a few of the patterns given. For all levels of ability. 128 pages, $3.50, plus 85¢ postage. Published by Dover Publications, Inc.

120 PATTERNS FOR TRADITIONAL PATCHWORK QUILTS by Maggie Malone. Here is a fine collection of traditional quilt patterns gleaned from the *Kansas City Star*, *Hearth and Home*, *Godey's Lady's Book*, and other needlework sources. Each pattern is accompanied by a scale drawing, full-size templates, and block assembly instructions, as well as dimensions and fabric requirements for completing a bed-size quilt. For all levels of quilting experience. 239 pages, $9.95. Published by Sterling Publishing Co., Inc.

1001 PATCHWORK DESIGNS by Maggie Malone. The author has compiled yet another valuable collection of traditional patchwork patterns, including nine, four, five, and seven patch designs, as well as hexagonal, circular, diamond, and star patterns. There are no full-size templates, but easy drafting instructions and scale block drawings using a grid system will help the quilter make her own accurate pattern pieces. Yardage charts and rudimentary construction methods are also included. For all levels of quilting ability. 224 pages, $9.95. Published by Sterling Publishing Co., Inc.

PATCHING THINGS UP by Jan Halgrimson. Well-planned scrap quilts can create a remarkable visual experience. Begin your scrap quilt with one of the 150 patchwork and appliqué patterns shown here, including such designs as Georgetown Circle, Country Roads, and Mexican Rose. Each is accompanied by a scale block drawing and full-size templates which

indicate the correct number of patches required per block. Sizes range from 2″ to 28″ square, with many designs reproduced in several convenient sizes. For the beginner, intermediate, and advanced quilter. 102 pages, $9.95, plus $1.25 postage. Published by Weaver-Finch Publications.

PATCHWORK PICTURES, 1001 PATTERNS FOR PIECING by Carol LaBranche. Create an original and imaginative picture quilt from any combination of over 1,000 designs in this patchwork picture collection. All patterns are drawn on graph paper for easy transfer and include houses, flowers, baskets, people, alphabets, and more. Twenty full-color photographs of antique and contemporary picture quilts provide an interesting look at this unique quilt style. For intermediate to advanced levels. 127 pages, $14.95, plus $1.75 postage. Published by The Main Street Press.

PLASTIC TEMPLATES FOR TRADITIONAL PATCHWORK QUILT PATTERNS by Rita Weiss. Hand or machine piece twenty-seven old-fashioned patchwork patterns easily and accurately using the set of four durable plastic templates tucked into an envelope inside the back cover of this book. Each 12″-square pattern has its own block diagrams, fabric requirements, and cuting charts. Windmill, Susannah, and Road to Oklahoma are just a few of the patterns given. For beginner to intermediate levels of ability. 32 pages, $3.95, plus 85¢ postage. Published by Dover Publications, Inc.

QUILT DESIGNS FROM INDIAN ART by Kittie Spence. Accurate templates, helpful construction diagrams, and expert instructions are provided for each of

the twenty original pieced and appliquéd designs inspired by Native American pottery and basketry. Here is certainly an important tribute to a seldom-explored design source. Spiral-bound. Requires intermediate and advanced quilting skills. 64 pages, $11.50, plus $1 postage. Published by Mosi Publications.

THE QUILTER'S ALBUM OF BLOCKS AND BORDERS by Jinny Beyer. This is a neatly organized and well-illustrated dictionary of over 700 geometric block and border patterns, grouped into eight basic design categories. Tips for using fabrics to maximize the overall visual impact of any design are also included. For all levels of skill. 198 pages, $15.95. Published by EPM Publications.

THE SAMPLER QUILT by Diana Leone. An exceptionally well-organized and illustrated teaching manual whose expert instructions and encouragement guide the beginner through every aspect of quiltmaking. Thirty full-size patterns, presented in a logical order of complexity, help the beginner (and the more experienced) develop skills that will ensure a lifetime of successful quiltmaking. 68 pages, $9.95, plus 15% postage. Published by Leone Publications.

SAMPLER SUPREME by Catherine H. Anthony. Challenge your creative thinking abilities and needleworking skills by designing an extraordinary sampler quilt from any combination of the thirty-four complex patchwork patterns given here. Accurate, full-scale drawings, con-

struction diagrams, and hints for precision piecing will help you stitch the 6″ blocks with expert ease. For the intermediate to advanced levels of ability. 80 pages, $11.95, plus 15% postage. Published by Leone Publications.

THE SCRAP LOOK by Jinny Beyer. Arranging fabric scraps of various colors and prints into a successful, well-balanced design scheme requires as much skill as intuition. Uncomplicated instructions, diagrams, and photographs, along with several one-patch patterns, show you how to achieve exciting results. A brief history of charm quilts and humorous accounts of "fabric addicts" contribute to some enjoyable reading. 129 pages, $19.95. Published by EPM Publications.

SCRAP QUILTS by Judy Martin. Scrap quilts, originally born out of necessity and economy, have been recognized by many as the most favored and perhaps truest form of quilt art. Here the quilter will learn how to collect and organize scraps into a pleasing visual statement. Full-size patterns and instructions for twenty quilts, plus patterns for seventy-two traditional block designs suitable for scrap quilts, are also included. For all levels of ability. 96 pages, $13.95, plus $1.25 postage. Published by Moon Over the Mountain Publishing Co.; order from Leman Publications.

THE SECOND QUILTMAKER'S HANDBOOK: CREATIVE AP-PROACHES TO CONTEMPORARY QUILT DESIGNS by Michael James. Fabric geometry, color design, curved seams, and strip piecing are some of the techniques Michael James offers intermediate and advanced quilters who wish to refine and revitalize their designing and quiltmaking skills. Detailed drawings and photographs illustrate each topic, and there is a special color section on contemporary quilt designs. 184 pages, $10.95. Published by Prentice-Hall, Inc.

SHADOW QUILTING by Marjorie Puckett. Easy-to-understand step-by-step directions, patterns, and photographs for thirty delightful projects show the quilter how to achieve the delicate pastel appearance of shadow appliqué. For all levels of experience. 202 pages, $24.95, hardcover edition. Published by Charles Scribner's Sons.

SHADOW TRAPUNTO by Nancy Donahue. Shadow trapunto, known for its soft, pastel coloring, can be used for creating quilts, pillow tops, clothing trims, and fashion accessories. Basic instructions, full-size floral designs, and individual project plans offer an introduction to this popular technique. Requires only beginner to intermediate skills. 72 pages, $8, plus $1.50 postage. Published by

Patchwork Patterns; order from Dicmar Publishing.

SMALL QUILTS by Marsha McCloskey. If you've ever longed for a lap quilt to snuggle under on a cold winter's evening or hoped to make a simple but special crib quilt for a soon-to-arrive baby, then perhaps one of the eighty traditional quilt patterns shown here will help you get started. All blocks are easy to construct and are accompanied by full-size templates, complete piecing instructions, and yardage requirements for both lap quilts and crib quilts.

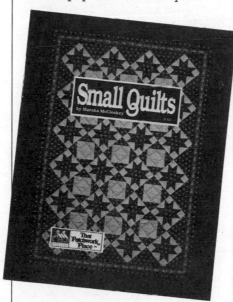

For beginner to intermediate levels of skill. 47 pages, $6, plus $2 postage. Published by That Patchwork Place.

THE STANDARD BOOK OF QUILTMAKING AND COLLECTING by Marguerite Ickis. This venerable handbook has enjoyed a long reputation for being one of the most comprehensive guides to traditional quiltmaking. Forty-six appliqué and patchwork patterns, such as Oak Leaf and Storm at Sea, are

presented with full-size patterns and instructions. An additional 150 designs with drafting instructions are included, along with a brief history of quilting. Contemporary quilters may find some of the information not quite as thorough or up-to-date as the information found in more recent publications, but the material is nevertheless timeless and worth including in any quilter's library. For all levels of ability. 273 pages, $5.95, plus 85¢ postage. Published by Dover Publications, Inc.

STORYBOOK QUILTING by Jennifer L. Baker and Laurie E. Mchalko. Give your child a gift to treasure—perhaps a Jack and the Beanstalk quilt or a Sleeping Beauty dress. Complete instructions and full-size storybook appliqué designs will turn commercial clothing patterns and ordinary childhood accessories into something special. For all levels of experience. 195 pages, $15.95. Published by Chilton Book Co.

SUPER QUILTER II by Carla J. Hassel. The author has designed thirteen advanced level projects aimed at challenging basic quilting skills and teaching new skills to raise the quality of workmanship from adequate to "super." Lessons on pattern analysis and drafting, color theory, and problem solving are thoroughly discussed in Hassel's logical but easy-going manner. *Super Quilter II* is an indispensible reference for every serious quilter. Spiral-bound, with full-size templates included. 175 pages, $12.95. Published by Wallace-Homestead Book Co.

TAKING THE MATH OUT OF PATCHWORK QUILTS by Bonnie Leman and Judy Martin. Just as the title suggests, this handbook will help the quilter plan and figure the yardage requirements for any size quilt, any number size and shape patch, and any width and length for borders, sashing strips, lining, and bias bindings. Easy to read charts with clear explanations for their correct usage will put an end to time-consuming and troublesome mathematics. 35 pages, $4.95, plus $1 postage. Published by Moon Over the Mountain Publishing Co.; order from Leman Publications.

TEMPLATE-FREE QUILTMAKING by Trudie Hughes. Rotary cutting techniques have been carefully organized and explained to help the quilter construct quilts faster, easier, and with fewer problems. Eight block patterns and plans for nineteen quilts are included. Intermediate skills are required. 96 pages, $11.95, plus $1.50 postage. Published by That Patchwork Place.

THE TIED QUILT by Diana Leone. Nicely detailed, easy to follow directions for tying a baby quilt, lap robe, or other small quilted items are given in this instructional leaflet. Also included are directions for making a rolled hem. For all levels of experience. 4 pages, $2.95, plus 15% postage. Published by Leone Publications.

TRIP AROUND THE WORLD QUILTS by Blanche Young and Helen Young. Whether it has been done in bright, strong colors, or soft, subdued shades, a Trip Around the World creates a striking visual impact. Time-saving, easy to follow instructions, diagrams, and full-size posterboard templates will encourage the quilter to try at least one variation shown here. 87 pages, $11.95 plus $1 postage. Published by Young Publications.

VESTING by Jean Wells. From one basic vest pattern many interesting and unique versions can be made by using a variety of patchwork, stenciling, and quilting adornments. Included with the helpful design and construction tips is a full-size vest pattern in three basic sizes. For the beginner or intermediate needleworker. 16 pages, $5. Published by Yours Truly/Burdett Publications.

WALL QUILTS by Marsha McCloskey. Sunshine and Shadow, Baskets, and Log Cabin are among the ten traditional patchwork designs adapted for creating decorative wall quilts and companion pillows. Competent, well-organized instructions discuss everything from fabric selection to machine piecing techniques, stencil making, hand quilting, and mounting and displaying methods. Full-size templates and quilting designs, plus helpful diagrams and attractive color photographs, add to the pleasure of making these wall quilts. Requires basic and intermediate skills. 76 pages, $8, plus $1.50 postage. Published by That Patchwork Place.

WORKING IN MINIATURE, A MACHINE PIECING APPROACH TO MINIATURE QUILTS by Becky Schaefer. Miniature patchwork presents new challenges and problems not always encountered in its full-size

counterpart. Presented here is a very professional, but easy to follow, guide to miniature patchwork. Numerous diagrams, clear step-by-step instructions, and beautiful color photographs illuminate the author's special techniques. Included are complete and specific directions for making charming adaptations of Irish Chain, Churn Dash, Grape Basket, Lone Star, and Schoolhouse designs. 59 pages, $14.95, plus $1.50 postage. Published by C & T Publishing.

YOU CAN BE A SUPER QUILTER by Carla J. Hassel. This handbook will guide the self-taught beginner through every aspect of quiltmaking, from gathering tools and fabrics to completing a full-size quilt. The basic techniques for piecing, appliqué work, and hand quilting are presented in a series of lessons, each clearly described and well-illustrated with diagrams and photographs. Accurate full-size templates are included in a special section, printed on heavy stock for the quilter to cut and use as desired. Quilters of all levels of ability will refer to *Super Quilter's* expert information again and again. Spiral bound. 136 pages, $10.95. Published by Wallace-Homestead Book Co.

Quilting Pattern Collections

Whether plain or fancy, quilting stitches add the final—and often most beautiful—touch to patchwork and appliqué quilts. Included here are a variety of pattern books for traditional hand quilting, machine quilting, trapunto, and other forms of quilting.

BIG BOOK OF QUILTING PATTERNS by Virginia Robertson. Among this basic collection of attractive, old-fashioned quilting patterns are florals, cables, feathers, hearts, and more. Many of the designs are drawn in several useful sizes and may be used for other techniques, such as appliqué and trapunto, as well. Brief instructions for all techniques are scattered throughout. Spiral-bound on over-sized pages and designed for all levels of ability. 56 pages, $14.50 postpaid. Published by The Osage County Quilt Factory.

CONTINUOUS CURVE QUILTING: MACHINE QUILTING THE PIECED QUILT by Barbara Johannah. The instructions and diagrams describing Johannah's innovative machine quilting technique are complete and surprisingly uncomplicated. Thoughtful consideration is given not only to time-saving methods, but also to the pattern and beauty of the patchwork

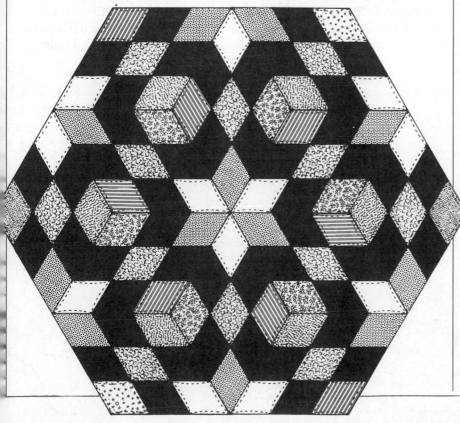

and the quilting. 53 pages, $8.95, plus $1 postage. Published by Pride of the Forest.

CONTINUOUS LINE QUILTING DESIGNS ESPECIALLY FOR MACHINE QUILTING by Pat Cody. Eighty-six machine quilting patterns designed to maximize creativity and minimize time and effort are presented with concise, easy-to-follow directions. All patterns are printed against a background grid for re-sizing if necessary. For all levels of ability. 96 pages, $7.95. Published by Chilton Book Company.

THE DESIGNER'S TOUCH, VOL. 1 by Mary Blaylock. Dainty hearts, flowers, cupids, and butterflies, each drawn in several block sizes, will make a pleasant addition to any quilting pattern library. Printed on loose-leaf pages, the twenty patterns will appeal to quilters of all levels of ability. 32 pages, $5.75, plus $1.50 postage. Published by The Pocket Gallery.

DESIGNS FOR TRAPUNTO AND QUILTING by Jacquelyn Canavan. The history and techniques of trapunto are thoroughly explored, with special emphasis on instructions and materials for the beginner and the expert. Twenty-one full-size designs, some antique and some original, along with suggestions for new uses of trapunto, are also included. 40 pages, $8, plus $1 postage. Published by Jacquelyn Canavan; order from Designs.

EVERY STITCH COUNTS by Patricia Cox. Stars, flowers, hearts, and feathers highlight this collection of 100 full-size quilting patterns for the 12" square. All designs are available in other sizes by special order from the author. Spiral-bound on heavy paper and designed to appeal to all levels of ability. 100 pages, $13.50 postpaid. Published by One of a Kind Quilting Designs.

FEATHERS AND OTHER FANCIES by Marguerite Wiebusch. Over twenty irresistable feather, flower, bird, and heart designs are found in this outstanding quilting pattern collection for blocks and borders. All are full-size and are printed on fold-out, spiral-bound pages. For beginner to advanced levels of ability. 47 pages, $9 postpaid. Published by Feathers and Other Fancies.

THE FINISHING TOUCH by Shirley Thompson. A wonderful source book of enchanting quilting designs that will provide many years of joyful stitching. One hundred full-size patterns for borders, blocks, and lattice strips of various sizes are printed on large, spiral-bound pages. For beginners and experts alike. 56 pages, $9.95, plus $1 postage. Published by Powell Publications.

HEIRLOOM QUILTING DESIGNS FROM THE WOODBOURNE QUILT by the Montgomery County Historical Society. Over fifty authentic antique quilting designs derived from the extraordinary Woodbourne quilt (c. 1852) comprise this breathtaking collection of patterns. Most designs are for large and small blocks and include many floral, bird, and folk art themes. All patterns are shown full-size on the fold-out, spiral-bound pages. For intermediate to advanced levels of ability. 43 pages, $8, plus $2 postage.

Published by The Montgomery County Historical Society, Inc.

HERITAGE QUILTING DESIGNS FROM THE COLLECTION OF DORATHY FRANSON by Bertha Reth Tribuno. One-hundred traditional and elegant flower, feather, cable, bird, and heart designs comprise a most impressive collection of full-size block and border quilting patterns. Each is shown full size and is printed on large, spiral-bound pages. For beginners and experts alike. 49 pages, $9.25, plus $1.50 postage. Published by Bertha Reth Tribuno.

HERITAGE QUILTS AND QUILTING DESIGNS II: ANOTHER COLLECTION FROM GRANDMA FRANSON'S ATTIC by Bertha Reth Tribuno. Complete patterns, diagrams, and instructions for eight old-fashioned patchwork quilts, each with its own charming quilting designs, are combined into one valuable source book. All patterns are full size and are printed on large, spiral-bound pages. Intermediate and advanced level quilters will enjoy working such patterns as Japanese Fan, Wishing Star, and Double Wedding Ring. 60 pages, $9.95, plus $1.50 postage. Published by Bertha Reth Tribuno.

AN INDIANA LEGACY by Millie Leathers. An attractive collection of thirty full-size quilting designs for blocks and borders, reflecting a piece of Indiana quilting history and natural beauty. The fold-out pages are printed on both sides and are spiral-bound. For all levels of ability. 32 pages, $9, plus $1 postage. Published by Millie Leathers.

IT'S NOT A QUILT UNTIL IT'S QUILTED by Shirley Thompson. A classic among quilting pattern collections with over 100 traditionally inspired designs for large and small blocks, borders,

and sashing strips. All patterns are shown full size and are printed on large, spiral-bound pages. For all levels of ability. 64 pages, $12.95, plus $1 postage. Published by Powell Publications.

MORE FEATHERS AND OTHER FANCIES by Marguerite Wiebusch.

Graceful flowers, charming folk-art motifs, leaves, and hearts are certain to make this collection a long-time favorite. All fifty block and border patterns are full size and are printed on spiral-bound, fold-out pages.

Both beginners and experts alike will find some lovely quilting patterns to add the perfect finishing touch to their patchwork. 96 pages, $13 postpaid. Published by Feathers and Other Fancies.

NEW STITCHES: ORIGINAL QUILTING DESIGNS by Dianna Vale. Twenty-four refreshingly original quilting patterns for blocks and borders include flowers, leaves, feathers, and birds. The beginner and the in-termediate quilter will appreciate the full-size patterns printed on convenient spiral-bound pages. 21 pages, $5, plus $1 postage. Published by Dianna Vale.

NEW STITCHES: BOOK II by Dianna Vale. An attractive collection of twenty-one full-size quilting patterns for blocks and borders, highlighted by several lovely floral, fan, basket, and ribbon designs. Quilters from beginning to advanced levels of ability will appreciate the variety of patterns printed on spiral-bound pages. 21 pages, $5, plus $1 postage. Published by Dianna Vale.

NEW STITCHES: BOOK III by Dianna Vale. Especially beautiful among the twenty-three full-size quilting patterns for blocks and borders are the Amish feathers, distlefink, and friendship quilting designs. For all levels of quilting ability. 21 pages, $5, plus $1 postage. Published by Dianna Vale.

NEW STITCHES: BOOK IV by Dianna Vale. Enjoy stitching the stork scissor design, or perhaps the feathered fan or the geo-

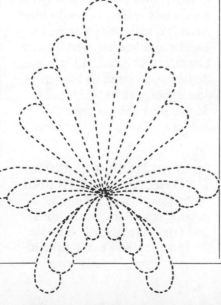

metric Navaho pattern from this delightful array of twenty-four original quilting designs. All patterns for blocks and borders are shown full size and are printed on spiral-bound pages. For the beginner to the advanced quilter. 21 pages, $5, plus $1 postage. Published by Dianna Vale.

NEW STITCHES: BOOK V by Dianna Vale. Small cables, spring flowers, fans, and country folk are included in the twenty-one imaginative full-size quilting patterns for blocks and borders. Spiral-bound convenience for beginners and experts alike. 21 pages, $5.95, plus $1 postage. Published by Dianna Vale.

ORIGINAL QUILTING DESIGNS by Loraine Neff. Beautifully embellished feather and flower quilting patterns, several of which are suitable for white-on-white quilting, are presented in a collection of forty-two designs for various size blocks and borders. All patterns are drawn full size and are printed on spiral-bound pages. Geared toward the intermediate to advanced levels of quilting ability. 48 pages, $7.95, plus $1 postage. Published by The American Quilter's Society.

QUILTING DESIGNS FROM THE AMISH by Pepper Cory. From private collections that have served generations of quilters comes a collection of authentic and unusual Amish quilting patterns. Fiddlehead ferns, pie crusts, and stars are just some of the 170 designs for blocks 2″ to 18″ and borders 1″ to 12″. Printed on oversized spiral-bound pages, each design is

shown full size. Commentaries, recipes, and the author's personal observations of Amish people and their lives are found throughout. For all levels of ability. 90 pages, $14.95, plus $1.75 postage. Published by C & T Publishing.

QUILTING PATTERNS by Linda Macho. An attractive variety of traditional and contemporary

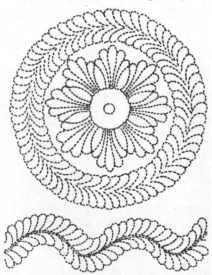

quilting designs, as well as complete instructions for transferring patterns, assembling the quilt layers, and for the actual quilting process help make this a valuable reference book. More than 100 full-size patterns for blocks and borders will inspire countless design combinations. To be appreciated by beginners and experts alike. 32 pages, $4.50, plus 85¢ postage. Published by Dover Publications.

QUILTING TECHNIQUES AND PATTERNS FOR MACHINE STITCHING by Maggie Malone. Florals, geometrics, stars, medallions, and fairy-tale figures, suitable for machine and hand quilting,

form a collection of over 150 different patterns for blocks and borders. The author includes her own brief, uncomplicated approach to machine quilting. 160 pages, $8.95. Published by Sterling Publishing Co., Inc.

SHASHIKO QUILTING by Kimi Ota. A short history of Shashiko, a Japanese style of stitchery similar to American quilting and embroidery, is accompanied by well-illustrated instructions and twenty traditional designs. Complete directions and diagrams for constructing and quilting a Japanese-style jacket in the Sashiko technique are included. For the intermediate to advanced levels of ability. 43 pages, $7.50, plus $1 postage. Published by Kimi Ota.

WHITE-ON-WHITE (WHO SAID IT HAD TO BE WHITE) by Doris Y. Garrett and RoseMary Fosner. Cables, flowers, and hearts are among the twenty-two block and border designs suitable not only for whole-cloth quilts, but also for patchwork and appliqué quilts. All patterns are full size and can be used for pillows, wall hangings, and other small projects. Beginner through advanced levels of quilting ability will appreciate this collection. 16 pages, $5, plus $1 postage. Published by Designs by RD.

Art, History, and Social Fabric

Quilters, quilt collectors and folk-art specialists, historians, and just about anyone with an interest in Americana will be pleased with the titles offered here as a unique visual, intellectual, and reading experience.

ALL FLAGS FLYING: AMERICAN PATRIOTIC QUILTS AS EXPRESSIONS OF LIBERTY by Robert Bishop and Carter Houck. Featured in this pictorial essay on patriotic quilts are 110 antique and contemporary examples, including the 51 winning quilts from the Great American Quilt Contest. Attractive color photographs and brief commentaries accompany each quilt. 102 pages, $14.95. Published by E.P. Dutton.

AMERICA'S PICTORIAL QUILTS by Caron L. Mosey. The author presents an interesting survey of contemporary pictorial quilts and their creators. Numerous color photographs and the artists' own comments on their work are offered as encouragement and inspiration for prospective quilt artists to channel their creative energies into visible form. 112 pages, $19.95, plus $1 postage. Published by American Quilter's Society.

AMERICA'S QUILTS AND COVERLETS by Carlton L. Safford and Robert Bishop. Special attention is given to the patchwork and appliqué quilt in this historical perspective of American bedcoverings from the 17th through the early 20th centuries. The luxurious color and black-and-white photographs speak for themselves, leaving no question as to why early domestic decorative arts deserve our appreciation and careful preservation. 314 pages, $16.50. Published by Crown Publishers, Inc.

AMISH CRIB QUILTS by Rachel and Kenneth Pellman. Often created as an outward expression of parental affection, Amish crib quilts have cradled

generations of children not only in love, but also in the religious beliefs of the Amish. They duplicate in miniature the patterns, vivid colors, fine workmanship, and enduring spirit found in full-size Amish quilts. Handsome color photographs of these rare quilts, along with stories and poems written by Amish children, make this a memorable visual and reading experience. 96 pages, $15.95, plus 5% postage. Published by Good Books.

AUNT JANE OF KENTUCKY by Eliza Calvert Hall. Full of warmth and wisdom, this American classic pays tribute to

the human experience that mysteriously remains unchanged despite the passage of time and the ever-changing cast of players. Quilters will especially enjoy the chapter "Aunt Jane's Album." 283 pages, $15.95, plus $1 postage. Originally published in 1907 by Little, Brown and Co.; facsimile published by R. & E. Miles.

CHINTZ QUILTS: UNFADING GLORY by Lacy Folmar Bullard and Betty Jo Shiell. Chintz

quilts have often been given little attention in quilting histories. Here their elegance and romantic appeal is unfolded through numerous color photographs of historic examples in the whole-cloth, broderie perse, patchwork, and appliqué styles. Several chapters offer inspiration and practical advice for using chintz fabrics in today's quilts. 88 pages, $14.95, plus $1.50 postage. Published by Serendipity Publishers.

COLLECTING QUILTS by Cathy Gaines Florence. Quilt collectors will find this to be a helpful guide for determining the current value of both antique and contemporary quilts. The attributes of each quilt—its condition, size, history, and style—are briefly stated opposite a full-color photograph. 207 pages, $19.95, plus $1 postage. Published by American Quilter's Society.

CRAZY QUILTS by Penny McMorris. During the years 1876-1900, crazy quilts were at the height of their popularity. Lavishly embroidered silk and velvet coverlets adorned every fashionable Victorian drawing room, and less extravagant versions were made by frugal country wives. Here is a fascinating history that traces the development of various crazy quilt styles. Numerous color photographs reveal the fine details and construction methods that make the crazy quilt unique. 127 pages, $19.95. Published by E.P. Dutton.

CRIB QUILTS AND OTHER SMALL WONDERS by Thomas K. Woodard and Blanche Greenstein. Attractive color photo-

graphs and historical information abound in this survey of crib quilts and other small, unusual quilted items, such as pillow shams, table covers, and doll quilts. Authentic full-size patterns for thirteen small quilts are included. 136 pages, $15.75. Published by E.P. Dutton.

DRESSING THE BED by Donald Hoke. Thirty-five of the finest quilts and woven coverlets from the Milwaukee Public Museum's textile collection are illustrated in both black-and-white and color photography. Appliqué and patchwork quilts of notable color, design, and workmanship display the skills of several 19th-century Wisconsin quilters. 65 pages, $9.95, plus $1.50 postage. Published by Milwaukee Public Museum.

THE ESPRIT QUILT COLLECTION by Julie Silber. Approximately twenty vintage Amish quilts from the Esprit Collection have been beautifully photographed for this catalog. Their colors seem to glow with an unforgettable vibrancy; their intricate stitches appear as if in relief against the plain fabric backgrounds. A documented and annotated list of the entire collection is included. 40 pages, $3.50, plus $1.25 postage. Published by Esprit De Corp.

FORGET ME NOT, A GALLERY OF FRIENDSHIP AND ALBUM QUILTS by Jane Bentley Kolter. *Forget Me Not* is a colorful tribute to an ongoing tradition in American life and artistry—friendship and album quilts. It is a wonderful source of design, as well as an interesting collection of stories behind the quilts and

their creators. Attractive color and black-and-white photographs illustrate intricately pieced and appliquéd album quilts from the 1840s through the 1970s. 127 pages, $14.95, plus $1.75 postage. Published by The Main Street Press.

A GALLERY OF AMISH QUILTS by Robert Bishop and Elizabeth A. Safanda. A comprehensive and revealing study of the Amish and their quilts, complete with

splendid color photographs and pertinent commentaries for over one hundred vintage Pennsylvania and Mid-western Amish quilts. Careful analysis of these quilts within their proper context—Amish religious and social life—uphold the author's premise that Amish quilts display "diversity within conformity." 96 pages, $12.50. Published by E.P. Dutton.

HAWAIIAN QUILTING—A FINE ART by Elizabeth A. Akana. The history and artistic development of the Hawaiian appliqué quilt are discussed. Black-and-white photographs of notable examples are included. 48 pages,

$2.95. Published by The Hawaiian Mission's Children's Society; order from The Pacific Trade Group.

HOMAGE TO AMANDA by Edwin Binney and Gail Binney-Winslow. Two hundred years of American quiltmaking—its history, artistic expression, and craftsmanship—have been beautifully documented in this collection of fine heirloom quilts. 96 pages, $16.95, plus

$1.75 postage. Published by RK Press; order from The Quilt Digest Press.

IN THE HEART OF PENNSYLVANIA, 19th AND 20th CENTURY QUILT-MAKING TRADITIONS by Jeannette Lasansky. From seven central Pennsylvanian counties comes a collection of quilts reflecting not only the ethnic backgrounds of the women who made them, but also a variety of geographical, occupational, and fashionable trends that had a profound effect on their maker's lives. The fine workmanship of many of the quilts has been beautifully reproduced in color.

Interspersed throughout is a text which explains the findings of this research project. The quilt historian will find this to be a handsome addition to her personal library. 102 pages, $15.95, plus $1.50 postage. Published by The Oral Traditions Project of the Union County Historical Society.

JUST A QUILT OR JUSCHT EN DEPPICH by Nancy Roan and Ellen J. Gehret. Through intuitive foresight, many quilters and historians have wisely sought to preserve and document the artistic and cultural heritage of a particularly unique region before it has been assimilated into the mainstream and lost forever. Such is the purpose of *Just a Quilt*, which focuses its attention on the Goschenhoppen region of southeastern Pennsylvania. Filled with charming quotations and observations from local quiltmakers, this folk study holds an endless fascination. Scale drawings of patchwork, appliqué, and quilting designs favored in the Goschenhoppen region are included. 40 pages, $6, postpaid. Published by Goschenhoppen Historians, Inc.

KENTUCKY QUILTS AND THEIR MAKERS by Mary Washington Clarke. Clarke's microcosmic view of Kentucky quilts and their makers has a universal appeal. Both the past and present traditions are explored in a communal and an individual context, revealing that Kentucky quilts exhibit an "infinite and continuing variety." This rich quiltmaking heritage, coupled with an unwavering commitment to the craft, has spanned the centuries. And, as

the author contends, it is clear why quilting has never actually died out in Kentucky despite outside influences. Several color and numerous black-and-white photographs illustrate the text. 120 pages, $12. Published by The University Press of Kentucky.

KENTUCKY QUILTS 1800-1900 by Jonathan Holstein and John Finley. This handsome book documents the first undertaking of its kind, the Kentucky Quilt Project, which set the precedent for gathering and documenting quilts that had hitherto been unrecognized, but nevertheless represent a vital part of our regional and national quilting legacy. An historical text and full descriptive commentaries complement color photographs of forty-four of the finest quilts gleaned from the hills, back roads, and villages of the Kentucky countryside. 80 pages, $14.95, plus $1.50 postage. Published by Pantheon Books; order from Dicmar Publishing.

LONE STARS, A LEGACY OF TEXAS QUILTS by Karoline Patterson Bresenhan and Nancy O'Bryant Puentes. Following the example set by the Kentucky Quilt Project, a two-year state-wide search directed by two Texas women documented over 3,000 quilts from family and other private collections—most of which had never before been seen in public. From these, sixty-two quilts were chosen for this catalog because of their fine aesthetic qualities, extraordinary needleworking skills, and historical significance. A color photograph of each quilt is accompanied by complete artistic analysis and historic documentation. Not to be overlooked are the brief glimpses into the quiltmakers' lives, dispelling for a moment the anonymity history has imposed on them as individuals and as artists. This handsome volume is a wellspring of valuable information and a proud tribute to the quilters and the rich quiltmaking traditions of Texas. 156 pages, $18.95, plus $2 postage. Published by The University of Texas Press.

LONE STARS
A Legacy of Texas Quilts, 1836–1936

BY KAROLINE PATTERSON BRESENHAN
AND NANCY O'BRYANT PUENTES
FOREWORD BY JONATHAN HOLSTEIN

THE MAIN STREET POCKET GUIDE TO QUILTS by Phyllis Haders. Quilters and collectors will find this to be a perfect companion at quilt shows, auctions, and antique markets. Dozens of color photos and pertinent information offer guidance in determining the age, style, and value of antique quilts. 256 pages, $6.95, plus $1.25 postage. Published by The Main Street Press.

A MEETING OF THE SUNBONNET CHILDREN by Betty J. Hagerman. Here is a well-researched and documented survey of the origin and development of the Sunbonnet family of patterns. Approximately twenty full-size patterns are included, along with numerous illustrations of the various styles in this pattern group. 80 pages, $7, plus $1 postage. Published by Betty J. Hagerman; order from Helen M. Ericson.

MENNONITE QUILTS AND PIECES by Judy Schroeder Tomlonson. In stark contrast to the harsh realities of the Kansas prairie are the beauty and comfort of Kansas Mennonite quilts. Yet these were not just bedcovers— they were portraits of the peoples' lives, records of their joys and sorrows, and a testament to their abiding faith. Splendid color photographs of the quilts and the Kansas prairie are interwoven with first-hand accounts of Mennonite farm life in such a way that one appears to be synonymous with the other. 96 pages, $15.95, plus 5% postage. Published by Good Books.

MISSOURI HERITAGE QUILTS by Betina Havig. Outstanding quilts gathered from private collections and documented for the

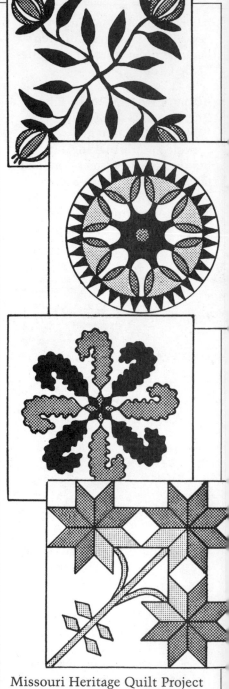

Missouri Heritage Quilt Project are presented in an attractive photographic essay. Historical information and brief artistic comments accompany each of the forty-two examples. Full-size templates for six of the quilts are included. 104 pages, $14.95, plus $1 postage. Published by American Quilter's Society.

NEW DISCOVERIES IN AMERICAN QUILTS by Robert Bishop. As a supplement to *American Quilts and Coverlets*, this volume presents recently discovered examples of American quilts and bedcoverings whose individual beauty adds an extra measure of richness to our quilting heritage. Handsome color photographs of quilts from sixteen stylistic groups, such as Amish, patriotic, and children's quilts, accompany brief historical notes. 127 pages, $15.95. Published by E.P. Dutton.

NORTH CAROLINA COUNTRY QUILTS: REGIONAL VARIATIONS by Ackland Art Museum. During a research project in North Carolina, over 450 antique quilts were examined and documented to help establish and record any similarities and dissimilarities in the quiltmaking traditions of three distinct geographical regions. A brief informative essay, along with black-and-white photographs of fifteen notable examples, illustrates the important results of this study. 56 pages, $2.50, plus $1 postage. Published by The Ackland Art Museum, University of North Carolina at Chapel Hill.

OLD PATCHWORK QUILTS AND THE WOMEN WHO MADE THEM by Ruth Finley. A fascinating blend of history and legend and artistic and social commentary has been woven together into a comprehensive view of American quilting traditions. Several chapters discuss the development of traditional patchwork and appliqué patterns and the origin of their names, as well as the migration of patterns with American pioneers as they set-

tled the frontier. Insights are given on the drafting techniques, construction methods, quilting designs, and dyeing recipes used by quilters of a bygone era. This is a classic among quilting publications that is as enjoyable to read as it is informative. 202 pages, $9.75. Published by Charles T. Branford Co.

A PEOPLE AND THEIR QUILTS by John Rice Irwin. From the cover photograph to the last simple, but wisdom-filled, quotation, the reader is captivated by the spirit of a people who have created so much beauty from so few and such precious raw materials. Irwin's interviews with quilters from the southern Appalachian regions of Tennessee are sensitive, respectful, and always in the speakers' own words. Handsome color and black-and-white portraits of the quilts and their makers or inheritors are the perfect complement to the text. 214 pages, $19.95. Published by Schiffer Publishing, Ltd.

THE PIECED QUILT, AN AMERICAN DESIGN TRADITION by Jonathan

Holstein. Holstein presents an interesting and personal view of American quilts based on their remarkable visual impact. Ninety-six color plates and fifty-six black-and-white photographs illuminate the author's study of this unique art form. 192 pages, $25. Published by New York Graphic Society Books/Little, Brown and Co.

PIECED QUILTS OF ONTARIO by Dorothy K. Burnham. Twenty-seven 19th-century Canadian quilts from the Royal Ontario Museum collection have been assembled into this modest but appealing catalog. Photographs, historical and stylistic commentaries, as well as full-size patterns, have been included for each example. Quilters from the United States will appreciate this rare glimpse at Canadian interpretations of such favorites as Delectable Mountains, Lemoyne Star, and English Ivy. 64 pages, $3.50, Canadian funds. Published by The Royal Ontario Museum.

THE POLITICAL AND CAMPAIGN QUILT by Katy Christopherson. Thirty quilts expressing diverse political themes and opinions are presented in this catalog from a 1984 exhibition held in the Old State Capitol, Frankfort, Kentucky. Commentaries and photographs are included for each quilt. 64 pages, $7.50, plus $1.50 postage. Published by The Kentucky Heritage Quilt Society.

THE QUILT DIGEST, VOLS. 1-4, edited by Roderick Kiracofe and Michael Kile. The eyes and heart of every quiltmaker and collector, folklore and folk art enthusiast will delight in the many attractive features found in each volume of this series. Interesting histories, interviews, and stories will provide hours of enjoyable reading. Luxurious color photographs of antique and contemporary quilts are beautifully displayed in a chapter appropriately titled "Showcase." Some of the highlights of *Quilt Digest 1* are an interview with Michael James, a discussion of Log Cabin quilts, and an article on documentation techniques. 70 pages, $12.95. *Quilt Digest 2* offers an article entitled "A Piece of Ellen's Dress," an essay on Hawaiian Flag quilts, and notes on quilt care and preservation. 79 pages, $12.95. *Quilt Digest 3* presents a rare glimpse at Quaker quilts, an article by Barbara Brackman called "Out of Control—Quilts That Break the Rules," and an interesting account of an early Alabama pioneer and her quilts. 87 pages, $15.95. Besides an interview with quilt collector Sandy Mitchell, *Quilt Digest 4* contains the story of a 19th-century spinster and the Friendship quilt made for her by her girlhood friends. The reader will be inspired by the story of Alabama's Freedom Quilting Bee and its members who now earn their living through their needleworking talents. 87 pages, $16.95. Postage is $1.75 for the first book ordered and $1 for each additional book. Published by The Quilt Digest Press.

THE QUILT ENGAGEMENT CALENDAR TREASURY by Cyril I. Nelson and Carter Houck. Browsing through this portrait gallery of exquisite quilts will provide hours of visual enjoyment and plenty of inspiration for the

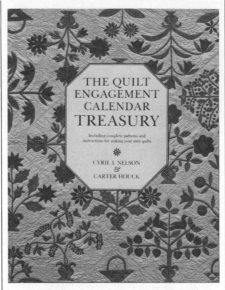

modern quilter to create her own works of art. Over 180 of the finest quilts gleaned from the *Quilt Engagement Calendars* of 1975 through 1982 are pictured in color, representing a wide variety of quilt styles. Brief commentaries are given for each example, and a useful cross-reference system has been devised for easy comparison of similarly styled quilts. Full-size patterns and instructions offer the intermediate and advanced quilter the opportunity to reproduce twenty-one of these beautiful quilts. 272 pages, $24.95. Published by E.P. Dutton.

THE QUILTERS, WOMEN AND DOMESTIC ART by Patricia Cooper and Norma Bradley Buferd. Occasionally, there are books written that defy analysis or criticism. *The Quilters* is one such book. The women who speak plainly and directly about their individual lives on Texan and New Mexican homesteads and about the quiltmaking traditions that are so inextricably linked to their lives make such a remarkable im-

pression on the reader that anything else seems pale by comparison. 157 pages, $12.95. Published by Doubleday & Co., Inc.

QUILTING 1915-1983, AN ANNOTATED BIBLIOGRAPHY by Colleen Lahan Makowski. The author has compiled a valuable aid for intensive research into quilting. Included are annotated lists of books, exhibition catalogs, periodical articles, non-print media, museum collections, and periodicals. 151 pages, $15. Published by Scarecrow Press, Inc.

QUILTS AMONG THE PLAIN PEOPLE by Rachel T. Pellman and Joanne Ranck. The authors offer sensitive insights into Amish and Mennonite life and the spirit of love and community that nurtures the creation of beautiful quilts. 96 pages, $3.95, plus 5% postage. Published by Good Books.

QUILTS FROM THE INDIANA AMISH by David Pottinger. The quilts made by the Indiana Amish represent a distinct regional variation of the design category

known generally as Amish quilts. Here is a colorful gallery of over 100 Amish quilts gleaned from Lagrange and Elkhart counties in rural Indiana, dated prior to 1940. The author and owner of the collection presents a warm and sensitive view of the Amish and their quilts. 88 pages, $15.95. Published by E.P. Dutton.

QUILTS, THE GREAT AMERICAN ART by Patricia Mainardi. The author has developed a thought-provoking essay on the quilter's role as artist. 58 pages, $3.95, plus $1 postage. Published by Miles & Weir, Ltd.; order from R. & E. Miles.

QUILTS: THEIR STORY AND HOW TO MAKE THEM by Marie D. Webster. Webster's book might very well be considered a quilting and needleworking encyclopedia, for it contains an enormous amount of information that few other single publications can rival. Beginning with its roots in antiquity, the art of quilting is traced from the Middle Ages, to old England, and finally to America—both past and present. Additional chapters discuss quilt construction, quilt names, and quilt collections. Black-and-white photographs of artistically and historically important quilts illustrate the text. Valuable to quilters, collectors, and researchers alike. 178 pages, $36. Originally published by Doubleday, Page & Co.; reprinted by Gale Research Co.

REMEMBER ME, WOMEN AND THEIR FRIENDSHIP QUILTS by Linda Otto Lipsett. *Remember Me* is a friendship quilt in its own right. Careful research has pieced together with intricate precision the lives of seven 19th-century women into a captivating narrative. And though the course of each woman's life was quite different, a thread of similarity is visible through their friendship quilts and their desire to preserve precious memories. 133 pages, $19.95, plus $1.75 postage. Published by The Quilt Digest Press.

STITCHES IN TIME: A LEGACY OF OZARK QUILTS by Michael Luster. Searching for and documenting quilts indigenous to six Ozark counties became part of the sesquicentennial celebration of the state of Arkansas. From over 200 quilts brought to the "quilt sharings," 30 were chosen to be photographed for this catalog, not only because of their artistry and remarkable condition, but also because of their regional and historical significance. Portraits of the women who created these quilts have been skillfully interwoven into a well-researched and interesting history of the Ozark region. 49 pages, $10, postpaid. Published by Rogers Historical Museum.

SMALL ENDEARMENTS by Sandi Fox. Nineteenth-century children's quilts served not only to wrap a precious child in warmth and love, but also as a woman's expression of pride in herself as expert needlewoman and dutiful mother. Color and black-and-white photographs of familiar and unusual children's quilts illustrate the informative and interesting text, focusing on the historical, sociological, and artistic aspects of this genre.

164 pages, $24.95. Published by Charles Scribner's Sons.

SOCIAL FABRIC, SOUTH CAROLINA'S TRADITIONAL QUILTS by Laurel Horton and Lynn Robertson Myers. The unique quiltmaking traditions found in the Low Country, the Midlands, and the Piedmont regions of South Carolina are illuminated in a series of well-documented and researched essays that discuss the cultural, geographical, and historical forces that influenced the quilting artisans of South Carolina's past. 56 pages, $10, plus $1 postage. Published by The University of South Carolina; order from the McKissick Museum.

THE STATE OF THE ART QUILT: CONTEMPORARY QUILTS FOR THE COLLECTOR edited by Barbara Packer. The catalog for Quilt Expo '85 presents a gallery of contemporary quilts, each one of which serves to recommend contemporary quiltmaking as a viable art form. A color photograph of each example and brief comments are included. 80 pages, $12.95, plus $2 postage.

Published by Friends of Nassau County Recreation, Inc.

SUNSHINE AND SHADOW by Phyllis Haders. *Sunshine and Shadow* contains a wealth of information on Amish quilt patterns and materials. Sixteen examples of Amish design, each shown in color and in black-and-white detail, are introduced by a relevant biblical passage or Amish prayer. Appropriate historical and artistic commentaries further describe each quilt. 88 pages, $7.95, plus $1.25 postage. Published by The Main Street Press.

TEXAS QUILTS, TEXAS WOMEN by Suzanne Yabsley. Quilts are symbolic not only of the people who have made them, but also of various cultural, historical, and geographical forces that have influenced their creation. In this well-researched and often touching essay, Yabsley describes those factors that have shaped the lives of Texas women, and ultimately the quilts they have produced. Photographs of the quilts have been kept to a minimum,

perhaps to focus attention on the importance of the text. Historians and folklorists, as well as quilters, will welcome the emphasis placed on the human spirit that has created some of America's most beautiful artifacts even in the face of great adversity. 99 pages, $19.95. Published by Texas A & M University Press.

THE WORLD OF AMISH QUILTS by Rachel and Kenneth Pellman. Amish quilts have been noted by quilters and folk art enthusiasts for their exquisite craftsmanship, brilliant colors, and often unique format. But only when viewed against the background of the simple daily life and deep religious faith of the Amish can these quilts be fully appreciated. Thirty designs typical of the Amish patchwork repertoire are fully illustrated and described. Interesting correlations are drawn between the patterns most often used and the aspects of Amish life that have inspired their use. Attractive color photographs, combined with a well-written text, offer a respectful glimpse into Amish life and quiltmaking traditions. 128 pages, $15.95, plus 5% postage. Published by Good Books.

Publishers' Addresses

*The Ackland Art Museum
The University of North
    Carolina at Chapel Hill
Ackland 003
Chapel Hill, NC 27514*

*Acropolis Books, Ltd.
2400 17th St., NW
Washington, DC 20009*

*American Quilter's Society
P.O. Box 3290
Paducah, KY 42001*

*Amity Publications
78688 Sears Rd.
Cottage Grove, OR 97424-9470*

*Pat Andreatta
626 Shadowood Ln.
Warren, OH 44484*

*Barbara Bannister
Needlecraft Books
5811 U.S. 31 N.
Alanson, MI 49706*

*Better Homes and Gardens
    Books
Meredith Corporation
1716 Locust St.
Des Moines, IA 50336*

*Dorothy Bond
34706 Row River Rd.
Cottage Grove, OR 97424*

*Betty Boyink Publishing
818 Sheldon Rd.
Grand Haven, MI 49417*

*Charles T. Branford Co.
P.O. Box 41
Newton Center, MA 02159*

*Karen Bray
21 Birch Dr.
Walnut Creek, CA 94596*

*C & T Publishing
P.O. Box 1456
Lafayette, CA 94549*

*Cabin Fever Calicoes
Box 54, Range Rd.
Center Sandwich, NH 03227*

*The Charleston Museum
360 Meeting St.
Charleston, SC 29403*

*Chilton Book Company
201 King of Prussia Rd.
Radnor, PA 19089*

Corona Publishing Company
1037 South Alamo
San Antonio, TX 78210

Covered Bridge Quilters
4308 Blueberry Rd.
Fredonia, WI 53021

Crown Publishers, Inc.
225 Park Ave. S.
New York, NY 10003

Culver Publications
P.O. Box 3103
Kingston, NY 12401

Dav-a-lyn Enterprises
P.O. Box 88682
Seattle, WA 98188

David & Charles
Box 257
North Pomfret, VT 05053

Designs, Jaquelyn Canavan
8000 Monte Dr.
Cincinnati, OH 45242

Designs by RD
260 Crestwood Circle
High Point, NC 27260

Dicmar Publishing
P.O. Box 3533
Georgetown Sta.
Washington, DC 20007

Donagil Publications
P.O. Box 7000-173
Redondo Beach, CA 90277

Doubleday & Company, Inc.
501 Franklin Ave.
Garden City, NY 11530

Dover Publications, Inc.
31 E. 2nd St.
Mineola, NY 11501

E.P. Dutton, Inc.
2 Park Ave.
New York, NY 10016

EPM Publications, Inc.
1003 Turkey Run Rd.
McLean, VA 22101

Helen M. Ericson
P.O. Box 650
Emporia, KS 66801

Esprit De Corp
900 Minnesota St.
San Francisco, CA 94107

Evening Star Farm, Inc.
P.O. Box 23094
Stanley, KS 66223

Farm Journal Books
230 W. Washington Sq.
Philadelphia, PA 19105

Feathers & Other Fancies
Marguerite Wiebusch
5440 W. 300 S.
Russiaville, IN 46979

Friends of Nassau County
Recreation, Inc.
P.O. Box 456
East Meadow, NY 11554

Gale Research Company
Book Tower
Detroit, MI 48226

Gick Publishing, Inc.
9 Studebaker Dr.
Irvine, CA 92718

Good Books
Main St.
Intercourse, PA 17534

Goschenhoppen Historians, Inc.
Red Men's Hall
Green Lane, PA 18054

Gutcheon Patchworks
P.O. Box 57
Prince St. Sta.
New York, NY 10012

Hawaiian Designing Collection
P.O. Box 1396
Kailua, Hawaii 96734

Hot Fudge Press
Suite 444
4974 N. Fresno St.
Fresno, CA 93726

Illinois Quilters, Inc.
P.O. Box 39
Wilmette, IL 60091

Imbach Publications
246 Greengates
Corona, CA 91719

Kentucky Heritage Quilt
Society
P.O. Box 23392
Lexington, KY 40523

Millie Leathers
P.O. Box 273
Vernon, IN 47282

Leman Publications
Moon Over the Mountain
6700 W. 44th Ave.
P.O. Box 394
Wheatridge, CO 80034-0394

Leone Publications
2721 Lyle Ct.
Santa Clara, CA 95051

The Main Street Press
William Case House
Pittstown, NJ 08867

R.&.E. Miles
P.O. Box 1916
San Pedro, CA 90733

McKissick Museum
University of South Carolina
Columbia, SC 29208

Milwaukee Public Museum
Publication Section—Orders
800 W. Wells St.
Milwaukee, WI 53233

The Montgomery County
Historical Society, Inc.
103 W. Montgomery Ave.
Rockville, MD 20850

Mosi Publications
1348 E. Edison St., Dept. E
Tucson, AZ 85719

New York Graphic Society
Little, Brown and Co.
34 Beacon St.
Boston, MA 02106

One of a Kind Quilting Designs
6601 Normandale Rd.
Minneapolis, MN 55435

Oral Traditions Project of the
    Union County Historical
    Society
County Courthouse
Lewisburg, PA 17837

The Osage County Quilt
    Factory
400 Walnut, Box 490
Overbrook, KS 66524

Kimi Ota
10300 61st Ave. S.
Seattle, WA 98178

Oxmoor House
P.O. Box 2262
Birmingham, AL 35201

The Pacific Trade Group
P.O. Box 668
Pearl City, Hawaii 96782-0668

Patchwork House Patterns
Loveland Pattern Co.
P.O. Box 891
Loveland, CO 80537

The Patchwork Press
P.O. Box 183
Bemidji, MN 56601

The Pocket Gallery
580 Pintaura Dr.
Santa Barbara, CA 93111

Powell Publications
P.O. Box 513
Edmonds, WA 98020

Prairie Flower Publishing
Barbara Brackman
500 Louisiana St.
Lawrence, KS 66044

Prentice-Hall, Inc.
Sylvan Road
Englewood Cliffs, NJ 07632

Pride of the Forest
P.O. Box 7266
Menlo Park, CA 94025

The Quilt Digest Press
955 14th St.
San Francisco, CA 94114

Quiltwork Publications
2600 Oak Valley Dr.
Vienna, VA 22180

Rita's Quiltn' Sewing Center
P.O. Box 2793
Santa Fe, NM 87504

Rogers Historical Museum
322 S. 2nd St.
Rogers, AR 72756

Royal Ontario Museum
Publication Services
100 Queen's Park
Toronto M5S 2C6
Canada

Scarecrow Press, Inc.
52 Liberty St.
Metuchen, NJ 08840

Schiffer Publishing, Ltd.
Box E
Exton, PA 19341

The School for Inquiring Mynds
241 E. 6th Ave.
Tallahassee, FL 32303

Charles Scribner's Sons
115 Fifth Ave.
New York, NY 10003

Serendipity Publishers
241 E. 6th Ave.
Tallahassee, FL 32303

Jan Stehlik
Sod House Treasures
Rt. 1, Box 11
Dorchester, NE 68343

Sterling Publishing Company,
    Inc.
2 Park Ave.
New York, NY 10016

Sudz Publishing
2931 Albee St.
Eureka, CA 95501

Sunset Publications
1655 Makaloa St.
Suite 906
Honolulu, Hawaii 96814

Texas A & M University Press
Drawer C
College Station, TX 77843

That Patchwork Place
P.O. Box 118
Bothell, WA 98041-0002

Thimbles 'n Roses
Box 18524
Greensboro, NC 27419

Bertha Reth Tribuno
4111 Woodridge Dr. NE
Cedar Rapids, Iowa 52401

The University of Texas Press
P.O. Box 7819
Austin, TX 78713

The University Press of
    Kentucky
102 Lafferty Hall
Lexington, KY 40506-0024

Dianna Vale Quilting Supplies
1294 32nd Ave. NW
Salem, OR 97304

Wallace-Homestead
P.O. Box 6500
Chicago, IL 60680

Weaver-Finch Publications
P.O. Box 353
Edmonds, WA 98020

Yankee Books
Yankee Publishing Inc.
Main St.
Dublin, NH 03444

Young Publications
P.O. Box 925
Oak View, CA 93022

Yours Truly/Burdett
    Publications
5455 Garden Grove Blvd.
Westminster, CA 92683

Periodicals

Periodicals contribute generously to the intense and ever-growing interest in quilting. They introduce the newcomer to all aspects of quilting and help to keep the more experienced quilter well informed of current events, new techniques, and new products designed especially for the quilter. In the same respect, periodicals help to preserve the best of our past quilting heritage through essays, photographs, and notices of important museum exhibitions. Often, periodicals offer quilting lessons, patterns, and answers to patchwork difficulties. Every serious quilter should consider a subscription to one or more periodicals.

AMERICAN QUILTER, edited by Marty Bowne and Mary Lou Schwinn. *American Quilter*, a newcomer in the field of quilting periodicals, offers the contemporary quilter a medium through which ideas and information can be exchanged and shared with other quilters. Regular features of this quarterly publication include full-size patterns for original quilt designs, articles written by well-known and knowledgeable quilting personalities, useful information on quilting techniques, and a calendar of quilting events. Attractive full-color photographs enhance the text. Approximately 60 pages per issue, $15 yearly subscription rate, plus $5 postage and handling for subscribers in foreign countries. Published by American Quilter's Society.

CANADA QUILTS, edited by Marilynn Holowachuk. For information on the myriad activities of Canadian quilting guilds, this publication is essential. It also provides useful how-to material from experienced Canadian quilters. Published five times a year: February,

April, June, September, and November. Canada, $12; $15 U.S. and overseas. Published by Canada Quilts.

COUNTRY QUILTS, edited by Jean Eitel. *Country Quilts*, identical in content and format to its sister publication *Quilt*, appears once a year to pay special homage to country-style quilts. Over twenty traditional appliqué and patchwork patterns, complete with full-size templates, block diagrams, and basic instructions are furnished for each design. Refer to the listing for *Quilt* in this section for a complete description of the regular features found in both publications. Approximately 100 pages per issue, $4 postpaid, U.S. funds only. Published by Harris Publications, Inc.

LADY'S CIRCLE PATCHWORK QUILTS, edited by Carter Houck. Published bi-monthly, each issue of *Lady's Circle Patchwork Quilts* explores the traditional and contemporary quilts and quilting trends indigenous to one state or geographical region in the United States. Color

photographs of heirloom quilts, displayed in historic settings, form the main attraction of this periodical. The pattern section includes full-size templates for at least ten of the quilts, as well as templates for an occasional original design. Construction details, however, are minimal, so some quilting experience is necessary to use the patterns. In addition, there are articles on special techniques and quilting "insight" and "humor," book reviews, and notices of shows and competitions. *LCPQ* will serve the quilter as a basic source for traditional patterns and for current events in the quilting world. Approximately 80 pages per issue, $15.95 yearly subscription rate, Canada add $3, other foreign countries add $4.50, U.S. funds only. Published by Lopez Publications, Inc.

THE PROFESSIONAL QUILTER, edited by Jeannie M. Spears. Anyone involved in the business of quilting—whether teacher, designer, shop owner, or writer—will appreciate the information contained in this quarterly publication. Articles cover such subjects as organization, marketing, professional image, teaching skills, and discussions of current issues in the quilt world. $15 yearly subscription rate, $18 in foreign countries. Published by Oliver Press, Publications for Quilters.

QUILT, edited by Jean Eitel. *Quilt,* published quarterly, abounds with patterns, ideas, and articles of interest to quilters of all levels of ability. Approximately twenty patchwork and appliqué patterns (mostly traditional) are reproduced in each issue and are accompanied by full-size templates, block diagrams, rudimentary instructions, and color or black-and-white photographs of the completed quilt. Articles offer information on quilting techniques and styles, current events, and the contributions of individuals, groups, or businesses to the contemporary quilting scene. Regular features found in *Quilt* and its sister publication, *Country Quilts,* include book reviews, a calendar of quilting events, and a display of new quilting products. Approximately 100 pages per issue, $11.80 yearly subscription rate, U.S. funds only. Published by Harris Publications, Inc.

QUILTER'S NEWSLETTER MAGAZINE, edited by Bonnie Leman. Since the publication of its first issue in 1969, *QNM* has sought to preserve and perpetuate the art and craft of quiltmaking. Its modest newsletter format has gradually developed into a full-color, well-organized, and carefully written magazine that has had a profound effect on quilting not only in the United

States, but throughout the world. Many quilting experts consider *QNM* to be the foremost quilting periodical available. Published ten times a year, *QNM* caters to the needs of all quilters, quilt lovers, and pattern collectors. Each issue includes valuable information on traditional and contemporary techniques and designs, as well as the history of quilting and current trends in the quilting forum. There are also listings for shows and competitions, book reviews, articles written by quilting professionals, and advertisements for quilting supplies and services. Patterns—both traditional and contemporary—are one of *QNM*'s most notable and standard features. Full-size, accurate templates, excellent piecing diagrams, complete construction details, and full-color drawings or photographs are included for each quilt design. This feature has proven to be a unique opportunity to learn basic and advanced quilting techniques, and an inexpensive way to collect patterns. Approximately 50 pages per issue, $13.95 yearly subscription rate, Canada add $4, overseas add $8.50 for

postage and handling, payable in U.S. funds only. Published by Leman Publications, Inc.

QUILTING USA, edited by Christiane C. Abdale. Currently published as a special edition of *Craftworks for the Home,* *Quilting USA* has so far been very popular and seems likely to become an independent magazine in the near future. A wide variety of articles, good in-depth research, and lots of color make this an enjoyable magazine to read cover to cover. Approximately 60 pages per issue,

$3.50 individual issues; $15.90 yearly subscription to *Craftworks for the Home* (six issues); overseas add $6, U.S. funds. Published by All American Crafts, Inc.

QUILTMAKER, edited by Bonnie Leman and Judy Martin. *Quiltmaker,* published twice a year, is a treasure trove of patterns and ideas for the active quiltmaker. Each issue contains between fifteen and twenty original designs complete with full-color pictures, step-by-step illustrated directions, full-size templates, and yardage requirements for quilts worked in a variety of styles, sizes, and techniques. All patterns are rated according to the level of skill and the amount of time required for completion. Basic quiltmaking lessons and articles which describe special design and sewing methods are also included. Approximately 40 pages per issue, $6.50 yearly subscription rate, plus $2.50 postage and handling outside the U.S., payable in U.S. funds only. Published by Leman Publications, Inc.

STITCH 'N SEW QUILTS, edited by Ruth M. Swasey. *Stitch 'N Sew Quilts*, a bi-monthly publication is a quaintly disorganized, often poorly photographed periodical modeled after some of the better known quilting magazines. The value of *Stitch 'N Sew Quilts*, however, lies in its excellent patterns—many of which are unusual traditional or original designs. The full-size templates are accurately reproduced and are drawn for both hand and machine piecing. Scaled block diagrams, a list for cutting the correct number of patches, and a small black-and-white photograph of a completed square are included for each pattern. Prior quilting experience may be required since the actual construction details are limited. Regular features include book reviews, articles about quilts and quilters, and a list of shows, competitions, and other quilting events. Approximately 60 pages per issue, $8 yearly subscription rate, $10 in Canada, $14 in other foreign countries. Published by The House of White Birches.

Pubishers of Periodicals

All American Crafts, Inc.
70 Sparta Ave., CN 1003
Sparta, NJ 07871

American Quilter's Society
P.O. Box 3290
Paducah, KY 42002-3290

Canada Quilts
P.O. Box 326
Grimsby, ON L3M 4G5
Canada

Harris Publications, Inc.
1115 Broadway
New York, NY 10010

The House of White Birches,
Inc./Tower Press
P.O. Box 337
Seabrook, NH 03874

Leman Publications, Inc.
Box 394
Wheatridge, CO 80034-0394

Lopez Publications, Inc.
602 Montgomery St.
Alexandria, VA 22314-1576

Oliver Press, Publications for
Quilters
P.O. Box 4096
St. Paul, MN 55104

Out-of-Print Classics

Quilters have inherited not only a rich and varied quilting legacy, but also a distinct and equally rich literary tradition. Unfortunately, many of the fine quilting books written during the early part of this century, as well as in recent years, are no longer in print, and as a result, are quite rare.

Determined quilters and students of quilting history and art, however, may search for and borrow copies of these books from local, state, or university library collections. Used and rare book shops, university book sales, and even flea markets often yield surprising finds. Another alternative is to enlist the services of a reputable title searcher, either through a local book shop or through a mail-order book dealer who offers this service for a nominal fee. Certainly, whenever a precious copy of an out-of-print quilting classic is found, the search will have been well worth the effort and will forever enrich the quilter's knowledge and appreciation of this unique art form.

Albacete, M.J., Sharon D'Atri, and Jane Reeves. *Ohio Quilts: A Living Tradition.* Canton, Ohio: The Canton Art Institute, 1981.
American Pieced Quilts. Washington, D.C.: Smithsonian Institution, 1972.
Bacon, Lenice I. *American Patchwork Quilts.* New York: William Morrow & Co., Inc., 1973.
Carlisle, Lillian Baker. *Pieced Work and Appliqué Quilts at the Shelburne Museum.* Shelburne, Vermont: Shelburne Museum, 1957.
Clark, Ricky. *Quilts and Carousels: Folk Art in the Firelands.* Oberlin, Ohio: FAVA, 1983.

Colby, Averil. *Patchwork*. Newton Center, Massachusetts: Charles T. Branford, 1958.

Conroy, Mary. *300 Years of Canada's Quilts*. Toronto: Griffin House, 1976.

Davidson, Mildred. *American Quilts from the Art Institute of Chicago*. Chicago: The Art Institute of Chicago, 1966.

Dunton, Dr. William Rush, Jr. *Old Quilts*. Catonsville, Maryland, 1946.

FitzRandolph, Mavis and Florence M. Fletcher. *Quilting Traditional Methods and Designs*. Leicester: Dryad Press, 1968.

Frye, L. Thomas. *American Quilts: A Handmade Legacy*. Oakland, California: The Oakland Museum, 1981.

Hall, Carrie A. and Rose G. Kretsinger. *The Romance of the Patchwork Quilt in America*. New York, 1935. Reprint, New York: Bonanza Books, n.d.

Johnson, Bruce. *A Child's Comfort: Baby and Doll Quilts in American Folk Art*. New York: Harcourt, Brace, Jovanovich, Inc., 1977.

Katzenberg, Dena S. *The Great American Cover-Up, Counterpanes of the 18th and 19th Centuries*. Baltimore: The Baltimore Museum of Art, 1971.

_____. *Baltimore Album Quilts*. Baltimore: The Baltimore Museum of Art, 1981.

Lane, Rose Wilder. *Woman's Day Book of American Needlework*. New York: Simon & Schuster, 1963.

Laury, Jean Ray. *Quilts and Coverlets, A Contemporary Approach*. New York: Van Nostrand Reinhold, 1970.

_____. *Appliqué Stitchery*. New York: Van Nostrand Reinhold, 1966.

Lewis, Alfred Allan. *The Mountain Artisans Quilting Book*. New York: Macmillan, 1973.

Lithgow, Marilyn. *Quiltmaking and Quiltmakers*. New York: Funk & Wagnalls, 1974.

Mary McElwain. *The Romance of Village Quilts*. Walworth, Wisconsin, 1936.

_____. *Notes on Applied Work and Patchwork*. London: His Majesty's Stationery Office, 1949.

_____. *Notes on Quilting*. London: His Majesty's Stationery Office, 1949.

New Jersey Quilters: A Timeless Tradition. Morristown, New Jersey: Morris Museum of Arts and Sciences, 1983.

150 Years of American Quilts. Lawrence, Kansas: University of Kansas Museum of Art, 1973.

Orlofsky, Patsy and Myron. *Quilts in America*. New York: McGraw Hill Book Co., 1974.

Peto, Florence. *Historic Quilts*. New York: American Historical Co., 1939.

_____. *American Quilts and Coverlets*. New York: Chanticleer Press, 1949.

Quilter's Choice, Quilts from the Museum Collection. Lawrence, Kansas: University of Kansas, Helen Foresman Spencer Museum of Art, 1978.

Quilts and Coverlets. Denver: The Denver Art Museum, 1974.

Ramsey, Bets. *Quilt Close-Up: Five Southern Views*. Chattanooga, Tennessee: The Hunter Museum of Art, 1983.

Renshaw, Donna. *Quilting: A Revived Art*. Los Altos, California, 1966.

Robertson, Elizabeth Wells. *American Quilts*. New York: The Studio Publications, Inc., 1948.

Sears Century of Progress in Quilting. Chicago: Sears, Roebuck & Co., 1934.

Sexton, Carlie. *Early American Quilts*. Southampton, New York: Crackerbarrel Press, 1924.

_____. *Yesterday's Quilts in Homes of Today*. Des Moines, Iowa: Meredith Publications, Co., 1930.

Something to Keep You Warm: The Roland Freeman Collection of Black American Quilts from the Mississippi Heartland. Jackson, Mississippi: Mississippi Department of Archives and History, 1981.

Southern Comfort: Quilts from the Atlanta Historical Society Collection. Atlanta: Atlanta Historical Society, 1978.

White, Margaret E. *Quilts and Counterpanes in the Newark Museum*. Newark, New Jersey: Newark Museum Association, 1948.

Mail-Order Book Suppliers

Consult Directory of Suppliers for Addresses

The Brass Goose, Front Royal, VA

Brewer Fabric Shop, Brewer, ME

Cabin Fever Calicoes, Center Sandwich, NH

Calico House, Scottsville, VA

Come Quilt with Me, Brooklyn, NY

Community Quilts, Bethesda, MD

Contemporary Quilting, Fairfield, CT

The Cotton Patch, Lafayette, CA

Country House Quilts, Zionsville, IL

Creative Stitches, Honolulu, HI

Cross Patch Quilting Center, Garrison, NY

Dorr Mill Store, Guild, NH

Bette S. Feinstein, Newton, MA

G Street Fabrics, Rockville, MD

Hearthside Quilts, Shelburne, VT

Needlearts International, Glendale, CA

Norton House, Wilmington, VT

Patience Corner Quilt Shop, Portsmouth, NH

The Quilt Patch, Marlboro, MA

Quilter's Peace, Garrison, NY

Quilting Books Unlimited, Aurora, IL

Quilts & Other Comforts, Wheatridge, CO

Quiltwork Patches, Corvallis, OR

I. Ronin & Co., Chicago, IL

Seminole Sampler, Ellicott City, MD

Silver Thimble Quilt Shop, Hampton Falls, NH

Treadleart, Lomita, CA

Tumbleweed, Cambridge, MA

The Vermont Patchworks, Shrewsbury, VT

6. Buying Antique and Contemporary Quilts

Today's quilt buyer is generally drawn to an antique or contemporary patchwork or appliqué bedcovering because of its beauty rather than its utility. After all, a goose-down comforter or even a plebian electric blanket provides more warmth. As quilts are no longer really necessary for their original practical purpose, why the burgeoning popularity of the craft? Aesthetics plays a large part, of course, as does the mystique inherent in the needleworker's talent, and the continuing success of the "American country" look in interior design.

Fine antique quilts are all the rage and make a good investment. Major fine arts museums that once disdained the gift of great-grandmother's patchwork Lone Star are now represented in the feverish bidding for a simple Amish Diamond at a large auction house. Dealers rise before dawn to reach the country marketplace when quilts are likely to be offered for sale. Visitors from Japan, Italy, and France flock to the big city quilt galleries in search of this most American of decorative objects.

Quilters have a special interest in well-wrought antique quilts. They are not only attractive objects to display, but intriguing works to study, even to imitate. Every quilt tells a story in its composition, stitches, and use of materials. The quiltmaker can "read" this tale of artistry and craftsmanship better than anyone else. A new binding on an old quilt will be spotted immediately; so, too, will the substitution of new fabric for old.

In the same way, no one can appreciate a finely worked contemporary quilt more than a fellow quilter. Modern quilts are not given as much attention as the old and this is regrettable. But for the quilter with a good eye, collecting modern masterpieces can be a satisfying and a rewarding hobby.

Floral quilt detail, courtesy of Custom Patchwork, Glens Falls, New York.

Antique Quilts

Antique quilts are treasured today by quilters everywhere. Anyone who has attempted to piece a traditional pattern, to match a fine stitch, or to duplicate a fancy appliqué design has a special appreciation for the artistry of the past. Now that a very fine example can bring up to $30,000 at a major New York auction house, the masterpieces of design and craftsmanship are being guarded with special care and rarely change hands. The majority of antique quilts, however, are simply well-wrought objects and not *objects d'art*. Their supply is by no means exhausted. Many dealers throughout the country offer a good selection of patterns and prices. Among the most reasonably priced offerings are quilts made during the 1920s and '30s which are as traditional in design as quilts made fifty years earlier. Nearly all of the dealers included in the following listings possess a variety of quilt types; a few specialize in categories such as Amish and Mennonite, friendship appliqué, and early whitework. An appointment may be necessary to view the quilts since not all shops are open during regular business hours. Inquiries will be answered by mail or telephone, and, in some cases, dealers can supply photos of quilts in stock.

Arizona

JUST US
P.O. Box 50023
Tucson, AZ 85703-1023
(602) 622-3607

California

MARGARET CAVIGGA QUILT COLLECTION
8648 Melrose Ave.
Los Angeles, CA 90069
(213) 659-3020

Margaret Cavigga Quilt Collection.

THE GAZEBO OF NEW YORK
South Coast Plaza
3333 Bristol St.
Costa Mesa, CA 92626
(714) 540-0209

KIRACOFE AND KILE
955 14th St.
San Francisco, CA 94114
(415) 431-1222

CASKY LEES GALLERY
1325 W. Washington Blvd.
Venice, CA 90291
(213) 296-0876

PEACE AND PLENTY
7320 Melrose Ave.
Los Angeles, CA 90046
(213) 937-3339

Colorado

HOMESPUN HEART ANTIQUE QUILTS
208 W. 8th St.
Leadville, CO 80461

Connecticut

JUDI BOISSON
89 Main St.
Westport, CT 06880
(203) 226-4100

PATTY GAGARIN ANTIQUES
Banks North Rd.
Fairfield, CT 06430
(203) 259-7332

PHYLLIS HADERS
158 Water St.
Stonington, CT 06378
(203) 535-4403

MARTHA JACKSON ANTIQUES
Riverside, CT 06878
(203) 637-2152

IRIS AND MEL PENNER
Stamford, CT 06902
(203) 329-1702

District of Columbia

MARSTON LUCE
1314 21st St., NW
Washington, DC 20036
(202) 775-9460

Georgia

GRANNY TAUGHT US HOW
1921 Peachtree Rd., NE
Atlanta, GA 30309
(404) 351-2942

Idaho

**THE HISSING GOOSE: A GALLERY
 OF FINE AMERICANA**
4th and Leadville Sts.
P.O. Box 597
Ketchum, ID 83340
(208) 726-3036

THE QUILT BARN
P.O. Box 1252
421 S. River and Elm
Hailey, ID 83333
(208) 788-4011

Illinois

**CARROW AND McNERNEY COUN-
 TRY ANTIQUES**
P.O. Box 125
Winnetka, IL 60093
(312) 441-7197 or 446-7516

Courtesy of Phyllis Haders.

Courtesy of The Fosters.

THE FOSTERS
R.R. 2
Pittsfield, IL 62363
(217) 285-4588

Indiana

ALCORN'S ANTIQUES
214 W. Main St.
Centerville, IN 47330
(812) 855-3161

FOLKWAYS
R.R. 2, Box 365
Georgetown, IN 47122
(812) 951-3454

REBECCA HAARER
P.O. Box 52
Shipshewana, IN 46565
(219) 768-4787

Iowa

JENSEN ANTIQUES
2017 E. 13th St.
Davenport, IA 52803
(319) 322-4905

Kansas

**MARK'S INTERNATIONAL ORIENTAL
 RUGS AND CARPETS**
5512 Johnson Dr.
Mission, KS 66202
(913) 722-2242

Kentucky

BRUCE AND CHARLOTTE RIDDLE
116 W. Broadway
Bardstown, KY 40004
(502) 348-2275

SHELLY ZEGART'S QUILTS
12-Z River Hill Rd.
Louisville, KY 40207
(502) 897-7566

Louisiana

THE SALT BOX
2310 Fagot St.
Metairie, LA 70001
(504) 837-0539

Maine

PATRICIA STAUBLE ANTIQUES
P.O. Box 265
Pleasant and Main Sts.
Wiscasset, ME 04578
(207) 882-6341

Maryland

"ALL OF US AMERICANS" FOLK ART
P.O. Box 5943
Bethesda, MD 20814
(301) 652-4626

COUNTRY ANTIQUES
Pry Mill, P.O. Box 35
R.D. 1
Keedysville, MD 21756
(301) 797-3895

STELLA RUBIN ANTIQUES
12300 Glen Rd.
Potomac, MD 20854
(301) 948-4187

Stella Rubin Antiques.

CATHY SMITH ANTIQUE QUILTS
P.O. Box 681
Severna Park, MD 21146
(301) 647-3503

Massachusetts

MOUNTAIN COLORS
41 Elm St.
Marblehead, MA 01945
(617) 631-7599

MOUNT VERNON ANTIQUES
P.O. Box 66
Rockport, MA 01966
(617) 546-2434

Michigan

THE PATCHWORK PARLOUR
109 Petoskey Ave.
Charlevoix, MI 49720
(616) 547-5788

Minnesota

ATTIC WORKSHOP QUILTS
4033 Linden Hills Blvd.
Minneapolis, MN 55410
(612) 920-6268

Missouri

SUSAN DAVIDSON ANTIQUES
102 S. Elm
St. Louis, MO 63119-3018
(314) 454-1020

PATCHWORK SAMPLER
168 Parsons
St. Louis, MO 63119
(314) 997-6116

New Jersey

AMANDA'S ANTIQUES
R.D. 1, Box 243
Pittstown, NJ 08867
(201) 730-9114

KAROLEE'S QUILTS
155 Stephens Park Rd.
Hackettstown, NJ 07840
(201) 852-2847

PENNY'S CORNER
1833 Front St.
Scotch Plains, NJ 07076
(201) 232-9584

TEWKSBURY ANTIQUES
The Crossroads
Oldwick, NJ 08858
(201) 439-2221

Tewksbury Antiques.

New York

AMERICA HURRAH
766 Madison Ave.
New York, NY 10021
(212) 535-1930

AMERICAN COUNTRY ANTIQUES
315 E. 68th St.
New York, NY 10021
(212) 628-3697

AMERICAN FOLK ART GALLERY
180 Rock Creek Ln.
Scarsdale, NY 10583

**ANTIQUE BUYERS INTERNATIONAL,
INC.**
790 Madison Ave.
New York, NY 10021
(212) 861-6700

JUDI BOISSON
Studio 3F
4 E. 82nd St.
New York, NY 10028
(212) 719-5188 or 734-5844
and
28C Job's Ln.
Southampton, NY 11968
(516) 283-5466

BONNER'S BARN
25 Washington St.
Malone, NY 12593
(518) 483-4001

BRIDGEHAMPTON QUILT GALLERY
Main St.
Bridgehampton, NY 11932
(516) 537-0333

C.J. BROWN
P.O. Box 226
Staten Island, NY 10308
(718) 967-4755

ANTHONY CIBELLI
50 Hamden Ave.
Staten Island, NY 10306
(718) 351-6528

A COUNTRY STORE
1262 Madison Ave.
New York, NY 10128
(212) 875-5775

CUSTOM PATCHWORKS
202 Aviation Rd.
Glens Falls, NY 12801
(518) 793-0935

DALVA BROTHERS, INC.
44 E. 57th St.
New York, NY 10022
(212) 758-2297

**LAURA FISHER ANTIQUE QUILTS
AND AMERICANA**
Gallery 57
1050 Second Ave.
New York, NY 10022
(212) 838-2596 or 866-6033

THE GAZEBO OF NEW YORK
660 Madison Ave.
New York, NY 10021
(212) 832-7077

JANOS AND ROSS
110 East End Ave.
New York, NY 10028
(212) 988-0407

KELTER-MALCE
361 Bleecker St.
New York, NY 10014
(212) 989-6760

**SUSAN PARRISH AT SPIRIT OF
AMERICA**
269 W. 4th St.
New York, NY 10014
(212) 645-5020 or 807-1561

PILLOW FINERY
979 Third Ave., 709M
New York, NY 10022
(212) 935-7295

**JUDITH SELKOWITZ FINE ARTS,
INC.**
c/o Levy and Cantor
745 Fifth Ave.
New York, NY 10151-0001
(212) 755-3924

JUDY S. SHORT ANTIQUES
R.R. 1, Dunbar Rd.
Cambridge, NY 12816
(518) 677-5155

SWEET NELLIE
1262 Madison Ave.
New York, NY 10128
(212) 876-5775

VAN VRYLING
Rt. 22
Essex, NY 12936
(518) 963-7210

**THOS. K. WOODARD, AMERICAN
ANTIQUES AND QUILTS**
835 Madison Ave.
New York, NY 10021
(212) 988-2906

North Carolina

BOONE'S ANTIQUES, INC.
Hwy. 301 S.
P.O. Box 3796
Wilson, NC 27893
(919) 237-1508

Ohio

DARWIN BEARLEY
98 Beck Ave.
Akron, OH 44302
(216) 376-4965

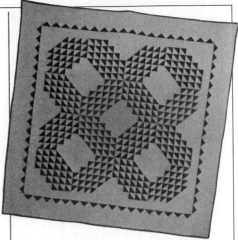

Courtesy of Darwin Bearley.

CALICO, WICKER & THYME, INC.
4205 State Rt. 43
Brimfield, OH 44240
(216) 678-3220

BRUCE AND MARGIE CLAWSON
Blue Creek, OH 45616
(513) 544-3263

MICHAEL COUNCIL
583 S. Fifth St.
Columbus, OH 43208
(614) 221-4119

FEDERATION ANTIQUES, INC.
2030 Madison Rd.
Cincinnati, OH 45208
(513) 321-2671

MIDWEST QUILT EXCHANGE
495 S. 3rd St.
Columbus, OH 43215
(614) 221-8400

SANDRA MITCHELL
739 Mohawk
Columbus, OH 43206
(614) 443-6222

OH SUZANNA
6 S. Broadway
Lebanon, OH 45036
(513) 932-8246

OLDE HOUSE ANTIQUES AND QUILTS
5069 Township Rd. 56
Huntsville, OH 43324
(513) 686-2403

JOAN TOWNSEND
4215 Utica Rd.
Lebanon, OH 45036
(513) 932-3619

Oklahoma

JUNE BLACKBURN
4148 S. Norfolk
Tulsa, OK 74105
(918) 747-7152

BUCKBOARD ANTIQUES AND QUILTS
1411 N. May
Oklahoma City, OK 73107
(405) 943-7020

Oregon

DIANNA'S QUILTING SUPPLIES
1294 32nd Ave. NW
Salem, OR 97304
(503) 364-6355

Pennsylvania

COUNTRY PATCHWORK
1603 Carlisle Rd.
Camp Hill, PA 17011
(717) 761-2586

M. FINKEL AND DAUGHTER
936 Pine St.
Philadelphia, PA 19107
(215) 627-7797

JAMES AND NANCY GLAZER ANTIQUES
2209 Delancey Pl.
Philadelphia, PA 19103
(212) 732-8788

WILLIAM P. HAYES ANTIQUES
R.D. 1, Box 134
Belleville, PA 17004
(717) 935-5125

Great Expectations Quilts

JOE AND MARY KOVAL ANTIQUES
550 Lutz School Rd.
Indiana, PA 15701
(412) 465-7370

PIED PIPER GALLERY
537 E. Girard Ave.
Philadelphia, PA 19125
(215) 423-9669

THE PINK HOUSE
Rt. 179
New Hope, PA 18938
(215) 862-5947

J.D. QUERY ANTIQUES
R.D. 2
Martinsburg, PA 16662
(814) 793-3185

Rhode Island

QUILT ARTISAN
39 Memorial Blvd.
Newport, RI 02840
(401) 846-2127

Tennessee

AMERICAN COUNTRY FURNITURE AND ACCESSORIES
433 Scenic Dr.
Knoxville, TN 37919
(615) 525-6359

Texas

GREAT EXPECTATIONS QUILTS, INC.
14520 Memorial, Suite 54
Houston, TX 77079
(713) 496-1366

LARRY A. MULKEY & ASSOCIATES
World Trade Center 9074
P.O. Box 58547
Dallas, TX 75258
(214) 748-1361

Virginia

QUILTS UNLIMITED
The Homestead Resort
Hot Springs, VA 24445
(703) 839-5955
or
431 Prince George St.
Williamsburg, VA 23185
(804) 253-8700

ROCKY ROAD TO KANSAS
215 S. Union St.
Alexandria, VA 22314
(703) 683-0116

West Virginia

QUILTS UNLIMITED
203 E. Washington St.
Lewisburg, WV 24901
(304) 647-4208

Kentucky

AMERICAN QUILTER'S SOCIETY
P.O. Box 3290
Paducah, KY 42002-3290

PAULINE AND DONNA'S QUILTS
4333 N. Preston Hwy.
Shepherdsville, KY 40165
(502) 955-8673

New Quilts

Newly made quilts of traditional or contemporary design are sometimes handled by the same dealers who offer antique quilts. More often, however, new work is offered by the makers themselves at group shows, by quilt shops, or by direct-mail firms. There is a great demand for new Amish and Mennonite quilts in geometric patterns and for quilts in such commonly worked patterns as Log Cabin, Star of Bethlehem, and Schoolhouse. Some of the sources listed below sell only by mail; others combine a retail operation with a direct-mail service. Almost all the firms are small ones, the proprietor being an experienced quilter who can provide standard or custom-made designs and sizes. Prices will vary according to the complexity and size of the quilt.

Pauline and Donna's Quilts.

Arizona

PINE COUNTRY QUILTS
413 N. San Francisco
Flagstaff, AZ 86001
(602) 779-2194

Arkansas

DELTA COMFORTS
P.O. Box 88
Lexa, AR 72355
(501) 572-5565

PATCHWORK EMPORIUM
224 S. 2nd St.
Rogers, AR 72756
(501) 636-3385

California

APPALACHIA
14440-E Big Basin Way
Saratoga, CA 95070
(408) 741-0999

MARGARET CAVIGGA QUILT COLLECTION
8648 Melrose Ave.
Los Angeles, CA 90069
(213) 659-3020

THE GAZEBO OF NEW YORK
South Coast Plaza
3333 Bristol St.
Costa Mesa, CA 92626
(714) 540-0209

Florida

RAINBOW QUILTS
143 NE 4th Ave.
Delray Beach, FL 33444
(305) 278-8988

Illinois

QUILTING BOOKS UNLIMITED
156 S. Gladstone
Aurora, IL 60506
(312) 896-7331

Louisiana

THE SALT BOX
2310 Fagot St.
Metairie, LA 70001
(504) 837-0539

Massachusetts

LADYBUG QUILTING SHOP
612 Rt. 6A, P.O. Box 628
Dennis, MA 02638
(617) 385-2662

Michigan

AMISH QUILTERS
Box 438
Clarkston, MI 48016

Minnesota

KATHY'S QUILTS
Rt. 1
Isle, MN 56342
(612) 676-3359

Missouri

PATCHES QUILT SHOP
337 S. Main
St. Charles, MO 63301
(314) 946-6004

New York

AMISH CLASSICS
250 Crows Nest Rd.
Tuxedo Park, NY 10987

CUSTOM PATCHWORK
202 Aviation Rd.
Glens Falls, NY 12801
(518) 793-0935

Custom Patchwork.

THE GAZEBO OF NEW YORK
660 Madison Ave.
New York, NY 10021
(212) 832-7077

HANDS ALL AROUND, INC.
971 Lexington Ave., 1B
New York, NY 10021
(212) 744-5070

"Ohio Amish Star",
© 1986 by Cath Heslin; Quilter's Corner.

QUILTER'S CORNER
83 Main St.
Tappan, NY 10983
(914) 359-6866

Ohio

COMFORTS OF HOME
9441 Main St.
Cincinnati, OH 45242
(513) 793-0330

Schoolhouse Quilt Shop.

SCHOOLHOUSE QUILT SHOP
4315 Hills and Dales Rd., NW
Canton, OH 44708
(216) 477-4767

Pennsylvania

HAND MADE QUILTS
P.O. Box 215
Lampeter, PA 17537
(717) 464-4598

OLD COUNTRY STORE
Main St.
Intercourse, PA 17534
(717) 768-7101

PENN DUTCH COTTAGE CRAFTS
2323 Lincoln Hwy. E.
Lancaster, PA 17602
(717) 299-7251

QUILT PATCH
1897 Hanover Pike
Littlestown, PA 17340
(717) 359-5940

QUILT SQUARE
752 Main St.
Meadville, PA 16335
(814) 333-4383

QUILTING BEE
126 S. Market St.
New Wilmington, PA 16142
(412) 946-8566

QUILTS INCREDIBLE
Street Rd. and Rt. 202
P.O. Box 11
Lahaska, PA 18931
(215) 794-3107

Rhode Island

QUILT ARTISAN
39 Memorial Blvd.
Newport, RI 02840
(401) 846-2127

"Rhode Island Star" by Irene King; The Quilt Artisan.

Texas

GREAT EXPECTATIONS QUILTS, INC.
14520 Memorial, Suite 54
Houston, TX 77079
(713) 496-1366

Utah

MISTY ISLES DESIGNS
811 N. University Ave.
Provo, UT 84601
(801) 373-2415 or 225-6815

Virginia

QUILTS UNLIMITED
431 Prince George St.
Williamsburg, VA 23185
(804) 253-8700
or
The Homestead Resort
Hot Springs, VA 24445
(703) 839-5955

Canada

Ontario

MILLER'S BARN
R.R. 1
Mitchell, ONT N0K 1N0
(519) 229-6429
or
MILLER'S GENERAL STORE
221 Erb St. W.
St. Agatha, ONT N0B 2L0
(519) 886-9552

ROCKY ROAD TO KANSAS
215 S. Union St.
Alexandria, VA 22314
(703) 683-0116

West Virginia

QUILTS UNLIMITED
203 E. Washington St.
Lewisburg, WV 24901
(304) 647-4208

Miller's General Store.

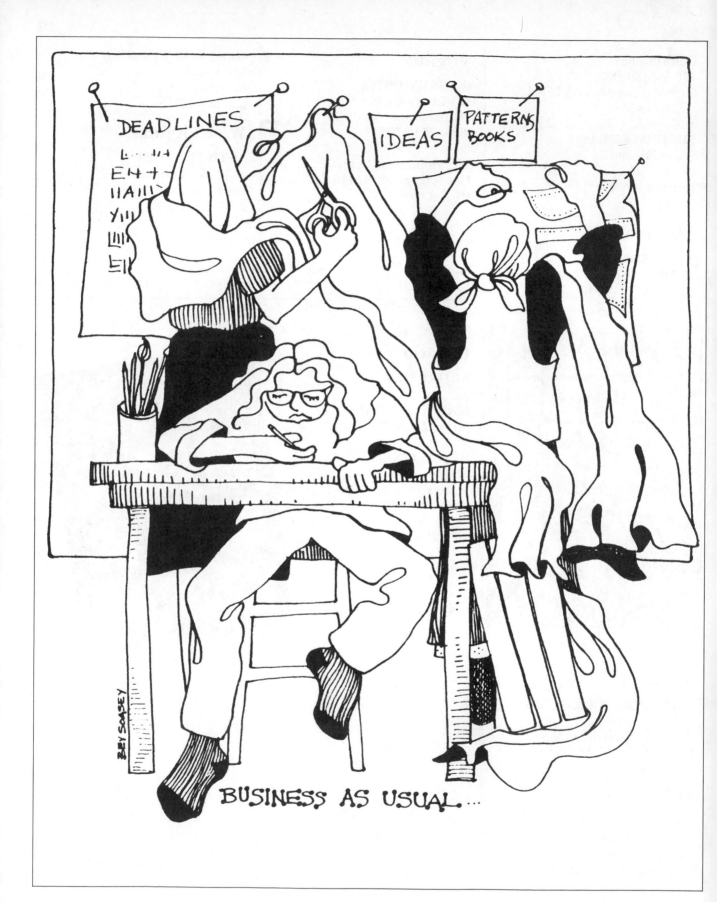

7. Back to School: Quilting Shows, Retreats, Workshops, and Teachers

Quilting is all about skills—the ability to combine forms and colors in proper proportions and in interesting ways, the talent to work a needle through a layer of material in a deft manner, the dexterity to shape the right curve or angle so that it meets its companion piece perfectly. To become an accomplished quilter is, for many, a lifetime profession. If practice does not make perfect, it at least makes the job easier and more pleasurable.

Quilting shows, many of which feature juried competitions, are held from coast to coast in large towns and small. It is at such events that the quilter can compare different approaches to the fabric art. There may even be a financial incentive to enter a show, the largest of which offer impressive prizes. New York City's Great American Quilt Festival of 1986 attracted thousands of visitors and the fortunate finalists in the competition received considerable recognition. Most shows, however, are relatively modest affairs, offering the average quilter—competitor or attendee—less tangible but no less educational rewards.

The quilting retreat, workshop, or conference is a relatively new phenomenon. Usually of two or three days duration, these concentrated educational sessions are sometimes held in vacation spots. Although one may attend several sessions a day, there is always time to relax, to enjoy the companionship of fellow quilters in a non-competitive atmosphere. Extended workshops of this sort usually involve a number of teachers with varied backgrounds and skills.

Individual and group classes ranging from beginning to advanced quilting techniques are offered by most quilt shops, of course, and by teachers throughout North America. Many of these experts will travel a considerable distance to lecture or work with local quilting organizations. A listing of teachers and lecturers is included in the following pages.

"Business as Usual" by Beverly Soasey, courtesy of Amity Publications.

Shows and Competitions

As the popularity of quiltmaking has grown, so, too, have the shows at which quilts are featured. Most of these events are held annually and are often sponsored by a local quilting guild or charitable organization. The majority of shows display only new quilts, with competitions to choose the very best a frequent highlight of the festive event.

January–February

THE TUCSON WOMAN'S CLUB ANNUAL QUILT SHOW is held at the club's headquarters, 6245 E. Bellevue, Tucson. Admission is free. The show includes a viewers' choice competition; ribbons are awarded to the winners. A boutique features quilts for sale. Demonstrations are held throughout the show.

Laurie Sivers
Annual Quilt Show
7776 E. Kenyon
Tucson, AZ 85710
(602) 296-2817

February-March

"OH, THOSE LOVELY QUILTS" ANNUAL QUILT SHOW is held at the Tennessee Wesleyan College Museum, Athens, Tennessee. There is a small admission charge. The show includes a competition that attracts some 200 entries. Ribbons are awarded to the winning quilts. For the competition, quilts are divided into two categories, pre- and post-1930. Quilts displayed in the show are not for sale. Workshops, demonstrations, and lectures are scheduled throughout the two-month exhibition.

Sheryl Richards
"Oh, Those Lovely Quilts"
* Annual Quilt Show*
P.O. Box 889
Athens, TN 37303
(615) 745-0329

Early to Mid-March

GREAT MIDWEST QUILT SHOW AND SALE is held at the Lebanon Expo Center, Lebanon, Ohio. Admission, $3 per person; the proceeds of the show are donated to the Warren County Historical Society. Many quilt dealers attend and over 300 antique and contemporary quilts are for sale.

Joan Townsend
Great Midwest Quilt Show and
* Sale*
6 S. Broadway
Lebanon, OH 45036

Third Weekend of March

DALLAS QUILT CELEBRATION is held at the Grand Place Fair Park, Dallas, Texas. Admission, $4 per day; $6 three-day pass. The show includes numerous demonstrations, a donation quilt, and a merchant mall. A competition is featured, with ribbons awarded to the winners; entry charge is $5 per quilt. The competition attracts approx-

imately 300 quilts of all types and from all periods.

Laura Hobby
Dallas Quilt Celebration
15775 N. Hillcrest, Suite 508
Dallas, TX 75248
(214) 783-4149

Last Week of March

NORTHWEST QUILTERS' QUILT SHOW is held at Portland State University, 1825 SW Broadway, Portland, Oregon. Admission, $2 adults; $1 children, senior citizens. The show does not include a competition, although the best quilts displayed receive rosettes. Quilts displayed are not for sale. A variety of lectures is held each day of the week-long show.

Cheryl Younger
Northwest Quilters' Quilt Show
7565 SW 102nd Ave.
Beaverton, OR 97005
(503) 641-2081

Fourth Weekend of March

ANNUAL PENNSYLVANIA NATIONAL ARTS & CRAFT SHOW is held at the State Farm Show Complex, Harrisburg, Pennsylvania. Admission, $4. The show does not include a competition. Quilts of all types are displayed, and all are on sale to the general public.

Kay Kishbaugh
Annual Pennsylvania National
* Arts & Crafts Show*
P.O. Box 11469
Harrisburg, PA 17108
(717) 763-1254

Early April

MID-KANSAS MCC RELIEF SALE is held at the State Fairgrounds, Hutchinson, Kansas. There is no charge for admission. Over

300 quilted items are for sale each year, all proceeds used to pay for relief work. The sale also includes a number of craft demonstrations.

Rose Haury
Mid-Kansas Relief Sale
P.O. Box 101
N. Newton, KS 67117
(316) 283-1531

First Saturday of April

PENNA RELIEF SALE is held at the Harrisburg Farm Show Building (Main Exhibition Area), Harrisburg, Pennsylvania. There is no admission charge. Over 300 quilts are displayed and offered for sale each year. A quilting demonstration is also featured and patterns are for sale.

Esther Hostetter
PENNA Relief Sale
121 Bomberger Rd.
Akron, PA 17501
(717) 859-2392

First or Second Weekend of April

WEST COAST MENNONITE RELIEF SALE is held at Fresno Pacific College, Fresno, California. Admission is free. At present the sale does not include a quilting competition; generally, the quilts offered are contemporary. All quilts are sold by auction.

Kathleen Heinrichs
West Coast Mennonite Relief
  Sale
42025 Rd. 42
Reedley, CA 93654
(209) 638-6447

Second Thursday of April

GENESSEE VALLEY QUILT CLUB SHOW is held at the Masonic Temple, Rochester, New York. Admission is free. The show, primarily a display of members' quilts, does not include a competition; both antique and contemporary quilts are shown. Only a few quilts at the show are for sale, by special arrangement with their owners. The show also includes demonstrations and a sale table.

Karen LaDuca
Genessee Valley Quilt Club
  Show
8 Thornwood Circle
Pittsford, NY 14534

Second Weekend of April

FESTIVAL OF QUILTS BY MAPLE LEAF QUILTERS is held at the College of St. Joseph, Rutland, Vermont. Admission, $3 per person. The show includes a viewers' choice competition for which there is a $2 entry fee to cover insurance. Over 200 quilts are on display; many are for sale. The show also includes demonstrations, films, and many exhibits by vendors of quilting supplies.

Kathy Schmidt
Festival of Quilts by Maple Leaf
  Quilters
Box 4137, RD 1
Rutland, VT 05701
(802) 775-7228

Fourth Weekend of April

AMERICAN QUILTER'S SOCIETY SHOW AND CONTEST is held at the Executive Inn Riverfront,

Paducah, Kentucky. The admission charge varies from year to year. The show includes a large quilt competition for which a jury selects 400 entries from many times that number of applications. Entry in the competition is free for members; $5 for non-members. Cash prizes totaling $30,000 are awarded to the winners; the competition is entirely composed of contemporary quilts, although some antique quilts are on display. Some of the quilts in the show are for sale. The event also includes a variety of workshops, lectures, and seminars.

American Quilter's Society
American Quilter's Society
  Show and Contest
P.O. Box 3290
Paducah, KY 42001
(502) 898-7903

Late April

VISIONS is held at Grand Tradition, Fallbrook, California; this biennial show takes place on years ending in odd numbers. Admission, $3 per person. The show includes a juried competition with cash prizes totaling over $1,300. An unlimited number of entries are accepted for judging; from these, eighty pieces are accepted for display at the show. Entry fee, $5 per quilt. A balance of traditional and contemporary designs are presented. Many of the quilts on display are for sale. A variety of workshops is offered.

Rose Turner
Visions
P.O. Box 26902
San Diego, CA 92126
(619) 578-5499

Last Weekend of April

KUTZTOWN AREA HISTORICAL SOCIETY QUILT SHOW AND SALE is held in the school building, Kutztown, Pennsylvania. Admission, $2 per person. The show's quilting competition, for which there is no entry fee, attracts approximately 150 entries each year; ribbons are awarded to the winners. Many, but not all, of the quilts on display are for sale.

Barbara Held
Kutztown Area Historical Society Quilt Show and Sale
R.D. 4, Box 329
Kutztown, PA 19530
(215) 683-3210

First Week of May

WORLD OF QUILTS, an annual quilting show, is held at the John F. Kennedy High School, Somers, New York, and is sponsored by the Northern Star Quilters' Guild.

Alice Dokken
World of Quilts
P.O. Box 232
Somers, NY 10589
(914) 232-4279

First Weekend of May

BOYERTOWN AREA HISTORICAL SOCIETY'S ANNUAL QUILT SHOW is held in Boyertown, Pennsylvania. Admission is nominal. Approximately 125 quilts are entered in the show's competi-

tion; entry in the competition is free. Winners are awarded non-monetary gifts. Quilts exhibited in the show are not for sale. The annual event features a variety of lectures.

Jane Blair
Boyertown Area Historical Society's Annual Quilt Show
341 W. Philadelphia Ave.,
Boyertown, PA 19505
(215) 367-9843

Mid-May

QUILTS: AN AMERICAN ROMANCE is held at the Somerset Mall, Troy, Michigan. Admission is free. This very large show does not feature a competition, but many quilts are displayed, most of them dating from before 1940 and many for sale. This outstanding quilting event features a comprehensive workshop program.

Merry Silber
Quilts: An American Romance
724 Lakeside
Birmingham, MI 48009
(313) 642-4371

Third Weekend of May

CROP FRIENDSHIP QUILT AUCTION is held at the Elkhart County Fairgrounds, Goshen, Indiana. Admission is free. The many quilts on display have been donated to CROP (Christian Response to Overseas Poverty) to be sold to raise funds. All are sold by auction.

R. Blake
CROP Friendship Quilt Auction
403 E. Plymouth St.
Bremen, IN 46506
(219) 546-2091

End of May

IOWA MENNONITE RELIEF SALE is held at the Johnson County Fairgrounds, Iowa City, Iowa. Admission is free. All quilts on display are for sale; the show includes a number of quilting demonstrations.

Jean Swartzendruber
Iowa Mennonite Relief Sale
P.O. Box 343
Kalona, IA 52247

Second Weekend of June

ANNUAL GARRISON HOUSE QUILT SHOW is held at 105 Garrison Rd., S. Chelmsford, Massachusetts. Admission, $2 per person. The show includes over 100 quilted items, covering all aspects of the craft. The quilts shown are not for sale.

Blanche Weeks
Annual Garrison House Quilt Show
6 Hillside Ln.
Chelmsford, MA 01824

Mid-June to Mid-July

ANNUAL QUILT COMPETITION AND SALE is held at the Western Heritage Center, Billings, Montana. Admission is free. A $2 entry fee entitles quilters to compete for cash prizes in six different quilting categories. All the quilts in the show are contemporary, and some can be bought from their makers.

Joan Ware
Annual Quilt Competition and
    Sale
2282 Montana Ave.
Billings, MT 59101
(406) 256-6809

End of June

GREAT LAKES QUILT SHOW AND EXHIBIT is held at the Lutheran High School North, Mt. Clemens, Michigan. This biennial show, for which a nominal admission is charged, is held in even-numbered years and is the largest of its kind in Michigan. The show features a competition with substantial cash prizes for the winners. The competition includes only contemporary quilts, although antique quilts are on display. Some of the many quilts shown are for sale. Also featured is a full program of workshops, lectures, and demonstrations.

Marilyn Albrecht
Great Lakes Quilt Show and
    Exhibit
221 Lonesome Oak Dr.
Rochester, MI 48064
(313) 651-7091

July

BRIGHAM CITY MUSEUM-GALLERY ANNUAL QUILT FESTIVAL is held at the Museum-Gallery in Brigham City, Utah. Admission is free. Both contemporary and antique quilts are displayed, although tied and painted quilts are excluded. Only a few of the quilts displayed are for sale. The local quilt guild conducts demonstrations and workshops throughout the time of the festival.

Larry Douglas
Brigham City Museum-Gallery
    Annual Quilt Festival
P.O. Box 583
Brigham City, UT 84302
(801) 723-6769

MIDWEST HERITAGE QUILT SHOW is held at the Vermillion County Museum, Danville, Illinois. Admission, $1 adults; 50¢ children. The show includes a competition for which there is a $1 entry fee; ribbons are awarded to the winner and first runner-up in each of several categories. Some of the quilts on display are for sale.

Ann Bauer
Midwest Heritage Quilt Show
116 N Gilbert St.
Danville, IL 61832
(217) 442-2922

First Week of July

HERITAGE QUILT SHOW AND SALE is held at the Lambton Heritage Museum, Grand Bend, Ontario. Admission, $1.75 per adult. The show includes a competition which is divided into three categories: quilting as a fine art, group sewn, family favorites. Entry fees vary, but all are under $5. Winners and runners-up in each category receive cash prizes. Many of the quilts on display are for sale. The show also features films, demonstrations, and lectures.

Gwen Watson
Heritage Quilt Show and Sale
Lambton Heritage Museum
R.R. 2
Grand Bend, ON N0M 1T0
Canada
(519) 243-2600

Weekend Nearest July 4th

GROVE BUSINESS & PROFESSIONAL WOMENS CLUB ANNUAL QUILT SHOW is held at the Grove Community Center, Grove, Oklahoma. Admission is free. The show includes a competition; winners receive trophies and ribbons. There is no entry fee. A different theme informs the show each year (e.g., the 1987 theme was Garden of Flowers). Many of the quilts displayed are for sale; to cover expenses, the Club receives a commission on each sale.

Clara Mills
Grove Business & Professional
    Womens Club Annual Quilt
    Show
P.O. Box 1551
Grove, OK 74344
(918) 786-3292 before 5 pm
(918) 786-6601 after 5 pm

Mid-July

ASHLAND'S ANNUAL QUILT SHOW is held at the First United Methodist Church, Ashland, Oregon. Admission, $1.25 per person. The quilts displayed are of all styles and periods; some can be purchased after the show.

Jean Strand
Ashland's Annual Quilt Show
1070 Terra Ave.
Ashland, OR 97520
(503) 482-3503

Third Sunday of July

ANNUAL QUILT SHOW, sponsored by the Delaware Piecemakers Quilt Guild, is held at the Delaware County District Library, Delaware, Ohio. A nominal admission fee is charged. Featured is a people's choice competition, with ribbons for the winners, and both antique and contemporary quilts included. Members of the Guild give quilting demonstrations throughout the show.

Rose Fitzgerald
Annual Quilt Show
644 Congress Ct.
Delaware, OH 43015
(614) 363-3677

Fourth Weekend of July

ANNUAL HERITAGE QUILT AUCTION is held at the Lion's Club Hall, Arnprior, Ontario. Admission is free. The show includes a competition; cash prizes are awarded to the best three quilts. There is no set charge for entering a quilt, but the Lionette Club retains twenty-five percent of the sale price of each quilt as a commission. Virtually all of the quilts are contemporary; many are variations on traditional designs. All quilts in the show are sold by auction.

Helen Hall
Annual Heritage Quilt Auction
P.O. Box 181
Arnprior, ON K7S 3H4
Canada

MAINE QUILTS is held at a different location in the Saco area each year. Admission, $2 per person. Maine's largest quilt show features exhibits and a comprehensive lecture and workshop program. Many of the quilts displayed are for sale.

Jane Eubanks
Maine Quilts
P.O. Box 395
Monmouth, ME 04259
(207) 933-4057

Last Week of July

AMISH QUILTS ACROSS AMERICA SHOW/SALE is held at the Chautauqua Institute, Mayville, New York. While the show itself is free, there is a small charge for admission to the Institute. All the quilts in the show have been made recently, but all employ old Amish colors and patterns. Some combine Amish and contemporary designs, producing an unusual and attractive effect. Most of the items on display are for sale. Featured in the show are Amish quilters demonstrating traditional techniques.

Millicent Agnor
Amish Quilts Across America
* Show/Sale*
1443 Arthur Ave.
Cleveland, OH 44107
(216) 226-1300

End of July-Early August

FESTIVAL OF THE AMERICAN WEST QUILT SHOW is held in the Hyper Building, Utah State University, Logan, Utah. A nominal admission fee is charged. The show includes a competition for which there is no charge to enter. Cash prizes are awarded to the winners. Although each show features a theme, quilts entered in the competition do not have to conform to that theme. Only a few of the quilts displayed are for sale. The festival's chosen theme is echoed in special lectures and workshops.

Louise Young
Festival of the American West
* Quilt Show*
UMC 2910, 314C
Logan, UT 84322
(801) 750-1566

First-Second Weekend of August

OUR HERITAGE IN QUILTS is held at the Folsom Society Museum, Folsom, California. Admission is free. All the quilts in the show were made prior to 1935; none are for sale. The event is run in conjunction with the festivities of Sacramento County's History Week.

Lenore Dean
Our Heritage In Quilts
411 Mormon St.
Folsom, CA 95630
(916) 985-2160

Second Week of August

EDMONDS QUILT SHOW AND SALE is held at Puget Sound Christian College, Edmonds, Washington. Admission, $2 adults; $1 senior citizens, children. The show features a competition, with ribbons and certificates for the winners. Some of the quilts displayed are for sale. Several workshops are given at the show.

Eileen Westfall
Edmonds Quilt Show and Sale
736 Dayton St.
Edmonds, WA 98020
(206) 775-5481

Second Week of August-Labor Day

QUILT SHOW, an annual event, is held at the Sesson Museum, Mount Shasta, California. Admission is free. Quilts of all styles are represented at the show. Those displayed are not for sale, but each year a quilt is raffled at the show by the local guild. A quilting workshop is also featured.

Lee Apperson
Quilt Show
1705 Holiday Ln.
Mount Shasta, CA 96067
(916) 926-4738

Second Weekend of August

COUNTERPANE CRAFTS QUILT SHOW is held at a number of different buildings, several of which are part of the Cedar Falls Historical Society, Cedar Falls, Iowa. There is a small entry charge. Lectures and workshops are given throughout the show; quilts on display are not for sale.

Rosemary Beach
Counterpane Crafts Quilt Show
303 Franklin St.
Cedar Falls, IA 50613
(319) 277-8817

Third Week of August

ANNUAL QUILT SHOW is held at the Raleigh County Armory/Civic Center, Beckley, West Virginia. There is an admission charge for entry to the Appalachian Arts & Crafts Festival of which the quilt show is a part. The show features a competition; entry fee is $1.50 per quilt. All the quilts are contemporary and ribbons and monetary prizes are awarded in ten different quilting categories. A portion of the quilts are for sale, but the majority are not. The Raleigh County Extension Homemakers, who sponsor the Quilt Show, also present an educational program on the opening day, featuring lectures and workshops.

Gail McCray
Annual Quilt Show
207 Elkins St.
Beckley, WV 25801
(304) 252-4863

Late August

QUILT SHOW AND SALE is held at the Sweeney Convention Center, Santa Fe, New Mexico. Admission, $2 per person. The 250 to 300 quilts on display are all for sale by the show's organizers, Buckboard Antiques and Quilts. Free brochures on quilt care and collecting quilts are available at the show.

Judy Howard
Quilt Show and Sale
1141 N. May
Oklahoma City, OK 73107
(405) 943-7020

September

MARIN NEEDLEWORK AND QUILT SHOW is held in San Rafael, California. Admission, $3.50 adults; $2 senior citizens, children. Featured is a needlework and quilt competition; entry, $8 for the first item; $5 for each additional item. Cash prizes are awarded to the best two entries in each of the twenty-three categories. Some of the quilts on display are for sale. Programs vary from year to year, although workshops, lectures, and a fashion show are always included.

Ann Kingsbury
Marin Needlework and Quilt Show
P.O. Box 2684
San Rafael, CA 94912-2684
(415) 388-9463

Early September

A HARVEST OF QUILTS: 200 YEARS OF AMERICAN QUILTING is held at the Armory Museum, Winona, Minnesota. Admission is nominal. Each year a different theme is chosen for the show. Some of the quilts displayed are for sale. Workshops, lectures, and films are scheduled throughout the show.

Mark Peterson
A Harvest of Quilts
160 Johnson St.
Winona, MN 55987
(507) 454-2723

First or Second Weekend of September

CLINTON COUNTY QUILT ASSOCIATION QUILT SHOW is held at the Clinton County Fairgrounds, Wilmington, Ohio, in conjunction with the County Corn Festival. Admission is charged for the festival; there is no additional fee to see the quilts. A quilt competition is featured, with ribbons awarded to the winners in each of the nine categories. There is no fee to enter a quilt in the competition. A few of the quilts displayed are for sale. The Association gives half-hourly demonstrations, making a full quilt during the time of the festival. It also raffles a quilt made by its members.

Anne Lynch
Clinton County Quilt Association Quilt Show
3235 Stone Rd.
Sabina, OH 45169

Second Weekend of September

ANNUAL QUILT SHOW AND SALE, sponsored by the Heritage Quilters Guild, is held at the Wolfe Community Building, Shipshewana, Indiana. The show is a three-day event. Admission, $1.50 adults; $1 senior citizens, children. Each show features a raffle and a people's choice competition.

Ruby Hostetler
R.R. 2, Box 84
Shipshewana, IN 46565
(219) 768-4244

MUSKINGUM COUNTY EXTENSION HOMEMAKERS QUILT SHOW AND SALE is held at the Salvation Army Citadel Building, Zanesville, Ohio. Admission, $1 adults, helps to endow a scholarship at Ohio State University. Some of the quilts displayed are for sale. Classes and workshops are offered on both days of the show as is the free use of a pattern tracing table to allow visitors to swap patterns.

Martha Briggs
M.C.E.H. Quilt Show and Sale
Court House, Fourth St.
Zanesville, OH 43701

SPRING VALLEY QUILT GUILD SHOW is held at the Historical Museum, Pendleton, Indiana. Admission, $2 per person. Most of the quilts in the show are of local origin and include all styles and periods. The quilts displayed are not for sale.

Elanor Hickman
Spring Valley Quilt Guild Show
747 Greenhill Way
Anderson, IN 46011

Third Weekend of September

WINGS 'N WATER FESTIVAL QUILT SHOW is held at St. Mary's Church, Stone Harbour, New Jersey. Admission, $4 per person. Although all styles of quilts are displayed, most are contemporary. The Wetlands Quilters make a quilt each year to raffle at the show for the benefit of the Wetlands Institute, which sponsors the show.

Olive Prout
Wings 'n Water Festival Quilt
  Show
Stone Harbour Blvd.
Stone Harbour, NJ 08247
(609) 465-5356

Last Weekend of September

BOSTON VALLEY CONSERVATION FALL QUILT SHOW AND SALE is held at the Boston Valley Conservation Club, Boston, New York. Admission, $1 per person. Ribbons are awarded to the viewers' choices in both antique and contemporary categories. Activities at the show include demonstrations, door prizes, a quilts-for-sale section, and a quilt raffle.

Isabelle Schmitt
Boston Valley Conservation Fall
  Quilt Show and Sale
5623 S. Fedick Rd.
Boston, NY 14025

HOUSE OF QUILTING QUILT SHOW is held at the Community Building, Lapaz, Indiana. Admission, $2 per person. A wide variety of quilts and quilted wall hangings are displayed, some of which are for sale. Quilting demonstrations are given throughout the show.

Ruby Salyer
R.R. 1, Box 245 Teegarden
Walkerton, IN 46574
(219) 784-2289

October

AMERICAN HERITAGE QUILT EXHIBIT is held at the First United Methodist Church, Ann Arbor, Michigan. Admission, $1 per person. Displayed are from 80 to 100 contemporary and antique pieces. The exhibition also includes a quilting demonstration and a quilters' question-and-answer session. The quilts on display are not for sale.

Lil Dehart
American Heritage Quilt
  Exhibit
2250 Ellsworth Rd.
Ann Arbor, MI 48104
(313) 971-4899

AUTUMN INSPIRATIONS is held at the Shaker Heritage Society Building, Loudonville, New York. The show is sponsored by Quilters United In Learning Together, Schenectady (Q.U.I.L.T.S.).

Dee Albert
Autumn Inspirations
27 Cresthaven Ave.
Albany, NY 12205
(518) 456-7603

QUILTS OF SOUTHERN INDIANA is held at the Floyd County Museum, New Albany, Indiana. Admission, $1 adults; 50¢ children. The show features a competition for which 100 entries are accepted. A $1 enrollment charge is used to pay the cash first prizes and for ribbons and rosettes for runners-up in each of nine quilting categories. All quilts in the show are less than ten years old; some can be purchased from their makers.

Helen Brown
Quilts of Southern Indiana
Floyd County Museum
201 E. Spring St.
New Albany, IN 47150
(812) 944-7336

Second Week of October

ROCKHILL COMMUNITY QUILT AUCTION is held at Rockhill Community, Sellersville, Pennsylvania. Admission is free. Fifty to eighty quilts are auctioned, with the proceeds benefiting the Community. The event lasts for two days and includes such events as craft demonstrations, a bake sale, and a dinner.

Rockhill Community
Rts. 152 and 309
Sellersville, PA 18960
(215) 257-2751

Third Week of October

BOONE COUNTY EXTENSION HOMEMAKERS QUILT SHOW AND SALE is held at the Ozark Mall, Harrison, Arkansas. Admission is free. The show features a competition for which 175 to 200 entries are accepted. There is no charge for entering the competition; cash prizes are awarded to the winners. On display are both antique and contemporary quilts, many of which are for sale. Among the other events are a number of quilting demonstrations.

Katie Kirk
Boone County Extension
*   Homemakers Quilt Show*
*   and Sale*
P.O. Box 848
Harrison, AR 72601
(501) 741-6168

Third Saturday of October

COLORADO MENNONITE QUILT AUCTION is held at the Fairgrounds in Rocky Ford, Colorado. Admission is free. The fifty-plus quilts and comforters that are auctioned are mostly contemporary. The event also features booths selling traditional Mennonite foods and home-crafted items.

Juanita Simonich
Colorado Mennonite Quilt
*   Auction*
4730 W. Temple Pl.
Denver, CO 80236
(303) 798-3518

Third Weekend of October

BERKSHIRE QUILT FESTIVAL is held at the Berkshire Community College, Pittsfield, Massachusetts. Admission, $4 per person. Featured is a competition for which a small entry fee is charged to cover the cost of insurance. Cash prizes are given to the three best quilts; honorable mention ribbons are awarded to the three runners-up. In addition, lectures are given each afternoon by well-known quilting teachers.

Martha Kulpinski
Berkshire Quilt Festival
P.O. Box D-13
Pittsfield, MA 01201

DEPOT MUSEUM QUILT SHOW is held at the Depot Museum, Henderson, Texas. Admission is free. The show includes a viewer-judged competition with ribbons awarded to the best quilts in several categories. There is no charge to enter the competition. Many of the quilts on display are for sale.

Susan Weaver
Depot Museum Quilt Show
514 N. High St.
Henderson, TX 75652
(214) 657-4303

Tuesday of the Fourth Week of October

ANNUAL WYANDOTTE COUNTY QUILT SHOW is held at the Wyandotte County Museum, Bonner

Springs, Kansas. Admission is free. There is no charge for displaying quilts, and up to three quilts are accepted per person. Quilts must be hand quilted, but may be antique or contemporary. None of the pieces on display are for sale.

Curator of Collections
Wyandotte County Museum
631 N. 126th St.
Bonner Springs, KS 66012
(913) 721-1078

Last Week of October

AMISH QUILTERS ACROSS AMERICA SHOW/SALE is held at the Pavillion Mall, Beachwood, Ohio. Admission is free. The show includes only new quilted pieces using traditional Amish colors and patterns. Featured are from fifty to eighty full-size quilts and hundreds of wall hangings, purses, aprons, and other quilted items. Most of the pieces in the show are for sale. Demonstrations are given by Amish quilters throughout the week.

Millicent Agnor
Amish Quilters Across America
*   Show/Sale*
1443 Arthur Ave.
Cleveland, OH 44107
(216) 226-1300

Last Week of October —First Week of November

NORTH CENTRAL FLORIDA ANNUAL QUILT SHOW is held at the Cox Furniture Store, Gainesville, Florida. Admission, $1 per person. About 300 entries covering all aspects of quilting are accepted; some of the quilts displayed are for sale.

Stephanie Metts
North Central Florida Annual
 Quilt Show
3846 NW 39th Ave.
Gainesville, FL 32606
(904) 375-1369

Last Weekend of October—First Weekend of November

INTERNATIONAL QUILT FESTIVAL is held in Houston, Texas. Admission, $5 per person. The show includes the judged show of the American/International Quilt Association. Over 200 entries are accepted, covering all aspects of quilting, past and present, around the world. About 2,500 quilts are for sale at the show, which includes the largest selection of seminars and lectures at any American quilt show.

Katie Bresenhan
International Quilt Festival
P.O. Box 79164
Houston, TX 77279

Early November

LDS HOSPITAL HOLIDAY QUILT SHOW AND AUCTION is held at the Little America Hotel, Salt Lake City, Utah. Admission, $2.50 per person. All styles of quilt are displayed at the show; they are sold on the final evening with the proceeds donated for medical research and education at LDS Hospital.

Melissa Phillips
LDS Hospital Holiday Quilt
 Show and Auction
8th Ave. and C St.
Salt Lake City, UT 84143
(801) 321-1775

Mid-November

ANNUAL HOLIDAY QUILT SHOW is held in New York City. All the quilts displayed are of American origin, antique, and for sale. Visitors to the show can bring along their own quilts to be appraised or sold.

Shelly Zegart
12-Z River Hill Rd.
Louisville, KY 40207
(502) 897-7566

End of November

THE ANNUAL HARVEST QUILT COMPETITION is held in Miami, Florida. Cash awards or gift certificates are awarded to the winners and runners-up in each of eight quilting categories.

Annual Harvest Quilt
 Competition
P.O. Box 55-0822
Miami, FL 33255

LANCASTER MENNONITE HIGH SCHOOL BENEFIT AUCTION is held at the high school in Lancaster, Pennsylvania. Admission is free. Displayed is a wide range of quilts, all of which are sold at auction.

School Office
Lancaster Mennonite High
 School Benefit Auction
2176 Lincoln Hwy. E.
Lancaster, PA 17602
(717) 299-0436

November-December

QUILTS-ART-QUILTS ANNUAL JURIED QUILT SHOW is held at the Schweinfurth Art Center, Auburn, New York. Admission is free. Featured is a competition in which the winners receive cash, merchandise, and gift certificates as well as ribbons. The 120 quilts and quilted wall hangings displayed maintain a balance between the traditional and non-traditional elements of quiltmaking. Some of the quilts in the show are for sale by their makers. A program of workshops, demonstrations, lectures, and slide shows that runs throughout the show provides first-rate educational entertainment that will appeal to quilters of all interests and abilities.

Kristin Hauge
Quilts-Art-Quilts Annual Juried
 Quilt Show
P.O. Box 916
Auburn, NY 13021
(315) 255-1553

Additional Biennial Shows

LOVE APPLE QUILT SHOW, sponsored by the Love Apple Quilt Guild, is held in the vicinity of Philadelphia, Pennsylvania, every second year. All entries are submitted by members of the Guild, who display their expertise with various techniques of quilting, both traditional and contemporary. None of the quilts displayed are for sale, although some owners may wish to sell privately. There is a small admission charge which covers costs; the Guild's boutique table sells donated objects. Lectures by well-known quilting personalities and various workshops are also featured.

Anne Donofry
Love Apple Quilt Show
1351 71st Ave.
Philadelphia, PA 19126
(215) 927-0475

MONTSHIRE QUILT SHOW is held in even-numbered years at a different location in northern New England for four to five weeks during the summer. The show, sponsored by the Montshire Museum of Science, which chooses the quilts to be displayed, is based on the theme "nature-inspired small quilts by New Hampshire, Vermont, and Maine quilters." Various lectures and workshops are generally scheduled during the run of the show; a small admission fee is charged to cover costs, and at the close of the exhibit, the winning quilter receives a cash prize. Many of the quilts on display are for sale by their makers.

Joan Waltermire
Montshire Quilt Show
Montshire Museum of Science
45 Lyme Rd.
Hanover, NH 03755

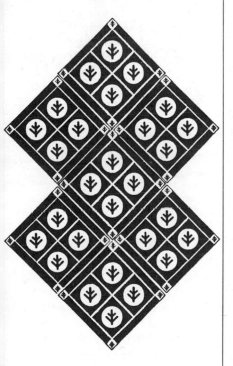

Retreats and Conferences

For any serious quilter who can spare the time, a quilting retreat or workshop will prove a rewarding experience. Whether termed a conference, workshop, retreat, or seminar, such an extended event affords true hands-on instruction in special areas of skill. Most of these events are held during the summer months in very pleasant settings.

End of January

THE JINNY BEYER HILTON HEAD ISLAND QUILTING SEMINAR is held annually at Mariner's Inn, Hilton Head Island, South Carolina. A known and respected author of quilting books, Jinny Beyer has taught at the Smithsonian Institution in Washington, D.C. Both expert and novice quilters will find the variety of topics offered by Ms. Beyer and her guest lecturers challenging and inspiring. The four-day event is packed with classes and lectures, yet time is allowed for recreational activities.

Jinny Beyer
The Jinny Beyer Hilton Head
  Island Quilting Seminar
600 Insbruck Ave.
Great Falls, VA 22066

Second Weekend of March

"SPRING FLING" ATLANTA QUILT FEST is held at the Lanier Plaza Hotel and Conference Center, Atlanta, Georgia. Two-and-a-half days of workshops and lectures are scheduled, with classes attended by some of America's best-known quilters, who are drawn to the wide selection of topics offered. An added fillip is a quilt show; judges award cash prizes to the best quilts entered.

Rita Barber
"Spring Fling" Atlanta Quilt
  Fest
R. 3, Box 119
Carlinville, IL 62626
(217) 854-9323

Late March

ANNUAL QUILTING WORKSHOP AND COLLOQUIUM is organized by the Empty Spools quilt shop, Alamo, California. This five-day colloquium offers workshops led by some of America's finest quilting teachers. Experts who have chaired past sessions include Jean Ray Laury, Edward Larsen, Michael James, Yvonne Porcella, and Judi Warren. An impressively wide range of workshop topics is offered each day; lectures are given after dinner each evening.

Suzanne Cox, Empty Spools
Annual Quilting Workshop and
  Colloquium
Dept. S, 140-B Alamo Plaza
Alamo, CA 94507
(405) 838-2737

Early April

QUILTER'S HERITAGE CELEBRATION is held at the Americana Host

Farm Resort, Lancaster, Pennsylvania. A large variety of workshops is offered during this four-day event.

Rita Barber
Barber Diversified
R. 3, Box 119
Carlinville, IL 62626
(217) 854-9323

Late April

SEA TURTLE RETREAT is held twice a year, in late April and early October, in the relaxed environment of two large private homes in Edisto Beach, South Carolina (not far from historic Charleston). Retreat organizer Kaye Evans builds the event around a different theme each year—scrap quilting is one current subject. During the three-day event, participants receive approximately ten hours of classroom instruction, as well as personal attention and helpful advice. Quilters of all levels of skill are welcome.

Kaye Evans
Sea Turtle Retreat
P.O. Box 675
St. George, SC 29477
(803) 563-4832

May

QUILTERS' RETREAT is a biannual event, held in a pleasant lake setting near Minneapolis, with sessions in May and September. The three-day retreat, run by well-known teachers Pat Cox and Helen Kelley, is crammed with lectures and workshops. Meals and accommodations are supplied.

Patricia Cox
One of a Kind Quilting Designs
6601 Normandale Rd.
Minneapolis, MN 55435
(612) 922-8083

End of May

CARLINVILLE QUILT CONFERENCE is held on the campus of Blackburn College, Carlinville, Illinois. While the highlight of this event is the large assortment of workshops offered, a juried exhibit and a large merchant mall are among the other features. Over forty separate workshops are available to choose from; fees vary from class to class. Blackburn College provides dormitory housing and food services for quilters who attend.

Rita Barber
Barber Diversified
R. 3, Box 119
Carlinville, IL 62626
(217) 854-9323

July

WEST COAST QUILTERS' CONFERENCE is held annually; the location changes from year to year. Attracting some of America's best known teachers and lecturers, among them Roberta Horton, Michael James, Jean Ray Laury, Marsha McCloskey, and Michael Kile, the four-day conference includes workshops, seminars, and lectures covering topics as diverse as quilting geometric surfaces and designing work spaces for quiltmaking. Both one- and two-day workshops are offered; participants will want to make time to visit the adjacent quilt show and to peruse the exhibitors' booths, with their displays of new tools and accessories.

Herb Stude
West Coast Quilters' Conference
P.O. Box 13677
Portland, OR 97213
(503) 281-0800

July-August

AUGUSTA HERITAGE ARTS WORKSHOP offers a number of comprehensive quilting and general needlework courses as part of a wide-ranging summer program of folk-art classes held on the campus of Davis and Elkins College. Classes vary in length (one to two weeks), in subject, and in skill level recommended for enrollment. Among the recent offerings have been advanced quilt design, taught by fabric artist Nancy

Crow, and basic quilting, taught by Barbara Caron. A complete list of necessary supplies is sent to registrants, who are required to bring all materials and notions with them, including their sewing machines (a basic mastery of the machine is a requisite). Dormitory housing is available at the college residence halls, and registrants are invited to participate in extracurricular activities such as concerts, films, and lectures.

*Doug Hill
Augusta Heritage Arts
 Workshop
Davis and Elkins College
Elkins, WV 26241
(304) 636-1903*

Late July-Early August

QUILTING-BY-THE-LAKE WORKSHOPS are held at the Cazenovia College Conference Center, Cazenovia, New York, during the last week of July and the first week of August. Various workshops are offered, ranging in duration from one to four days, and in subject area from machine appliqué to foundation in color, dyeing, pattern drafting, and Islamic design. Special events such as lectures, fashion shows, and merchants' exhibits augment the workshop sessions. Two well-known quilters are invited to act as artists-in-residence; other experts chair the workshop sessions (Virginia Avery, Yvonne Porcella, Judi Warren, and Hellen Kelley are among recent participants). Meals and accommodations are available at the College.

*Mary Lou Schwinn
Quilting-By-The-Lake
P.O. Box 282
Cazenovia, NY 13055
(315) 655-9009*

September

QUILTERS' RETREAT has its second session of the year; for more information see the May listing.

Mid-September

Gwen Marston and Joe Cunningham with "Birds in Flight", 1984.

BEAVER ISLAND QUILT RETREAT is held at the Central Michigan University Conference Center, located on a bucolic Michigan island. Hosted by quilters Gwen Marston and Joe Cunningham, who live and work nearby, the retreat is a small, intimate annual gathering (limited to thirty-five participants) which boasts special touches such as gourmet meals prepared by food consultant and author Fran Gordenker and lodging which includes antique quilts on every bed. The four days of workshops are run by Marston and Cunningham and by collector Merry Silber; past topics have included Design and Construction, The Antique Quilt: An Overview, Crib and Doll Quilts, Quilting Designs, and Quilting your Quilt.

*Gwen Marston and Joe
 Cunningham
Beaver Island Quilt Retreat
155 Beaver Island
St. James, MI 49782
(616) 448-2565*

Late September-Early October

ROAD TO CALIFORNIA QUILTERS CONFERENCE, held annually at the Grand Hotel in Anaheim, California, features three jam-packed days of workshops and programs run by nationally known teachers such as Nancy Crow, Judi Warren, Elly Senkiewicz, Moneca Calvert, and Marsha McCloskey. Participants may choose among different classes, opting to take one in-depth course for the three full days, three day-long courses, or a two-day and a one-day class. Luncheon and dinner programs features lectures and slide presentations; a quilt show and a fashion show are extra attractions.

Brenda Webelow
Road to California Quilters
*   Conference*
1435 Birchmont Dr.
Anaheim, CA 92801
(714) 991-5635

Late October

SEA TURTLE RETREAT has its second session of the year; for more information see the April listing.

Teachers and Lecturers

Quilters are known for their enthusiasm and willingness to share their expertise with others. Some of the very best quilters today are among the most active teachers of other needlecrafters. Many of these professionals regularly teach special workshops throughout the country. Others lecture on traditional quilts and are experts on antique examples.

VIRGINIA AVERY conducts workshops and lectures and is a well-known show judge. She has taught extensively overseas, including such diverse places as Australia, France, New Zealand, and Switzerland. Brochure available on request.

Virginia Avery
Great Sew-ciety
731 King St.
Port Chester, NY 10573
(914) 939-3605

SONYA LEE BARRINGTON holds workshops and lectures across North America. Topics include curved seams, how to use dark fabrics, and themes in tradi-

tional quilts. Brochure available at no charge.

Sonya Lee Barrington
837 47th Ave.
San Francisco, CA 94121
(415) 221-6510

BARBARA BRACKMAN is a teacher, lecturer, and consultant. She teaches classes in antique quilt dating and identification and also in quilt design.

Barbara Brackman
500 Louisiana
Lawrence, KS 66044
(913) 842-8242

KAREN BRAY teaches machine appliqué at stores and at group meetings in the San Francisco Bay Area.

Karen Bray
21 Birch Dr.
Walnut Creek, CA 94596
(415) 934-2414

PAULIE CARLSON is a teacher of both traditional and contemporary quilting techniques, using both hand and machine piecing methods. She teaches for the National Quilting Association and for the Gulf States Quilting Association and travels frequently, giving speeches and workshops for quilt guilds and private groups. Details are available on request.

Paulie Carlson
6353 Briar Rose Dr.
Houston, TX 77057
(713) 783-7718

MARY CROSS is a central figure for quilting activities in the Northwest; she is a lecturer, historian, judge, consultant, and curator and has been associated with the Columbia-Wilamette Quilt Study Group and the American Quilt Study Group. She has also served as the curator of several exhibitions at the Oregon School of Arts and Crafts. Resumé available on request.

"Cross and Crown" by Mary Cross.

Mary Cross
805 NW Skyline Cres.
Portland, OR 97229
(503) 292-6350

CHRIS WOLF EDMONDS teaches at symposiums, conferences and meetings throughout the country by invitation. A list of workshops and lectures is available free of charge on request.

Chris Wolf Edmonds
Pine Hill Farm
Rt. 2
Lawrence, KS 66046
(913) 542-2517

BETTY FERGUSON is nationally

known as the leading contemporary experimenter with the cyanotype process of printing designs on textiles. Her quilts are distinctive and unusual because of this process; she offers lectures, workshops, and demonstrations on many quilting subjects, but cyanotypes are her chief topic. Write for brochure.

Betty Ferguson
1013 Marshall
Richland, WA 99352
(509) 946-0370

MARIANNE FONS offers classes

and lectures to groups nationwide; many are given in conjunction with her partner, Liz Porter. Free brochure available.

Marianne Fons
Fons-Porter Designs
RR. 3, Box 95
Winterset, IA 50273
(515) 462-2608

SANDY FOX is well known to quilters for her 19th-century-style quilts. She lectures frequently at museums and universities throughout the country and often gives workshops for quilt guilds and clubs.

Sandy Fox
100 W. Kensington Rd.
Los Angeles, CA 90026
(213) 250-4032

FLAVIN GLOVER is a lecturer and workshop instructor in such areas as creative patchwork, Log Cabin variations, and patchwork-quilted clothing. She also presents a variety of slide presentations.

Flavin Glover
861 Ogletree Rd.
Auburn, AL 36830
(205) 821-7091

ROBERTA HORTON taught the first state-accredited quilting course in San Francisco in 1972; since then she has gone on to teach extensively both in the United States and overseas. She offers a wide variety of workshops and lectures. A brochure is available on request.

Roberta Horton
1929 El Dorado Ave.
Berkeley, CA 94707
(415) 526-5086

MICHAEL JAMES is a well-known contemporary quilter whose work is frequently displayed in museums across the country. His use of shapes and colors results in quilts of great beauty. He lectures and gives workshops for quilt festivals, shows, and meetings across the country.

Michael James
Studio Quilts
258 Old Colony Ave.
Somerset Village, MA 02726
(617) 672-1370

MARGOT STRAND JENSEN offers a wide variety of slide lectures, seminars, and lectures. A brochure giving details is available at no charge.

Margot Strand Jensen
18365 E. Mansfield Ave.
Aurora, CO 80013
(303) 693-9642

JEAN JOHNSON is a very experienced workshop teacher and lecturer specializing in strip-pieced pictures, curved seam piecing, and creative design. She teaches for guilds, conferences, and shops on request. Readers can write for a brochure at no cost.

"Four Seasons" by Jean Johnson, 1983.

Jean Johnson
12 Park Rd.
Maplewood, NJ 07040
(201) 762-4523

HELEN KELLEY conducts classes in her Minneapolis studio and also teaches and lectures throughout the United States. Her workshops and lectures can be tailored to individual groups' needs. Send a self-addressed,

stamped envelope for information.

Helen Kelley
2215 Stinson Blvd.
Minneapolis, MN 55418
(612) 789-8207

MICHAEL KILE is perhaps best known as the publisher and co-founder of the Quilt Digest Press; as such he is a well-qualified commentator on current quilting trends. In addition, his schooling in the fine arts has given him the technical knowledge necessary to become a respected antique quilt expert. A brochure describing his lectures is available.

Michael Kile
The Quilt Digest Press
955 14th St.
San Francisco, CA 94114
(415) 431-1222

EDWARD LARSEN is primarily a picture-quilt maker; his work is well-known nationally. He gives lectures and conducts workshops across the country. Write for details.

Edward Larsen
208 Broadway
Libertyville, IL 60048
(312) 362-4614

JEAN RAY LAURY leads workshops throughout North America and

at her home studio. She is very accomplished as an author of quilting books. Information about lectures and workshops is available on request.

Jean Ray Laury
194 Tollhouse Rd.
Clovis, CA 93612
(209) 297-0228

PAULA LEDERKRAMER offers lectures and workshops; further in-

"Technicolor Dream Quilt" by Paula Lederkramer.

formation is available on request. Her best-known workshop, "Undulations," is devoted to quilts composed entirely of straight lines that, through optical illusion, appear to be curved.

Paula Lederkramer
25 Swing Ln.
Levittown, NY 11756
(516) 735-7878

LINDA OTTO LIPSETT is a quilt collector, author, and lecturer with a special interest in the lives of the women whose signatures appear on the friendship quilts in her collection. Information on her lectures and seminars can be obtained on request.

Linda Otto Lipsett
The Quilt Digest Press
955 14th St.
San Francisco, CA 94114
(818) 984-0311

DIANN LOGAN is a free-lance designer who teaches and lectures frequently. Her teaching portfolio is available on request.

Diann Logan
435 S. Pennsylvania
Denver, CO 80209
(303) 777-5102

MARY MASHUTA is originally from the world of interior design; she offers a selection of quilting lectures and workshops that includes such diverse topics as wearable art and story quilts.

Mary Mashuta
1929 El Dorado
Berkeley, CA 94707
(415) 526-5086

JUDY MATHIESON offers a wide assortment of topics for lec-

tures, slide shows, and workshops; she holds regular classes at Los Angeles fabric shops but also travels nationally. Free brochure available.

Judy Mathieson
5802 Jumilla Ave.
Woodland Hills, CA 91367
(818) 347-3247

MARSHA McCLOSKEY has been involved with quilting for nearly twenty years. She teaches at quilting shops and for groups around the country and specializes in feathered star designs. Write for information.

Marsha McCloskey
2151 7th Ave. W.
Seattle, WA 98119
(206) 285-7342

PENNY McMORRIS is best known in the quilting world as the producer and host of the PBS television series *Quilting* and *Quilting II*. She is also an author and lecturer, speaking primarily on crazy quilts and contemporary quilting in general. Write for details.

Penny McMorris
The Quilt Digest Press
955 14th St.
San Francisco, CA 94114
(415) 431-1222

MARGARET MILLER conducts lectures and workshops for quilting groups; teaching color and design skills for contemporary quiltmaking, among other subjects, she uses the techniques of block manipulation, borders and sets, and strip piecing. Classes range in duration from six hours to five days, and all levels of skill are encouraged. A listing of her lecture and workshop topics is available on request.

Margaret Miller
1798 Curry Comb Dr.
San Marcos, CA 92069
(619) 727-1256

MARGE MURPHY teaches throughout the United States and specializes in the incorporation of trapunto into quilts. Her special method allows her quilts to be fully reversible. She also designs patterns for quilting motifs. Write for information.

Marge Murphy
P.O. Box 6306
Biloxi, MS 39532
(601) 392-3731

KATIE PASQUINI teaches contemporary quiltmaking throughout the United States and abroad; the Mandala design and a dazzling array of textured and colored fabrics make many of her quilts instantly recognizable as hers alone. Information about lectures and workshops is available on request.

Katie Pasquini
Sudz Publishing
2931 Albee St.
Eureka, CA 95501
(707) 443-7478

CHARLOTTE PATERA is very much

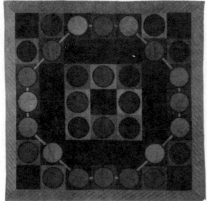

"String of Pearls" by Charlotte Patera, 1985.

"At Last" by Charlotte Patera, 1985.

an ethnic quilter; she conducts workshops in Mola techniques. Molas are panels of intricate appliqué made by Kuna Indians of the San Blas Islands of Panama. She also offers classes in more

conventional appliqué techniques. Write for free brochure.

Charlotte Patera
15 Sequoia Glen Ln.
Novato, CA 94947
(415) 892-4562

MARY COYNE PENDERS' services include a complete selection of workshops, professional development seminars, and lectures for quilt conferences, group meetings, and retreats. She has taught throughout the United States; a brochure describing her programs, including details of fees and references, is available at no charge.

Mary Coyne Penders
2600 Oak Valley Dr.
Vienna, VA 22180
(703) 938-6175

YVONNE PORCELLA has written several quilting and pattern books; she offers a number of lectures and workshops nationwide. Write for brochure.

Yvonne Porcella
3619 Shoemake Ave.
Modesto, CA 95351
(209) 524-1134

LIZ PORTER offers many classes, featuring such topics as design, color sense, vestmaking, and whole cloth quiltmaking. Brochure available on request.

THE QUILT TEACHERS' CO-OP represents many professional quilting teachers and presents a schedule of quilting classes quarterly. The teachers involved all travel regularly; for information about engaging the Co-op's teachers, send a self-addressed, stamped envelope. To be placed on the group's quarterly mailing list, send name and address.

Quilt Teachers' Co-op
5100 S. 19th Rd.
Bozeman, MT 59715
(406) 587-8213

MOANI REVOIR is an expert in Hawaiian quiltmaking; she offers workshops and lectures that fully cover this aspect of the American quilting heritage. A brochure giving details of classes is available.

Liz Porter.

Liz Porter
Fons-Porter Designs
R.R. 1, Box 127
Lorimar, IA 50149
(515) 763-2159

Moani Revoir
Misty Isles Designs
811 N. University Ave.
Provo, UT 84604
(801) 373-2415

DEANNA POWELL conducts a very wide selection of lecture and workshop topics. Write for brochure.

Deanna Powell
702 Endicott Rd.
Melbourne, FL 32935
(305) 259-0140

"Bravissemo" by Deanna Powell, 1983.

HELEN RICHARDS has been a traveling teacher for over twenty-five years; her specialties include new designs from old patterns, mirror-image designing, and quilted garments in ethnic styles. Brochure available at no charge.

Helen Richards
10131 Trask Ave., #5
Garden Grove, CA 92643
(714) 539-4633

VIRGINIA ROBERTSON conducts lectures and workshops nationwide; each presentation is tailored to the specific audience. Presentations are accompanied by a collection of over eighty quilts, garments, and quilt-related projects that illustrate the topic of the lecture or workshop. Where applicable

she offers patterns, kits, and notions for sale to the audience.

Virginia Robertson
Osage County Quilt Factory
3632 SW 38th
Topeka, KS 66610
(913) 665-7500

JOAN SCHULZE is a veteran of over twenty one-woman shows; she offers a variety of workshops and lectures. Included are workshops in design, machine quilting, and cloth painting.

Joan Schulze
808 Piper Ave.
Sunnyvale, CA 94087
(408) 736-7833

JANE SMITH is famous for her "Trip Around the World" workshops where the participants each make an entire quilt in one day. She has also written extensively on quilting and offers a variety of lectures and workshops to interested organizations. For details, write for free brochure.

Jane Smith
R.D. 1, Box 518A
South Berwick, ME 03908
(207) 676-2209

Jane Smith.

JEANNIE SPEARS is an author and quilt show judge, as well as a teacher; she offers a variety of workshops, many of which are specifically designed to help quilters become professionals.

Jeannie Spears
1409B Farrington
St. Paul, MN 55117
(612) 488-0974

DOREEN SPECKMANN became a quiltmaker a decade ago after many years of involvement with other fiber arts. She teaches and lectures extensively and offers a variety of programs to suit those at all levels of quilting ability.

Doreen Speckmann
3118 Cross St.
Madison, WI 53711
(608) 231-1563

JUDI WARREN, who teaches at Bowling Green State University and at the Toledo Museum School of Design, offers a considerable assortment of workshops and lectures. Details of her programs are available on request.

Judi Warren
114 E. Harrison
Maumee, OH 43537
(419) 893-4957

PHILOMENA WIECHEC has created a unique and beautiful style of quilting by combining ancient Celtic designs with modern quilting techniques. She conducts lectures and workshops across North America. Write for details.

Philomena Wiechec
Celtic Design Co.
834 W. Remington Dr.
Sunnyvale, CA 94087
(408) 735-8049

COLETTE WOLFF teaches and lectures frequently, often at quilt festivals and shows throughout the country. Details of her workshops and lectures are available on request.

Colette Wolff
Platypus
P.O. Box 396, Planetarium Sta.
New York, NY 10024
(212) 874-0753

BLANCHE AND HELEN YOUNG are a mother and daughter team that teaches and lectures frequently; experienced quilters, they have written several books together. Write for details of the Youngs' lecture and workshop programs.

Blanche Young
14271 Middletown Ln.
Huntington Beach, CA 92683
(714) 894-8145

Helen Young
10340 Russett Ave.
Sunland, CA 91040
(818) 353-5494

8. The World of Quilting: A Directory of North American Quilting Guilds and Other Organizations

Quilters have always been noted for their friendliness and sociability; the very term "quilting bee" suggest an air of cooperation and conviviality. For generations, the making of quilts has often been an activity associated with the church, and it is here that so many friendship and album quilts have been created. In many communities today, the base for quilting activity has shifted from the church to the guild which may meet in a member's home, a community center, or even a bank. There are well over a thousand such organizations in North America which make a valuable contribution to the art of quilting.

Leading national organizations, regional guild associations, and over 250 local quilting groups are described in the following pages. In each case, there is a sketch of the organization's activities and information regarding dues, meeting times, and locations; a contact person is also provided. Only organizations that responded to a *Quilter's Catalog* questionnaire are included in the listings. For the most part, these are groups with twenty or more members.

Information on quilting organizations not included in this chapter can often be found at a local quilting shop. It is here that so many needleworkers gather for supplies, instruction, and the exchange of information. A new group is always in formation somewhere. Publications such as *The Quilter's Newsletter Magazine* often include information on the organizing of new guilds. This periodical also issues a biennial *International Quilt Guild Directory* which may be of help to the needleworker in search of companionship and advice.

Detail, Buttercup quilt, 1978. Owner, Eleanor Jones. Courtesy of Patchworkers Quilt Club, La Plata, Maryland. Photo by John Kopp.

National Organizations

AMERICAN/INTERNATIONAL QUILT ASSOCIATION meets at the end of October in Houston, Texas. In conjunction with the meeting, the group holds its annual quilt festival which lasts for three or four days. The Association has a membership of over 1,000, which is spread throughout the United States and Europe. Members are kept informed of activities through *Quiltmaker*, the Association's quarterly newsletter. Annual dues are $15. The group has an extensive slide library that is rented to members for local guild meetings. The Association maintains a grant program for quilters who are doing research, mounting shows, offering demonstrations, or planning other worthy activities.

Lynn Young
American/International Quilt
* Association*
P.O. Box 19126
Houston, TX 79126
(713) 978-7054

AMERICAN QUILT STUDY GROUP, a nonprofit organization established in 1981, is dedicated to the development of a "responsible and accurate body of information regarding the history of quiltmaking in America." Research into the history of quilts, quiltmaking, and textiles is encouraged and supported by the AQSG and is presented to its membership and the general public through seminars and publications. Membership in the AQSG is open to anyone interested in the history of quiltmaking and textile arts; individual annual dues are $15. The AQSG's major activities include an annual seminar for the presentation of research papers and the publication of those research papers in an annual volume entitled *Uncoverings*. The AQSG also publishes guides which discuss research methods, quilt care, and other related topics, as well as *Blanket Statements*, a newsletter for members. The AQSG serves as a consultant to students, writers, curators, and others needing quilt-related information and is presently developing a resource center to house a library and archival collections.

American Quilt Study Group
105 Molino Ave.
Mill Valley, CA 94941
(415) 388-1382

CANADIAN QUILTERS' ASSOCIATION aims to promote a greater understanding, appreciation, and knowledge of the art, techniques, and heritage of patchwork, appliqué, and quilting. Each year the CQA annual meeting is held in a different part of the country. The "Quilt Canada" conference is often held in conjunction with the annual meeting; the conference is sponsored by an individual quilters' guild and not by the Association. Annual dues are $10; this includes a subscription to the Association's quarterly newsletter. While the CQA does not sponsor or maintain local guilds, it will put members in contact with local groups.

Valerie McMillin
Canadian Quilters' Association
1354 Queen St., #3
Halifax, NS B3J 2H5
Canada
(902) 425-6664

CONTINENTAL QUILTING CONGRESS is a nonprofit organization founded to promote quilting as an art form, to provide education on all aspects of quilting, and to create a record of quilting's rich history. Unlike other quilting organizations there is no formal membership; information regarding the group's activities is available to all who are interested. The Congress hosts an annual convention and organizes occasional educational quilting tours. In the past these tours have visted England, Ireland, Hong Kong, New Zealand, Australia, and Japan, as well as extensively covering the United States and Canada. Another feature of the Congress is its Quilter's Hall of

Fame, initiated in 1979 to recognize those persons who have made outstanding contributions to quilting.

The Continental Quilting Congress, Inc.
P.O. Box 561
Vienna, VA 22180
(703) 938-3246

EMBROIDERER'S GUILD OF AMERICA

EMBROIDERER'S GUILD OF AMERICA is a nonprofit organization founded in 1958 "to foster high standards of design, color, and workmanship in embroidery; to teach the embroidery arts; and to preserve our national needle arts heritage." Membership is open to all people who work with a threaded needle; annual dues for members-at-large are $17, which includes a subscription to *Needle Arts*, the official publication of the EGA. Among the numerous programs run by the EGA are group and individual courses, a master craftsman program, a teacher certification course, and a judge's certification program. The Guild also sponsors a week-long national seminar every Fall which offers a variety of intensive classes and exhibits.

The Embroiderer's Guild of America, Inc.
200 Fourth Ave.
Louisville, KY 40202
(502) 589-6956

NATIONAL QUILTING ASSOCIATION

NATIONAL QUILTING ASSOCIATION, a nonprofit organization established in 1969, is dedicated to promoting quality quiltmaking activities through its numerous educational programs. Membership is open to all who are interested in quilting; annual dues are $10. The NQA sponsors an annual quilt contest and exhibition held during one of the Summer months at a different location each year. Educational seminars are held each Spring and Fall, also at various locations throughout the United States. A teachers' and judges' certification program, a Masters' Guild, and a scholarship fund are among the other important features of the NQA. In addition, the Quilt Registry Program has been established to provide a permanent archive of quilts and their makers.

National Quilting Association, Inc.
P.O. Box 393
Ellicott City, MD 21043-0393
(301) 461-5733

THE QUILT CONSERVANCY is an organization established to assist museums and other qualified institutions in acquiring quilts for their collections. Membership is open to any individual, guild, or other organization interested in preserving the quilting heritage for future generations to enjoy. Tax-deductible dues are available in various categories and amounts; individual dues are $15 per year. There are no meetings, but all members receive periodic updates on the activities of the Quilt Conservancy and are eligible to vote for its officers. All dues received from its membership will be used to "purchase quilts and quilt-related items which are representative of or contribute to the history of the quilting arts in the United States." The Quilt Conservancy will then donate all acquisitions to qualified institutions that "agree to preserve and display the quilts for viewing, education, and enjoyment of the public."

Bettina Havig
The Quilt Conservancy
1108 Sunset Ln.
Columbia, MO 65203
(314) 449-1602

Regional Organizations

ARIZONA

ARIZONA QUILTERS GUILD is an umbrella organization for over fifteen groups throughout the state. The Guild meets twice yearly as a full body—in Phoenix each April, and elsewhere in the state each Fall. Most of the affiliated groups meet monthly. Annual dues for Guild membership are $10; there are also individual group dues that vary from group to group. The Guild publishes a quarterly newsletter, *The Patchwork Chatter*, the subscription to which is covered by dues. The Guild's primary function is to coordinate the activities of the goups; it runs workshops, gives demonstrations, organizes speakers, and holds a quilt show every two or three years.

Debbie Bobo
Arizona Quilters Guild
3841 W. Teim Dr.
Phoenix, AZ 85019
(602) 246-4783

NORTHERN CALIFORNIA

NORTHERN CALIFORNIA QUILT COUNCIL meets on the third Thursday during the months of January, April, July, and October at St. Jerome's Church, El Cerrito. Any group, business, or individual interested in quilting is invited to join. Annual dues for a business, teacher, or individual are $25; dues for a guild with under 100 members, $20; dues for a guild with over 100 members, $30; dues for a guild with over 300 members, $40. Northern California Quilt Council provides a forum for quilters, quilt shop owners, quilt groups, and teachers to communicate and share their ideas on all aspects of quilting. Panel discussions touch on such subjects as organizing a quilt show, contract guidelines, and fabric quality.

Janet Shore
Northern California Quilt
* Council*
715 Gelston Pl.
El Cerrito, CA 95430
(415) 527-1341

SAN DIEGO COUNTY, CALIFORNIA

QUILT SAN DIEGO is a nonprofit organization established by the San Diego County quilt guilds in an effort to "produce a juried quilt exhibit that will increase the awareness of quilting in the community." All members of San Diego County quilt guilds are automatically members of Quilt San Diego; there are no dues. The organization's first exhibit, "Visions," held in April 1987, featured contemporary quilts displaying growth in the quiltmaking process based on traditional methods and designs. Quilt San Diego also hopes to sponsor special programs for children, organize special exhibits, and offer other quilting events such as lectures and fashion shows.

Rose Turner
Quilt San Diego
P.O. Box 26902
San Diego, CA 92126
(619) 578-5499

COLORADO

COLORADO QUILTING COUNCIL holds its meeting on the fourth Saturday of each month. Because the group's membership is statewide, each meeting is held in a different part of the state. The Council organizes demonstrations, lectures, and workshops for its members; it hosts an annual quilt fair and sale. The group holds its Colorado Quilt Symposium about every five years.

Elaine Thomas
Colorado Quilting Council
582 Galaxy Circle
Denver, CO 80221
(303) 320-8500

GULF STATES

GULF STATES QUILTING ASSOCIATION meets four times a year. Anyone with a desire to quilt, whether a beginner or an expert, is invited to join; annual dues are $5, $3 for senior citizens. The Association hosts a biennial quilt show, annual seminars, and annually stitches a fund-raising quilt.

Marion Maerke
Gulf States Quilting
* Association*
1717 Auburn Ave.
Metairie, LA 70003
(504) 888-1674

ILLINOIS

LAND OF LINCOLN QUILTER'S ASSOCIATION meets during the months of February, April, June, August, and October at different locations throughout the state. The only membership requirement is an interest in quilts and in the craft of quilting; annual dues are $10. The guild is presently involved in the Illinois Quilt Project; other activities include making raffle quilts and offering quilting-education classes.

Edie Idelman
Land of Lincoln Quilter's
* Association*
417 Holly Ct.
Decatur, IL 62526
(217) 877-4055

IOWA

IOWA QUILTER'S GUILD meetings move from place to place across the state; meetings are held on one Saturday of the month during January, March, May, July, September, and November. The September gathering is always the annual general meeting and is held in Des Moines. There are usually workshops on the Fridays before meetings. Annual dues are $15; many members also belong to non-affiliated local quilt guilds. The Guild organizes a biennial May quilt show. The group occasionally makes a quilt to raffle for charity; the principal benefactor has been the Living History Museum in Des Moines. The group often gives quilting demonstrations; occasionally there is a small charge.

Marcene Tack
Iowa Quilter's Guild
Box 624
Hudson, IA 50643
(319) 988-4649

KANSAS

KANSAS QUILTER'S ORGANIZATION meets twice a year, Spring and Fall. Anyone with an interest in quilting is invited to join; annual dues are $10. The group, which is the official state quilting organization, offers educational programs and weekend retreats.

Virginia Lamb
Kansas Quilter's Organization
519 N. B St.
Arkansas City, KS 67005
(316) 442-6687

KENTUCKY

KENTUCKY HERITAGE QUILT SOCIETY is the parent organization for eight chapters throughout the state. Board meetings are held monthly, with the annual general meeting in April. Annual dues are $10 for the Society and a further $15 for the individual chapters. The Society organizes an annual show in May, which is timed to coincide with the Kentucky Derby. The Society also plans the Shaketown

Retreat, a quilter's retreat which is held in Pleasant Hill each October. Each June there is a three-day seminar. The Society has its own quilt documentation program, Quilters on File, which is preserving the otherwise oral history of today's Kentucky quiltmakers. The information is shared with local museums.

Marie Salazar
Kentucky Heritage Quilt
  Society, Inc.
P.O. Box 23392
Lexington, KY 40503
(606) 581-4368

NEW ENGLAND

NEW ENGLAND QUILTER'S GUILD founded in 1976 by a small group of quilting teachers, holds meetings in April and October. Membership has now grown to over 1,800 men and women in over sixty charter groups from six New England states. The purpose of the Guild is to promote the art of quiltmaking through exhibitions and lectures. Annual dues of $15 entitle members to a subscription of *The Compass*, the NEQG newsletter. Guild meetings feature guest speakers who share their knowledge through lectures, workshops, and demonstrations. Regional workshops are held throughout the New England area and are taught by qualified instructors. For students under nineteen years of age the Guild sponsors an annual quilt contest with cash prizes. New England Images is an important triennial juried quilt show that is organized by the Guild. In 1981 the NEQG decided to establish a quilt museum to promote

quiltmaking and to document and research its rich history.

Jeanne Osbourne
New England Quilter's Guild,
  Inc.
P.O. Box 73
Carlisle, MA 01741
(617) 646-5939

MID-ATLANTIC STATES

TRI-STATE QUILTMAKING TEACHERS is open to all quilting teachers in New Jersey, Delaware, Pennsylvania, and surrounding areas; annual dues are $7. The purpose of the organization is to serve as a support group for quilting teachers in order to encourage the exchange of methods, concerns, and innovations in the fields of quilting and teaching. It also aids members in the preparation of materials for class use and sponsors educational activities for members and students of quiltmaking.

Jeannette Muir
Tri-State Quiltmaking Teachers
623 Devon Rd.
Moorestown, NJ 08057
(609) 235-6854

OHIO

OHIO QUILT RESEARCH PROJECT meets irregularly at the Dublin Church, Columbus; there are usually four or five meetings each year. This organization is devoted to researching Ohio quilts and collecting and compiling information on local quilts and their makers. The group is partially funded by the Ohio Arts Council. Annual dues are $12. The group's newsletter is printed intermittently and keeps members informed of activities and meetings.

Poppy Sanks
Ohio Quilt Research Project
7983 Executive Ct.
Cincinnati, OH 45244
(513) 474-2577

TENNESSEE

TENNESSEE VALLEY QUILTERS' ASSOCIATION is a coordinating organization for sixteen guilds within the state. Its board of directors meets quarterly to plan activities. Annual Association dues are $2.50; individual guild dues vary in amount and are additional to Association dues. The cost of subscription to the Association's quarterly newsletter is included in the dues. The group is primarily an advisory and cooperative service to provide educational programs. It sponsors an "Assembly Day" each August where members can attend lectures, slide shows, and demonstrations. The Association organizes an annual show, the White Glove Quilt Show, which is held in a different area of the state each year. A biennial quilters' retreat and a biennial bus tour are held by the group. The Association is involved with several national shows and provides information on these to its members. Each June the Association hosts a three-day quilting seminar.

Norma Bagley
Tennessee Valley Quilters'
  Association
Rt. 2, Box 165
Fayetteville, TN 37334
(615) 433-2940

UTAH

UTAH QUILT GUILD is composed of over two dozen chapters across the state which are coordinated by an executive body. The Guild meets as a whole at the annual meeting, which is held each September. The meeting is a three-day event with a judged show, a dinner, and many workshops and classes. Annual dues are $10. The Guild offers lectures once or twice a year and also publishes a newsletter, *Beeline*, eleven times a year. Annually the chapters present a combined exhibition at the Springville Art Museum in Springville, Utah, and at the Festival of the American West in Logan. Most of the chapters meet monthly or bi-monthly.

Charlotte Warr-Anderson
Utah Quilt Guild
5740 Wilderland Ln.
Kearns, UT 84118
(801) 967-8112

NORTHERN VIRGINIA

QUILTERS UNLIMITED consists of ten quilting chapters spread across Northern Virginia. The individual chapters meet locally; there are four general meetings a year. The major meeting is held each May and includes speakers, workshops, and demonstrations. Activities include a Spring quilt show, a Fall luncheon, and a Winter quilt-in.

Leslie McGregor
Quilters Unlimited
9013 Penn Manor Ct.
Springfield, VA 22153
(703) 455-2237

WISCONSIN

WISCONSIN QUILTERS meets four times a year at locations throughout the state. Anyone who enjoys quilting and wants to preserve the art of quilting is welcome to join. Annual dues are $12; $10 for senior citizens. The organization hosts a quilt show every eighteen months that features an auction, workshops, lectures, and a fashion show. In conjunction with the show a quilt teachers' symposium is held featuring noted quilting teachers from across the nation. The group also runs Summer and Fall lecture programs and holds a Spring meeting for quilting teachers with day-long workshops.

Wisconsin Quilters, Inc.
Box 344
Germantown, WI 53022

Local Organizations

United States

ALABAMA

Birmingham

BIRMINGHAM QUILTER'S GUILD meets on the fourth Monday of each month at the Vestavia Library. Annual dues are $15. The Guild is involved in an annual quilt show and in quilting demonstrations at community events.

Jean Vance
4160 Churchill Dr.
Birmingham, AL 35213
(205) 879-4637

Montgomery

KUDZU QUILTERS GUILD meets on the third Tuesday of the month at the County Extension Auditorium, 4576 S. Court St; meeting times alternate between 9 am and 7 pm. Annual dues are $10. There is a lecture or workshop at each meeting. The group occasionally makes quilts for local charities; it sponsors a quilt block contest at the County Fair. The Guild has a program to teach beginners from the local military base and hosts a biennial quilt show.

Janice Jarrett
Kudzu Quilters Guild
4576 S. Court St.
Montgomery, AL 36196
(205) 281-1293

ALASKA

Anchorage

ANCHORAGE LOG CABIN QUILTERS meets every Thursday during the day and on the third Wednesday of each month during the evening, at the Central Lutheran Church. Annual membership dues are $15. The guild has invited several well-known quilting teachers to speak to its membership, and has also sponsored the first statewide quilter's conference. To raise funds for various purposes, a quilt is raffled each year.

Anchorage Log Cabin Quilters
7853 Spruce St.
Anchorage, AK 99507
(907) 344-0829

Fairbanks

CABIN FEVER QUILTER'S GUILD holds a general meeting on the third Tuesday of the month at the Lathrop High School Library. Informal meetings are also held every Thursday. There are no requirements for membership; annual dues are $15. The Guild hosts a biennial quilt show at the Fairbanks Civic Center Gallery and sponsors the quilt show division at the Tanana Valley Fair each August. Other activities include community service projects, workshops with well-known speakers, and the making of a Fairbanks historical quilt.

Cabin Fever Quilter's Guild
Box 83608
Fairbanks, AK 99708
(907) 479-3961

ARKANSAS

Hot Springs

HOT SPRINGS AREA QUILT GUILD meets on the first Monday of each month at the First National Bank Community Room. Annual dues are $7. The group is currently working on a quilt to be raffled as a fund-raiser.

Arlene Dexter
Hot Springs Area Quilt Guild
9 Arias Way
Hot Springs, AR 71909
(501) 922-3317

Little Rock

ARKANSAS QUILTERS GUILD meets on the second Monday of each month at the North Little Rock Community Center. Annual dues are $10 and includes a subscription to the Guild's monthly newsletter. The Guild annually holds a three-day Spring workshop at the 4-H Center. There are many workshops each year and every meeting features a lecture. The group makes one quilt each year which is either raffled as a fund-raiser or donated to a charity. The Guild is working on a book documenting the quilts of Arkansas. In order to find quilts that are in private hands, the Guild has been sponsoring Quilt Days where the best quilt brought in receives a cash prize. The Guild hosts a quilt show each October.

Barbara Neil
Arkansas Quilters Guild
108 King Pine Rd.
Sherwood, AR 72116
(501) 835-7217

Springdale

QUILTERS UNITED IN LEARNING TOGETHER meets on the fourth Thursday evening of each month at the Wesley United Methodist Church, Springdale. Annual dues are $10. There is either a lecture or a workshop at each meeting. The group has an on-going program of making quilts for local charities. A quilt show and sale is hosted biennially.

Sharon Phillips
Quilters United in Learning
*   Together*
Rt. 1, Box 102C
Gentry, AR 72734
(501) 248-7358

ARIZONA

Tucson

TUCSON QUILTER'S GUILD meets on the second Wednesday of each month at the Rincon Congregational Church. A love of quilts is the only requirement for membership; annual dues are $10. The Guild hosts an annual quilt show, presents quilting demonstrations at local libraries and schools, and raffles quilts to help raise funds for various charities.

Betty Haydon
Tucson Quilter's Guild
122 N. Richey
Tucson, AZ 85716
(602) 326-0180

CALIFORNIA

Antioch

DELTA QUILTERS meets on the first Thursday of every month at the Homestead Savings building, Antioch. Membership is open to anyone with an interest in quilting; annual dues are $12. Every October the guild hosts its annual quilt show. Members enjoy a variety of activities such as films, lectures, demonstrations, and the sharing of projects.

Delta Quilters
P.O. Box 154
Antioch, CA 94509
(415) 757-4933 or
(415) 757-8359

Bakersfield

COTTONPATCH QUILTERS meets on the third Thursday of the month at Veteran's Hall on Norris Rd., Bakersfield. Membership is open to quilters of all levels of ability; annual dues are $15. The guild hosts a biennial quilt show, demonstrates quilting at local events, and decorates the Howell House at Pioneer Village Museum each Christmas.

Juanita Hamilton
Cottonpatch Quilters
P.O. Box 9944
Bakersfield, CA 93389
(805) 831-4674

Carpinteria

CARPINTERIA QUILTERS meets every Thursday at the Carpinteria Community Church. The only requirements for membership are a love of quilts and quilting and an ability to hand sew; annual dues are $12. The

guild is involved in quilt shows and fund-raising projects.

Carpinteria Quilters
c/o Community Church
1111 Vallecito Rd.
Carpinteria, CA 93013

Chula Vista

CRAFTY QUILTERS meets every Wednesday at the Loma Verde Recreation Center, Chula Vista. Members must be willing to work for charitable causes and have a desire to learn and share their quilting ideas; annual dues are $10. The guild hosts an annual quilt show during June, donates the funds raised from a raffle quilt to Meals on Wheels, and makes toys for abused children. A center medallion quilt, entitled "The Chula Vista Square," was designed by a guild member and then presented to the City of Chula Vista as the official quilt block for the city.

Patsy A. Goodman
Crafty Quilters
468 Rivera Ct.
Chula Vista, CA 92017
(619) 421-7093

Cotati

MOONLIGHT QUILTERS OF SONOMA COUNTY meets on the first and third Wednesday of each month at the Coddingtown

Community Center. Members include quilters of all skill levels. Dues are $15 annually. The guild hosts a biennial quilt show and also makes quilts to be raffled for charities.

Carla Schoental
Moonlight Quilters of Sonoma
* County*
8955 Cypress Ave.
Cotati, CA 94928
(707) 795-3099

El Cajon

SUNSHINE QUILTERS OF SAN DIEGO meets on the second Tuesday of the month at the First Christian Church of El Cajon. Anyone interested in the art of quilting is invited to join, but membership is limited to 150 active members so that the proper attention can be given at each meeting to the individual's work. Annual dues are $15. Activities include involvement in a yearly "opportunity quilt" made as a cooperative project, assistance at a community quilt show, and sundry lectures and workshops.

Arlene Watters
Sunshine Quilters of San Diego
P.O. Box 20483
El Cajon, CA 92022
(619) 583-8123

Fairfield

NORTH WIND QUILTERS meets each Wednesday at the Senior Center, Fairfield. Quilters of all levels of experience are welcome; annual dues, $6. The guild hosts a quilt show and is involved in making raffle quilts.

North Wind Quilters
P.O. Box 2891
Fairfield, CA 94533
(707) 428-7421

La Canada

THE FOOTHILL QUILTERS meets every Wednesday morning and on the first and third Thursdays during the evening at members' homes. Quilters of all levels of experience are welcome; annual dues are $10. The guild has made group quilts and raffle quilts and has hosted guest speakers and workshops.

Ellen Christensen
The Foothill Quilters
1315 Olive Ln.
La Canada, CA 91011
(818) 790-6655

Los Angeles

LOS ANGELES QUILTMAKER'S GUILD meets once a month at the California Federal Savings and Loan, Los Angeles. Membership is open to beginners as well as to advanced quilters; annual dues are $12. The Guild is involved in several fund-raising projects and workshops throughout the year.

Mary Ann Knox
Los Angeles Quiltmaker's Guild
4101 W. 22nd Pl.
Los Angeles, CA 90018
(213) 732-4792

Mt. Shasta

ALPINE QUILTER'S GUILD meets on the first Thursday of the month, 11 am, at the Sissou Hatchery Museum. Quilters of all levels of expertise are welcome. The Guild makes a quilt each year to donate to the Sissou Hatchery Museum.

Andrea Nibecker
Alpine Quilter's Guild
303 E. Lake St.
Mt. Shasta, CA 96067
(916) 926-2583

Oakhurst

SIERRA MOUNTAINS QUILTER'S ASSOCIATION holds a program night on the first Thursday of each month in addition to three monthly working meetings. A love of quilting is the only requirement for membership. Annual dues are $15, $10 for senior citizens. The guild hosts an annual quilt show, "For the Love of Quilting," each June. Guest speakers are presented each month and at two large workshops held each Fall and Spring. Other activities include making a raffle quilt and displaying members' quilts at a local library.

Marge Hoyt
Sierra Mountains Quilter's
* Association*
P.O. Box 1359
Oakhurst, CA 93644
(209) 742-7942

Pioneer

SIERRA GOLD QUILTER'S GUILD meets on the second and fourth Tuesdays of the month, 11 am, at the Faith Lutheran Church, Highway 88 and Volcano Rd., Pioneer. Beginners and experts alike are welcome; annual dues are $10 for active members and $5 for associate members. The Guild sponsors a quilt show each April and organizes several fund-raising projects, including a raffle quilt, to benefit the Amador County Museum's quilt collection and the Amador County Library's quilting book selection.

JoAnn Marshall
Sierra Gold Quilter's Guild
12400 El Del Rd.
Pine Grove, CA 95665
(209) 296-7065

Porterville

PORTERVILLE QUILTERS meets on the third Thursday of each month, 10 am, at the Community Center, Porterville. Anyone living in southern Tulare County who has an interest in quilting is invited to join; annual dues are $10. The guild is a member of the NQA and the Southern California Council of Quilt Guilds. Activities include an annual quilt show, workshops, and quilting demonstrations at community fairs and local schools. Guild members have also made group quilts that have been used to raise funds for scholarships and to help support the California Heritage Quilt Project.

Doris Pyland
Porterville Quilters
P.O. Box 1881
Porterville, CA 93258
(209) 784-3497

Poway

FRIENDSHIP QUILTERS OF SAN DIEGO meets on the second Monday of the month, September through May, at the Tierra Bonita School, Poway. Anyone with an interest in quilts or quilting is welcome; annual dues are $18. The guild participates in the San Diego Quilt Show each year. Many members also assist in coordinating Quilt San Diego, a biennial juried quilt show.

Peggy Martin
Friendship Quilters of San
  Diego
P.O. Box 1108
Poway, CA 92064
(619) 484-1412

Redlands

CITRUS BELT QUILTERS, INC., meets on the last Friday of the month at the Contemporary Club, 173 S. Eureka, Redlands. The November and December meetings are combined into a single meeting. The guild is open to all quilters, but membership is limited to 250 people; an unlimited number of associate memberships, however, is offered. Annual dues are $20 for full membership, $12 for associate membership. Citrus Belt Quilters, Inc., is primarily a social/recreational organization and currently does not sponsor any shows.

Citrus Belt Quilters, Inc.
P.O. Box 626
Bryn Mawr, CA 92318
(714) 797-3815

Sacramento

RIVER CITY QUILTER'S GUILD meets on the third Thursday of every month at St. Mark's Church. Quilters of all levels of expertise are welcome; dues are $20 annually. The Guild hosts an annual show, presents monthly speakers, and schedules a weekend of workshops every three years.

Elizabeth Ringler
River City Quilter's Guild
P.O. Box 21483
Sacramento, CA 95821
(916) 923-3638

San Diego

SEASIDE QUILT GUILD meets on the first Tuesday of the month at the Mission Beach Women's Club, San Diego. Annual membership dues are $15. The Guild supports two major quilt shows in the area and par-

ticipates in an annual meeting with other guilds in the San Diego area.

Seaside Quilt Guild
108 Little Oaks Rd.
Encinitas, CA 92024
(619) 436-4852

Saratoga

SANTA CLARA VALLEY QUILT ASSOCIATION meets on the last Thursday of each month, 9:30 am, at the Westhope Presbyterian Church, Saratoga. Anyone with an interest in quilting is invited to join; annual dues are $20, $12 for senior citizens. The guild hosts an annual quilt show and supports the American Museum of Quilts in San Jose through various fund-raisers. In addition, the guild has published a series of original pattern books entitled *I'd Rather Be Quilting*.

"Olympic Quilt" by Phyllis Dale, 1984.

Santa Clara Valley Quilt
  Association
P.O. Box 792
Campbell, CA 95009
(408) 289-1217

Simi Valley

SIMI VALLEY QUILT GUILD meets on the third Wednesday of each month at the Simi Valley Senior Center. Anyone with an interest in quilting is welcome; annual dues are $16. This newly formed guild is involved in many community projects and

"Friendship Circle Quilt", Simi Valley Quilt Guild.

participated in the California Heritage Quilt Project.

Simi Valley Quilt Guild
P.O. Box 3689
Simi Valley, CA 93062
(805) 522-2743

Torrance

SOUTH BAY QUILTER'S GUILD holds general meetings on the third Wednesday of each month, with individual sewing circles meeting once or twice a week at Arlington Elementary School, 17800 Van Ness Ave., Torrance. Membership is open to anyone interested in quilting; annual dues are $16. The Guild sponsors a quilt show every one or two years, teaches Girl Scouts to quilt, and is involved in charity work.

South Bay Quilter's Guild
P.O. Box 6115
Torrance, CA 90504
(213) 426-4231

COLORADO

Canon City

ROYAL GORGE QUILT COUNCIL meets quarterly during the months of January, April, July, and October at the First National Bank community room. Membership is open to all women with an interest in quilting; annual dues are $5. The guild hosts an annual quilt show in February at the Fine Arts Center, annually stitches a raffle quilt, and publishes a quarterly newsletter. Several of the guild's members have made prize-winning quilts or have had

their work featured in *Quilter's Newsletter.*

Laura Kozubik
Royal Gorge Quilt Council
1242 Park Ave.
Canon City, CO 81212
(303) 275-8585

Pueblo

PRIDE CITY QUILT GUILD meets on the third Monday of the month, 9 am, at the Chapel Building, State Hospital, in Pueblo. Anyone interested in quilting is welcome; annual dues are $5. Monthly meetings always include a program for teaching and learning some phase of quilting. The Guild creates quilts to be used as fund-raisers for hiring guest speakers.

Pride City Quilt Guild
6 Brooks Pl.
Pueblo, CO 81001
(303) 543-2975

CONNECTICUT

Enfield

ENFIELD QUILTERS meets on the third Wednesday of the month, 7 pm, at the Enfield Library. Quilters of all levels of ability are welcome; annual dues are $7. The guild stitches a raffle quilt each year to raise funds for various purposes and hosts at least two well-known quilters to speak at guild meetings.

Celeste Unsworh
Enfield Quilters
12 Light St.
Enfield, CT 06082
(203) 763-1626

Glastonbury

THE GREATER HARTFORD QUILT GUILD holds a general meeting twice a year. Its Steering Committee is made up of two representatives from each of the fourteen chapters and meets every two months. Individual chapter meetings are scheduled once a month. Anyone with an interest in quilts and quilting is invited to join. Activities include an annual meeting with guest speakers and vendors, and a "Sharing Day" where each chapter displays its current projects. The Guild also coordinates a quilt show in which all the chapters take part.

Diane Obernesser
Greater Hartford Quilt Guild
63 Belridge Rd.
Glastonbury, CT 06033
(203) 633-7930

Old Mystic

THAMES RIVER QUILTERS GUILD meets on the first Tuesday of the month at the Old Mystic Baptist Church. Annual dues are $12. The group sponsors occasional shows, makes raffle quilts, and publishes a monthly newsletter. A speaker highlights every meeting, and prominent speakers are brought in once or twice a year. At least one workshop is held each month.

Mary Granata
Thames River Quilters Guild
P.O. Box 529
Gales Ferry, CT 06335-0529
(203) 739-0854

Richfield

NUTMEG QUILTER'S GUILD meets on the second Wednesday of every second month, beginning in February; meetings are held at the Jesse Lee Methodist Church, Main St. Annual dues are $10. The group holds workshops for its members and

has had three shows in the past. The Guild is involved in many charity projects, including lap quilts for nursing homes and quilts for the local Ronald McDonald House.

Susan Bisanzo
Nutmeg Quilter's Guild
21 Brook Crossway
Greenwich, CT 06831
(203) 531-0427

DISTRICT OF COLUMBIA

Washington

BEAUVOIR QUILTERS meets every Thursday morning, September through June. Parents of children attending Beauvoir School as well as friends of the school, are eligible for membership. The guild makes a quilt to be raffled at the annual auction which raises money for the school's scholarship fund.

Judith Smith
Beauvoir Quilters
1717 Lamont St., NW
Washington, DC 20010
(202) 332-3020

PM PATCHWORK meets once a month on the third Thursday at Chevy Chase Community Center, 5601 Connecticut Ave., NW. Anyone who enjoys quilting is welcome. The guild has donated quilts to the local Ronald McDonald House and has hosted guest speakers at guild meetings.

Margaret McKenzie
PM Patchwork
4500 Connecticut Ave., NW
Washington, DC 20008
(202) 244-6815

DELAWARE

Newark

LADYBUG CHAPTER OF THE NATIONAL QUILTING ASSOCIATION meets at 7:30 pm on the third Wednesday of each month; meetings are held at the Christiana Mall, Newark. Annual dues are $7. The group hosts a biennial quilt show, makes occasional raffle quilts as fundraisers, and presents a speaker or workshop at most meetings.

Nancy Davis
Ladybug Chapter of NQA
26 Austen Rd.
Wilmington, DE 19810
(302) 478-7529

FLORIDA

Boca Raton

GOLD COAST QUILTERS' GUILD meets on the third Tuesday of each month at the Boca Raton Community Center on Crawford Blvd. Anyone interested in quilting is welcome. Annual dues are $15. Most monthly meetings feature a speaker, a hands-on project, or another activity of interest. The Guild also organizes quilting bees and demonstrations at community functions.

Jane Hill
Gold Coast Quilters' Guild
716 NW 6th Dr.
Boca Raton, FL 33432
(305) 395-7694

Bradenton

MANATEE PATCHWORKER'S QUILT GUILD meets on the second Monday of the month, 7 pm, at the Florida Power and Light

Building. Smaller groups within the Guild meet once a week. An interest in quilting is the only requirement for membership; annual dues are $12. Guild activities include an annual quilt show held during March, and raising funds for Meals on Wheels and for needy families in the area.

Kathy Curtin
Manatee Patchworker's Quilt
*   Guild*
P.O. Box 356
Bradenton, FL 33506
(813) 747-4134

Largo

LARGO CRACKER QUILTERS meets every Monday, 10 am, at the Prince of Peace Lutheran Church, Largo. Beginners as well as more experienced quilters are welcome; annual dues are $12. A biennial show is the guild's primary activity. Many members have entered quilted projects in local and national competitions and have won prizes.

Betty Sarine
Largo Cracker Quilters
709 Grovewood Ln.
Largo, FL 33540
(813) 581-8193

Sanford

CENTRAL FLORIDA QUILTER'S GUILD holds a general meeting once a month at a local church. Smaller groups meet twice a month at members' homes. Anyone interested in quilts or quilting is invited to join; annual dues are $8. The Guild hosts a biennial quilt show and a quilt symposium during the year between shows. Other activities include making raffle quilts, donating quilts to a local

home for troubled youth, contributing quilting books to the public library, and presenting well-known speakers at meetings and workshops.

Central Florida Quilter's Guild
P.O. Box 50
Sanford, FL 32771

Satellite Beach

SEASIDE PIECEMAKERS meets on the fourth Wednesday of the month at the Satellite Beach Civic Center. Quilters of all levels of expertise are invited to join; annual dues are $7. The guild hosts an annual quilt show in March and is presently making quilts to donate to a local home for abused girls.

Marion Richardson
Seaside Piecemakers
655 Caribbean Rd.
Satellite Beach, FL 32937
(305) 773-5165

GEORGIA

Gainesville

HALL COUNTY QUILT GUILD meets on the first and third Mondays of the month at the Home Federal Bank, College Square Branch. Anyone with an interest in quilting is welcome; annual dues are $10. The Guild sponsors a biennial workshop and juried quilt show during the month of August at the Gainesville Junior College.

Sandy Myers
Hall County Quilt Guild
5845 Hidden Cove Rd.
Gainesville, GA 30501
(404) 536-0406

Lilburn

GWINNETT QUILTER'S GUILD meets on the third Tuesday of the month at the Lilburn City Hall. Anyone with an interest in quilting is welcome; annual dues are $10. The Guild stitches a group quilt each year as a fund-raising project, presents an annual quilting workshop for Guild members, and participates in quilting demonstrations at local events such as the Old South Celebration at Stone Mountain Park. Members also participate in the North Georgia Quilt Council quilt show.

Linda Huff
Gwinnett Quilter's Guild
2207 Camp Circle
Lilburn, GA 30247
(404) 972-7099

Macon

HEART OF GEORGIA QUILT GUILD meets on the third Thursday of the month, 1:30 pm, at the Museum of Arts and Sciences. Members must be active in the craft of quilting or genuinely interested in the future development and preservation of the art form. The Guild hosts an annual quilt show each November featuring over 100 quilts, many of which are for sale.

Ann Boyd
Heart of Georgia Quilt Guild
1092 River N. Blvd.
Macon, GA 31211
(912) 746-5526

Stone Mountain

YELLOW DAISY QUILTERS meets once a month at the Stone Mountain Women's Club. Membership dues are required. The guild participates in quilting demonstrations at

Stone Mountain's Old South Days.

Pat Shumacher
Yellow Daisy Quilters
890 Post Rd. Circle
Stone Mountain, GA 30088
(404) 498-5105

HAWAII

Kailua

HAWAII QUILT GUILD meets on the fourth Monday of the month at local libraries and churches. Membership is open to anyone with an interest in making, collecting, or enjoying quilts; annual dues are $10. The Guild sponsors the Pacific Friendship Fibre Arts Conference.

Hawaii Quilt Guild
P.O. Box 810
Kailua, HI 96734
(808) 259-7473

IDAHO

Boise

BOISE BASIN QUILTERS meets on the third Tuesday of each month at the Church of Christ, 2000 Eldorado St. Annual dues are $12. A lecture is featured at most meetings. The group hosts a biennial quilt show and organizes many quilt exhibits, often at local businesses. Members have documented much of the local historical society's quilt collection.

Cheryl Little
Boise Basin Quilters
P.O. Box 2206
Boise, ID 83701
(208) 345-5567

Council

COUNCIL MOUNTAIN QUILTERS meets on the first and third Mondays of the month at the local library. Quilters of all levels of expertise are welcome; there are no annual dues. Guild members stitch one raffle quilt each year and donate the proceeds to a worthy cause.

Cathy Gross
Council Mountain Quilters
HC62 Box 1207
Council, ID 83612
(208) 253-4503

ILLINOIS

Atlanta

QUILTERS AT HEART holds its monthly meetings at the Logan County Farm Bureau Building, Lincoln. Anyone with an interest in quilting is invited to join; membership fees are $5. Several members of the guild have won prizes in national competitions and have had their work featured in quilting magazines and other publications. Guild meetings are designed to keep members informed of important up-coming events, to learn new techniques, and to exchange patterns and fabrics.

Georgia Green
Quilters At Heart
R.R. 2, Box 170
Atlanta, IL 61723
(217) 648-2973

Champaign

HEARTLAND QUILTERS meets once a month in members' homes. The only criteria for membership is an interest in quilting; annual dues are $5. Guild activities include making friendship quilts and attending quilt shows.

Rebecca Grant
Heartland Quilters
2314 Carlisle Dr.
Champaign, IL 61821
(217) 351-5109

Chicago

GARFIELD RIDGE QUILT GROUP meets once a month at the Garfield Ridge Branch of the Chicago Public Library. Beginners, as well as advanced quilters, are welcome; there are no annual dues at the present time. The guild's activities include making fund-raising quilts for the Ronald McDonald House and for the Battered Women's Crisis Center.

Carol McKernan
Garfield Ridge Quilt Group
6249 W. 59th St.
Chicago, IL 60638
(312) 582-6094

RATHER BEE QUILT CLUB meets every two weeks in members' homes. Quilters of all levels of ability are welcome; dues are $1 per meeting. Guild members attend quilt shows and workshops and support and encourage each other in their quilting endeavors.

Nancy Roate
Rather Bee Quilt Club
4915 N. Harding
Chicago, IL 60625
(312) 478-4262

Crete

PIECES & PATCHES OF ILLINOIS holds a general meeting on the second Wednesday of each month, 7 pm, at the Steger Village Hall. Quilters of all levels of ability are welcome. Annual chapter dues arc $10; annual NQA dues are an additional $10. The guild organizes a biennial quilt show during April of odd-number years. Other activities include making raffle quilts and hosting guest speakers and teachers at guild meetings.

Pat English
Pieces & Patches of Illinois
R.R. 3, Box 1095
Crete, IL 60417
(312) 672-5942

Freeport

COUNTRY CROSSROAD QUILTER'S GUILD meets on the third Monday of the month at the Forreston Methodist Church. Anyone interested in quilting is welcome. The Guild sponsors a quilt show and stitches a raffle quilt as a fund-raising project.

Helen Hartog
Country Crossroad Quilter's
* Guild*
1342 Empire Ct.
Freeport, IL 61032
(815) 232-7580

Ingleside

QUILTING QUEENS meets every Monday, September through May, at the Ingleside Town Hall. An interest in quilting is the only criterion for membership; dues are required. The guild has made and donated quilts to the Ronald McDonald House in Chicago and is planning quilt shows for the near future.

Eleanor Klein
Quilting Queens
407 Lincoln Ave.
Ingleside, IL 60041
(312) 587-2350

McHenry

COUNTRY QUILTERS meets on the first Thursday of the month at Granny's Quilts in McHenry. Members must have a desire to promote the art of quilting; annual dues are $5. The guild has hosted a successful quilt show and has another planned. Members are also involved in various service projects such as donating quilting books to local libraries and supporting a scholarship fund at a community college.

Country Quilters
4509 W. Elm St.
McHenry, IL 60050
(815) 455-2818

Moline

MISSISSIPPI VALLEY QUILTERS GUILD meets at 7 pm on the first Tuesday of each month; meetings are held at the First Congregational Church, Moline. Annual dues are $12. Most meetings feature a speaker. The Guild hosts a biennial quilt show, and members often give demonstrations at community events.

Barbara Tennyson
Mississippi Valley Quilters
* Guild*
514 6th St.
Bettendorf, IA 52722
(319) 359-1443

Plainfield

PRIDE OF THE PRAIRIE QUILT GUILD meets on the third Thursday of the month at the Plainfield United Methodist Church. Membership is open to quilters of all ages and levels of experience; annual dues arc $10. The Guild has donated four tied quilts to the church which hosts its meetings and has raised funds for various purposes by making raffle quilts.

Pat Pruss
Pride of the Prairie Quilt Guild
131 E. Pennington Ln.
Plainfield, IL 60544
(312) 369-8392

Shorewood

JOLIET QUILT GUILD meets on the first and third Monday of each month at the Joliet Park District. Quilters of all levels of ability are welcome; annual dues are $10. Members participate in making a raffle quilt to benefit Guild activities.

Rosemary Bruckner
Joliet Quilt Guild
312 Greenfield Dr.
Shorewood, IL 60435
(815) 744-6454

South Holland

HERITAGE QUILT GUILD OF SOUTH SUBURBIA meets on the third Tuesday of each month, except July, August, and December, at the meeting room of a local nursing home. Only a strong interest in quilting is required for membership; annual dues are $15. The Guild sponsors occasional quilt shows and makes quilts for the benefit of the Ronald McDonald House in Chicago.

Heritage Quilt Guild of South
* Suburbia*
P.O. Box 932
South Holland, IL 60473
(312) 339-9423

Sycamore

DEKALB COUNTY QUILT GUILD
meets on the fourth Thursday of
the month at the Ben Gordon
Health Center, located between
Sycamore and DeKalb. Anyone
interested in the preservation,
history, appreciation, and application of quilting is welcome
to join; annual dues are $15.
The Guild sponsors a quilt
show every other year. Other activities include hosting nationally known speakers and offering quilting workshops.

Sondra Tague
DeKalb County Quilt Guild
P.O. Box 385
Sycamore, IL 60178
(815) 784-3359

Urbana

ILLINI COUNTRY STITCHERS
meets on the second and fourth
Thursdays of the month at St.
Patrick's Church, Urbana.
Quilters of all levels of expertise
are welcome; annual dues are
$10. The guild sponsors an an-
nual quilt show and is involved
in civic activities such as providing lap robes for nursing
homes.

Cheryl Kennedy
Illini Country Stitchers
R.R. 3, Box 52
Mahomet, IL 61853
(217) 586-3748

Wilmette

ILLINOIS QUILTERS, INC., meets
on the first Thursday of the
month, September through
June, at the Beth Hillel Con-
gregation, Wilmette. Membership is open to anyone with an
interest in quilting; regular annual dues are $20, and newslet-
ter membership dues are $10.

The guild presents an annual
quilt show at the Chicago
Botanic Gardens during
November, hosts speakers and
workshops, and is involved in
community service projects
that benefit such organizations
as the Battered Women's
Shelter. The group occasionally
offers a quilter's retreat.

Mary Ray
Illinois Quilters, Inc.
P.O. Box 39
Wilmette, IL 60091
(312) 251-8938

INDIANA

Bloomington

BLOOMINGTON QUILTER'S GUILD
meets on the first Tuesday of
the month, September through
June, at 1514 E. Third St.,
Bloomington. Quilters of all
levels of expertise are welcome;
annual dues are $10. The Guild
makes raffle quilts as a fund-
raising project, is involved in
several community events, and
hosts an annual workshop or
lecture featuring a nationally
known quilter or teacher.

Bloomington Quilter's Guild
3311 Piccadilly St.
Bloomington, IN 47401
(812) 333-1705

Columbus

COLUMBUS STAR QUILTERS meets
on the first Wednesday of the
month at the Sandy Hook
United Methodist Church, Columbus. An interest in quilting
is the only requirement for
membership; annual dues are
$10. The guild hosts a biennial
quilt show, offers workshops
featuring well-known quilting

instructors, and donates several
quilts each year to charitable
causes.

Catherine Bahnsen
Columbus Star Quilters
3701 Balsam Ct.
Columbus, IN 47203
(812) 372-5484

Fort Wayne

CROSSROADS QUILT CLUB meets
once a week at 6110 Manchester
Dr., Fort Wayne. A love of
quilting is the only membership
requirement; there are no annual dues. The guild holds
classes for beginners within its
membership.

Joan Stolle
Crossroads Quilt Club
6110 Manchester Dr.
Fort Wayne, IN 46815
(219) 485-4140

Indianapolis

**THE QUILTER'S GUILD OF IN-
DIANAPOLIS** meets every month
on the second Thursday, 7 pm,
at St. Pius X Church, In-
dianapolis. A smaller group
meets on the fourth Thursday of
the month at 10 am in
Laughner's Cafeteria, In-
dianapolis. Membership is open
to quilters of all ages and levels
of experience; annual dues are
$10. The Guild hosts a biennial
quilt show, offers workshops for
beginning quilters, and presents
quilting demonstrations at
museums. Members have also
made numerous quilts and wall
hangings for the Ronald
McDonald House in In-
dianapolis, the Julian Center for
Abused Women and Children,
and the Christamore Aid
Society.

The Quilter's Guild of Indianapolis
607 W. Ralston Rd.
Indianapolis, IN 46217
(317) 888-8513

LaPorte

"Vesterheim Rosemaling" by Charlotte Bass.

PURDUE QUILTERS meets on the third Thursday of each month at Purdue North Central Campus. Quilters of all levels of experience and with a strong interest in learning more about quilting are welcome to join; annual membership dues are $10. The guild participates in a biannual quilt display at the historic Barker Mansion in Michigan City. Several of the group's members are currently working on quilts to be entered in national competitions.

Marlene Woodfield
Purdue Quilters
7101 W. 125 N.
LaPorte, IN 46350
(219) 362-4406

Noblesville

HOOSIER HERITAGE QUILT GUILD meets on Tuesdays. There are no requirements for membership; annual dues are collected. Each year the Guild enters a quilt in a local quilt competition. In addition, members have assisted in organizing the First Annual Quilting Party at the Indiana State Fairgrounds and hope to continue in this endeavor.

Cindy Boden
Hoosier Heritage Quilt Guild
R.R. 4, Box 258
Noblesville, IN 46060
(317) 773-4103

North Vernon

WINDING WATER QUILT CLUB meets once a month at members' homes. Anyone interested in quilting is invited to join. The guild holds an annual quilt exhibit at a local bank, and many members also display their work at the county fair.

Sheila Kane
Winding Water Quilt Club
701 N. Elm
North Vernon, IN 47265
(812) 346-4941

Shipshewana

HERITAGE QUILTERS GUILD meets at 7 pm on the first Tuesday of each month. Meetings are held in private homes or at the public library. Quilters of all levels of expertise are welcome; the only requirements are that members attend monthly meetings and help with the Guild projects. The Guild hosts

Heritage Quilt Guild member Mrs. Yoder with an award-winning quilt.

an annual quilt show which features a "People's Choice" competition and a charity raffle.

IOWA

Cedar Rapids

EAST IOWA HEIRLOOM QUILTERS meets on the fourth Monday of each month at the Ambrose Recreation Center, Cedar Rapids. Annual dues are $12. Each February and July workshops with lectures are held. The group hosts a biennial

Ruby Hostetler
Heritage Quilters Guild
R.R. 2, Box 84
Shipshewana, IN 46565
(219) 768-4244

Spring quilt show; several conferences have been held in the past.

Dianne Karr
East Iowa Heirloom Quilters
1275 Lindale Dr.
Marion, IA 52302
(319) 377-4701

Creston

"Patches and Pieces" raffle quilt (and lucky winner).

PATCHES AND PIECES QUILTER'S GUILD holds two business meetings during the year. Membership is open to anyone interested in quilts and quilting; annual dues are $2. The Guild hosts an annual quilt show in July and offers lectures, workshops, and other programs

of special interest to members throughout the year.

Sarah Harvey
Patches and Pieces Quilter's
* Guild*
519 New York Ave.
Creston, IA 50801
(515) 782-2206

Des Moines

DES MOINES AREA QUILTERS' GUILD, INC., meets on the fourth Tuesday of each month at the Westminster Presbyterian Church; there are two groups: one meets at 1 pm, the other at 7 pm. Annual dues are $10. Each meeting has a special speaker or project. Every year an outside teacher is brought in to lecture and give workshops. The Guild holds an annual quilt show in the last week of September.

Kathie Anderson
Des Moines Area Quilters'
* Guild, Inc.*
3502 SW 2nd St.
Des Moines, IA 50315
(515) 288-3571

Dubuque

CABLE CAR QUILTER'S GUILD meets on the third Monday of every month except August and December, 7 pm, at the Holy Trinity Lutheran Church, 1755 Delhi, Dubuque. Annual membership dues are $10. The Guild participates in a quilt show with the Dubuque County Historical Society and also sponsors its own show. Quilting demonstrations at museums and malls, making guild quilts, and hosting speakers and workshops are just some of the group's other activities.

Ruth Lyon
Cable Car Quilter's Guild
1915 Admiral
Dubuque, IA 52001
(319) 583-7285

Fairfield

PRAIRIE QUILTERS meets once a month in the meeting room of a local bank. Anyone interested in

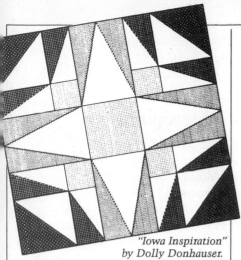

"Iowa Inspiration"
by Dolly Donhauser.

quilts and quilting is welcome; annual dues are $5. The guild hosts an annual quilt show during April. Members also work on one quilt a year which is sold to raise funds to hire special teachers or hold workshops.

Dolly Donhauser
Prairie Quilters
707 W. Taylor
Fairfield, IA 52556
(515) 472-2684

Iowa City

QUILTING FOR FUN, INC., meets at 7 pm on the second Monday of each month; meetings are held at Our Redeemer Lutheran Church, 1st Ave. Annual dues are $10. The group sponsors occasional educational trips; most group activities are involved with making the very large number of quilts that the members donate to charities every year.

Anna Murphy
Quilting For Fun, Inc.
123 Stevens Dr.
Iowa City, IA 52240
(319) 351-3829

Madrid

MADRID CENTENNIAL HERITAGE QUILTERS meets once a month

in members' homes. Membership is open to quilters of all levels of ability and to those who wish to preserve the quilting heritage. There are no dues. The guild participates in occasional fund-raising activities.

Lorna Carlson
Madrid Centennial Heritage
Quilters
802 S. Kennedy
Madrid, IA 50156
(515) 795-2559

Mason City

NORTH IOWA QUILTER'S GUILD meets on the second Wednesday of each month at the Mason City Public Library, September through June. Annual membership dues are $5. The Guild sponsors a biennial quilt show and offers workshops, lectures, and slide presentations at its meetings.

Jan Garrard
North Iowa Quilter's Guild
606 S. Virginia
Mason City, IA 50401
(515) 424-2785

Waukon

NORTHEAST IOWA QUILTERS GUILD meets on the first Tuesday of each month; meetings are usually held in Waukon, but they are sometimes in Decorah. Annual dues are $5. Each meeting features a show-and-tell; most include workshops or lectures. To raise funds, a raffle quilt is made each year; there is a quilt show every two years.

Jandice Arp
Northeast Iowa Quilters Guild
R.R.
Decorah, IA 52101
(319) 382-4394

KANSAS

Great Bend

CENTRAL KANSAS THREAD-BENDERS meets on the third Friday of the month, 1 pm, at First Presbyterian Church. Membership is open to all who are interested in quilts; annual membership dues are $12. The guild holds a biennial quilt show as well as various workshops and special programs throughout the year.

Maggie Bleeker
Central Kansas Thread-Benders
5343 Quail Creek
Great Bend, KS 67530
(316) 792-7779

Hutchinson

HEART OF KANSAS QUILTERS meets on the last Monday of the month at the Trinity United Methodist Church. Anyone who enjoys quilting is invited to join; annual dues are $10. The guild sponsors a biennial quilt show, donates books to the Hutchinson Public Library, and is supporting the Reno County Museum in its efforts to purchase a quilt display case.

Billie Elliott
Heart of Kansas Quilters
202 W. 23rd
Hutchinson, KS 67502
(316) 669-0547

Paola

MIAMI COUNTY QUILTER'S GUILD meets on the first Thursday of the month at the Kansas City Power and Light Building. Anyone interested in learning to quilt, in improving their quilting skills, or in preserving the art of quilting is welcome to join; annual dues are $10. Members make a group quilt every year to raise funds for the Guild's annual quilt show in September. Other activities include making doll quilts and dressing dolls to give to underpriviledged children in the area, stitching lap quilts for the elderly, and contributing quilting books to the local library.

Naomi Clifton
Miami County Quilter's Guild
P.O. Box 453
Paola, KS 66071
(913) 294-4961

Parsons

QUILTER'S GUILD OF PARSONS meets on the third Wednesday of each month, except during December, at the Parsons Recreation Center. A love of quilts and quilting is the only requirement for membership; annual dues are $12. The Guild has supported and worked at the county fair and has also made raffle quilts as fund-raisers.

Sandy Wagerle
Quilter's Guild of Parsons
1029 S. 28th St.
Parsons, KS 67357
(316) 421-9534

Wichita

PRAIRIE QUILT GUILD meets on the second Tuesday of the month at the Downtown Senior Center, Wichita. Membership is open to anyone with an interest in quilting; annual dues are $12. The Guild hosts a large quilt show every two years, supports the local Ronald McDonald House with donated quilts, and co-sponsors the Heartland Quilt Symposium. Guild members are

presently working on a project that will reproduce quilts from watercolors painted during the Depression as part of a WPA project.

Norma Johnston
Prairie Quilt Guild
432 S. Winterset Ct.
Wichita, KS 67209
(316) 943-4387

KENTUCKY

Highland Heights

LICKING VALLEY QUILTERS is a chapter of the Kentucky Heritage Quilt Society, Inc. Meetings are held on the third Wednesday of each month at Kroger Technical Center, Highland Heights. Each meeting features a workshop, lecture, or demonstration. The group has made several raffle quilts in the past and has helped with a number of state quilt projects.

Alice Heath
Licking Valley Quilters
107 Memorial Pkwy.
Bellevue, KY 41073
(606) 781-4427

LOUISIANA

New Orleans

JAMBALAYA GEMS meets twice a month at a local library. There is presently a waiting list for new members; annual dues are $22. The guild is associated with the Gulf States Quilting Association and participates in its activities.

Jambalaya Gems
1514 Athis St.
New Orleans, LA 70122
(504) 283-5901

Shreveport

RED RIVER QUILTERS holds a general meeting on the first Monday of the month at the Barnwell Center. In addition, five tributary groups meet in members' homes either monthly or weekly, depending on how active members want to be. Anyone who expresses interest in promoting the knowledge and understanding of all aspects of quilting is welcome. Annual membership dues are $12. The guild's primary activity is its annual educational seminar featuring nationally and regionally known quilting instructors, a fashion show, and a quilt show. Members also participate in several community events and festivals such as the Red River Revel and contribute quilts and other items to local charitable organizations.

Pat Lonnecker
Red River Quilters
727 Thora Blvd.
Shreveport, LA 71106
(318) 865-4701

MAINE

Houlton

FRIENDS & NEEDLES QUILTER'S GUILD meets once a month at various locations in the Houlton area. Anyone interested in quilting is encouraged to join; annual dues are $8, which includes chapter dues to the Pine Tree Quilters Guild of Maine. The group hosts an annual quilt show at the end of

August during Houlton's Potato Feast Days. Raffle quilts are made to benefit guild activities such as acquiring books for the local library and helping to underwrite the airing of a quilting series on the Public Broadcasting network.

Ellen Cyr
Friends & Needles Quilter's
*   Guild*
12 Johnson St.
Houlton, ME 04730
(207) 532-7180

South Paris

PINE NEEDLES QUILTERS meets every Thursday at 9 am in the community room of a local bank. Quilters of all levels of expertise are welcome, but many members have completed a basic quilting course before joining. The guild is a chapter of the Pine Tree Quilters Guild, the state quilting organization. Annual dues are $8, which includes dues to the state Guild. Pine Needles Quilters has hosted its own quilt shows and has participated in the annual show sponsored by the Pine Tree Quilters Guild. Other activities include visiting nursing homes for a quilt show-and-tell and making quilts to benefit local organizations.

Barbara Swan Frost
Pine Needles Quilters
Hooper Lodge
South Paris, ME 04281
(207) 743-8337

MARYLAND

Annapolis

ANNAPOLIS QUILT GUILD meets at 7:30 pm on the first Monday

of the month; meetings are held in the Board of Education Building. Annual dues are $10. A lecture or a workshop is given at each meeting. Each Spring the Guild sponsors a quilt show and a retreat; there is also a Fall retreat. The group makes and raffles at least one quilt a year; it also occasionally makes and donates quilts to local charities.

Rhoda Miller
Annapolis Quilt Guild
1020 Forest Hills Ave.
Annapolis, MD 21403
(301) 268-5337

Fulton

PIECEMAKER'S QUILTING CLUB meets on the second and fourth Tuesday of the month, 9 am, at the CEC Building located on Highway 545 South. An interest in quilting is the only requirement for membership; dues are 25¢ per meeting. At the present time, members are involved in helping each other quilt patchwork tops.

Susan Harrison
Piecemaker's Quilting Club
Rt. 3, Box 45A
Fulton, MD 65251
(314) 642-8608

LaPlata

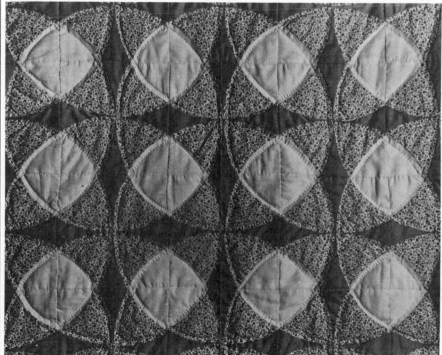

"Buttercup", Patchworker's Quilt Club, 1978. Photo by John Kopp.

PATCHWORKER'S QUILT CLUB holds a business meeting once a month and quilting meetings once a week at members' homes. A basic knowledge of quilting techniques and a completed example are required for membership; annual dues are $10. Members must also be willing to contribute at least ten hours' work on group quilts. The guild hosts an annual quilt

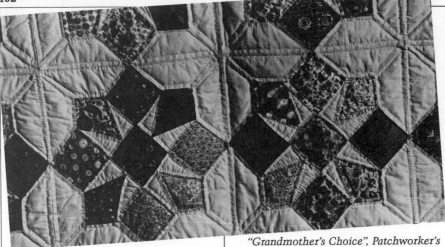

"Grandmother's Choice", Patchworker's Quilt Club, 1977. Photo by John Kopp.

show in the Spring, demonstrates quilting at the county fair and other local events, and donates the proceeds from a raffle quilt to a worthy charity.

Dolores Eckman
Patchworker's Quilt Club
P.O. Box 718
LaPlata, MD 20646
(301) 934-4874

Fort Washington

QUILTER'S WORKSHOP OF OXON HILL meets once a month, except during July and August, at the Harmony Hall Regional Center, Fort Washington. Members must have some prior quilting experience before joining the guild; annual dues are $10. The group hosts an annual quilt show and quilting demonstration. Members also display their completed quilts at the National Needlework Exhibition at Woodlawn Plantation in Virginia.

Shirley Elliott
Quilter's Workshop of Oxon Hill
2204 Piermont Dr.
Fort Washington, MD 20744
(301) 248-9166

Glen Burnie

ETERNAL QUILTERS meets monthly at Christ Lutheran Church. Members vary in their levels of quilting skill, and all with an interest in the craft are welcome. Nominal dues cover the cost of a newsletter, coffee, and paper supplies. The group sponsors occasional speakers and workshops and every two or three years hosts a fund-raising quilt show.

Betty Bulich
Eternal Quilters
622 Newfield Dr.
Glen Burnie, MD 21061
(301) 766-8150

MASSACHUSETTS

Amherst

HANDS ACROSS THE VALLEY QUILTER'S GUILD meets on the second Sunday of the month, September through May, at the Masonic Hall, Amherst. Membership is open to anyone living in the Pioneer Valley who shares an interest in the art and craft of quilting; annual dues are $10. The Guild has hosted successful quilt shows and has completed fund-raising raffle quilts. Other activities include workshops in special techniques, lectures by nationally recognized quilters, and field trips.

Linda Pelletier
Hands Across the Valley
* Quilter's Guild*
P.O. Box 831
Amherst, MA 01004
(413) 967-5882

Arlington

QUILTER'S CONNECTION meets on the fourth Wednesday of the month; there are no meetings in July or August; the November and December meetings are combined into one meeting. Meetings are held at the Universalist Unitarian First Parish Church. Annual dues are $12.50. The guild brings in guest speakers to lecture and give workshops about four times a year. A pot-luck supper is held each January which is also the principal work meeting for the group's annual collective quilt. The quilt is raffled at the group's quilt show in April. The group often helps local students to learn quilting skills. It also sponsors a comfort-quilt program which makes and donates several quilts annually to local charities.

Rosemary Koch
Quilter's Connection
100 Brand St.
Arlington, MA 02174
(617) 646-1293

Burlington

BURLINGTON QUILTER'S GUILD meets on the second Thursday of each month at the Ethan Allen Furniture Store. Annual dues are $10. The group is making several quilts to raffle for the benefit of the New England Quilt Museum.

Sally Bates
Burlington Quilter's Guild
2 Grandview Ave.
Burlington, MA 01803
(617) 272-2795

Cape Cod

BAYBERRY QUILT GUILD OF CAPE COD meets on the fourth Wednesday of each month in Brewster. Annual dues are $10. There is a speaker at each meeting, and usually there is also a workshop. The Guild welcomes members from the entire Cape Cod area and hosts the Cape Cod Quilt Show each August.

Barbara Hedlund
Bayberry Quilt Guild of Cape Cod
P.O. Box 1327
North Eastham, MA 02651
(617) 255-2377

Chatham

"The Wildflower Garden", Beach Plum Quilt Guild.

BEACH PLUM QUILT GUILD meets on the second Thursday of the month, except during July and August, at St. Christopher's Church, Main St., Chatham. Quilters of all levels of ability are welcome. An annual quilt show is held each July. Contributing books to the local library and funding three scholarships for local schools are among the Guild's activities.

Pricilla Harding
Beach Plum Quilt Guild
P.O. Box 131
Chatham, MA 02633
(617) 945-0863

Haverhill

MERRIMACK VALLEY (MASSACHUSETTS) QUILTERS meets on the third Thursday of each month at the Universalist Unitarian Church. Annual dues are $10. The group annually holds a May quilt show and a Fall crafts fair; both are held at the Church. The group makes one raffle quilt for each event.

Doreen Burbank
Merrimack Valley (Massachusetts) Quilters
16 W. Shore Rd.
Windham, NH 03087
(603) 893-3029

Newton

NEWTON PATCHWORKS meets at 7:30 pm on the first and third Wednesdays of the month; meetings are held at the Horace Mann Elderly Apartment Complex, Watertown St. Annual dues are $15. Every third meeting an outside speaker is brought in to give a lecture or workshop. The group makes two quilts per year: one is raffled as a fund-raiser, the other is donated to a local charity. The group organizes an annual show.

Suzanne Breslouf
Newton Patchworks
327 Tremont St.
Newton, MA 02158
(617) 527-7110

North Reading

NORTH PARISH QUILTERS meets on the first Thursday of the month, September through June, at the Congregational Church, North Reading. Quilters of all levels of expertise are welcome; annual dues are $10. The Guild hosts an annual quilt show, makes raffle quilts, and offers workshops with guest speakers.

Diana DiPaolo
North Parish Quilters
175 Forest St.
Middleton, MA 01949
(617) 774-6140

MICHIGAN

Battle Creek

CAL-CO QUILTER'S GUILD meets on the second Monday of each month at the Calhoun County Center. Annual dues are $12. Annually the Guild offers a February quilters' retreat and a September quilt show.

Juanita Bogart
Cal-Co Quilter's Guild
22109 Waubascon Rd.
Battle Creek, MI 49017
(616) 963-9443

Detroit

QUILT GUILD OF METRO DETROIT meets eight times a year on the third Tuesday of the month; meetings are held at Christ the King Lutheran Church, 20339 Mack Ave., Grosse Pointe Woods. Annual dues are $10. The Guild hosts a biennial Spring quilt show where a raffle quilt, a juried exhibition, and an exhibition of members' work are featured. The group organizes show-and-tells, lectures, and workshops throughout the year.

Pat Beninati
Quilt Guild of Metro Detroit
27861 Sylvan
Warren, MI 48093
(313) 754-4493

Fremont

TALL PINE QUILTERS meets on the second Thursday of each month at the Congregational Church, Fremont. Anyone interested in quilting is welcome; annual dues are $10. The guild presents quilting demonstrations and quilt displays at the annual city art fair. In addition, it contributes special-interest books to the local public library.

Milly Splitstone
Tall Pine Quilters
2073 Baldwin
Fremont, MI 49412
(616) 924-0629

Grand Rapids

WEST MICHIGAN QUILTER'S GUILD meets on the fourth Tuesday of February, April, September, and November. Meetings are held at the West Christian School in Grand Rapids; annual dues are $7. The group holds a biennial quilt show, organizes occasional educational trips and hosts a quilt picnic each July.

Judy Nayhak
West Michigan Quilter's Guild
9250 Ten Mile Rd. NE
Rockford, MI 49341
(616) 874-9226

Iron Mountain

SPINNING SPOOLS QUILTER'S GUILD meets at 7 pm on the fourth Monday of every month; meetings are held at the Iron Moutain Public Library. Dues are $1 per annum or $5 for life membership. The group collectively makes a quilt every two years; it is currently involved with teaching quilting skills to local high school students. The Guild has also hosted several quilt shows.

Melissa Meyers
Spinning Spools Quilter's Guild
Rt. 1, Box 185
Vulcan, MI 49892
(906) 563-5099

Kalamazoo

KALAMAZOO AREA QUILT GUILD is an umbrella organization for all Kalamazoo area quilt groups. It meets four times a year at the Crossroads Mall Community Room, Portage. Annual dues are $8; members are informed of activities and meetings through a newsletter. The Guild occasionally makes quilts for worthy charities and also holds special classes annually.

Cindy Whittingham-Neill
Kalamazoo Area Quilt Guild
205 Berkeley
Kalamazoo, MI 49007
(616) 388-5274

Lansing

CAPITOL CITY QUILT GUILD meets on the third Thursday of each month at the Valley Court Community Center in East Lansing. Annual dues are $6. A speaker or workshop is featured at each monthly meeting. For its biennial Fall quilt show, the group makes a quilt to raffle at the event; in showless years a quilt is made for charity, often as a subscription quilt.

Ruth Dukelow
Capitol City Quilt Guild
520 N. Fairview
Lansing, MI 48912
(517) 372-4383

Marquette

MARQUETTE COUNTY QUILTERS' ASSOCIATION meets at the Marquette Township Building on the first Wednesday of each month. Annual dues are $1. The group actively participates in charity fund-raising events; a quilt is made and raffled each year for the Association's own fund-raising. The group also hosts a biennial quilt show.

Carole Prisk
Marquette County Quilters'
* Association*
P.O. Box 411
Marquette, MI 49855
(906) 475-4810

Pontiac

QUAINT QUILTERS meets every Tuesday, 9 am-3 pm, at the Bethel United Church of Christ. Meetings serve as informal workshops for working on individual projects. Annual dues are $10. There are occasional lectures and demonstrations, and the group makes one quilt a year collectively which is raffled for charity. The group has held one show so far and hopes to make future shows a biennial event.

Ruth Huntington
Quaint Quilters
c/o Bethel United Church of
* Christ*
6650 Elizabeth Lake Rd.
Pontiac, MI 48054
(313) 673-2880

Saginaw

PIECEMAKER'S QUILT GUILD meets on the third Monday of each month at the Butman-Fish Library, Saginaw. Annual dues are $5. Sponsored are occasional lectures, demonstrations, and an infrequent show. The group makes a quilt to raffle once a year. The Guild has been very involved with the Michigan Quilt Project.

Linda Tesch
Piecemaker's Quilt Guild
1061 Glendale
Saginaw, MI 48603
(517) 799-4140

Sylvania

GATHERING OF QUILTERS GUILD meets on the third Thursday of January, May, and September; meetings are held at the First United Methodist Church, 7000 Erie St., Sylvania. Yearly dues are $7. Among the group's activities is an occasional doll's quilt auction for charity.

Virginia Soss
Gathering of Quilters Guild
P.O. Box 41
Ottawa Lake, MI 49267
(313) 856-2905

West Branch

TGIW-OTLB QUILTERS meets once a week at members' homes. Anyone with a love of quilting is invited to join. The guild participates in an annual folk art show, prepares demonstrations for local festivals, and stitches a fund-raising quilt for the Creative Arts Association.

Nancy Ehinger
TGIW-OTLB Quilters
2831 Highland Dr.
West Branch, MI 48661
(517) 345-2418

MINNESOTA

Bloomington

MINNESOTA QUILTERS, INC., holds daytime and evening meetings once a month. Quilters of all levels of expertise are welcome; annual dues are $15 and include a monthly newsletter and a resource directory of shops, services, and workshops. The guild sponsors an annual quilt show.

Minnesota Quilters, Inc.
5053 Nine Mile Creek Circle
Bloomington, MN 55437
(612) 776-6120

Delano

CALICO QUILTERS meets once a month at the local library. A love of quilting is the only requirement for membership.

Joan Otto
Calico Quilters
417 E. Elm Ave.
Delano, MN 55328
(612) 972-2413

International Falls

NORTHERN LIGHTS QUILTER'S GUILD meets once a month at various locations in the area. All quilters are welcome; annual dues are $5. The Guild hosts a biennial quilt show, makes two raffle quilts each year, donates lap quilts to nursing homes, and assists in the documentation of antique quilts at the County Historical Museum.

Helen Caswell
Northern Lights Quilter's Guild
Rt. 9, Box 518
International Falls, MN 56649
(218) 377-4437

Mankato

DEEP VALLEY QUILTERS meets on the second Thursday or the second Saturday of each month, except during July, August, and December, at the Unitarian Center, Mankato. Anyone with an interest in quilting is invited to join; annual dues are $6. The guild offers workshops and lectures and presents quilting demonstrations at community events.

Marcia T. Schuster
Deep Valley Quilters
R.R. 6, Box 234
Mankato, MN 56001
(507) 625-6314

Spring Grove

PIECEMAKERS QUILTING GUILD OF SPRING GROVE meets on the third Monday of each month at the Spring Grove Hospital. Quilters of all levels of experience are welcome; annual dues are $10. An annual quilt show, workshops, and fundraising projects are among the group's activities.

Mary Deters
Piecemakers Quilting Guild of Spring Grove
Rt. 2
Spring Grove, MN 55974
(507) 498-3993

MISSISSIPPI

Hattiesburg

PINE BELT QUILTERS meets on the third Wednesday of the month at the Extension Conference Room in Hattiesburg. An interest in quilting is the only requirement for membership; annual dues are $10. The guild hosts a biennial quilt show during odd-numbered years and features a guild quilt that is raffled at the show. The group also organizes educational programs and encourages the sharing of ideas at guild meetings.

Martha Ginn
Pine Belt Quilters
909 N. 31st Ave.
Hattiesburg, MS 39402
(601) 264-6884

MISSOURI

Chesterfield

PIECE MILL QUILTERS meets on the first Friday of each month at members' homes. Membership is limited to thirty people who live in the West St. Louis County area; annual dues are $5. The guild hosts an annual quilt show each September which features a raffle quilt, workshops, vendors, a speaker, and a show-and-tell. Members also offer quilting demonstrations at local shopping malls and craft shows.

Karen Compton
Piece Mill Quilters
P.O. Box 653
Chesterfield, MO 63017
(314) 878-0708

Columbia

BOONESLICK TRAIL QUILTER'S GUILD meets on the first Monday of each month at St. Andrew's Lutheran Church, Columbia. Membership is open to anyone with an interest in quilting; annual dues are $10. The Guild hosts an annual quilt show, sponsors workshops and lectures by nationally known speakers, and features a Christmas fund-raising project.

Pam Gainor
Booneslick Trail Quilter's Guild
P.O. Box 542
Columbia, MO 65205
(314) 445-7774

Kansas City

QUILTER'S GUILD OF GREATER KANSAS CITY meets on the second Tuesday of each month at the Roanoke Presbyterian Church, 1617 W. 42nd St. Annual dues are $15. The monthly meeting always features a guest speaker. The group's varied activities include an annual quilt show, demonstrations, exhibitions, and the donation of quilts to worthy charities. To perpetuate the quilting tradition, the Guild's educational committee works directly with the local school system.

Barbara Bruce
Quilter's Guild of Greater Kansas City
P.O. Box 22561
Kansas City, MO 64113
(913) 888-7311

St. Louis

BITS 'N' PIECES meets on the fourth Tuesday of each month, 7:30 pm, at the Germania Savings and Loan Building. An interest in quilting is the only membership criterion, so all levels of quilters are welcome. The group sponsors monthly speakers and other educational events and holds occasional quilt shows to raise money for charities.

Anna Mae Brown
Bits 'n' Pieces
214 Orrick
Kirkwood, MO 63122
(314) 821-3130

CIRCLE IN THE SQUARE QUILTERS is a piecing group that meets at members' houses. Meetings are held on the third Tuesday of the month during January, March, May, and October at the University City Library Auditorium. Annual dues are $8, $7.50 for senior citizens. The group newsletter is issued five times yearly; non-members can subscribe for $2 per annum. A workshop or lecture is offered at each meeting. The group makes a fund-raising quilt about once every nine months; in addition, one or two quilts are made and donated to charities every year.

Pat Owoc
Circle in the Square Quilters
2508 Bremerton
St. Louis, MO 63144
(314) 968-1393

THIMBLE AND THREAD QUILT CLUB meets on the second Friday of the month at the fellowship hall of Webster Groves Presbyterian Church. Members range from very experienced quiltmakers to beginners. Non-members are welcome to attend meetings as a visitor twice, paying a visitor fee of $1 each time, and then they must become members if they wish to attend subsequent meetings. Annual dues are $10. A quilt show for members' work is held approximately once a year. Each Spring, a speaker/ teacher with a national reputation visits the guild to lecture and lead a workshop.

Barbara Gambrel
Thimble and Thread Quilt Club
P.O. Box 5201
St. Louis, MO 63139
(314) 394-3562

Springfield

OZARK PIECEMAKERS QUILT GUILD meets at 9:30 am on the fourth Thursday of the month; meetings are held at Christ Episcopal Church, 601 E. Walnut. Annual dues are $8 and include a monthly newsletter. In addition to making one fund-raising quilt each year, the Guild pieces quilts for the local children's home. The group is very involved with Public Television, often giving demonstrations and sponsoring shows. The Guild holds a quilt show in the first week of October each year where the fund-raising quilt is raffled. Every year the group brings in an outside teacher to lecture and lead a workshop. It also organizes annual bus trips to the Paducah and Kansas City quilt shows as well as occasional trips to shows in Arkansas.

Toni Smith
Ozark Piecemakers Quilt Guild
521 S. Forest Ct.
Springfield, MO 65806
(417) 866-7809

MONTANA

Bozeman

QUILTER'S ART GUILD OF THE NORTHERN ROCKIES meets four times a year at various locations in the area. Annual membership dues are $10. The Guild sponsors an annual quilt workshop, distributes a newsletter, and promotes other educational activities.

Quilter's Art Guild of the
*   Northern Rockies*
P.O. Box 4117
Bozeman, MT 59772
(406) 587-8213

Great Falls

FALLS QUILT GUILD meets once a month at 1004 Central Ave., Great Falls. An interest in quilting is the only requirement for membership; annual dues are nominal. The Guild organizes a biennial quilt show.

Falls Quilt Guild
P.O. Box 6592
Great Falls, MT 59406
(406) 727-8799

Helena

HELENA QUILTER'S GUILD meets once a month at St. Paul's United Methodist Church.

Members are required to have an interest in quilts and quilting; annual dues are nominal. The Guild sponsors a quilt show every eighteen months and makes a quilt to be raffled at this show.

Helena Quilter's Guild
P.O. Box 429
Helena, MT 59601
(406) 442-2731

NEBRASKA

Beatrice

BEATRICE QUILTER'S GUILD holds a business meeting on the first Tuesday of each month and a workshop meeting on the last Tuesday of each month in the meeting room at the Bonanza Restaurant. Anyone who is interested in promoting and preserving the art of quilting is welcome; annual dues are $3. An annual quilt show, hosted by the Guild each October, features a raffle quilt made by Guild members. Other activities include hands-on demonstrations, lectures, and videos at the workshop meetings.

Marilyn Maurstad
Beatrice Quilter's Guild
416 N. 5th St.
Beatrice, NE 68310
(402) 223-5937

Columbus

CALICO QUILT CLUB meets once a month at the Columbus Public Library. Only an interest in quilting and needlecraft is required for membership. The guild hosts an annual quilt show, makes raffle quilts, and donates books and tapes to the Columbus Library.

Calico Quilt Club
Rt. 1, Box 18
Richland, NE 68657
(402) 564-5763

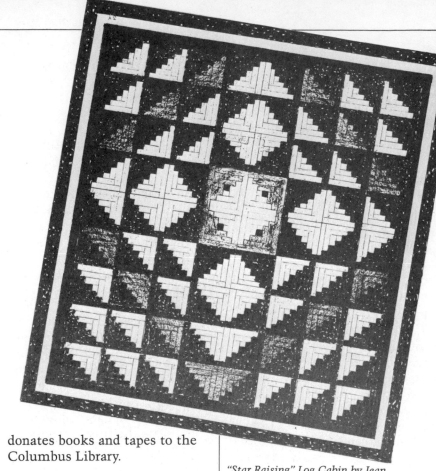

"Star Raising" Log Cabin by Jean Younkin and Joan Waldman, 1985.

Fremont

PRAIRIE PIECEMAKERS meets once a month, except during July and December, at a local city-owned facility. The group is made up of women interested in needle-work; annual dues are $6. The guild hosts a biennial quilt show.

Prairie Piecemakers
P.O. Box 1202
Fremont, NE 68025
(402) 721-2733

Lincoln

LINCOLN QUILTERS GUILD meets on the second Monday of the month, except in June, July, August, and December. Meetings are held at the Westminster Presbyterian Church; annual dues are $10. The group is involved in the documentation of quilts across the state; this work is assisted by a federal grant. The Guild holds four workshops each year and offers numerous lectures. It sponsors a biennial Fall quilt show and participates in charity work by making quilts and either donating or raffling them.

Jo Baxter
Lincoln Quilters Guild
6001 Southdale Rd.
Lincoln, NE 68516
(402) 423-1059

North Platt

NEBRASKA STATE QUILT GUILD meets once a year, in July, in North Platt. Annual dues are $10. In conjunction with its annual meeting, the Guild sponsors a show with workshops, a merchant's mall, a show-and-tell, exhibitions, and lectures. To keep its members informed, it publishes a quarterly newsletter. The group is currently planning a quilter's symposium to be held in Omaha.

Sara Dillow
Nebraska State Quilt Guild
2228 Teakwood Dr.
Fremont, NE 68025
(402) 727-5138

Omaha

OMAHA QUILTER'S GUILD meets on the second Tuesday of each month, except during June, July, and August. Anyone interested in any aspect of quilting is invited to join. The Guild sponsors an annual quilt show, makes raffle quilts, organizes field trips, and hosts nationally recognized quilters for lectures and workshops.

Omaha Quilter's Guild
P.O. Box 24614
Omaha, NE 68124
(402) 895-2225

Waterloo

COTTONWOOD QUILTERS OF ELKHORN meets at 7:30 pm on the fourth Monday of each month; meetings are held at the United Presbyterian Church, Waterloo. Annual dues are $6. The guild invites guest speakers three times annually, holds workshops every month, and sponsors an annual quilt show.

The group donates several quilts each year to worthy causes.

Debbie Titus
Cottonwood Quilters of Elkhorn
P.O. Box 27
Elkhorn, NE 68022
(402) 333-5212

NEVADA

Henderson

DESERT QUILTERS meets on the second Wednesday of the month at 3232 Bluebird St. There is also a meeting at 1 pm on the last Thursday of the month at the Rainbow Craft Shop. Annual dues are $6. The group holds monthly workshops and an annual two day symposium, and it makes and donates quilts to local charities. The group participates in the local Jayccccs Fair and in the Annual Hobby Show at Meadows Mall in the first week of August.

Kate Nelson
Desert Quilters
333 Esquina St.
Henderson, NV 80195
(702) 458-8053

Reno

TRUCKEE MEADOWS QUILTERS meets at 9:30 am on the second and fourth Fridays of each month and again at 7 pm on the first and third Mondays. The group meets at the First Federal Savings Building in S. Virginia St. Annual dues are $12. Two of the monthly meetings are reserved for workshops, lectures, or demonstrations; socializing and group business are covered at the other two. The group makes a quilt for charity annually and occa-

sionally holds a Spring quilt show.

Pearl Cartwright
Truckee Meadows Quilters
Box 5502
Reno, NV 89513
(702) 747-5378

NEW HAMPSHIRE

Peterborough

MONADNOCK QUILTER'S GUILD meets on the third Friday of every month, except December, at the Peterborough Library. Quilters of all levels of experience are welcome, but members must be willing to learn and share with others; annual dues are $8. The Guild offers quilting demonstrations at local crafts events, makes raffle quilts, sponsors well-known quilters at Guild workshops, and hosts occasional quilt shows.

Monadnock Quilter's Guild
P.O. Box 241
Peterborough, NH 03458
(603) 924-3247

Rochester

COUNTRY ROADS QUILT GUILD meets on the second Monday of each month, 7 pm, at the Profile Bank, Rochester. Membership is open to all who are interested in the art of quilting; annual dues are $12. The Guild is involved in several community projects such as donating quilts to local fire victims and raffling a quilt to benefit charitable organizations. Members also participate in the annual Somersworth Children's Festival.

Marilyn Wallace
Country Roads Quilt Guild
P.O. Box 1332
Rochester, NH 03867
(603) 332-6644

Wolfeboro

LADIES OF THE LAKES QUILTER'S GUILD meets once a month except in January, July, and August. The only criterion necessary for membership is an appreciation of quilting; quilters of all levels of expertise are welcome. Annual dues are $10. Among the activities sponsored is an annual raffle as well as a children's quilt-block contest and a children's workshop. The Guild also holds adult quilt-block contests as a means of collecting blocks for quilts to raffle or donate to worthy charities.

Marie Doubleday
Ladies of the Lakes Quilter's
* Guild*
P.O. Box 552
Wolfeboro, NH 03894
(603) 859-6911

NEW JERSEY

Bordentown

TURTLE CREEK QUILTERS GUILD meets at 2 pm on the third Sunday of the month at the Bordentown Township Northern Community Park; annual dues are $12. The Guild sponsors occasional workshops and lectures, it has made several charity quilts, and it participates in local quilt shows. To keep members informed of activities, the Guild publishes a newsletter two or three times a year.

Ronnie Shea
Turtle Creek Quilters Guild
22 Spruce Ave.
Bordentown, NJ 08505
(609) 766-3102

Chatham

GARDEN STATE QUILTERS meets on the second Tuesday of each month, except July and August, at St. Paul's Church, Chatham. Quilters of all levels of expertise are invited to join; annual dues are $15. The Guild, just recently organized, hopes to become actively involved in quilting events in the near future.

Betty Lou Wilder
Garden State Quilters
Llewellyn Park
West Orange, NJ 07052
(201) 736-0138

"The Mandarin's Garden" by Jean V. Johnson, 1983.

"Starshine" by Judy B. Dales.

Cherry Hill

BARCLAY FARMSTEAD QUILTERS holds a business meeting on the first Monday of the month and quilting meetings every Tuesday morning at the Barclay Farmstead. Members must be willing to devote their time to working on guild projects. The group hosts a biennial quilt show and makes custom quilts and quilted gift items to benefit the Barclay Farmstead.

Barclay Farmstead Quilters
114 Barclay Ln.
Cherry Hill, NJ 08034
(609) 429-3791

Gloucester City

LOVE APPLE QUILTERS meets from 8 to 10 pm on the second Tuesday of each month; meetings are held at the Highland Park Volunteer Fire Hall, Highland Blvd. Annual dues are $10, $7 for senior citizens. Dues include a subscription to the group's quarterly newsletter. The group hosts a biennial October quilt show at the National Guard Armory, Grove St., Cherry Hill. There are frequent lectures and mini-workshops; occasionally there are bus trips. The group makes several quilts each year. One is raffled to bring in extra funds; the others are donated to worthy causes.

Anne Donofry
Love Apple Quilters
1351 71st Ave.
Philadelphia, PA 19126
(215) 927-0475

Manalapan

MOLLY PITCHER STITCHERS meets on the second Monday of each month at the Old Tennent Church, Manalapan. Annual dues are $10. Activities include occasional lectures, workshops, and trips to nearby shows. The group is currently organizing a show.

Eleanor Vasso
Molly Pitcher Stitchers
62 Thomas Dr.
Manalapan, NJ 07726
(201) 446-1144

Waldwick

BROWNSTONE QUILTERS meets on the first Friday of each month at the Waldwick Ambulance Building. Anyone who expresses an interest in quilting is welcome; annual dues are $15. The guild offers workshops, demonstrations, and lectures and has also sponsored bus trips to quilt shows.

Maureen Papola
Brownstone Quilters
P.O. Box 228
Waldwick, NJ 07463
(201) 652-8638

Willingboro

GRAPEVINE QUILTERS meets on the first Tuesday of each month at the Florence Township Municipal Building. Quilters of all levels of skill are welcome; annual dues are $5. Guild members work collectively on projects as a means of exchanging skills and learning new techniques.

Laurie Heller
Grapevine Quilters
11 Minstrel Ln.
Willingboro, NJ 08046
(609) 835-2315

NEW MEXICO

Albuquerque

NEW MEXICO QUILTER'S ASSOCIATION meets on the last Monday of the month either at the Church of Jesus Christ of the Latter Day Saints or at St. Paul's Methodist Church. Membership is open to all persons interested in quilting; annual dues are $10. The guild hosts an annual non-competitive quilt show at the State Fair. Members also stitch a balloon quilt each year to be raffled at the International Balloon Festival in Albuquerque.

Gail Garber
New Mexico Quilter's
*   Association*
P.O. Box 20562
Albuquerque, NM 87154
(505) 892-3354

NEW YORK

Arkville

CATSKILL MOUNTAIN QUILTER'S GUILD meets every Monday, 10 am, at the Catskill Cultural Center, Arkville. Basic quilting skills are the only requirement for membership. The Guild sponsors an annual quilt show, presents workshops and demonstrations, and makes friendship quilts.

Nancy Smith
Catskill Mountain Quilter's
*   Guild*
P.O. Box 213
Pine Hill, NY 12465
(914) 254-5517

Blauvelt

HERITAGE QUILTERS OF THE HUDSON PALISADES meets on the second Wednesday of each month, except July and August, at the Greenbush Presbyterian Church, Blauvelt. Anyone who wishes to broaden her knowledge of quilting is welcome; annual dues are $12. The guild offers workshops, hosts a biennial quilt show with the Rockland County Community College Foundation, and presents smaller exhibits, lectures, and hands-on projects to educate the public.

Joyce Murrin
Heritage Quilters of the Hudson
*   Palisades*
19 Cairngorm Rd.
New City, NY 10956
(914) 638-0350

Delmar

Q.U.I.L.T. meets once a month, September through June, at a church in Delmar. An interest in the craft of quilting and a desire to improve skills and share ideas are the requirements for membership. Activities include monthly programs to teach new techniques and to show artists' interpretations of traditional or contemporary quilt designs. Members also make a quilt annually as a fund-raising project.

Grace Weatherley
Q.U.I.L.T.
2209 Western Ave.
Guilderland, NY 12084
(518) 456-5674

Fulton

LAKE COUNTRY QUILT GUILD meets on the second Wednesday of the month at the Volney School, Route 3, Fulton. Membership is open to anyone with an interest in quilting; annual dues are $15. The Guild presents lectures and workshops on all aspects of quilting. Members also donate quilts to the Burn Unit of Upstate Medical Center and to the pediatric units at three area hospitals.

Elizabeth Granholm
Lake Country Quilt Guild
R.D. 7
Oswego, NY 13126
(315) 343-5916

Merrick

LONG ISLAND QUILTER'S SOCIETY meets once a month, October through July, at the United Methodist Church, Merrick. Quilters of all levels of experience are invited to join; annual dues are $18. The guild hosts an annual convention, offers workshops and bus trips, and has recently completed fifty-four quilts for the Ronald McDonald House.

Linda Denner
Long Island Quilter's Society
P.O. Box 3020
Garden City, NY 11530
(516) 747-5227

North Syracuse

PLANK ROAD QUILTER'S GUILD meets on the second and fourth Wednesdays of each month at Andrews Memorial Church, North Syracuse. Quilters of all levels of expertise are invited to join; annual dues are $10. The Guild sponsors an annual quilt raffle whose proceeds are donated to local organizations in need of extra funds.

Linda Meyer
Plank Road Quilter's Guild
8046 Crockett Dr.
Clay, NY 13041
(315) 699-8574

Rochester

GENESEE VALLEY QUILT CLUB meets on the second Thursday of the month, September through June, at the Masonic Auditorium, Rochester. All quilters are welcome, but members must be willing to help others with their projects; annual dues are $2. The guild has hosted an annual quilt show ever since it was founded in 1936.

Peg Ames
Genesee Valley Quilt Club
225 Lanning Rd.
Honeoye Falls, NY 14472
(716) 624-2533

Schenectady

Q.U.I.L.T.S. (Quilters United in Learning Together, Schenectady) meets on the first Thursday of the month, 7 pm, at the Unitarian Church in Schenectady. Membership is open to anyone interested in quilting; annual dues are nominal. The guild hosts a quilt show every two years and donates a portion of the proceeds to a charitable cause. Workshops, lectures by well-known artists, and a contest for guild members are just some of the group's other activities.

Dee Albert
Q.U.I.L.T.S.
27 Cresthaven Ave.
Albany, NY 12205
(518) 456-7603

Smithtown

SMITHTOWN STITCHERS meets on the second Monday of the month at Nesaquake Junior High School, Smithtown. Quilters of all levels of experience are welcome; annual dues are $10. The guild organizes a "quilt extravaganza" every two years and stitches a raffle quilt each year.

Smithtown Stitchers
P.O. Box 311
Smithtown, NY 11787
(516) 724-5794

Somers

NORTHERN STAR QUILTER'S GUILD LTD., meets on the third Tuesday of the month at the Somers Intermediate School. Anyone with a genuine interest in quilting is welcome. The Guild sponsors a large quilt show each May.

Northern Star Quilter's Guild, Ltd.
P.O. Box 232
Somers, NY 10589
(914) 232-4279

Staten Island

STATEN ISLAND QUILTER'S GUILD meets on the fourth Friday of the month, 10 am, at the New Dorp Moravian Church. Members must have a knowledge of basic quilting skills; annual dues are $12. The Guild hosts a quilt show every other year and

Staten Island Quilter's Guild exhibit. Photo by Irving Silverstein.

has made over fifty quilts for the Ronald McDonald House in Manhattan.

Suzanne Appelman
Staten Island Quilter's Guild
332 Hillbrook Dr.
Staten Island, NY 10305
(718) 273-9081

Warwick

WARWICK VALLEY QUILTER'S GUILD meets on the second and fourth Thursday of each month at Christ Church, Warwick. Membership is open to quilters of all levels of ability; annual dues are $10. The Guild sponsors a biennial quilt show which features a raffle quilt made by Guild members.

"A Bounty of Quilts", Warwick Valley Quilt Guild, 1986.

Warwick Valley Quilter's Guild
P.O. Box 23
Warwick, NY 10990
(201) 764-6556

NORTH CAROLINA

Asheville

BEAUCATCHER QUILTERS meets every Thursday, 10:30 am, at the North Ashcville Community Center. Anyone interested in quilting, whether a beginner or an expert, is welcome; annual dues are $6. The guild participates in the Bel Cher Quilt Show and the Western North Carolina Quilter's Guild Quilt Show. Members also make an annual raffle quilt for the benefit of the University of North Carolina.

Beaucatcher Quilters
14 Edgemont Rd.
Asheville, NC 28801
(704) 252-1471

Calabash

CAROLINA SHORES QUILTER'S GUILD meets once a month at a local clubhouse. All quilters from the Carolina Shores area are welcome to join; annual dues are $5. The Guild has recently completed its first group project, a raffle quilt, which will help to raise funds for the local volunteer fire department and rescue squad.

Chris Alcorn
Carolina Shores Quilter's Guild
Carolina Shores, 22 Calabash Dr.
Calabash, NC 28459
(919) 579-3459

Fayetteville

TARHEEL QUILTER'S GUILD meets on the third Sunday of each month at the Westminster Presbyterian Church, Fayetteville. Quilters of all levels of ability are welcome; annual dues are $8. The Guild hosts an annual quilt show, sponsors workshops, and is involved in many community activities.

Tarheel Quilt Guild raffle quilt, 1986.

Penelope Snyder
Tarheel Quilter's Guild
P.O. Box 36253
Fayetteville, NC 28303
(919) 484-4412

Greensboro

PIEDMONT QUILTER'S GUILD
meets on the second Thursday
of each month, 7 pm, at the
Starmount Presbyterian Church,
Greensboro. Quilters of all
levels of expertise are welcome;
annual dues are $10. The Guild
is a co-sponsor of the North
Carolina Quilt Symposium.
Members make lap quilts for
nursing home residents and
baby quilts for the Children's
Home Society. Other activities
include participation in various
community events and giving
quilt talks at local schools.

Pamela Smith
Piedmont Quilter's Guild
P.O. Box 10673, Friendly
*   Center Sta.*
Greensboro, NC 27404
(919) 292-6978

Hendersonville

**WESTERN NORTH CAROLINA
QUILTER'S GUILD** meets on the
third Thursday of the month at
the Blue Ridge Technical College in the evenings and at the
Mud Creek Church during the
day. Only an interest in quilting
is required for membership; annual dues are $6. The Guild par-
ticipates in the Harvest of
Quilts Show each October in
Hendersonville.

Western North Carolina
*   Quilter's Guild*
P.O. Box 3121
Hendersonville, NC 28793
(704) 697-2600

Hickory

CATAWBA VALLEY QUILTER'S GUILD
meets on the second Thursday
of the month at the Holy Trinity Lutheran Church, Hickory.
Quilters of all levels of ability
interested in preserving the art
of quilting are welcome. The
Guild offers public quilting
demonstrations, classes, and
workshops.

Catawba Valley Quilter's Guild
1880 6th St. NW
Hickory, NC 28601
(704) 324-8932

Morehead City

CRYSTAL COAST QUILTER'S GUILD
meets on the third Thursday of
each month at the Webb
Library, Morehead City. Quilters
of all levels of expertise are
welcome; annual dues are $12.
An annual quilt show held in
May and a fund-raising raffle
quilt are among the Guild's
many activities.

Crystal Coast Quilter's Guild
P.O. Box 1819
Morehead City, NC 28557
(919) 728-4739

Washington

PAMLICO RIVER QUILTERS' GUILD
offers day meetings on the second and fourth Wednesdays of
the month, 10 am, at members'
homes, and evening meetings
on the second Monday of the
month, 7:30 pm, at the East
Haven Apartment social room.
A Board of Directors meets on
the first Monday of the month,
7 pm, in the study room of
Brown Library, Washington. Any
person with an interest in
quilting and who resides in the
Pamlico River or Pamlico Sound
region is welcome to join; an-

nual dues are minimal. The
Guild's activities include an annual quilt show, workshops for
members, making raffle quilts,
and making quilts for the
Ronald McDonald House. The
Guild also hosts an annual
quilt-in and salad-bar lunch for
its own members and for
members of other guilds in the
area.

Margot Hicking
Pamlico River Quilters' Guild
P.O. Box 905
Washington, NC 27889
(919) 946-1727

Winston-Salem

**FORSYTH PIECER'S AND QUILTER'S
GUILD** meets on the second
Monday of each month, 7:30
pm, at the Wesley United
Methodist Church, Winston-
Salem. The only requirement
for membership is a love of
quilting; annual dues are $10.
The Guild organizes an annual
quilt show, sponsors a symposium, presents quilting
demonstrations to the general
public, and makes raffle quilts
as fund-raisers.

Fannye Hall
Forsyth Piecer's and Quilter's
*   Guild*
P.O. Box 10666, Salem Sta.
Winston-Salem, NC 27108
(919) 724-0307

NORTH DAKOTA

Fargo

**QUILTERS GUILD OF NORTH
DAKOTA, INC.,** meets on the third
Saturday of each month at the
Westacre Community Room.
Annual dues are $10. Workshops
are held in the mornings before

meetings. The Guild makes a raffle quilt annually, gives occasional public demonstrations, has a show at Westacre each September, and publishes a monthly newsletter. The group is very much involved with community service work for local charities.

Ednabelle Kuehl
Quilters Guild of North Dakota, Inc.
P.O. Box 2662
Fargo, ND 58108
(218) 233-1226

Grand Forks

THE NORTH STAR QUILTER'S GUILD meets on the first Saturday of the month in the Community Room at the Columbia Mall. Membership is open to all persons interested in quilting; annual dues are $5, $3 for senior citizens. An additional $3 is required if members wish to receive the Guild's newsletter. Members participate in the annual quilt show at the Columbia Mall every March and at many other community festivals and events.

North Star Quilter's Guild
P.O. Box 814
Grand Forks, ND 58206
(701) 775-8587

Williston

DAKOTA PRAIRIE QUILTERS' GUILD meets the second Saturday of each month, except July and August, 1 pm, at the Williston Community Library. Quilters of all levels of experience are welcome; annual dues for the first year are $10, $5 thereafter. The Guild participates in local art shows each year and also hosts occasional quilt exhibitions. Raffle quilts, baby quilts

for expectant mothers, friendship quilts, and a Williston Centennial Quilt are just some of the projects this group has undertaken.

Ginger Mitchell
Dakota Prairie Quilters' Guild
1216 8th Ave. NW
Williston, ND 58801
(701) 572-5389

OHIO

Brimfield

PORTAGE PATCHERS QUILT GUILD meets on the third Wednesday of the month at the Kelso House, Brimfield. Membership is open to anyone interested in the art of quilting; annual dues are $10. Guild activities include workshops, lectures, slide presentations, and making raffle quilts. The Guild is participating in the Ohio Quilt Research Project.

Portage Patchers Quilt Guild raffle quilt, 1986.

Susan Meindl
Portage Patchers Quilt Guild
1055 Merydith St.
Kent, OH 44240
(216) 678-5852

Chillicothe

Freda Stewart with "Sampler."

Helen Dailey with "Interlocked Squares."

ROSS COUNTY QUILTER'S GUILD meets once a month, with smaller groups meeting twice a month to quilt. Anyone with a love of quilts and quilting is welcome; annual dues are nominal. The Guild participates in an annual county show, demonstrates quilting at local events, and makes a yearly raffle quilt.

Ross County Quilter's Guild
9 Leeds Rd.
Chillicothe, OH 45601
(614) 773-5927

Cincinnati

OHIO VALLEY QUILTERS GUILD
meets at 7:30 pm on the first
Tuesday of each month; meetings are held at the Montgomery Presbyterian Church.
Annual dues are $8. The Guild
conducts a quilter's retreat each
October, an annual three-day
seminar, and an occasional
show. Every meeting features a
lecture or a workshop; the group
makes comforters for local institutions and undertakes other
charitable projects.

Mary Stegman
Ohio Valley Quilters Guild
7332 Zig Zag Ln.
Cincinnati, OH 45242
(513) 791-0387

Delaware

**DELAWARE PIECEMAKERS QUILT
GUILD** meets on the last Monday of each month; meetings
are held at the Liberty Community Center, London Rd.,
Delaware. Since the group
formed only recently, there are
no dues as such yet: a collection
is taken at each meeting to
cover costs. The Guild organizes
an annual quilt show each July.

Rose Fitzgerald
Delaware Piecemakers Quilt
* Guild*
644 Congress Ct.
Delaware, OH 43015
(614) 363-3677

Greenville

TOWNE SQUARES QUILT CLUB
meets on the third Tuesday of
the month at the Brickroom
Brethren Home. Quilters of all
levels of ability are welcome.
The group hosts an annual quilt
show, organizes a quilting field
trip each year, and invites a

well-known teacher to speak to
guild members.

Leola Crowell
Towne Squares Quilt Club
730 E. Water St.
Greenville, OH 45331
(513) 548-7084

Millbury

THE GATHERING OF QUILTERS
meets on the third Monday of
each month. Anyone interested
in quilting can become a
member, but membership is
limited to twelve. The annual
membership fee is $12. The
group makes charity quilts for
worthy organizations to raffle or
auction. It also sponsors occasional quilting seminars.

Sue Smith
The Gathering of Quilters
29495 Millbury Rd.
Millbury, OH 43447
(419) 836-9285

North Royalton

KEEP US IN STITCHES QUILTERS
meets at 7 pm on the third
Monday of each month;
meetings are held in the North
Royalton Library. Annual dues
are $10. Activities include an
extensive lecture and workshop
program, hosting a biennial
Spring quilt show, and making a
charity quilt to be donated or
raffled. Many activities occur
informally outside the meetings
with small groups of members
meeting in each others' homes
to quilt together.

Jan Burgwinkle
Keep Us In Stitches Quilters
5814 Allanwood Rd.
Parma, OH 44129
(216) 845-6695

Ravenna

CALICO HEARTS QUILT GUILD
meets on the first Wednesday of
each month at a local elementary school. Additional
meetings are held during the
month at members' homes.
New members are required to
have a beginner's knowledge of
quilting; annual dues are $10.
Activities include donating
quilts to the Ronald McDonald
House, sponsoring lectures and
workshops that feature nationally known quilting
teachers, making a raffle quilt,
and participating in the Ohio
Quilt Research Project. The
Guild is also searching for a
sister Guild in a foreign country
with whom they hope to
establish an international
quilting relationship.

Diana Smicklevich
Calico Hearts Quilt Guild
263 Jefferson St.
Ravenna, OH 44266
(216) 297-9277

Streetsboro

STREETSBORO QUILTER'S GUILD
meets twice a month at the
Streetsboro United Methodist
Church. Quilters of all levels of
experience are welcome; membership, however, is limited to
thirty. Annual dues are $10. The
Guild hosts an annual show
each October.

Streetsboro Quilter's Guild
4217 Dudley Rd.
Mantua, OH 44255
(216) 274-2427

Versailles

QUILT & SHARE CLUB meets on
the first Thursday of the month
at the Versailles Town House.
Some quilting experience is re-

quired for membership; annual dues are $3. The guild invites a well-known speaker or teacher to its annual seminar, raffles quilts as fund-raisers, and donates quilting books to the local library.

Rosemarie Pierron
Quilt & Share Club
135 Virginia St.
Versailles, OH 45380
(513) 526-3549

Wilmington

CLINTON COUNTY QUILT ASSOCIATION meets on the first Thursday of each month at the Friendly Center, Wilmington. Annual dues are $2. Every second meeting features a lecture, workshop, or demonstration. Each September, the group hosts a show at the Corn Festival, where a fund-raising quilt is raffled.

Anne Lynch
Clinton County Quilt
　Association
3235 Stone Rd.
Sabina, OH 45169
(513) 584-4179

Worthington

QUINTESSENTIAL QUILTERS meets on the second Monday of the month, September through June, at the Lord of Life Lutheran Church, Worthington. Anyone interested in quilts and quilting is welcome, but members are required to join the NQA; annual dues are $10. The guild's primary goal is to share quilting knowledge. An annual workshop which features a nationally recognized quilting teacher is the group's main activity.

Ellen Hess
Quintessential Quilters
7393 Rings Rd.
Amlin, OH 43002
(614) 876-4284

OKLAHOMA

Bartlesville

JUBILEE QUILT GUILD meets on the second Friday of the month at the First Church of the Nazarene, Bartlesville. Quilters of all levels of experience are welcome; annual dues are $10. The group hosts a bazaar each Fall for which members make a quilt to be raffled.

Ruth Cozad
Jubilee Quilt Guild
1601 SE Whitney Ln.
Bartlesville, OK 74006
(918) 335-3861

Clinton

WESTERN OKLAHOMA QUILTER'S GUILD meets once a month in Clinton. Membership dues are nominal. The Guild makes fund-raising quilts to benefit local charities.

Janet Bonny
Western Oklahoma Quilter's
　Guild
Box 595
Burns Flat, OK 73624

Oklahoma City

CENTRAL OKLAHOMA QUILTER'S GUILD, INC., meets on the fourth Thursday of each month at the Antioch Christian Church, 119th and S. Portland, Oklahoma City. Anyone with an interest in quilting is welcome to join. The group

hosts quilt shows and exhibitions at art galleries and museums and is involved in a heritage project and the Kansas City Block project.

Pat Higgins
Central Oklahoma Quilter's
　Guild, Inc.
P.O. Box 23916
Oklahoma City, OK 73123
(405) 364-5451

OREGON

Albany

WILLAMETTE VALLEY QUILT GUILD meets once a week at a local church. Anyone with a love of quilting is welcome; weekly dues are $1.25, most of which is donated to the church where the group meets. The Guild offers quilting demonstrations at community functions and donates quilting books to the local library.

Willamette Valley Quilt Guild
1221 SW Calapooia
Albany, OR 97321
(503) 926-7916

Garibaldi

TILLAMOOK COUNTY QUILTERS meets on the third Thursday of the month at the Miami Cove Grange Hall, Garibaldi. The guild welcomes anyone interested in any aspect of quiltmaking and encourages mutual support among its members. Activities include an annual quilt show, several group projects, and assisting the County Museum with quilts for its displays.

Tillamook County Quilters
6735 Tillamook Ave.
Bay City, OR 97107
(503) 377-2342

Grants Pass

MOUNTAIN STARS QUILTER'S GUILD hosts four business meetings per year. Anyone interested in any aspect of quilting and who lives in the southern Oregon or northern California area is welcome; annual dues are $5. The group offers numerous classes featuring well-known quilting instructors and makes several quilts each year to benefit various charities.

Joyce Coulter
Mountain Stars Quilter's Guild
201 Hitching Post Rd.
Grants Pass, OR 97526
(503) 476-0050

Jacksonville

"Medford Centennial Train Quilt",
Jacksonville Museum Quilters, 1985.

JACKSONVILLE MUSEUM QUILTERS meets every Wesnesday and Thursday at 9 am. A desire to learn to quilt and to help maintain and improve the quilt collection at the Jacksonville Museum are the only criteria for joining the group. An annual quilt show held during July is sponsored by the guild to raise money for supplies and learning materials.

Dora Scheidecker
Jacksonville Museum Quilters
United States Hotel
California St., P.O. Box 59
Jacksonville, OR 97530
(503) 899-7009

Portland

COLUMBIA-WILLAMETTE QUILT STUDY GROUP meets once a month, October through July, usually in members' homes. Membership is open to all with an interest in quilts and with a desire to learn more about the art of quilting. Membership fees are $25 annually or $3 per meeting for guests. The guild is primarily a study group whose activities have included producing a quilt show; touring galleries, exhibitions, and private collections; and hosting lecturers.

Columbia-Willamette Quilt
  Study Group
P.O. Box 10212
Portland, OR 97210
(503) 292-6350

NORTHWEST QUILTERS, INC., meets on the first Monday of each month in the Selwood Community Center. The group holds a non-juried quilt show at Portland State University each March. The show includes an eight-day symposium with a different speaker each day. Annual dues are $7 including a subscription to *Patchwork* for $3 a year. The group sponsors workshops, public demonstrations, and occasional classes for beginners.

Patricia Evans
Northwest Quilters, Inc.
P.O. Box 3405
Portland, OR 97218
(503) 472-2494

PENNSYLVANIA

Annville

LEBANON QUILTER'S GUILD meets on the second Monday of the month at the South Lebanon Elementary School. Membership is open to quilters of all levels of experience, annual dues are $10. The Guild hosts an annual quilt show, raffles quilts for the benefit of worthy charities, and donates quilts to various organizations.

Jo Lynn Gerber
Lebanon Quilter's Guild
1025 Willow Dr.
Annville, PA 17003
(717) 867-5156

Boalsburg

CENTER PIECES holds general meetings four times a year, with smaller interest groups meeting about once a month. Quilters of all levels of expertise are welcome and are encouraged, but not required, to join the NQA; annual dues are $3. The group demonstrates quilting at local arts and agricultural festivals and has sponsored workshops and lectures.

Becky Shirer
Center Pieces
P.O. Box 657
Boalsburg, PA 16827
(814) 237-6009

Carlisle

LETORT QUILTERS meet September through May on the first Sunday of the month at 2 pm, and the third Monday of the month at 1 pm, at the First Church of Christ, Carlisle. Membership is open to quilters of all levels of experience; an-nual dues are $18, which includes membership in the NQA. Activities include workshops, group projects, hosting guest speakers, quilt shows, raffle quilts, and other fund-raising projects.

Julianne Bruetsch
LeTort Quilters
P.O. Box 372
Carlisle, PA 17013
(717) 766-5199

LeMoyne

LEMOYNE STAR QUILTERS meets on the first, third, and fifth Thursday of each month, except December, at the Grace United Methodist Church, LeMoyne. Quilters of all levels of expertise are welcome; annual guild dues are $8 and annual NQA dues are $10. The guild offers classes to its members on old and new techniques and an all-day Saturday workshop to keep members informed of new ideas.

Jewel Stailey
LeMoyne Star Quilters
Box 52F, R.D. 1
Newport, PA 17074
(717) 567-9770

Philadelphia

WILD GEESE QUILTERS meets at members' homes on the third Wednesday of each month. Membership is open to all quilters; annual dues are $10. Guild activities include an ex-hibition of members' work held every other year, plus numerous group projects and workshops. Recently, Wild Geese Quilters won the $1,000 prize in the 1986 Laura Ashley Quilt Contest (*see below*).

Tina Gravatt
Wild Geese Quilters
1308 E. Columbia Ave.
Philadelphia, PA 19125
(215) 423-7338 or
(215) 423-9669

RHODE ISLAND

Pawcatuck

NINIGRET QUILTERS meets on the second Wednesday of the month at the Pawcatuck Neighborhood Center, Pawcatuck. Quilters of all levels of experience are welcome. The guild hosts a biennial quilt show, makes raffle quilts, offers workshops and lectures by nationally recognized quilters, and helps to promote quilting at local festivals.

Ninigret Quilters
P.O. Box 475
Westerly, RI 02891
(401) 322-7906

Portsmouth

QUILTERS BY THE SEA meets on the first Thursday of the month at the Portsmouth Middle School. Membership is open to quilters of all levels of expertise; annual dues are $5. The guild hosts an annual quilt show and has completed several fund-raising quilts for charitable causes.

Helen Babcock
Quilters by the Sea
P.O. Box 708
Portsmouth, RI 02871
(401) 624-9873

SOUTH CAROLINA

Landrum

LANDRUM LIBRARY QUILTERS meets on the second Thursday of the month at the Landrum Library Building. The group is sponsored by the Friends of the Library and there are no dues as such. There is an annual $8 charge for the monthly newsletter. Meetings are open to the public, and many feature a visiting speaker or a workshop. There is a show-and-tell every other month. Members participate in the Hendersonville show every year and occasionally make a group quilt to auction as a fund-raiser for the group and for the Friends of the Library.

Ruth Farrow
Landrum Library Quilters
400 Rutherford Rd.
Landrum, SC 29356
(803) 457-2218

Columbia

LOGAN LAP QUILTERS meets on the third Tuesday of each month, 9:30 am, at the Logan Community School, Columbia. Members are recruited by invitation or request and must be actively interested in the art of quilting. Annual dues are $12. The guild hosts an annual quilt show, organizes bus trips, works on group quilts, and sponsors workshops.

Beth Howell
Logan Lap Quilters
3144 Cimarron Trail
West Columbia, SC 29169
(803) 794-4202

SOUTH DAKOTA

Rapid City

BLACK HILLS QUILTER'S GUILD holds a monthly business meeting and weekly workshop meetings where members work on guild or individual projects. The group hosts an annual quilt show and sponsors a convention. Other activities include making raffle quilts, donating quilts to needy families, and promoting the art of quilting at many festivals and local events.

Black Hills Quilter's Guild
P.O. Box 2495
Rapid City, SD 57709
(605) 342-4126

TENNESSEE

Memphis

THE MEMPHIS COTTON PATCHER'S QUILT CLUB meets on the first and third Thursday of the month, 10 am, in the public meeting room at the Main Public Library. Beginning as well as expert quilters are welcome; yearly dues are minimal. Among its many functions, the group demonstrates quilting at community crafts fairs and on local television.

Clare G. Steinfeld
The Memphis Cotton Patcher's
* Club*
4160 Argonne
Memphis, TN 38127
(901) 357-7234

Oak Ridge

SMOKY MOUNTAIN CHAPTER OF THE TENNESSEE VALLEY QUILTER'S ASSOCIATION meets six to eight times a year on the second

Monday of the month at various locations in Oak Ridge and Knoxville. Membership is open to anyone interested in quilting or collecting quilts; annual dues of $14.50 include membership in the National Quilter's Association and the Tennessee Valley Quilter's Association. The group hosts a quilt show and competition each April in Oak Ridge. Other activities include workshops with renowned teachers, mini-workshops by the guild's own members, and demonstrations presented at fairs, schools, and art museums.

Smoky Mountain Chapter of
*   the TVQA*
20 Argonne Plaza, Suite 114
Oak Ridge, TN 37830
(615) 482-6914

TEXAS

Austin

AUSTIN AREA QUILT GUILD holds a general membership meeting on the first Monday of each month at the Central Library. Each of its twenty chapters meets once a week in members' homes, local libraries, or schools. Membership is open to all quilters and quilt admirers; annual dues are $10, $7.50 for senior citizens. The Guild holds a biennial quilt show, offers workshops and quilting demonstrations at community events, and has mounted exhibits at area museums. Recently, the Guild assisted in the conservation and documentation of quilts in the collection at the Texas Memorial Museum.

Austin Area Quilt Guild
P.O. Box 5757
Austin, TX 78753
(512) 443-2776

Beaumont

GOLDEN TRIANGLE QUILT GUILD meets on the third Thursday of every month at 12:30 pm, and also at 7 pm; meetings are held at the First Baptist Church, Beaumont. Everyone from ardent admirer to expert quilter is invited to join; annual dues are $12. The Guild sponsors a biennial quilt show, raffles a quilt each year, and displays quilts at several local events.

Norma Clubb
Golden Triangle Quilt Guild
Rt. 1, Box 912
Beaumont, TX 77706
(409) 892-9114

Dallas

QUILTER'S GUILD OF DALLAS meets on the first Thursday of the month, 7:30 pm, at the Preston Hollow Presbyterian Church. Anyone with an interest in quilting is invited to join; annual membership dues are nominal. Activities include an annual quilt show in March, workshops and special programs for Guild members, stitching quilts for the Ronald McDonald House in Dallas, and making and filling Christmas stockings for needy children. To celebrate Texas's sesquicentennial, Guild members completed an anniversary quilt which won the honor of Best of Show at the 1986 State Fair.

Marilou C. Wimmer
Quilter's Guild of Dallas
15775 N. Hillcrest, Suite 508
P.O. Box 304
Dallas, TX 75248
(214) 733-1387

Del Rio

PIECEMAKERS QUILTERS meets every Monday, 7 pm, at the Little Schoolhouse and every Thursday, 9 am, at the Firehouse Art Center. Quilters of all levels of interest and expertise are welcome; there are no dues. The guild sponsors an annual quilt show and workshops and is involved in making quilts for donation to worthy causes.

Del Woodward
Piecemakers Quilters
Box 1236
Del Rio, TX 78840
(512) 775-3990

VAL VERDE HERITAGE QUILTER'S GUILD meets on the first and third Thursday of the month from 7 pm to 9 pm. Meetings are held in the Directors' Room of the Del Rio Bank and Trust. Annual dues are $5, $2.50 for senior citizens. The Guild sponsors the South West Texas Quilt Festival, which is held each Spring in the Plaza del Sol Mall, Del Rio. Occasional workshops are held at meetings, and the group periodically visits other guilds in the region. The Guild makes a fund-raising quilt once a year for auction. Quilts are made from time to time to be donated to, or auctioned for, a local charity.

Lottie Salinas
Val Verde Heritage Quilter's
*   Guild*
500 E. Losoya
Del Rio, TX 78840
(512) 775-0332

Denton

DENTON QUILT GUILD meets on the third Thursday of the month at the Trinity Presbyterian Church, Denton. Annual dues are $12 and include a subscription to the monthly Guild newsletter. The group holds occasional workshops, puts on public demonstrations, participates in local quilt shows, and makes quilts for auction within the membership for fund-raising. The Guild also makes doll quilts as fund-raisers.

Carole Normile
Denton Quilt Guild
2108 Kayewood
Denton, TX 76201
(817) 382-5071

El Paso

EL PASO QUILTERS ASSOCIATION meets at 7 pm on the third Thursday of the month; there is no June meeting. Meetings are held at the Meneely Presbyterian Church, El Paso. Annual dues are $15. The group sponsors a show about every two or three years. During the membership year, the Association holds a weekend workshop and three or so smaller workshops, and makes a fund-raising quilt. Two sub-groups meet weekly to work on individual projects. In the past, the guild has hosted the Regional Quilt Seminar for the Texas/New Mexico area, donated thirty quilts to a local charity, and helped to support a local children's home.

Nannette Strain
El Paso Quilters' Association
5220 Chateau
El Paso, TX 79924
(915) 755-6500

Houston

BAY AREA QUILT GUILD meets on the fourth Monday of the month at a local utility building. Anyone with an in-terest in quilting is invited to join; annual dues are $15. The Guild offers quilting demonstrations to the public, presents workshops and organizes field trips, makes raffle quilts, and displays quilts at community events.

Pat Bishop
Bay Area Quilt Guild
11539 Sageking
Houston, TX 77089
(713) 481-3335

QUILT GUILD OF GREATER HOUSTON meets at 7 pm on the third Tuesday of each month; meetings are held at St. Christopher's Episcopal Church, Blaylock St. Annual dues are $15. In conjunction with the American International Quilt Association, the group holds an annual quilt show at the end of November. The group also has a biennial fund-raising show of its own, and it makes one fund-raising quilt per year. The Guild gives public demonstrations at several community events annually. Several small quilting circles exist within the Guild and make quilts for local charities.

Sarah Tammer
Quilt Guild of Greater Houston
Box 79035, Memorial Park Sta.
Houston, TX 77024
(713) 729-3493

Kerrville

HILL COUNTY QUILT GUILD meets on the third Monday of the month at the First Christian Church in Kerrville. Annual dues are $15. Each meeting includes a workshop or a lecture. The group periodically makes quilts as fund-raisers or to give to local charities. Each June the Guild sponsors a quilt show.

Joan Karaus
Hill County Quilt Guild
118 Spanish Oak Ln.
Kerrville, TX 78028
(512) 367-4533

Longview

COUNTY PATCHES QUILT GUILD meets on the third Thursday of the month at the Eastman Road Activity Building; there is a 9 am morning meeting and a 7 pm evening meeting. Annual dues are $15, $10 for senior citizens. Within the Guild there are two quilting circles, one meeting weekly and the other meeting monthly; each makes quilts mainly to donate to local charities. The Guild hosts a quilt show each October and also organizes a bus trip to the annual Dallas Quilt Show.

Becky Prior
County Patches Quilt Guild
P.O. Box 3411
Longview, TX 75606
(214) 759-6407

Odessa

ODESSA QUILTER'S GUILD meets on the third Tuesday of each month at the Asbury Methodist Church, Odessa. Membership is open to anyone who is interested in promoting the art of quilting; annual dues are $10. The Guild offers community workshops and has stitched quilts for such charities as the Ronald McDonald House.

Odessa Quilter's Guild
2203 E. 11th
Odessa, TX 79762
(915) 332-2638

San Angelo

CONCHO VALLEY QUILTER'S GUILD meets every Wednesday at the

Cutting Corner, 1815 Freeland St., San Angelo. The only requirement for membership is a love of quilting; annual Guild dues are $5 and annual NQA dues are $10. The Guild hosts an annual quilt show, works on a yearly fund-raising project, and initiates an annual membership drive.

Ernie Williams
Concho Valley Quilter's Guild
3301 Stanford Ave.
San Angelo, TX 76904
(915) 949-1656

San Antonio

GREATER SAN ANTONIO QUILT GUILD meets on the second Saturday of the month at St. Anthony's Church Hall. Annual dues are $12. The Guild holds workshops four times a year; to supplement the workshops, lectures and demonstrations are offered throughout the year. As a community service the group presents quilting demonstrations at local public schools. A small sub-group makes quilted items to donate to local organizations. The Guild makes a fund-raising quilt annually and sponsors a biennial Fall quilt show. The group also organizes bus trips to the Austin, Dallas, and Houston quilt shows.

Bonnie McCoy
Greater San Antonio Quilt
 Guild
P.O. Box 65124
San Antonio, TX 78265
(512) 696-4140

Tyler

QUILTERS' GUILD OF EAST TEXAS meets at 10 am on the second Thursday of every month; meetings are held at the First

Christian Church in Tyler. Annual dues are $15, $10 for senior citizens. A lecture or workshop is featured at each meeting, and several small sewing groups within the Guild meet during the month. The Guild sponsors the Azalea Quilt Show each Spring and a scholarship for the Homemaking Department at Tyler Junior College, and it makes an annual donation to the Athens Public Library to buy quilting books. Annually, the group makes a fund-raising quilt and organizes a get-away weekend.

Marilyn Hardy
Quilters' Guild of East Texas
P.O. Box 130773
Tyler, TX 75713
(214) 561-8407

VERMONT

Hanover

NORTHERN LIGHTS QUILTING GUILD meets once a month at the Howe Library, Hanover. The only requirement for membership is an interest in some aspect of quilting. The group

hosts periodic shows and workshops and is involved in fund-raising projects that benefit local charities.

Nanine Hutchinson
Northern Lights Quilting Guild
Godfrey Rd.
E. Thetford, VT 05043
(802) 785-2946

Kirby

KIRBY QUILTERS meets once a week in members' homes or in the Kirby Town Hall. The only requirement is for members to live in the vicinity of Kirby. The group holds an annual quilt show, makes raffle quilts, and participates in the local Christmas Fair.

Sue Willey
Kirby Quilters
R.F.D. 2
Lyndonville, VT 05851
(802) 626-3207

Rutland

GREEN MOUNTAIN QUILTER'S GUILD holds a Saturday meeting in October and May. Only a love of quilting is required for membership; annual dues are $5. The Guild hosts a quilt show every other year.

Mary Ryan
Green Mountain Quilter's Guild
Grandview Terr.
Rutland, VT 05701
(802) 773-6563

VIRGINIA

Middletown

BELLE GROVE QUILTER'S GUILD meets on the first and third Thursday and on the second and fourth Tuesday of each month.

New members must be experienced quilters and must be approved by a membership committee. Annual dues are $5. The Guild sponsors a quilt show every two years and makes two raffle quilts annually.

Belle Grove Quilter's Guild
P.O. Box 137
Middletown, VA 22645
(703) 869-2028

Philomont

WATERSFORD QUILT GUILD meets once a month on the second Wednesday, 10 am, at the Watersford Historical Foundation. Members must have a sincere interest in quilts and quiltmaking and be willing to participate in public quilting demonstrations. The Guild makes several quilts to be raffled, the proceeds from which are donated to a non-profit historic preservation society. Annual quilting demonstrations are offered by the group at Watersford Fair, the Lucketts Fair, and the Oatlands Plantation in Leesburg.

Pricilla Godfrey
Watersford Quilt Guild
P.O. Box 252
Philomont, VA 22131
(703) 687-5689

Richmond

RICHMOND QUILTERS' GUILD meets annually, with five chapters meeting monthly in local community rooms, libraries, and churches. Anyone interested in quilting and in preserving the tradition is welcome to join; annual dues are $15. The Guild sponsors an annual exhibit and quilt show, holds demonstrations at schools and festivals, and makes raffle quilts to raise funds for various purposes.

Arie M. Brandon
Richmond Quilters' Guild
7820 Wilton Rd.
Richmond, VA 23231
(804) 222-9211

Roanoke

STAR QUILTER'S GUILD meets on the first Monday of each month at the Valley View Mall Community Room, Roanoke. A love of quilting is the only criterion for membership; annual dues are $10. The Guild offers quilting demonstrations, donates a quilt each year to a worthy community cause, and hosts monthly workshops.

Cyndy Szarzynski
Star Quilter's Guild
R.F.D. 1, Box 46-B
Glasgow, VA 24555
(703) 291-2712

Virginia Beach

TIDEWATER QUILTER'S GUILD meets on the first Monday of the month, 7 pm, and on the second Tuesday, 10 am, at the Norfolk Botanical Gardens. An interest in quilts and quilting is required for membership; annual dues are $10, $8 for senior citizens. The Guild sponsors an annual show to display members' work.

Tidewater Quilter's Guild
P.O. Box 62635
Virginia Beach, Va 23462

WASHINGTON

Anacortes

FIDALGO ISLAND QUILTERS meets every Monday at the Westminster Presbyterian Church Parish House. Anyone with an interest in quilting is welcome; annual dues are $8. The guild hosts a large quilt show each August, and members make at least one raffle quilt for fund-raising.

Diana Smith
Fidalgo Island Quilters
3009 K Ave.
Anacortes, WA 98221
(206) 293-8053

Mukilteo

LADIES OF THE BLOCK meets every Thursday at 10 am. Membership is limited to those living in South Snohomish County, Washington. The guild participates in festivals and other local events.

Teresa Haskins
Ladies of the Block
5902 94th St. SW
Mukilteo, WA 98275
(206) 347-3806

Olympia

QUILTMAKERS meets on the second and fourth Thursday of each month in the Community Room at the Capital Mall. Beginners and experts alike are welcome; annual dues are $10. The guild is presently making doll quilts for the benefit of the Salvation Army.

Patricia Isaacson
Quiltmakers
527 Stoll Rd.
Olympia, WA 98501
(206) 491-9216

Washougal

CLARK COUNTY QUILTERS holds a general meeting once a month in a local community room, with smaller groups meeting once a week in members' homes. An interest in quilting and community service is the only requirements for membership; annual dues are $5. Besides sponsoring an annual quilt show, the guild participates in various local quilting demonstrations and craft festivals.

Phyllis Gildehous
Clark County Quilters
37116 SE Sunset View Rd.
Washougal, WA 98671
(206) 835-5351

WEST VIRGINIA

Buckhannon

THE QUILTERS meets on the second Thursday of each month at the local YWCA or in members' homes. Membership is open to quilters of all levels of expertise. Since the guild is sponsored by the local chapter of the YWCA, the only membership dues required are those for the Y. The guild hosts an annual quilt show in September and arranges day trips for its members to attend quilt shows throughout the state.

Kay Sienkiewicz
The Quilters
26 Meade St.
Buckhannon, WV 26201
(304) 472-3546

Charleston

KANAWHA VALLEY QUILTERS holds a business meeting once a month and a working meeting once a week at the local library. Anyone who enjoys quilting is welcome; annual dues are $10. The guild stitches raffle quilts and participates in workshops

and quilt-ins with neighboring guilds.

Barbara Lantz
Kanawha Valley Quilters
1612 Berkshire Pl.
Charleston, WV 25314
(304) 346-9776

Flemington

FRIENDSHIP STAR QUILTERS meets on the third Tuesday of each month at the Taylor County Court House. Quilters of all levels of ability are welcome; annual dues are $6. The guild organizes several workshops for its members.

Donna Carnegie
Friendship Star Quilters
P.O. Box 252
Flemington, WV 26347
(304) 739-4648

Huntington

CREATIVE QUILTERS meets on the second Monday of the month, 7:30 pm, at the Enslow Park Presbyterian Church. Membership is open to anyone interested in quilting, whether beginner, expert, or simply a quilt appreciator; annual dues are $10 and include a monthly newsletter. The guild sponsors a biennial juried quilt show, offers workshops and classes during the summer months, and hosts field trips to places of interest. Guild-made quilts have been donated to the Ronald McDonald House Foundation and to the patients at Veteran's Hospital.

Sara Campbell
Creative Quilters
5107 Pea Ridge Rd.
Huntington, WV 25705
(304) 736-3108

WISCONSIN

Cedarburg

CEDAR CREEK QUILTERS meets once a month in members' homes. Anyone interested in quilts and quilting and willing to share ideas and projects is invited to join. The guild instituted Wisconsin Quilters, Inc., and helps to organize its symposiums.

Holly Seymour
Cedar Creek Quilters
1654 Summit Dr.
Cedarburg, WI 53012
(414) 377-8667

Franksville

LIGHTHOUSE QUILTER'S GUILD, INC., meets on the last Monday of the month, except during December, at the Franksville United Methodist Church. Quilters of all levels of ability are welcome, but membership is limited to 130. The Guild sponsored its first quilt show in 1986 and hopes to make its show a biennial event. Members have made and donated quilts to the Milwaukee Ronald McDonald House, participated in local festivals, and presented a wall hanging to the city of Racine to display at the new festival site on Lake Michigan.

Dianne Zimmerman
Lighthouse Quilter's Guild
4903 Charles St.
Racine, WI 53402
(414) 681-0753

Janesville

ROCK VALLEY QUILTER'S GUILD meets on the third Tuesday of the month, September through July, at the Janesville Public

Library. Quilters of all levels of expertise are welcome; annual dues are $7.50. Guild activities include an annual quilter's retreat, a raffle quilt to raise funds for quilt restoration at the local historical society, and two workshops each year. The group also offers monthly quiltmaking classes and a quilt show-and-tell.

Rock Valley Quilter's Guild
P.O. Box 904
Janesville, WI 53547-0904
(608) 756-2509

Montello

CALICO CAPER QUILTER'S GUILD
meets on the first Monday of the month at various locations throughout a two-county area. Quilters of all levels of ability and who are willing to share their love of quilts are welcome; annual dues are $5. The Guild hosts an annual quilt show, makes a raffle quilt as a fundraiser, and participates in public events.

Jane Oravetz
Calico Caper Quilter's Guild
Rt. 2, Box 333
Montello, WI 53949
(608) 742-4772

Sun Prairie

PRAIRIE HERITAGE QUILTERS
meets weekly for two months prior to its annual Spring quilt show and once after the show and once in the Fall. Members are encouraged to complete a quilting course through the local adult education program and must be willing to work together on the guild's quilt show. The annual Spring quilt show, which runs for two days and draws 5,000 people and exhibits 300 quilts, is the group's principal activity.

Klaudeen Hansen
Prairie Heritage Quilters
P.O. Box 253
Sun Prairie, WI 53590
(608) 837-2298

WYOMING

Powell

PAINTBRUSH PIECERS QUILT GUILD meets on the fourth Monday of the month at the American National Bank Meeting Room. Annual dues are $12. The Guild has organized shows in the past, but is currently involved with preparations for the Wyoming centennial celebration in 1990. The group made the flag quilt that represented Wyoming at the Statue of Liberty celebration in 1986. The group occasionally makes and donates quilts for local charities.

Carlie Otto
Paintbrush Piecers Quilt Guild
P.O. Box 258
Powell, WY 82435
(307) 754-3388

CANADA

BRITISH COLUMBIA

Cranbrook

CRANBROOK QUILTER'S GUILD meets twice a month at a local senior citizen's pavilion. Membership is open to quilters of all levels of experience; annual dues are $10. The Guild makes group quilts to be raffled and sponsors a tea/quilt show.

Pat Hall
Cranbrook Quilter's Guild
3512 9th St. S.
Cranbrook, BC V1C 4M3
Canada
(604) 426-8508

Kelowna

ORCHARD VALLEY QUILTER'S GUILD meets every Tuesday at the Kelowna Curling Club. Membership is open to anyone interested in quilting; annual dues are $25. The Guild hosts a biennial quilt show and donates lap quilts and crib quilts to organizations for the needy.

Diane Elliott
Orchard Valley Quilter's Guild
P.O. Box 585, Station A
Kelowna, BC V1Y 7P2
Canada
(604) 860-3342

Kitimat

KITIMAT QUILTER'S GUILD meets on the fourth Monday of the month at the Kildala Elementary School Library. Additional meetings are held every Monday morning at members' homes. An interest in quilting is the only requirement for membership; annual dues are $10. Activities include making raffle quilts and organizing workshops and quilt shows.

Kitimat Quilter's Guild
28 Amos St.
Kitimat, BC V8C 1A6
Canada
(604) 632-7813

Vancouver

FRASER VALLEY QUILTER'S GUILD meets on the second Monday of the month, September through June. Membership is open to anyone with an interest in quilting; annual dues are $15. The Guild sponsors an annual quilt show and offers several public quilting demonstrations and displays throughout the year.

Ethel Snow
Fraser Valley Quilter's Guild
1195 Hazelton St.
Vancouver, BC V5K 4H8
Canada
(604) 253-0637

Victoria

VICTORIA QUILTER'S GUILD meets every other month at the Gordon Head United Church Hall. Membership is open to all quilters; annual dues are $5. The group participates in shows, conferences and craft shows throughout the year.

Joan Ruxton
Victoria Quilter's Guild
17 Torey Crescent
Victoria, BC V9B 1A4
Canada
(604) 727-6050

MANITOBA

Winnipeg

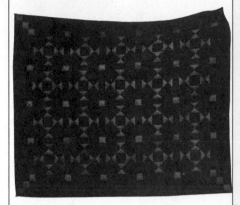

MANITOBA PRAIRIE QUILTERS meets once a month on alternate Friday evenings, with an all-day Saturday workshop held at Crafts Guild, 183 Kennedy, Winnipeg. Quilters of all levels of ability are welcome; annual active membership dues are $15 or $5 for a newsletter membership only. The guild works on group quilts that are raffled for fund-raising.

Pat Borecky
Manitoba Prairie Quilters
Box 2276
Winnipeg, MB R3C 4A6
Canada
(204) 475-3074 or
(204) 667-4708

NEW BRUNSWICK

Fredericton

FREDERICTON QUILTER'S GUILD meets on the third Tuesday of January, March, May, September, and November at the Monsignor Boyd Family Centre. Membership is open to anyone interested in quilts or quilting;

annual dues are $10. The Guild hosts an annual quilt show.

Fredericton Quilter's Guild
64 Sunset Dr.
Fredericton, NB E3A 1A1
Canada
(506) 472-5330

NOVA SCOTIA

Halifax

MAYFLOWER HANDQUILTER'S SOCIETY OF NOVA SCOTIA meets once a month from September through June. Quilters of all levels of expertise are welcome; annual dues are $10, $2 for senior citizens. The guild sponsors quilt shows and presents workshops for its members. It makes quilts to benefit the Red Cross, the Ronald McDonald House, and the Children's Hospital.

Phyllis Rowland
Mayflower Handquilter's
* Society of Nova Scotia*
Box 3664 Halifax S.
Halifax, NS B3J 3K6
Canada
(902) 423-5923

ONTARIO

Oakville

HALTON QUILTER'S GUILD meets at 7:30 pm on the third Thursday of each month, except July, August, and December, at the Central Baptist Church, Oakville. Anyone with an interest in quilting is invited to join; annual dues are $12. The Guild hosts an annual quilt show, gives demonstrations at local events, offers workshops, and raffles a quilt to raise funds for local charities.

Ruth Landon
Halton Quilter's Guild
644 Trafford Crescent
Oakville, ON L6L 3T5
Canada
(416) 827-3088

Sarnia

SARNIA QUILTER'S GUILD holds its general meetings once a month from September to May and its quilting meetings twice a month at the Grace United Church. Quilters of all levels of expertise are invited to join; annual dues are $10. Members stitch one quilt each year to be raffled and then donate the proceeds to a charity of their choice. The Guild also organizes workshops to keep members well-informed of new techniques and subjects.

Vivian Cothros
Sarnia Quilter's Guild
1290 Errol Rd. E.
Sarnia, ON N7S 5L2
Canada
(519) 542-3310

Windsor

WINDSOR QUILTER'S GUILD meets on the first Monday of each month, September through June, at the Budimir Library, Windsor. Anyone with an interest in quilting is welcome; annual dues are $10. The Guild sponsors a quilt show every other year, participates in craft and art shows, and displays its work at local libraries.

Dorothy McMurdie
Windsor Quilter's Guild
1020 Watson Ave.
Windsor, ON N8S 3T4
Canada
(519) 948-0976

9. Touring the Museums: The Best North American Quilt Collections

Appliqué quilt, c. 1825, Frederick County, Maryland. Made by Anna Catherine Hummell Markey. Courtesy of The Daughters of the American Revolution Museum, Washington, D.C. Photo by Helga Studios.

Art and historical museums now house important collections of antique quilts. It was not always so. Only in the mid-1970s did one leading Pennsylvania museum, located in the heart of the state's historic Amish country, begin to acquire examples of quilts made within an hour's drive of the institution. Public interest in the art of the quilt is now so widespread that no general museum can ignore the form.

Quilts have always been an important part of a few general museum collections. Notable among them are The Oakland Museum, The Denver Art Museum, the Daughters of the American Revolution Museum, the Honolulu Academy of Arts, the Spencer Museum of Art, the Baltimore Museum of Art, the Maryland Historical Society, The Newark Museum, The Brooklyn Museum, the Shelburne Museum, and the State Historical Society of Wisconsin. The Los Angeles County Museum of Art is now in the process of establishing the American Quilt Research Center.

In addition to the general museums of art and history are institutions specializing in the history and art of the quilt. The Museum of American Folk Art in New York City has been a pioneer in the study and exhibition of antique quilts. In the past several years MAFA has been joined by others, including the Esprit Corporate Offices collection, the American Museum of Quilts, and the newly formed New England Quilt Museum.

At any given time, only a small proportion of the quilts housed in a museum is likely to be on display. Because of the large dimensions of most examples, it is impossible to install the entire collection on a permanent basis. In almost all cases, however, arrangements can be made in advance with the curator or registrar to view quilts held in storage.

UNITED STATES

ALABAMA

Birmingham

BIRMINGHAM MUSEUM OF ART.
Open Tuesday-Saturday except Thursday, 10 am-5 pm; Thursday, 10 am-9 pm; Sunday, 2 pm-6 pm. An appointment must be made to view the quilt collection, which is not on permanent display. Admission is free.

The quilt collection consists primarily of Alabama-made quilts, but there are also several Southern and New England examples. The collection contains one of the Alabama Gunboat quilts: these were auctioned in various cities during the Civil War to raise money for a gunboat. A great deal of historical information about the quilts is available at the museum, which also hosts occasional quilts exhibitions.

Birmingham Museum of Art
2000 8th Ave. N.
Birmingham, AL 35203
(205) 254-2565

ARIZONA

Tucson

ARIZONA HISTORICAL SOCIETY.
Open Monday-Saturday, 10 am-4 pm; Sunday, 12 pm-4 pm. As only portions of the collection are on display, an appointment with the registrar or assistant registrar is necessary to view the collection. Admission is free.

The quilt collection contains ninety-one quilts in a wide variety of styles and patterns, including thirteen crazy quilts, ten Log Cabin patterns, eight Star patterns, and five Pineapple patterns. Other patterns in the collection include Oak Leaf and Reel, Triple, Irish Chain, Dresden Plate, Drunkard's Path, Sherman's March, Streak O'Lightning, and Rose Wreath. Most are regionally concentrated, particularly from the Kentucky area.

Arizona Historical Society
949 E. Second St.
Tucson, AZ 85719
(602) 628-5774

CALIFORNIA

Los Angeles

AMERICAN QUILT RESEARCH CENTER AT THE LOS ANGELES COUNTY MUSEUM OF ART. Open only by appointment during Museum hours: Tuesday-Friday, 10 am-5 pm; Saturday-Sunday, 10 am-6 pm. Admission, $1.50 adults; 75¢ senior citizens, students.

The collection contains 125 quilts, primarily American, although a number are European. The collection dates from 1760 to 1940, but most pieces are pre-1850. The collection contains four late-18th-century linsey-woolseys, five Amish quilts, a W.C.T.U. signature quilt, several stenciled quilts, a number of friendship quilts, and the only Baltimore album quilt known that was a child's quilt.

American Quilt Research
Center at the Los Angeles
County Museum of Art
5905 Wilshire Blvd.
Los Angeles, CA 90036
(213) 857-6083

Oakland

THE OAKLAND MUSEUM. Open Wednesday-Saturday, 10 am-5 pm; Sunday, 12 pm-7 pm. Portions of the collection are permanently displayed in the History galleries and are rotated with those in storage. For serious research, specific pieces can be viewed by appointment. Admission is free.

The museum has an acquisitions policy that favors items that pertain to California history, and the quilt collection reflects this. The collection includes 130 quilts, as well as numerous patterned quilt-pieces and supportive literature. Crazy quilts, many with a strong Japanese influence, predominate. One of the finest pieces in the collection is the More Family quilt—this was made by the five More children for their grandmother in the late 19th century. It is made of alternating blocks of wine and black velvet plush which are appliquéd with themes relating to the family history, e.g. grapes, California, dogs.

The Oakland Museum
1000 Oak St.
Oakland, CA 94607
(415) 273-3402

San Francisco

ESPRIT CORPORATE OFFICES.
Open Monday-Friday, 9 am-4:30 pm. After hours curator-led tours for groups of six or more are available by appointment. The quilt collection is on permanent display. There is no formal admission charge, although visitors are asked to purchase a catalogue/gallery guide ($3.50).

The collection consists of 248 pieces and includes a great deal of Amish and Amish-influenced work from the early part of this century. The catalogue/gallery guide gives details for each quilt as to type, place and date of origin, materials used, and a brief history of the quilt itself.

Esprit Corporate Offices
900 Minnesota St.
San Francisco, CA 94107
(415) 648-6900

THE FINE ARTS MUSEUMS OF SAN FRANCISCO.
Open Wednesday-Sunday, 10 am-5 pm. The collection is not on permanent display, and a minimum of fourteen days notice is required to view it. Admission is $3 for adults. Free on first Wednesday of each month and Saturday mornings, 10 am-12 pm.

The collection comprises some forty quilts. Dates range mainly from mid-19th century to early 20th-century, with two quilts dated to the 1820s. Many typical patterns are represented, and the collection includes both pieced and appliqué quilts.

The Fine Arts Museums of San
*   Francisco*
M.H. de Young Memorial
*   Museum*
Golden Gate Park
San Francisco, CA 94118
(415) 751-4432

San Jose

AMERICAN MUSEUM OF QUILTS.
Open Tuesday-Saturday, 10 am-4 pm. While there are some permanent exhibits, much of the collection is in storage. The stored quilts can be viewed for research purposes by appointment with the curator. Admission is free.

"Erica's Poppy."

The collection ranges from mid-18th century to the present; most of the pieces are from the 1920s. There are also many pieces from the Depression. Among the 200 quilts are several exquisite Victorian quilts, including one that survived the 1906 San Francisco earthquake and fire. There are also 3 Amish quilts and a very fine white trapunto, c. 1850. The museum annually sponsors a lecture series on quilts. There is also an on-going program of quilting classes.

American Museum of Quilts
766 S. 2nd St.
San Jose, CA 95112
(408) 971-0323

COLORADO

Denver

THE DENVER ART MUSEUM.
Open Tuesday-Saturday, 9 am- 5 pm; Wednesday, 9 am-8 pm; Sunday, 12 pm-5 pm. Twenty-five to thirty quilts are on view at all times; the display is changed annually. Admission, $3 adults; $1.50 senior citizens and children under six.

The quilt collection is found on the sixth floor and, while comparatively small, is very high in quality.

The Denver Art Museum
100 W. 14th Ave. Pkwy.
Denver, CO 80204
(303) 575-2793

CONNECTICUT

Hartford

WADSWORTH ATHENEUM.
Open Tuesday-Friday, 11 am-7 pm; Saturday-Sunday, 11 am-5 pm. The collection is not on permanent display, but quilts can be seen by appointment. Admission, $3 adults; $1.50 senior

citizens, students; free on Thursdays and on Saturdays, 11 am-1 pm.

The collection of forty quilts contains mostly pieced quilts with some wholecloths. Included are ten black-printed and five copper-plate-printed quilts from France, as well as two quilts of English origin. The collection contains pieces from 1795 to 1889. The 1795 quilt is of exceptional beauty: it is a mosaic-pattern pieced quilt with a border of pink calamanco. Sewn with both linen and cotton thread, the quilt is backed with homespun fabric giving it two very interesting sides. The Costumes and Textiles Society is a museum support group which sponsors lectures and trips for its members.

Wadsworth Atheneum
600 Main St.
Hartford, CT 06103
(203) 278-2670

DELAWARE

Winterthur

HENRY FRANCIS DU PONT WINTERTHUR MUSEUM. Open Tuesday-Saturday, 9 am-5 pm; Sunday, 12 pm-5 pm. There are thirty-eight quilts on permanent display; approximately eighty others are in the Bedspread Storage Room. This can be seen on a needlework tour for which a reservation is necessary. A specially-trained guide leads the tour. Admission charges vary, as all viewing is by tour. Prices range from $6.50 to $12.50.

There are approximately 120 quilts in total, the earliest dated 1782. Almost all the quilts are American, and most are pre-1850. The museum also sponsors occasional quilting workshops and lectures.

Henry Francis du Pont Winterthur Museum
Winterthur, DE 19735
(302) 656-8591

DISTRICT OF COLUMBIA

Washington

Appliqué quilt by Anna Catherine Hummell Markey; Maryland, c. 1825. Photo by Helga Studios.

DAUGHTERS OF THE AMERICAN REVOLUTION MUSEUM. Open Monday-Friday, 9 am-4 pm; Sunday, 1 pm-5 pm. The quilt collection is not on permanent display, but it can be viewed by appointment. Admission is free.

The collection contains 200 to 250 quilts dating from 1770 to 1900 and exhibiting a virtually complete selection of all major styles of stitching and patterns. Lectures about the exhibits are given to groups on request.

Daughters of the American Revolution Museum
1776 D St., NW
Washington, DC 20006
(202) 879-3240

NATIONAL MUSEUM OF AMERICAN HISTORY. Open daily, 10 am-5 pm. The collection is not on permanent display, but there is a weekly showing of some of the stored quilts. Other stored quilts can be seen by appointment with the Division of Textiles. Admission is free.

There are 300 pieces in the collection, although this figure also includes unquilted tops. The collection ranges from 18th century to early 20th century. Pieces include Russellville Fair, which is an 1856 all-white quilted counterpane depicting a fair near Russellville, Georgia, and an 1835 pieced Rising Star pattern with an elaborate appliquéd surround. The museum holds occasional quilting workshops.

National Museum of American History
14th St. and Constitution Ave., NW
Washington, DC 20560
(202) 357-1300

GEORGIA

Atlanta

ATLANTA HISTORICAL SOCIETY. Open Monday-Friday, 9 am-5:30 pm; Saturday, 9 am-5 pm. The quilts on display regularly rotate with those in storage. Quilts that are in storage can be seen for scholarly purposes by appointment. Admission, $4.50 adults; $4 students.

The collection contains 200 quilts in varying states of repair. Most are late 19th century and early 20th century, but the collection includes some pieces from the 1840s. A conservation group is associated with the museum. Occasional quilting lectures are held by the museum's Education Department.

Atlanta Historical Society
3101 Andrews Dr. NW
Atlanta, GA 30305
(404) 261-1837

HAWAII

Honolulu

BERNICE PAUAHI BISHOP MUSEUM. Open Monday-Saturday, 9 am-5 pm. Some quilts are on display while others can be viewed through an appointment with the Anthropology Department. Admission, $4.50 adults; $2.75 children.

There are twenty-five quilts in the collection, mostly of vibrant floral patterns in a distinct Hawaiian style. The museum has an on-going program for quilters.

Bernice Pauahi Bishop Museum
1525 Bernice St.
P.O. Box 19000-A
Honolulu, HI 96817-0916
(808) 847-3511

HONOLULU ACADEMY OF ARTS. Open Tuesday-Saturday, 10 am-4:30 pm; Sunday, 1 pm-5 pm. The collection is not on permanent display; viewing is possible on Mondays and Tuesdays by appointment. Admission is free.

The collection consists of forty-eight very good pieces from both Hawaii and the Mainland. It includes four flag quilts and the well-known Garden of Elenale, the only known Hawaiian quilt with human figures. In conjunction with the museum's quilt shows, the Academy presents lecture/workshops for the public from time to time.

Honolulu Academy of Arts
900 S. Beretania St.
Honolulu, HI 96814
(808) 538-3693

ILLINOIS

Chicago

THE ART INSTITUTE OF CHICAGO. Open Monday, Wednesday-Sunday, 10:30 am-4:30 pm; Tuesday, 10:30 am-8 pm. The quilt collection is inaccessable until 1988 because of construction work. There is no admission charge, but a donation of $4.50 is suggested.

The collection contains 100 pieces, mostly 19th-century American and also some European examples of earlier dates.

The Art Institute of Chicago
Michigan Ave. at Adams St.
Chicago, IL 62706
(217) 782-7386

Springfield

ILLINOIS STATE MUSEUM. Open Monday-Saturday, 8:30 am-5 pm; Sunday, 1:30 pm-5 pm. Viewing of the collection is only by appointment as the collection is not on permanent display. Admission is free.

The collection of over sixty quilts contains fifty Illinois quilts, most dating from the 19th century. Types include appliqué, pieced, and trapunto. The museum has occasional

Crazy quilt by Clara Rush Moore; Illinois, c. 1880.

programs and exhibitions for quilters.

INDIANA

Indianapolis

INDIANA STATE MUSEUM. Open daily, 9 am-5 pm. The quilts on display are rotated with those in storage. The latter may be viewed by appointment. Admission is free.

The collection contains 150 quilts dating from the late 18th century to the present. The earliest quilts are two yard quilts made of roller-print chintz. Also featured is a white-on-white quilt purportedly from the 1750s although documentation is at present incomplete. The collection contains an 1860s political quilt made of

Lincoln campaign ribbons from the New Albany area of Indiana. The museum hosts occasional quilting workshops.

*Indiana State Museum
202 N. Alabama St.
Indianapolis, IN 46204
(317) 232-1637*

IOWA

Cherokee

SANFORD MUSEUM AND PLANETARIUM. Open Monday-Friday, 9 am-5 pm; Saturday-Sunday, 12 pm-5 pm. The collection is not on permanent display, but can be seen by appointment. Admission is free.

While the collection contains ony five complete quilts, it features several hundred quilt blocks. The quilts date from the late 19th and early 20th centuries, while the blocks were made in the 1950s.

*Sanford Museum and
    Planetarium
117 E. Willow St.
Cherokee, IA 51012
(712) 225-3922*

Pella

PELLA HISTORICAL VILLAGE. Open Monday-Friday, 9 am-5 pm; April-October and December, Saturday, 9 am-5 pm. Admission, $3.50.

The small permanent collection is expanded each Fall when the museum displays quilts from private collections.

*Pella Historical Village
507 Franklin St.
Pella, IA 50219
(515) 628-2409*

*Illinois State Museum
Cnr. Spring and Edwards Sts.
Springfield, IL 62706
(217) 782-7386*

KANSAS

Lawrence

SPENCER MUSEUM OF ART. Open Tuesday-Saturday, 8:30 am-5 pm; Sunday, 12 pm-5 pm. An appointment is essential to view the collection, which is not on permanent display. Admission is free.

Composed primarily of 19th- and 20th-century quilts, the collection contains some 170 American pieces. It includes the works of Rose Kretsinger and the quilt block collection of Carrie Hall, the latter a collection of 844 sample blocks. There are also works by many of America's best-known quilters including Christina Hay Malcom and Harriet Theetge.

Spencer Museum of Art
The University of Kansas
Lawrence, KS 66045
(913) 864-4710

KENTUCKY

Bowling Green

THE KENTUCKY MUSEUM. Open Tuesday-Saturday, 9:30 am- 4 pm; Sunday, 1 pm-4:30 pm. Although there is at least one quilt exhibit each year, the quilt collection is not on permanent display. Access to reserve collections may be obtained by appointment. Admission is free.

Fifty-nine of the museum's seventy-eight quilts are dated pre-20th century; most are pieced, but examples of appliqué, whole cloth (stuffed), and crazy are included. Significant pieces include the Henry Clay portrait quilt, the Calvert quilt, the Chester Dare quilt, the Logan County whitework quilt and the Spectrum quilt.

The Kentucky Museum
Western Kentucky University
Bowling Green, KY 42101
(502) 745-2592

Frankfort

KENTUCKY HISTORY MUSEUM. Open Monday-Saturday, 9 am-4 pm; Sunday, 1 pm-5 pm. The collection is not on permanent display, nor can it be viewed by appointment. The museum, however, offers slides of many of its quilts that can be viewed or purchased. Admission to the museum is free.

The collection is of Kentucky-related quilts, including pieced, appliquéd, and crazy quilts. Most are 19th and early 20th century works.

Kentucky History Museum
Old Capitol Annex
Cnr. Broadway and Lewis
Frankfort, KY 40601
(502) 564-3016

MARYLAND

Baltimore

BALTIMORE CITY LIFE MUSEUMS. Open Tuesday-Saturday, 10 am-4 pm; Sunday, 12 pm-4 pm. Some of the quilts are permanently displayed; the others can be seen by appointment with the Decorative Arts Curator. Admission, $4 adults; $3 senior citizens, students.

The collection, while small, includes a Baltimore album quilt c. 1845. Most of the other quilts are from 1860-1890.

Baltimore City Life Museums
800 E. Lombard St.
Baltimore, MD 21202
(301) 396-3523

THE BALTIMORE MUSEUM OF ART. Open Tuesday-Friday, 10 am-4 pm; Saturday-Sunday, 11 am-6 pm. The collection is not on permanent display, but exhibits within the museum are rotated with those in storage. Admission is free.

The collection contains over 200 quilts, including fifty children's quilts. The majority of the quilts are mid-19th century, but several date to the 18th century. The collection contains two very fine pieces of chintz appliqué—one each of English and American origin. The collection is famous for its twelve Baltimore album quilts; these exquisite pieces are usually on public display.

The Baltimore Museum of Art
Art Museum Drive
Baltimore, MD 21218
(301) 396-7101

MARYLAND HISTORICAL SOCIETY.
Open Tuesday-Friday, 11
am-4:30 pm; Saturday, 9
am-4:30 pm; October-April,
Sunday, 1 pm-5 pm. The collection is not on permanent
display, but photographs are
available for study. As the quilts
are stored on the fourth floor of
the museum's 19th-century
house, viewing is difficult;
usually a small charge is made
for this service. Viewing is only
possible for scholarly purposes
and must be by appointment.
Admission, $2.50.

The collection contains about
100 quilts that date from the
late 18th century to the present.
Particularly fine pieces include
the silk Lafayette quilt and
several Baltimore album quilts
—one incorporating an appliquéd picture of the Washington
Monument in Baltimore,
c. 1840, and another including
the Treadway of Baltimore.
Notable also are the Goodman
and Governor's quilts. The
museum's education department periodically offers quilting
workshops.

Maryland Historical Society
201 W. Monument St.
Baltimore, MD 21201
(301) 685-3750

MASSACHUSETTS

Boston

MUSEUM OF FINE ARTS. Open
Tuesday-Sunday, 10 am-5 pm;
Wednesday, 10 am-10 pm. The
quilt collection is not on
display on a permanent basis,
but may be seen by appointment. Admission, $5 adults
when all galleries are open, $4
adults when only some of the
galleries are open, $3 children;
free on Saturdays before noon.

The collection includes a selection of quilts from America and
England, dating from the 17th
to the 19th century. Most well-
known among these are two
American quilts: one, a patchwork and embroidered bed
quilt, is said to have been made
by Celestine Bacheller; the
other is an appliqué quilt made
by Mrs. Harriet Powers of
Georgia. Both date from the end
of the 19th century.

Museum of Fine Arts
465 Huntington Ave.
Boston, MA 02115
(617) 267-9300

Carlisle

NEW ENGLAND QUILT MUSEUM.
Call (617) 256-2738 for details
of hours. Portions of the collection are on display at all times;
these are rotated with those in
storage. Viewing of the quilts in
storage is possible, but only by
appointment.

The collection includes
"Archipelago" by Nancy
Halpern, who is well known for
her architectural-type designs;
the quilt depicts three islands
with buildings. Also in the collection is Ruth McDowell's
"Bloodroot," a beautiful example of contemporary design. The
museum maintains a library
and work areas for workshops
and lectures.

New England Quilt Museum
c/o N.E.Q.G., P.O. Box 73
Carlisle, MA 01741
(617) 256-2738

Fall River

FALL RIVER HISTORICAL SOCIETY.
Open Tuesday-Friday, 9 am-4:30
pm. Closed January and
February. The quilt collection is
on permanent display. Admission is free, although donations
are gratefully accepted.

The collection, although small,
contains a variety of interesting
variations on the familiar
themes: a postage stamp pattern, friendship quilts, several
quilts backed with flour bags.

Fall River Historical Society
451 Rock St.
Fall River, MA 02720
(617) 679-1071

Fitchburg

FITCHBURG HISTORICAL SOCIETY.
Open Monday-Thursday, 10 am-
4 pm; Sunday, 2 pm-4 pm. The
quilt collection is stored in the
Society's historical house, so
notice must be given if the collection is to be viewed. Admission is free.

The collection includes several
cotton quilts, one friendship
quilt, one Tumbling Blocks, and
three crazy quilts made of
velvet and silk.

Fitchburg Historical Society
50 Grove St.
P.O. Box 953
Fitchburg, MA 01420
(617) 345-1157

Lexington

**MUSEUM OF OUR NATIONAL
HERITAGE.** Open Monday-
Saturday, 10 am-5 pm; Sunday,
12 pm-5 pm. The collection is
not on permanent display; appointment must be made to
view it. Admission is free.

The collection consists of
twenty-five quilts, mostly
pieced or crazy. A point of interest is that many contain
unusual fraternal symbols.

*Museum of Our National
    Heritage*
33 Marrett Rd.
Lexington, MA 02173
(617) 861-6559

Wenham

WENHAM MUSEUM. Open Monday-Friday, 11 am-4 pm; Saturday, 1 pm-4 pm; Sunday, 2 pm-5 pm. While there are always one or two quilts on public display, the bulk of the collection is in visible storage. These quilts can be viewed at most times by request. Admission, $1.50 adults; 50¢ children.

The collection contains about 100 quilts; the majority are crazy quilts. The museum holds a quilt exhibition approximately every two years.

Wenham Museum
132 Main St.
Wenham, MA 01984
(617) 468-2377

MICHIGAN

Dearborn

GREENFIELD VILLAGE AND HENRY FORD MUSEUM. Open daily, 9 am-5 pm. The collection is not on permanent display, and appointments are essential to view it. Note, however, that appointments are granted only infrequently. Admission is $8 per person.

The collection of 200 quilts ranges over most construction types and periods and varies in quality as it does in age (1780-1950). Of special interest are 10 late-19th-century quilts by the famed Susan McCord. Classes on quilting are given through the Museum's Adult Education Department.

*Greenfield Village and Henry
    Ford Museum*
20900 Oakwood Blvd.
Dearborn, MI 48121
(313) 271-1620

Detroit

DETROIT HISTORICAL MUSEUM. Open Wednesday-Sunday, 9:30 am-5 pm. The quilt collection is not on permanent display, and at the present time it is not possible to make quilts available for viewing when they are not on display. Admission is free; voluntary contributions are encouraged.

The collection consists of approximately 150 quilts and throws of all types, including pieced, whitework, and appliqué. Many of the quilts are crazy patch. Of special note are several crib quilts and an extremely fine broderic perse.

Detroit Historical Museum
5401 Woodward Ave.
Detroit, MI 48202
(313) 833-1805

MINNESOTA

St. Paul

MINNESOTA HISTORICAL SOCIETY. Open by appointment, Monday-Friday, 8:30 am-5 pm. The quilt collection is not on permanent display. As the quilts are in boxed storage, an appointment is necessary. To secure one, contact the Collections Curator, (612) 296-0147. Admission is free.

The 250-quilt collection contains mainly Minnesota-made quilts. The period from the early 19th century to the present day is well covered.

Minnesota Historical Society
690 Cedar St.
St. Paul, MN 55101
(612) 626-6126

MISSISSIPPI

Jackson

MISSISSIPPI STATE HISTORICAL MUSEUM. Open Monday-Friday, 8 am-5 pm; Saturday, 9:30 am-4:30 pm; Sunday, 12:30 pm-4:30 pm. The collection is not on permanent display, but appointments to view the collection may be made with the Curator of Collections. Admission is free.

The museum has an outstanding collection of 125 19th- and 20th-century quilts, mostly Mississippi-made. Among the quilts are examples of pieced, appliquéd, embroidered, stuffed and corded, and homespun construction techniques. The collection includes thirty Afro-American quilts, including three 19th-century slave-made quilts. These three quilts were passed down through different families and each features a different appliquéd design: Princess Feathers, Flower Baskets, and Tulips. Also in the Afro-American section are strip quilts and quilts incorporating grain, flour, feed, and fertilizer sacks. There are a number of fine pieces, including a 1902 map of Mississippi with the counties pieced in silks and velvets, and also an 1880s quilt top with a pieced and appliquéd railroad train design. The museum periodically sponsors textile identification and conservation workshops.

Mississippi State Historical Museum
100 S. State St.
Jackson, MS 39201
(601) 354-6222

MISSOURI

Kansas City

THE KANSAS CITY MUSEUM OF HISTORY AND SCIENCE. Open Tuesday-Saturday, 9:30 am-4:30 pm; Sunday, 12 pm-4:30 pm. The collection is not on permanent display, but quilts can be viewed by appointment. Admission is free. Suggested donation, $3 adults; $2 children.

The museum has some eighty-five quilts, most dating from 1875 to 1920. There is a predominance of Log Cabin patterns and crazy quilts. The collection contains a red, white, and blue star-patterned pieced quilt with shields and flags on a background of white silk. The quilt was made in 1852 by Mrs. Harvey Smith and was exhibited at the 1853 New York Crystal Palace Exposition.

The Kansas City Museum of History and Science
3218 Gladstone Blvd.
Kansas City, MO 64123
(816) 483-8300

St. Louis

THE SAINT LOUIS ART MUSEUM. Open Tuesday, 1:30 pm-8:30 pm; Wednesday-Sunday, 10 am-5 pm. The quilt collection is not on permanent display. Researchers may make appointments to view quilts at the convenience of the museum staff. Admission is free.

The collection is composed of some thirty quilts in a variety of patterns. Most are 19th-century American.

The Saint Louis Art Museum
Forest Park
St. Louis, MO 63110
(314) 721-0067

NEW HAMPSHIRE

Concord

NEW HAMPSHIRE HISTORICAL SOCIETY. Open Monday-Saturday except Wednesday, 9 am-4:30 pm; Wednesday, 9 am-8 pm. The collection is not on permanent display, but access to the quilts is available by appointment. Work space is limited, but, with sufficient notice, scholars are welcome. Admission is free.

The collection consists of pieced and appliquéd quilts primarily dating from the 19th century. These include New Hampshire-made white-on-white, friendship, and crazy quilts. In addition there is an extensive collection of New Hampshire quilt patterns.

New Hampshire Historical Society
30 Park St.
Concord, NH 03301
(603) 225-3381

NEW JERSEY

Burlington

BURLINGTON COUNTY HISTORICAL SOCIETY. Open Monday-Thursday, 1 pm-4 pm; Sunday, 2 pm-4 pm. Part of the quilt collection is on permanent display and rotated periodically with other quilts in storage. Admission, $1.

The collection consists of approximately sixty-five quilts, representing sixteen different patterns: Birds in Flight, Botanical Album, Broken Dishes, Chinese Coins, Christmas Star, Diamond in a Square, Goose Tracks, Irish Chain, Honeycomb, Log Cabin, Nine Patch, Simple Patch, Sunflower, Tumbling Blocks, Twinkling Star, and Wild Goose Chase. Spanning a century, 1806-1906, the collection also contains six signature quilts and sixteen quilts identifiable by maker. Over a dozen utilitarian quilts complete the collection; these represent quilting at its most primitive level, as they are not ornate and were usually hastily fashioned.

Burlington County Historical Society
457 High St.
Burlington, NJ 08016
(609) 386-4773

Morristown

MORRIS MUSEUM OF ARTS AND SCIENCES. Open Monday-

Saturday, 10 am-5 pm; Sunday, 1 pm-5 pm. The collection is not on permanent display; for those involved in serious research, appointments can be made to view particular quilts. Admission, $1.50 adults; 50¢ children.

The seventy-five quilts that make up the collection range from the late 18th century to the present. There is a good representation of New Jersey quilts. Most are pieced or crazy, many are also appliquéd. One very fine crazy quilt was over fifty years in the making, having been started by one New Jersey woman and finished by her daughter. Included in the collection are a number of excellent album quilts.

Morris Museum of Arts and
*   Sciences*
Normandy Hts. and Columbia
*   Rd.*
Morristown, NJ 07960
(201) 538-0454

Newark

THE NEWARK MUSEUM. Open Tuesday-Sunday, 12 pm-5 pm. The collection is not on permanent display, but an appointment can be made if the viewing is for scholarly purposes. Admission is free.

The collection contains 200 pieces; New Jersey quilts predominate, although there are a number from New England. The quilts range in date from early 18th century to the present. The collection includes the Evelyn Dean bride's quilt, made in Orange County in 1860 and containing an ornate appliquéd picture of her house. Another quilt of note is the Hackensack Friendship Medly quilt. Made in 1876, the all-white stuffed quilt

is one of the finest of its type known. The Reasoner crazy quilt is unique in that it is a crazy quilt with a theme—the Hoboken to New York Railway. The museum's Arts Workshop offers adult classes in quiltmaking.

The Newark Museum
49 Washington St.
Newark, NJ 07101
(201) 596-6550

NEW MEXICO

Santa Fe

MUSEUM OF NEW MEXICO. Open Monday-Saturday, 10 am-4:45 pm. The quilts are not on permanent display, but may be viewed by appointment. Admission, $3 adults; $1.25 children.

Dating from 1790 to the present, the sixty quilts that make up the collection are predominantly piecework. Twenty-five New Mexican quilts dating from 1950 to 1986, a broderie perse (c. 1790), a very fine patchwork from New Jersey (c. 1842), and a Texan crazy quilt made of silks with appliquéd flags of various nations comprise the nucleus of the collection.

Museum of New Mexico
North Side of the Plaza
P.O. Box 2087
Santa Fe, NM 87501
(505) 827-8350

NEW YORK

Brooklyn

THE BROOKLYN MUSEUM. Open Monday, Wednesday-Friday, 10

am-5 pm; Saturday, 10 am-6 pm; Sunday, 12 pm-5 pm. Portions of the collection are on display at all times; these are rotated with quilts in storage. An appointment is required to view the quilts in storage. Admission, $2 per person.

The collection contains over 200 quilts dating from the 18th century to the present and displaying a wide variety of construction and pattern types. An interesting feature of the collection is its considerable number of European quilts.

The Brooklyn Museum
188 Eastern Pkwy.
Brooklyn, NY 11238
(718) 638-5000

Cooperstown

NEW YORK STATE HISTORICAL ASSOCIATION. Open May-October, daily, 9 am-5 pm; November-December, Tuesday-Sunday, 10 am-4 pm. The quilts are not on permanent display, but may be viewed by appointment for educational or scholarly purposes. Admission, $4.

Most of the 120 quilts in the collection are post-1850 and about thirty are related to New York State. The makers are known for some thirty of the quilts; six are dated before 1825.

New York State Historical
*   Association*
Fenimore House
Lake Rd.
P.O. Box 800
Cooperstown, NY 13326
(607) 547-2533

Cortland

CORTLAND COUNTY HISTORICAL SOCIETY. Open Tuesday-Saturday, 1 pm-4 pm. The col-

lection is not on permanent display, but viewing is possible by appointment. Admission, $1.

The collection comprises some thirty-five quilts dating from 1830 to 1976. A variety of techniques and patterns is present; many of the quilts are excellent examples of their various genres.

Cortland County Historical
* Society*
25 Homer Ave.
Corland, NY 13045
(607) 756-6071

New York

THE METROPOLITAN MUSEUM OF ART. Open Tuesday-Sunday, 9:30 am-5:30 pm. Because the collection is not on permanent display but in storage, an appointment must be made with the Decorative Arts Department to view the quilts. A donation of $4.50 per person is suggested.

About thirty quilts are in the collection; many are Amish or Amish-influenced; unfortunately the condition of some of these is poor.

The Metropolitan Museum of
* Art*
Fifth Ave. at 82nd St.
New York, NY 10028
(212) 879-5500

MUSEUM OF AMERICAN FOLK ART. Because of ongoing construc-

tion, hours currently vary. The quilt collection is not on permanent display, and appointments to view it are only given to specialized scholars.

The collection is very strongly Amish-orientated—about 125 of the 200 quilts in the collection are Amish pieces. The museum sponsors lectures and classes on quilts as an historic art form; to find out when lectures are scheduled, call the museum office.

Museum of American Folk Art
444 Park Ave. S.
New York, NY 10016
(212) 481-3080

NORTH CAROLINA

Winston-Salem

MUSEUM OF EARLY SOUTHERN DECORATIVE ARTS. Open Monday-Saturday, 10 am-5 pm; Sunday, 1:30 pm-4:30 pm. Portions of the collection are on display on a rotating basis. Quilts in storage may be seen by appointment. Admission, $4 adults; $2 students, children.

The collection contains fifty quilts spanning the years 1790 to 1910. Many have local histories; most are of pieced and appliquéd chintz, although there are some crazy quilts. Occasional seminars and workshops are held by the museum.

Museum of Early Southern
* Decorative Arts*
924 S. Main St.
Winston-Salem, NC 27108
(919) 722-6148

OHIO

Cincinnati

CINCINNATI ART MUSEUM. Open Tuesday-Saturday, 10 am-5 pm; Sunday, 1 pm-5 pm. The collection is not on permanent display, but it can be viewed by contacting the Curator and arranging an appointment. Admission, $2; free on Saturday.

Begun in 1911, the collection has grown slowly and is now a small but select collection of forty quilts. Examples range in date from the 18th century to several from recent years. Highlights include an 1811 John Hewson quilt, a "New York" blue and white quilt, and the Cincinnati quilt of 1973.

Cincinnati Art Museum
Eden Park
Cincinnati, OH 45202
(513) 721-5204

Cleveland

WESTERN RESERVE HISTORICAL SOCIETY. Open Tuesday-Friday, 10 am-3 pm; Saturday-Sunday, 12 pm-5 pm. Several quilts are on permanent display in the period rooms but there is no permanent display. Appointments to view the full collection will be made for scholars conducting research or for other museum curators working on an exhibit. Because of lack of staff, the museum cannot offer these services to the general public. Admission $2.50 adults; $1.50 senior citizens, students; free for children under seven.

The collection contains 225 quilts, ranging in date from 1785-1930. It includes appliquéd and pieced quilts, children's quilts, and quilt tops. Signature and friendship quilts, crazy quilts, and political and historical quilts are also included. One of the most famous pieces in the collection is the Mississippi Greetings quilt which was presented to President and Mrs. McKinley by the Daughters of the American Revolution (*below*).

Western Reserve Historical
* Society*
10825 East Blvd.
Cleveland, OH 44106
(216) 721-5722

Columbus

OHIO HISTORICAL CENTER. Open Monday-Saturday, 9 am-5 pm; Sunday, 10 am-5 pm. The collection is not on permanent display, but requests are taken to see specified quilts. Admission, $2 per car; $25 per bus.

The collection contains close to 200 quilts; most are from the late 19th and early 20th centuries.

Ohio Historical Center
1985 Velma Ave.
Columbus, OH 43211
(614) 466-1500

Lebanon

WARREN COUNTY HISTORICAL SOCIETY MUSEUM. Open Tuesday-Saturday, 9 am-4 pm; Sunday, 12 pm-4 pm. Portions of the collection are always on display, and these are rotated with those in storage. It is possible to view the quilts in storage, but an appointment is necessary. Admission, $3 adults; $1 students.

Representative of the year 1820 to the turn of the century, the collection contains fifty quilts and fifteen coverlets. The only contemporary quilt in the collection was made for the historical society and is stenciled with themes from the museum. The museum owns an exceptionally fine red, white, and blue Sunburst pattern quilt that was the Ohio State Fair winner in 1850. A quilt show and sale is held each March, and each Summer a quilt appraisal is conducted in which experts attempt to date and discuss quilts brought to them by the public.

Warren County Historical
* Society Museum*
105 S. Broadway
P.O. Box 223
Lebanon, OH 45036
(513) 932-1817

Massillon

THE MASSILLON MUSEUM. Open Tuesday-Saturday, 9:30 am-5 pm; Sunday, 2 pm-5 pm. Since the collection is not on permanent display, viewing is possible by appointment only. Admission is free.

Holdings consist of some thirty quilts, mostly made or used by Massillonians; signature, crazy, and Log Cabin quilts

predominate. The collection includes an 1830s hand-painted French chintz album quilt as well as several fascinating contemporary quilts.

The Massillon Museum
212 Lincoln Way
East Massillon, OH 44646
(216) 833-4061

Oberlin

ALLEN MEMORIAL ART MUSEUM. Open Tuesday, Wednesday, and Friday, 11 am-5 pm; Thursday, 11 am-8 pm. The collection is not on permanent display, but it can be viewed by appointment. Admission is free.

This small collection contains quilts dating from the late 19th century. There is a good representation of the best-known styles and patterns. The collection includes the Sarah Mahan quilt as well as a stunning fan-patterned patchwork quilt made of silks, satins, and velvets feather-stitched together.

Allen Memorial Art Museum
Oberlin College
Oberlin, OH 44074
(216) 775-8668

OKLAHOMA

Oklahoma City

OKLAHOMA HISTORICAL SOCIETY. Open Monday-Saturday, 8 am-5 pm. A small portion of the collection is on permanent display; the bulk of the quilts are in storage and are currently inaccessible. Admission is free.

Approximately seventy pieced quilts comprise the collection;

most are common patterns, but there are several of considerable interest. Occasional lectures on textile conservation are given.

Oklahoma Historical Society
2100 N. Lincoln Blvd.
Oklahoma City, OK 73105
(405) 521-2491

OREGON

Jacksonville

SOUTHERN OREGON HISTORICAL SOCIETY. Open Tuesday-Saturday, 10 am-5 pm; Sunday, 12 pm-5 pm. In summer, (Memorial Day-Labor Day), the museum is also open on Mondays, 10 am-5 pm. Only portions of the collection are on display at any one time. To view those quilts in storage, an appointment is necessary. Admission is free.

The collection contains a predominance of crazy quilts. The quilts are generally of local origin and date from the 1850s onwards. Holdings include several very fine examples of Log Cabin and Drunkard's Path variations. The museum hosts an annual quilt exhibition. Formed eight years ago as an auxillery unit of the museum, the Quilting Group acts as a permanent workshop. The group continuously restores old quilts and makes new quilts, thus giving participants hands-on experience.

Southern Oregon Historical
Society
206 N. Fifth St.
Jacksonville, OR 97530
(503) 899-1847

PENNSYLVANIA

Ambridge

OLD ECONOMY VILLAGE. Open Tuesday-Saturday, 9 am-5 pm; Sunday, 12 pm-5 pm. The collection is not on permanent display, but quilts can be viewed by appointment. Admission, $3 adults; $2 senior citizens, $1 children.

The collection contains thirty-five 19th-century quilts, but many are in poor condition. There are also thirty-three coverlets and fragments. Of particular interest is an 1824 Rising Sun-pattern cotton quilt which has puffed stitched-motif trapunto quilting and is also appliquéd.

Old Economy Village
14th and Church Sts.
Ambridge, PA 15003
(412) 266-4500

Harrisburg

THE STATE MUSEUM OF PENNSYL-VANIA. Open Tuesday-Saturday, 9 am-5 pm; Sunday, 12 pm-5 pm. The quilt collection is not on permanent display, but can be seen by small groups or

researchers if advance notice is given. Admission is free.

The collection contains over 200 pieces dating from the early 19th century to the present. A wide variety of styles is held, and most quilts have documented Pennsylvanian histories.

The State Museum of
Pennsylvania
3rd and North Sts.
P.O. Box 1026
Harrisburg, PA 17108-1026
(717) 787-4978

Lancaster

PENNSYLVANIA FARM MUSEUM OF LANDIS VALLEY. Open Tuesday-Saturday, 9 am-4:30 pm; Sunday, 12 pm-4:30 pm. The quilts on display are rotated with those in storage. To view those quilts in storage, an appointment must be made by writing to the director of the museum. Admission, $3 adults; $2 senior citizens, students.

The collection contains fifty quilts, mostly from the late 19th century. The museum holds biannual craft classes, including instruction in quilting.

Pennsylvania Farm Museum of
Landis Valley
2451 Kissel Hill Rd.
Lancaster, PA 17120
(717) 569-0401

Philadelphia

PHILADELPHIA MUSEUM OF ART. Open Tuesday-Sunday, 9 am-5 pm. The collection is not on permanent display, but is stored in the Costumes and Textiles department. Portions of the collection can be viewed by appointment. Admission, $4 adults; $2 senior citizens, students.

Admission is free on Tuesdays and on Sundays before 1 pm. Most of the fifty-seven quilts are 19th-century patchwork quilts of American origin. This very beautiful collection includes the Hancock quilt: a friendship quilt made in Philadelphia in 1842 for the wedding of Samuel P. Hancock. There is also an appliquéd 1840 Baltimore quilt with a Baskets and Flowers pattern in very vivid colors.

Philadelphia Museum of Art
26th and Benjamin Franklin
*   Pkwy.*
P.O. Box 7646
Philadelphia, PA 19101
(215) 785-5404

West Chester

CHESTER COUNTY HISTORICAL SOCIETY. Open Tuesday, Thursday-Saturday, 10 am-4 pm; Wednesday, 1 pm-8 pm; Sunday, 12 pm-4 pm. The quilt collection is not on permanent display but can be viewed by making an appointment with the curatorial staff ten to fourteen days in advance. Admission, $2 adults; $1 senior citizens; 50¢ students.

The collection numbers approximately 200 quilts that range in date from the early 19th century to the early 20th. In addition to complete quilts, the collection includes several quilt tops, and patterns and stencils used in quiltmaking.

Chester County Historical
*   Society*
225 North High St.
West Chester, PA 19380
(215) 692-4800

York

THE HISTORICAL SOCIETY OF YORK COUNTY. Open Monday-Saturday, 9 am-5 pm; Sunday, 1 pm-4 pm. The museum is closed January-March. The collection is not on permanent display, and a written request must be made in order to view the quilts. Admission, $1.50.

The collection contains sixty-five quilts, mostly pieced and ranging in date from the early 19th century to the 1930s. Of particular interest is a John Hewson quilt, c. 1790, which is in excellent condition.

The Historical Society of York
*   County*
250 E. Market St.
York, PA 17403
(717) 848-1587

RHODE ISLAND

Providence

RHODE ISLAND HISTORICAL SOCIETY. Open Tuesday-Saturday, 11 am-4 pm; Sunday, 1 pm-4 pm. The quilt collection is not on permanent display, but it can be viewed by contacting the Curatorial Department and arranging an appointment. Admission, $2.50 for house tour; no charge for an appointment with the curator.

The quilts are mainly 19th century, with several from the 18th century. One 18th-century piece of note is a Brown family quilted calamanco petticoat quilt. Most of the quilts are well documented, and all are repaired or conserved. Three 18th-century quilted calamanco petticoats—all in good condition—are also featured.

Rhode Island Historical Society
52 Power St.
Providence, RI 02906
(401) 331-8575

SOUTH CAROLINA

Charleston

CHARLESTON MUSEUM. Open Monday-Saturday, 9 am-5 pm; Sunday, 1 pm-5 pm. The quilt collection is not on permanent display. Because quilts are rolled and consequently difficult to view, they are only available for serious research. Photographs are available, however, and small portions of the collection can be viewed on specific request. Admission, $3 adults; $1 children.

The collection contains about 100 quilts, half dating from 1821 to 1900. Sixty-four are pieced, including some twenty-three paper-pieced mosaic designs. Twenty-three are appliquéd, many of which are very fine examples of chintz appliqué. Most of the quilts are South Carolina-made, although the origins of others are thus far undocumented.

Charleston Museum
360 Meeting St.
Charleston, SC 29403
(803) 722-2996

Columbia

MCKISSICK MUSEUMS. Open Monday-Friday, 9 am-4 pm; Saturday, 10 am-5 pm; Sunday, 2 pm-5 pm. Since the collection is not on permanent display, an appointment is necessary to view the quilts. Admission is free.

The collection contains twenty

quilts, but the museum also maintains a public collection of the slides and data resulting from the South Carolina Quilt History Project which stores information on 3,100 quilts. On permanent display in the museum is a slide/sound program, "Quilts Like My Mama Did," a study of Afro-American quilt design and its American and West African roots.

McKissick Museums
The University of South
* Carolina*
Columbia, SC 29208
(803) 777-7251

TENNESSEE

Chattanooga

HUNTER MUSEUM OF ART. Open Tuesday-Saturday, 10 am-4:30 pm; Sunday, 1 pm-4:30 pm. The collection is not on permanent display, but can be viewed by appointment. A donation is requested, $1 adults; 50¢ children.

In addition to its quilts, the collection includes the research work of the 1984 Tennessee Quilt Survey, incorporating photographs of 1,425 quilts, interviews with quilt owners and makers, and family history and information relevant to the quilts. The museum sponsors an annual quilt symposium during the first week of April. At least one exhibition of historic or contemporary quilts is held annually, usually in conjunction with the symposium.

Hunter Museum of Art
10 Bluff View
Chattanooga, TN 37403
(615) 267-0968

Norris

MUSEUM OF APPALACHIA. Open daily, 9 am-5 pm. The quilt collection is on permanent display, but an appointment should be made to visit the gallery where it is located. Admission, $2.75 adults; $1.75 children.

The collection contains about thirty quilts, most from the beginning of the 20th century but some from the Civil War period. Of particular interest are several very fine friendship quilts and a number of Victorian quilts with unusual motifs. All of the quilts have a regional history; some are of obviously local construction, using materials such as feed sacks made by area companies. The Museum of Appalachia is a "living" museum where hands-on experience is possible. A unique feature is a partially made quilt that any interested visitor can work on.

Museum of Appalachia
Hwy. 61 at Norris
Norris, TN 37828
(615) 494-7680

TEXAS

Dallas

DALLAS HISTORICAL SOCIETY. Open Monday-Saturday, 9 am-5 pm; Sunday, 1 pm-5 pm. The collection is not on permanent display; contact the Curator of Collections for an appointment. Admission is free.

The collection comprises approximately fifty quilts dating from 1800 to the present and forms a representative selection of Texan quilting in general. The collection contains a very

fine example of fabric stenciling, a technique which was created c.1825-1830. The stenciled quilt dates from c.1830 and has a homespun cotton front and back and a hand-carded cotton batt which makes it very unusual.

Dallas Historical Society
Hall of State
Grand Ave. at Nimitz
Fair Park
Dallas, TX 75226
(214) 421-5136

Edinburg

TEXANA MUSEUM. Open Tuesday-Friday, 1 pm-5 pm. Portions of the collection are on permanent display; the remainder of the collection is divided between temporary displays and the Museum storage areas. Admission is free.

The collection contains twenty-three quilts of assorted patterns.

Texana Museum
403 N. Wells St.
P.O. Box 401
Edinburg, TX 77957
(512) 782-5431

Houston

HARRIS COUNTY HERITAGE SOCIETY. Open Monday-Saturday, 10 am-4 pm; Sunday, 1 pm-5 pm. A selection of quilts is always on display; these rotate with those in storage. Quilts not on exhibit can be viewed for research by appointment. Admission, $4 adults; $2 senior citizens, students; $1 children.

The society currently has seventy quilts in its textile collection. These range from elaborate silk and velvet quilts of the late-Victorian era, to the more utilitarian cotton quilts of the 1840s. Quilt workshops are held at various times in conjunction with an on-going program of crafts classes.

Harris County Heritage Society
1100 Bagby
Houston, TX 77002
(713) 655-1912

VERMONT

Shelburne

SHELBURNE MUSEUM. Open mid-May to mid-October, daily, 9 am-5 pm. More than 200 quilts are permanently on display; quilts on display continually rotate with hundreds more in storage. Admission, $9.50 adults; $4 children.

The Shelburne has the largest public quilt collection in North America, with approximately 650 quilts and coverlets. Begun in 1947 by Mrs. Electra Havemeyer Webb, the collection includes very fine examples of bed rugs, linsey-woolseys, crewel work, candlewick, broderie perse, whitework, coverlets, appliqué, pieced quilts, and crazy quilts. The sheer volume of unusual and very fine pieces makes any brief listing impossible. Each May the museum sponsors a quilt show with lectures and demonstrations.

Shelburne Museum
U.S. Rt. 7
Shelburne, VT 05482
(802) 985-3346

VIRGINIA

Mount Vernon

MOUNT VERNON LADIES' ASSOCIATION OF THE UNION. Open

daily, 9 am-5 pm. The collection is not on permanent display, but the quilts can be viewed by appointment. Admission, $5 adults; $2.50 children.

Most of the twenty quilts in the collection are late 18th century, but some are from the 19th century. The collection contains six quilts attributed to Martha Washington, among them the Penn Treaty quilt.

Mount Vernon Ladies' Association of the Union
Mount Vernon, VA 22121
(703) 780-2000

WOODLAWN PLANTATION. Open daily, 9:30 am-4:30 pm. The quilts on display are rotated with those in storage; those stored may be seen by appointment. Admission, $4 adults; $3 children.

The twelve quilts in the collection are mostly from the mid-19th century. Among them is a very large Baltimore album quilt which displays most of the typical Baltimore bridal motifs. Of particular interest are an 1840 all-white quilt that belonged to Nellie Custis Lewis, and a 19th-century princess feathered quilt in blue and mustard. The Museum holds the materials and information collected by the 1985 Virginia Quilt Survey. Each March, the Museum holds several mini-seminars on quilts and quilting.

Woodlawn Plantation
P.O. Box 37
Mount Vernon, VA 22121
(703) 557-7881

Richmond

VALENTINE MUSEUM. Open Monday-Saturday, 10 am-5 pm; Sunday, 1 pm-5 pm. The collec-

Star of Bethlehem, 1860s.

tion is not on permanent display; viewing is possible by an appointment with the curator of Costumes and Textiles. Admission, $2.50 adults; $2 senior citizens; $1.50 children.

The collection contains over 200 quilts, primarily from Virginia. Documentation is very good as most of the quilts were gifts to the museum by the makers' descendants.

Valentine Museum
1015 E. Clay St.
Richmond, VA 23219
(804) 649-0711

Williamsburg

ABBY ALDRICH ROCKEFELLER FOLK ART CENTER. Open daily, 10 am-9 pm. Only a very small part of the collection is on display, but all the quilts have been photographed and can be seen in this way. Quilts in storage can be seen by appointment, but viewing space is very limited. Admission, $2.50 per person.

The collection contains nearly forty quilts, half of which are pieced. Most of the quilts date from 1840 to 1870, although there are a few 20th century pieces. Of particular interest are two Baltimore album quilts, three wholecloth quilts, and a stuffed whitework quilt c.1815.

*Abby Aldrich Rockefeller Folk
  Art Center
The Colonial Williamsburg
  Foundation
307 S. England St.
Williamsburg, VA 23185
(804) 229-1000*

DEWITT WALLACE GALLERY OF DECORATIVE ART. Open daily except Friday, 11 am-7 pm; Friday, 11 am-9 pm. Almost all the quilts are permanently in storage, but photographs are available for study. Specific quilts in storage can be seen by appointment. Admission, $5.

The collection contains 120 quilts dating from the late 18th century to 1830. Mostly English or American in origin, the quilts are generally cord-quilted, appliquéd, and made of calamanco. There are many very fine pieces in this collection, including a number with Williamsburg histories.

*DeWitt Wallace Gallery of
  Decorative Art
The Colonial Williamsburg
  Foundation
325 W. Francis St.
Williamsburg, VA 23185
(804) 229-1000*

WISCONSIN

Madison

STATE HISTORICAL SOCIETY OF WISCONSIN. Open Monday-Friday, 9 am-5 pm. The collection is not on permanent display, but may be seen by appointment. Admission is free.

The collection contains mainly patchwork pieced quilts. Some excellent examples of early whitework as well as sections of trapunto and appliquéd pieces are also held. The 350-piece collection contains mainly pieces from the 19th century. Of particular note are an exquisite linsey-woolsey, c. 1785, and six early calico quilts from the 1830s and 1840s. One quilt, a Star-of-Bethlehem variant, is made entirely of silks that were scraps from a parasol factory. A workshop on the cleaning, storing, and preservation of quilts, called Caring For Quilts, is held annually.

*State Historical Society of
  Wisconsin
816 State St.
Madison, WI 53706
(608) 262-2704*

Milwaukee

MILWAUKEE PUBLIC MUSEUM. Open daily, 9 am-5 pm. The collection is not on display, but quilts can be viewed by appointment. Admission, $2.50 adults; $1.50 children.

The collection numbers about seventy quilts dating from 1820 to 1930. It includes three trapunto white-on-white quilts, one of which is a very fine crib quilt, c. 1825. Also of interest are several silk quilts from the

1870s and 1880s, including Log Cabin and Tumbling Blocks variations.

*Milwaukee Public Museum
800 N. Wells St.
Milwaukee, WI 53233
(414) 278-2784*

WYOMING

Big Horn

BRADFORD BRINTON MEMORIAL MUSEUM. Open mid-May to Labor Day, 9:30 am-5 pm. Parts of the collection are on display at all times. Admission is free.

The collection contains about a dozen quilts made in the northern region of Wyoming for the Bunton family. All were made prior to 1930; their condition is excellent and the designs are quite unusual.

*Bradford Brinton Memorial
  Museum
239 Brinton Rd.
P.O. Box 23
Big Horn, WY 82833
(307) 672-3173*

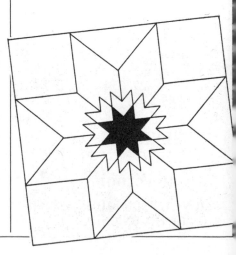

CANADA

ALBERTA

Calgary

GLENBOW MUSEUM. Open daily 10 am-9 pm. The collection is not on display, but can be seen by appointment. Admission, $2.

The collection numbers eighty quilts; half date from 1821 to 1900. Included are six pre-1820 quilts; nearly all the remaining quilts are pre-World War II. Of particular interest are two quilts made from silk cigar bands, three quilts made from commemorative ribbons, four signature quilts, and seventeen Log Cabin variations. The collection also includes ten utilitarian quilts, most in good condition and most made by local Mennonites.

Glenbow Museum
Glenbow-Alberta Institute
130 Ninth Ave. SE
Calgary, AB T2G 0P3
(403) 264-8300

BRITISH COLUMBIA

Victoria

BRITISH COLUMBIA PROVINCIAL MUSEUM. Open daily, summer, 7 pm-9:30 pm; winter, 10 am-5:30 pm. The quilt collection is not on permanent display but may be viewed by appointment. Admission is free.

Although the collection is made up of largely Eastern Canadian pieces, a few are from British Columbia and were mostly made in church groups by Eastern immigrants.

British Columbia Provincial
Museum
675 Belleville St.
Victoria, BC V8V 1X4
(604) 387-3014

MANITOBA

Winnipeg

MANITOBA MUSEUM OF MAN AND NATURE. Open May 15-September 15, Monday-Saturday, 10 am-9 pm; Sunday, 12 pm-9 pm. September 16-May 14, Monday-Saturday, 10 am-5 pm; Sunday, 12 pm-6 pm. The collection is not on permanent display but may be viewed by appointment with the Curator of History. Admission, $2.50 adults; $1.25 students, $1 senior citizens, children.

The collection consists of twenty quilts ranging in date from the 1850s to the 1950s. Most are from Manitoba or Ontario. Pieces of interest include an 1850s goose down, cotton, and silk Steps-to-the-Lighthouse pattern quilt with matching pillow shams, and a mid-20th-century appliquéd quilt of unbleached muslin that was used by Japanese-Canadians in the prairies during World War II.

Manitoba Museum of Man and
Nature
190 Rupert Ave.
Winnipeg, MB R3B 0N2
(204) 956-2830

NEW BRUNSWICK

Saint John

NEW BRUNSWICK MUSEUM. Open Tuesday-Sunday, 10 am-5 pm. Part of the collection is on permanent display; the remainder can be viewed by an appointment with the Curator of Decorative Art. Admission, $2 adults; 50¢ students, $4 family, free for senior citizens and children.

The collection contains some fifty pieces, most relating to New Brunswick. Most common styles and patterns are represented, including some excellent examples of white-on-white.

New Brunswick Museum
277 Douglas Ave.
Saint John, NB E2K 1E5
(506) 693-1196

NOVA SCOTIA

Halifax

NOVA SCOTIA MUSEUM COMPLEX. Open May 15-October 15, Monday-Saturday, 9:30 am-5:30 pm; Wednesday, 9:30 am-8 pm; Sunday, 1 pm-5:30 pm. October 16-May 14, Tuesday-Saturday, 9:30 am-5 pm; Wednesday, 9:30 am-8 pm; Sunday, 1 pm-5 pm. The collection is not on permanent display, but quilts can be seen by appointment. Admission is free.

The collection contains approximately 130 quilts, but these are contained in six historic houses as well as the museum building. The houses are: Haliburton

House, Windsor; Uniacke House, Mt. Uniacke; Sherbrooke Village, Sherbrooke; Ross Farm, New Ross; Fisherman's Life Museum, Jeddore; Lawrence House, Maitland. The collection dates from 1810 to the present and includes many pieced quilts of a simple style, most in Star pattern variations. These are generally set herringbone fashion and are of glazed chintz. The collection also includes an 1810 homespun and handwoven woolen utilitarian quilt and two outstanding appliquéd quilts from the 1870s—one made by Sady Warne of New Tusket and one made by Abigail Uniacke which is a Rose-Wreath pattern with a vining border. The museum holds occasional lectures on quilt-related topics and maintains a slide show called "Looking at Quilts" on permanent display.

Nova Scotia Museum Complex
1747 Summer St.
Halifax, NS B3H 3A6
(902) 429-4610

ONTARIO

Toronto

ROYAL ONTARIO MUSEUM. Open Monday-Sunday, 10 am-6 pm; Tuesday and Thursday, 10 am-8 pm. The collection is not on permanent display, but quilts can be viewed for scholarly purposes by appointment. Admission, $3 adults; $2 senior citizens, students.

The collection contains 200 quilts, of which nearly 150 are Canadian. The remainder are mainly English or American. The collection also includes small numbers of quilts from Ireland, France, China, Germany, Portugal, and India. Occasional lectures are sponsored by the museum's Textile Endowment Fund.

Royal Ontario Museum
100 Queen's Park
Toronto, ON M5S 2C6
(416) 978-3655

QUEBEC

Montreal

MCCORD MUSEUM. Open Wednesday-Sunday, 11 am-5 pm. The collection is not on permanent display, but an appointment can be made for serious researchers to view the quilts. Admission, $1.

Since the McCord Museum is dedicated to Canadian social history, the quilts in its collection were all used in Canada and most were also made there. The museum possesses one of the most interesting of all known North American quilts—a predominantly silk patchwork quilt dated 1726. While its origin cannot be securely traced, the McCord quilt's construction, design, and fabrics all clearly indicate that its appliquéd date is accurate. It is the earliest known example of a pieced bedcover in North America.

McCord Museum
690 Sherbrooke St. W.
McGill University
Montreal, PQ H3A 1E9
(514) 392-4778

*"McCord Quilt", 1726. The McCord
Museum.*

10. A Quilter's Scrap Bag

In the same way that many needleworkers are drawn to the special art of quilting because of the vibrant color combinations and eye-catching shapes of both patchwork and appliqué designs, so, too, are artists and manufacturers outside the sewing field inspired by antique and contemporary examples of the quilter's art. No longer are quilt designs found just on bed-coverings and pillow tops; such motifs now decorate objects with many other useful functions, as well.

Thus quilters can find samples of their favorite pastime reproduced on notecards, postcards, gift wrap, and stationery. Or they can make their own designs using one or several of the many rubber stamps made with quilt motifs. Prints and posters with colorful quilting themes abound, as do annual wall calendars with large, full-color quilt images suitable for framing at year's end, and weekly datebooks and notebooks with lots of room for entering reminders of important events. Makers of cloisonné, pewter, and sterling-silver jewelry adapt popular piecework designs into striking pins and pendants; some manufacturers will take your original design and reproduce it on a lapel pin.

Cheerful magnets with patchwork motifs can affix shopping lists and other memos to the refrigerator door; equally bright coffee mugs hold the morning brew. There are even wooden puzzles which replicate popular patchwork designs.

If you want to introduce your offspring to the joys of quilting, there are colorful children's books to explain some of its special attractions. And, if you find it difficult to attend quilting classes, some of North America's best teachers have now issued videotapes for private instruction at the touch of a button.

These are among the attractive peripheral items which are described in the pages that follow.

Detail, piecework and appliqué album quilt, 1985, Chattanooga, Tennessee. Made by members of the Eastside Branch of Senior Neighbors. Courtesy of Bets Ramsey. Photo by John Coniglio.

BARBIE BECK. Create your own unique stationery with one or more of the hundreds of rubber stamps illustrated in Barbie Beck's catalog. Needleworkers will find lots of different motifs to choose among, from a cross-stitch teddy bear or house to a quilting girl, woman hanging quilts, or a traditional quilt pattern—Ohio Star, Fan, or Bear Paw. Stamp pads come in ten different colors, from dark green and turquoise to burgundy and purple, or in one of three rainbow assortments, each featuring three separate complementary colors in one pad. Barbie Beck also sells plain paper products ready to decorate—letter sheets and envelopes, pads, labels, gift enclosures, boxes, and bags. Catalog, $1.

Barbie Beck
113 Caroline St.
Fredericksburg, VA 22401
(703) 371-3517

BETTY BOYINK. Needleworkers will appreciate Madonna Auxier Ferguson's purse-size *Quilter's Notebook*, which is illustrated with charming country scenes and traditional quilt block designs. Generous space is given for jotting down notes and ideas. Square, diamond, and hexagon grids are printed on the left-hand pages, facilitating quick sketches of design ideas. At your local quilt or fabric shop, or contact:

Betty Boyink Publishing
818 Sheldon Rd.
Grand Haven, MI 49417
(616) 842-3304

COUNTRY ART FOLKS. Artist Barbour Lee is an expert quilter who has won several prizes and has lectured on quilting technique and quilt patterns. Her quilting expertise is evident in the meticulously accurate patterns which are the centerpieces of her paintings. Four of those paintings have been carefully lithographed and the prints, each measuring 14″ by 20″, made available from The Country Art Folks. Each is printed on quality acid-free paper in a limited edition of 2,000 signed and numbered by the artist. Authentication is included. Color brochure, $1.

The Country Art Folks
P.O. Box 698
Centerville, MA 02632
(800) 223-6557

COUNTRY QUILTER. Cloisonné or pewter pins in favorite quilt patterns make ideal gifts for quilters and appropriate adornment on a suit lapel or coat collar. The Country Quilter offers cloisonné pins with the Peony, Stamp Basket, Schoolhouse,

Pine Tree, or Bear Paw motif. Pewter pins come in six patterns, among them Churn Dash, School, Sawtooth, and Basket of Grapes. Or choose a cloisonné sewing machine, thimble box, teddy bear, sewing basket, or miniature stencil. Catalog, $1.

The Country Quilter
Bonny Dr.
Somers, NY 10589
(914) 277-4958

NANCY CROW. A quilter for more than ten years, Nancy Crow works out of a studio on her Ohio farm. Her beautiful quilts are included in the collections of the Museum of American Folk Art and the American Crafts Museum, both in New York City. She has reproduced some of her designs in post-card form. The collection, called Quilts & Details, includes twelve full-color post cards

printed on quality cover stock. Each card measures 5″ by 8″ and features one of her quilts or a detail; all include descriptive information. Look for Nancy Crow post-card sets at your local quilt or fabric shop, or contact:

Nancy Crow
P.O. Box 37
Baltimore, OH 43105
(614) 862-6554

E.P. DUTTON. Cyril I. Nelson's classic *Quilt Engagement Calendar* has been a favorite among quilters and collectors for a number of years. Color photos of antique and contemporary quilts face each week's calendar page; space is provided for making daily notations. Look for *The Quilt Engagement Calendar* at your local quilt or book shop, or contact:

E.P. Dutton, Inc.
2 Park Ave.
New York, NY 10016
(212) 725-1818

GIFTED IDEAS. Highly polished magnets in special limited editions representing colorful quilts—both traditional and contemporary, patchwork and appliqué—are the specialty of Gifted Ideas. Dozens of different motifs are available; the magnets come in sets of four, no two of which are alike. What a delightful way to post notes on your refrigerator door! Brochure available.

Gifted Ideas
P.O. Box 4080
Highlands Ranch, CO 80126
(303) 791-0845

GOOD BOOKS. *Amish Quilts*, an annual calendar compiled by the editors of Good Books, features twelve full-color photos of antique quilts complementing monthly calendar pages. Available at many quilt shops, or contact:

Good Books
Main St.
Intercourse, PA 17534
(717) 768-7171

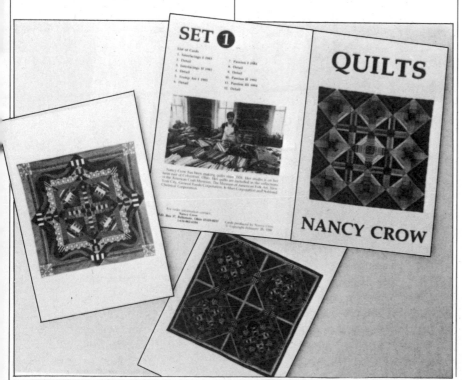

HB ENTERPRISES. Bonnie McCoy is a dedicated quilter, quilting teacher, and judge whose credentials include certification by the National Quilting Association and charter membership in several guilds and associations. She has cooperated with HB Enterprises in the production of a number of instructive video tapes, enabling quilters to take advantage of her classes without ever leaving home. Among the McCoy videos currently available are *The ABC's of Quiltmaking Pieced Quilts, The ABC's of Quiltmaking Appliquéd Quilts* (each 120 minutes in length), and hour-long tapes on specific subjects such as shadow quilting, quick machine techniques, stained-glass quilting, and more. Brochure available.

HB Enterprises
P.O. Box 161
Stockdale, TX 78160
(512) 996-3841

HOT FUDGE PRESS. In *Sunbonnet Sue Goes to the Quilt Show,* Jean Ray Laury presents a humorous and satirical portrait, intended for children of all ages, in which every quilting fanatic will recognize something of herself.

Hot Fudge Press
4974 N. Fresno St., Suite 44
Fresno, CA 93726

JOSEPH'S COAT. Print your favorite patchwork or appliqué design on stationery, gift wrap, cards, name tags, or book plates using one of the rubber stamps from Joseph's Coat. Among the available motifs are Lily, Wild Rose, Oak Leaf, Flying Geese, and Bridal Wreath. Stamp pads come in a choice of seven lively colors. Brochure available for SASE.

Joseph's Coat
26 Main St.
Peterborough, NH 03458
(603) 924-6683

KAYE'S ARTISTIC STITCHERY. Kaye Wood is a quilter and author who also finds the time to conduct workshops and seminars for groups of enthusiastic quilters. She has put together three video tapes on machine patchwork which are taken from her excellent books. Each is sixty minutes long and is available in VHS. Choose *Basic Log Cabin, Reversible Quilts*, or *Log Cabin Triangles.* Brochure available for SASE.

Kaye's Artistic Stitchery
4949 Rau Rd.
West Branch, MI 48661
(517) 345-3028

JEAN RAY LAURY. Jean Ray Laury is a talented quilter and designer whose work hangs in museum exhibitions, galleries, and corporate offices across the country. Full-color reproductions of eight of her original designs are now available in post-card form. The 5″ x 8″ cards include information on the original design. Shown is Lace Quilt, which features lace appliqué on velveteen. The 94″ x 103″ bed cover was commissioned by *Family Circle Magazine* in 1975. Brochure available.

Jean Ray Laury
19425 Tollhouse Rd.
Clovis, CA 93612
(209) 297-0228

THE MAIN STREET PRESS. Main Street's poster-size *Quilts Calendar* is without question the aristocrat of all quilt calendars. Its large format allows the fine details and stitching of superb quilts to be fully visible. Each month is illustrated with a glorious full-color photo of an outstanding antique patchwork or appliqué quilt. Each image is worthy of framing. Information about the quilts' history is included. Available at your local quilt shop or book shop, or contact:

*The Main Street Press
William Case House
Pittstown, NJ 08867
(201) 735-9424*

MARK DISTRIBUTORS. Pretty quilted stands and totes are the specialty of this manufacturer. Each is fully lined and fitted with inside pockets to keep small items readily at hand. Some of the totes come with matching needle cases, other needle cases in several styles are available separately.

*Mark Distributors, Inc.
5239 Commerce
Moorpark, CA 93020
(805) 529-0755*

WILLIAM MORROW & CO. Under its Greenwillow Books imprint, Morrow publishes *The Quilt*, by Ann Jonas, a lovely children's book which tells the story of a little girl who discovers the magic of a patchwork quilt made by her parents using scraps of fabric and tender loving care. Morrow's *Sam Johnson and the Blue Ribbon Quilt*, by Lisa Campbell Ernst, tells the heart warming story of a determined man who tries to invade woman's traditional domain of quiltmaking and, like many men in the past, succeeds.

*William Morrow & Co., Inc.
105 Madison Ave.
New York, NY 10016
(212) 889-3050*

NEEDLEARTS INTERNATIONAL.

Multicolored quilts patterns encircle sturdy, dishwasher-safe ceramic mugs from Needlearts International. Twelve separate patterns are offered, including Double Wedding Ring, Bear Paw, Triple Irish Chain, and Dresden Plate; the Little Red Schoolhouse pattern is available with either red or blue houses. Each mug holds a generous twelve ounces of coffee, tea, or other beverage. Catalog, $1 (refundable with order).

*Needlearts International
P.O. Box 6447
Glendale, CA 91205
(213) 227-1536*

O'CARROLL PRODUCTIONS. The Zachary Taylor Baltimore Album Quilt was made in the first half of the 19th century. Its exquisite blocks have been photographed and reproduced on a set of eight notecards and envelopes available from O'Carroll Productions. Each single-fold card measures 4¼'' by 5½''; the quilt detail is described on the reverse. Cabbage Roses, shown, features two sprays of red and white roses forming a wreath effect. The embroidery is silk and wool. Other quilt panels include an eagle with flag, a wreath with heart, and a cornucopia. Look for O'Carroll's notecards at your local quilt or fabric shop, or contact:

*O'Carroll Productions Ltd.
292 S. Green St.
Berkeley Springs, WV 25411
(304) 258-2732*

THE PATTERN FACTORY. Sally Broeker's Little Red Apples Designs for The Pattern Factory include innumerable kits for dolls, wall hangings, samplers, and clothing. Her talents can also be seen on magazine racks, folder holders, and handwork holders, all of which are

pliquéd quilt pattern you or your guild might have in mind. (Minimum order is 100 units). In addition, The Pin Place now stocks a number of ¾" lapel pins with quilt and country designs. Among the quilt patterns available are Pine Tree, Orange Peel, and Stepping Stone. Or chose an Amish doll, watermelon, or teddy bear. Look for the pins at your local quilt or fabric shop, or contact the firm for information on custom orders. Brochure available.

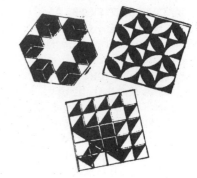

The Pin Place
1508 11th Ave. N.
Fort Dodge, IA 50501
(515) 573-8265

PRAIRIE FARM DESIGNS. In addition to its pre-cut stencils and quilting patterns, Prairie Farm Designs makes dual-purpose cross-stitch note cards. Each card features a full-color photo of a Terry Fatout design; on the overleaf the design is repeated in grid form for easy transfer, and instructions for counted

cross stitch are included. The recipient therefore not only has the pleasure of hearing from you, but gets a charming design to work at her leisure, to boot. Catalog available.

Prairie Farm Designs
578 S. Vine
Denver, CO 80209
(303) 778-7611

available in kit form. Each package includes wood parts, full-size patterns, complete instructions, and three different designs for the front panel. The handwork holder has a fabric liner with pockets to hold sewing, knitting, cross stitch, and small quilting projects and supplies. The Pattern Factory also sells full-color and black-and-white note cards and post cards featuring photos of Amish dolls completed using Broeker's patterns. Catalog $1.50.

The Pattern Factory
8724 104 St. E.
Puyallup, WA 98373
(206) 848-8490

THE PIN PLACE. The specialists at The Pin Place can create custom enamel lapel pins, stickpins, charms, and tie tacks to special order, reproducing from a color photo, sample, or detailed sketch any pieced or ap-

G.P. PUTNAM'S SONS. Award-winning artist Tomie de Paola's beautiful illustrations grace Tony Johnston's text in *The Quilt Story*, which relates the tale of a quilt and the comforts it provides to two little girls as they grow up in different centuries.

G.P. Putnam's Sons
200 Madison Ave.
New York, NY 10016
(212) 576-8900

QUILTS BY DESIGN. Quilts by Design specializes in original art and accessories based on designs from American quilts.

Included are limited-edition graphics, batiks, wooden quilts, quilt blocks, framed antique quilt tops, sweaters with quilt patterns, and stationery, as well as other paper products and gift items. Among the artists represented in the Quilts by Design collection is Judy Severson, whose embossed quilt prints are created from historical and traditional patterns. A number of her prints have been adapted for use in greeting cards. Brochure available.

Quilts by Design
311 Powder Point Ave.
Duxbury, MA 02332
(617) 934-0405

QUILTS OF THE PAST. Gaby Burkert, proprietor of Quilts of the Past, is a quilt collector and researcher interested not only in the fabrics and patterns of antique quilts, but also in the lives and feelings of their creators. Her annual *American Heirloom Quilts Calendar* presents twelve historic quilts in full color, selected not only for their appeal to the contemporary eye, but because they convey a sense of the lives and times of the women who made them. In addition, Burkert has chosen four of her favorite old quilts for reproduction on handsome notecards. Each card contains an explanation of the quilt's history and the pattern's derivation.

Quilts of the Past
943 Delano Ave.
San Francisco, CA 94112
(415) 334-4534

R & E MILES. Two publications from this small press will be of interest to quilters. *Patchwork Year—A Datebook*, by Elaine Miles, includes a poem, a patchwork pattern, and plenty of space to note appointments for each month of the year. In addition, full-size templates are given for making a miniature

quilt. Ms. Miles's *Quilts and Quotes: A Birthday Book* is designed to help you record and remember birthdays, anniversaries, and other important events. Small sketches of traditional quilt patterns and quotations appropriate to some aspect of quilting are included. Look for Miles's books at your local quilt shop, or contact:

R & E Miles
P.O. Box 1916
San Pedro, CA 90733
(213) 833-8856

MARY K. RYAN DESIGN. Mrs. Ryan's variation on the Feathered Star quilt was the recipient of a Judge's Choice Award at the 1986 Houston Quilt Festival. She has now made the quilt available in pattern form, and has also reproduced it in perfect miniature in a $\frac{7}{8}$''-square lapel pin. For further information, contact:

Mary K. Ryan Design
Grandview Terr.
Rutland, VT 05701
(802) 773-6563

SANPETE PUBLICATIONS. The Lone Stars quilt poster produced by Sanpete Publications features an extraordinary Sunburst quilt created circa 1885 by Texas

quiltmaker Sally Beaird Lewellin. The quilt is entirely hand pieced and quilted in double clamshells. In addition to the fine piecing in the sunburst, the vine sashing and border are also pieced, not appliquéd, into the quilt. The full-color poster measures 20″ by 28″. Other posters offered by Sanpete include "Homage to Amanda," a Mariner's Compass quilt circa 1840-1860, and "Quilters" a contemporary quilt featuring a vibrant Tree of Life central block. Brochures available.

Sanpete Publications
2751 W. Monte Vista
Tucson, AZ 85745
(602) 622-8957

SCREEN PROCESS PRINTERS. Among the innumerable gift items manufactured by Screen Process Printers are T-shirts, nightshirts, canvas totes, magnets, bumper stickers, aprons, gift wrap, note cards, bookplates, post cards, stationery, coffee mugs, and buttons. All feature quilting designs and/or humorous slogans, such as "Quilters make better comforters," "I'm a

Quilter, & my house is in pieces," "Quilting forever!... housework whenever," and many more. Look for the display at your local quilt or fabric shop, or send a SASE (with 39¢ stamp) for a brochure.

Screen Process Printers
R.D. 1, Box 2341
Schuylerville, NY 12871
(518) 695-3603

SEITZ HEIRLOOM COLLECTION. The magnetized solid-pine pieces in Quizzle quilt puzzles can be rearranged to form many different authentic quilt patterns. The Pierced Star shown, for instance, is from Seitz's Pinwheel puzzle, which measures 10″ square. The same colored wooden pieces that form the Pierced Star will also make a Windmill, Dutchman's Puzzle, Flock of Geese, Wild Goose Chase, and several other patterns. Three different puzzles are made by Seitz, each available in several different col-

or combinations. Look for Seitz's Quizzle puzzles at your local quilt shop, or contact the firm for a brochure.

Seitz Heirloom Collection
P.O. Box 1521
Barrington, IL 60011
(312) 382-3642 or
(312) 674-7854

SEMINOLE SAMPLER. Sterling-silver pins and pendants designed by Esther Blackburn, an award-winning jeweler, are available in three traditional quilt designs exclusively from Seminole Sampler. Choose Cake Stand, Variable Star, or Pine Tree, in either pin or pendant form (the pendant comes with an 18″ or 20″ sterling-silver chain). Catalog, $2 (refundable with order).

Seminole Sampler
P.O. Box 658
Ellicott City, MD 21043
(301) 465-6266

TAYLOR BEDDING. Morning Glory brand polyester batting manufactured by Taylor Bedding is a favorite among quilters across North America. The Taylor Company has produced a 22″ by 28″ full-color poster, "Batting a Thousand," whose photograph of stacks of antique quilts will inspire contemporary quilters and collectors alike. Brochure available.

Taylor Bedding Mfg. Co.
P.O. Box 979
Taylor, Texas 76574
(512) 352-6311

Other Suppliers of Quilter's Scrap Bag Items

Consult Directory of Suppliers for Addresses

And Sew On, El Segundo, CA
Betty Boyink Publishing, Grand Haven, MI
Cabin Fever Calicoes, Center Sandwich, NH
Iva Capps, Fredericksburg, VA
Country Crafts & Fabrications, Folsom, CA
Creative Stitches, Honolulu, HI
EA of Hawaii, Kailua, HI
Laura Fanclla's/BBP Designs, S. San Francisco, CA
Oaksprings Impressions, Fairfax, CA
The Quilt Patch, Marlboro, MA
Quilter's Peace, Garrison, NY
Quilts & Other Comforts, Wheatridge, CO
Quiltwork Patches, Corvallis, OR
Stencil Ease, New Ipswich, NH
Take One Productions, Silver Spring, MD
Treadleart, Lomita, CA

VANESSA-ANN COLLECTION. Illustrations taken from the pages of children's books are produced in 18″ x 24″ poster size by the Vanessa-Ann Collection. Of particular interest to quilters will be this illustration by award-winning artist Tomie de Paola from Clement Moore's *The Night Before Christmas*. "Take Time to Dream," also by de Paola, portrays a mother and daughter hard at work finishing a pieced quilt. Brochure available.

The Vanessa-Ann Collection
P.O. Box 9113
Ogden, UT 84409
(801) 621-2777

THE VERMONT PATCHWORKS. Unusual pin cushions created by Mary K. Ryan are among the gift items featured in The Vermont Patchworks catalog. All are backed with velveteen and filled with lamb's wool to keep your needles rust-free. Available in navy, green, or burgundy, their octagonal shape is roughly 4½″ in diameter. Other products of interest to quilters include bumper stickers and coffee mugs from Screen Process Printers; note cards from CVO Designs of Vermont, featuring six separate quilt designs; a collection of post cards illustrating antique quilts; and rubber stamps with quilt motifs. Catalog, $2 (refundable with order).

The Vermont Patchworks
229 Old Plymouth Rd.
Shrewsbury, VT 05738
(802) 492-3590

Directory of Selected Quilting Shops and Suppliers

Alabama

Attic Antiques
5620 Cahaba Valley Rd.
Birmingham, AL 35243

Calico Patch
5000 Sparkman Dr.
Hwy. 53
Huntsville, AL 35810

House of Quilts
P.O. Box 25, Main St.
Springville, AL 35146

Needle Arts Ltd.
5453 Old Shell Rd., #117
Mobile, AL 36608-3001

Patches & Stitches
2336A Whitesburg Dr.
Huntsville, AL 35801

Quiltique
110 Antigo Pl.
Oxford, AL 36203

Quilts Unlimited Inc.
3930 Crosshaven Dr.
Birmingham, AL 35243

Quilts 'n' Stuff
837 Williamson Rd.
Montgomery, AL 36109

Strawberry Patch Inc.
5336 Oporto Rd.
Birmingham, AL 35210

Alaska

Alaska Multi Crafts
3101 Penland Pkwy.
Anchorage, AK 99508

Country Classics
1104 E. Northern Lights
Anchorage, AK 99508

Muslin Moose
P.O. Box 154
Iliamna, AK 99606

Strawberry Ridge Store
32 College Rd.
Fairbanks, AK 99701

Arizona

American Star
P.O. Box 9
Arlington, AZ 85322

Crimson's Quilt Circus
25 E. Main
Mesa, AZ 85201

The Frame Mate
P.O. Box 26964
Tempe, AZ 84282

Homespun Quilts and Things
3530 W. Mescal St.
Phoenix, AZ 85029

Just Us
P.O. Box 50023
Tucson, AZ 85703-1023

Marie Products
P.O. Box 56000
Tucson, AZ 85703

Pine Country Quilts
413 N. San Francisco
Flagstaff, AZ 86001

Pollyanna
5645 E. 9th St.
Tucson, AZ 85711

The Quilt Basket, Inc.
3506 E. Grant Rd.
Tucson, AZ 85716

Quilter's Ranch
1042 E. Baseline Rd.
Tempe, AZ 85283

Quilter's Outpost
2240 Golf Links Rd.
Sierra Vista, AZ 85635

Sanpete Publications
2751 W. Monte Vista
Tucson, AZ 85745

Sedona's Country Store
P.O. Box 592
Sedona, AZ 86336

Arkansas

Boyce's
23600 Barry Ln.
Little Rock, AR 72204

Country Heirlooms
Rt. 5, 538 Patmos Rd.
Hope, AR 71801

Delta Comforts
P.O. Box 88
Lexa, AR 72355

Heirloom Creations Inc.
14722 Taylor Loop Rd.
Little Rock, AR 72212

Patchwork Emporium
224 S. 2nd St.
Rogers, AR 72756

Quilt House
10500 W. Markham
Little Rock, AR 72205

Strawberry Patch
708 Main
Van Buren, AR 72956

Sue's Calico Shop
Rt. 1, Box 142
Hensley, AR 72065

California

Abadine's Fabrics Inc.
657 Foothill Blvd.
La Canada, CA 91011

The American Quilter
P.O. Box 7455
Menlo Park, CA 94026

And Sew On
P.O. Box 386
El Segundo, CA 90245

Appalachia
14440-E Big Basin Way
Saratoga, CA 95070

Artistic Quilting Studio
524½ N. La Cienega
Los Angeles, CA 90048

Bits 'n' Pieces
155 Lincoln Center
Stockton, CA 95207

Branch of the Lily
Flower Hill Center, B-140
Del Mar, CA 92014

Calico Barn
138 W. 25th Ave.
San Mateo, CA 94403-2208

Calico Corner Quilt Shop
366 E. La Habra Blvd.
La Habra, CA 90631

Calico Crafts Fabrics
175 Cohasset Rd.
Chico, CA 95926

Calico Creations
12642 Poway Rd., C14
Poway, CA 92064-4416

Calico Cupboard
321 Redmond
El Segundo, CA 90245

Calico Horse
444 W. Highland Ave.
San Bernardino, CA 92405

Calico Mouse
924 Sespe Ave.
Fillmore, CA 93015

Calico Station
330 W. Felicita Ave., #A1
Escondido, CA 92284

Calico 'n' Canvas
398 Chorro St.
San Luis Obispo, CA 93401

Calico 'n' Quilts
1755 E. F St.
Oakdale, CA 95361

California Fiberloft Inc.
2167 E. 25th
Los Angeles, CA 90058

Caskey Lee's Gallery
P.O. Box 244
Venice, CA 90291-0244

Margaret Cavigga Quilt
  Collection
8648 Melrose Ave.
Los Angeles, CA 90069

Celtic Design Co.
834 W. Remington Dr.
Sunnyvale, CA 94087

Clever Lady
7356 Acoma Trail
Yucca Valley, CA 92284

Connection
5360 Fairfax Ave.
Oakland, CA 94601

Connie's Calicos
6122 Cardeno Dr.
La Jolla, CA 92037

Cotton Ball
75 Morro Bay Blvd.
Morro Bay, CA 93442

Cotton Blossom
12092 Royal Birkdale
San Diego, CA 92128

The Cotton Patch
1025 Brown Ave.
Lafayette, CA 94549

Country Cloth
17490 Monterey St.
Morgan Hill, CA 95037

Country Crafts & Fabrications
721 Sutter St.
Folsom, CA 95630

Country Patch
4350 Tyrolite
Riverside, CA 92509

Country Store
163 Guava Ave.
Chula Vista, CA 92010

Cozy Fabrics
14421 New Jersey Ave.
San Jose, CA 95124

Crafts and Ewe
1949 E. Valley Pkwy.
Escondido, CA 92026

Crazy Ladies & Friends
1606 Santa Monica Blvd.
Santa Monica, CA 90404

Creative Needle
1144 Main St.
St. Helena, CA 94574

Creative Touch
143 W. Walnut
Visalia, CA 93277-5366

Crestview Yardage Center
1428 Freedom Blvd.
Watsonville, CA 95078

Cuellar Quilting
2011 E. First St.
Los Angeles, CA 90033

Deutsch Quilting Co.
1135 S. Robertson Blvd.
Los Angeles, CA 90035

Elephant Quilts
234 Reina Del Mar Ave.
Pacifica, CA 94044

Empty Spools
140B Alamo Plaza
Alamo, CA 94507

Eye of the Needle
P.O. Box 2560
Yountville, CA 94599

Fabric Fair
40 E. Washington
Petaluma, CA 94952

The Fabric Patch
903A W. Foothill Blvd.
Upland, CA 91786

Fabric Showcase
487 Skyhill Ct.
Chula Vista, CA 92010

Fabric 'n' Things
P.O. Box 2560
Clearlake, CA 95422

Fabrications
118 Matheson St.
Healdsburg, CA 95448-4108

Fabulous Things Ltd.
1974 Union
San Francisco, CA 94123

The Gazebo of New York
South Coast Plaza
3333 Bristol St.
Costa Mesa, CA 92626

Ginger Designs
P.O. Box 3241
Newport Beach, CA 92663

Glenda's
369 W. Napa St.
Sonoma, CA 95476

Going to Pieces
1989F Santa Rita Rd.
Pleasanton, CA 94566

Grandma's House
1982 Sobre Vista Rd.
Sonoma, CA 95476

Granny's Quilts & Things
1500 8th St.
Manhattan Beach, CA 90266

Heartfelt
3053 Shattuck Ave.
Berkeley, CA 94705

The Hearth
2705 E. 4th
Long Beach, CA 90814

Heirloom
1143 Avenue E, J-5
Lancaster, CA 93535

Heritage Quilts
19680 Ojai Dr.
Cottonwood, CA 96022

Home Arts Center
P.O. Box 186
Covina, CA 91722

Hot Fudge Press
4974 N. Fresno St., Ste. 44
Fresno, CA 93726

Imperial Quilting
9540 Owensmouth Ave.
Chatsworth, CA 91311

It's a Stitch
1350 E. Glenoaks
Glendale, CA 91206-2612

J L Needlecraft
22547 Lassen St.
Chatsworth, CA 91311

Jacque's Quilt Gallery
312 Manhattan Beach Blvd.
Manhattan Beach, CA 90266

Jodi's Mercantile
710 Sutter St.
Folsom, CA 95630

Johnson Hand Sewn Quilts
12624 Felipe
El Monte, CA 91732

Kaleidoscope V
P.O. Box 572
Newhall, CA 91322

Katie's Quilt Shop
3147 Brian Ct.
Arcata, CA 95521

Kay's Fabrics
201 W. Napa St., #14
Sonoma, CA 95476

Kiracofe and Kile
955 14th St.
San Francisco, CA 94114

Laura Fanella's/BBP Designs
P.O. Box 5217
S. San Francisco, CA 94083

Jean Ray Laury
19425 Tollhouse Rd.
Clovis, CA 93612

Lexington Place
552 S. Lake
Pasadena, CA 91101

Lillian Sculpture Fabric
6657 Lankershim Blvd.
N. Hollywood, CA 91606

Louise's Fabrics/Quilts
13972 Riverside Dr.
Sherman Oaks, CA 91423

M & M Quilt Shop
5906 N. Figueroa
Los Angeles, CA 90003

The Mail Pouch
P.O. Box 1373
Monrovia, CA 91016

Manos Maravillosas
1057 Rosecrans St.
San Diego, CA 92106

Mark Distributors, Inc.
5239 Commerce
Moorpark, CA 93020

Mary Russell
398 Chorro St.
San Luis Obispo, CA 93401

Mary's Homespun Shop
111 Fletcher Pkwy.
El Cajon, CA 92020-2510

Material Pleasures
148 E. Duarte Rd.
Arcadia, CA 91006

Maudie's Place
37761 Niles Blvd.
Fremont, CA 94536

R. & E. Miles
P.O. Box 1916
San Pedro, CA 90733

The Mill
120 W. Main
Turlock, CA 95380

Miller Brown Gallery
335 Hayes St.
San Francisco, CA 94102

Needle Arts
206 G St.
Antioch, CA 94509

Needle Nook
35157 Yucaipa Blvd.
Yucaipa, CA 92339

Needlearts International
P.O. Box 6447
Glendale, CA 91205

Needlecrafters/Quilters
870 Grand Ave.
San Diego, CA 92109

Needlework Patch
18900½ Ventura Blvd.
Tarzana, CA 91356

Nimble Needles
1321 Sapphire Dr.
Santa Maria, CA 93454

Ninepatch
2001 Hopkins
Berkeley, CA 94707

Northern Feather Inc.
360 W. Victoria St.
Compton, CA 90220

Oaksprings Impressions
P.O. Box 340
Fairfax, CA 94930

Olympia Quilting Inc.
12220 Rivera Rd., #8
Whittier, CA 90606

Panache
24611 Shadow Fax Dr.
El Toro, CA 92630

Patches, Fabrics & Quilts
6362 Robertson Ave.
Newark, CA 94560

Patchwork Pansy
1830 Howard Rd.
Madera, CA 93637-5139

Patchwork Stitcher
5238 Arlington Ave.
Riverside, CA 92504

Patchwork 'n' Things
P.O. Box 3725
Granada Hills, CA 91344

Patti's Afghan Alley Gift Shop
2147 Foster St.
Oceanside, CA 92054

PC Quilt
7061 Lynch Rd.
Sebastopol, CA 95472

Peace and Plenty
7320 Melrose Ave.
Los Angeles, CA 90046

Pieceful Pleasures
566 30th Ave.
San Mateo, CA 94403

Piecemakers
1720 Adams Ave.
Costa Mesa, CA 92626-4863

Pin Cushion
111 Main
Half Moon Bay, CA 94019

Poppy Fabric
2072 Addison St.
Berkeley, CA 94704

Quality Quilters
13401 S. Western Ave.
Gardena, CA 90249

Quilt Basket
P.O. Box 3158
Quartz Hill, CA 93534

Quilt Emporium
4835 El Canon Ave.
Calabasas, CA 91302

Quilt Inn
362 N. Moorpack Rd.
Thousand Oaks, CA 91360

Quilt Patch
3423 E. Broadway
Long Beach, CA 90803

Quilt Peddler
1267 Hidden Mountain Dr.
El Cajon, CA 92020

Quilt Peddler
8580 La Mesa Blvd.
La Mesa, CA 92041

Quilt Sails
1020 S. Gaffey St.
San Pedro, CA 90731

Quilt & Quilt Studio
5369 Foothill Blvd.
Oakland, CA 94601

Quilted Counterpane
801 Los Robles
Davis, CA 95616

Quilter's Paradise
6716 N. Cedar, #101
Fresno, CA 93710

Quilting Bee
221 Main St.
Los Altos, CA 94022

Quilting House
18085 Euclid
Fountain Valley, CA 92708

Quilts Andsoforth
9589 Upland St.
Spring Valley, CA 92077

Quilts of the Past
943 Delano Ave.
San Francisco, CA 94112

Quilts Unlimited
2202 W. Artesia Blvd.
Torrance, CA 90504

Quilts West
501 San Mateo Rd.
Half Moon Bay, CA 94019

Quilts 'n' Things
3507 Tully Rd., #12
Modesto, CA 95356

Quiltworks
2855 Roosevelt St.
Carlsbad, CA 92008

Quiltworks
240 Loma Ave.
Tiburon, CA 94920

Quilt N Stuff
8302 E. Stewart at Gray Rd.
Downey, CA 90241

Sawtooth Quilt Shop
1560 4th St.
San Rafael, CA 94901

Schoolhouse Quilts
2452 Mission
Carmichael, CA 95608

Sew & Sew
P.O. Box 893
Aptos, CA 95003

Sewing Factory
1137 North 2nd St.
El Cajon, CA 92021

Sewing Shanty
25108 C Marguerite Pkwy.
Mission Viejo, CA 92692

Shirley's Quilts—Fabrics
928 Town & Country Village
San Jose, CA 95128

Soft Touch
P.O. Box 98
Rheem Valley, CA 94570

Solvang Needlework
1578 Mission Dr.
Solvang, CA 93464

South Bay Quilting
4702 Oyster Bay Dr.
San Jose, CA 95123

A Step Back
117 Crest Dr.
Manhattan Beach, CA 90266

Samuel Steward
2016-X Ninth St.
Berkeley, CA 94710

Stitch in Time
6193 Lake Murray Blvd.
La Mesa, CA 92041

Tahoe Textiles & Trims
P.O. Box 6985
Tahoe City, CA 95730

Thimbleweed
1895 Tulare Ave.
Richmond, CA 94805-2022

Thomasina Unlimited
17824 Tribune St.
Granada Hills, CA 91344

Treadleart
25834 Narbonne Ave., Ste. 1
Lomita, CA 90717

Tomorrow's Treasures
2836 Imperial Hwy.
Brea, CA 92621

Velona Needlecraft
5753 E. Santa Ana Canyon
Anaheim Hills, CA 92807

Wild Goose Designs
521 Castro St.
San Francisco, CA 94114

Barbara Williams
2642 Phaeton Dr.
Oroville, CA 95966

Yours Truly, Inc.
A Division of Burdett
  Publications
5455 Garden Grove Blvd.
Westminster, CA 92683

Colorado

Calico and Quilts
2700 W. Bowles, #C
Littleton, CO 80120-1836

Calico Sampler
Arapahoe Village Ctr.
Boulder, CO 80302

Counted Stitch Cottage
929 Magnolia
Colorado Springs, CO 80907

Gifted Ideas
P.O. Box 4080
Highlands Ranch, CO 80126

Gossip Bench
1581 York Rd.
Colorado Springs, CO 80918

Great American Quilt Factory
10101 E. Hampden Ave.
Denver, CO 80231

High Country Quilts
485A N. Academy Blvd.
Colorado Springs, CO 80907

Homespun Heart Antique Quilts
208 W. 8th St.
Leadville, CO 80461

Near and Far Bazaar, Inc.
2615 E. 3rd St.
Denver, CO 80206

Nine Patch Quilt Shop
511 N. Union Blvd.
Colorado Springs, CO 80909

Patchworks
700 Florida, #101
Longmont, CO 80501-6452

Prairie Farm Designs
578 S. Vine
Denver, CO 80209

Quilt Array
133 La Plata Ln.
Durango, CO 81301-7003

Quilt Patch
2313 17th St.
Greeley, CO 80631

Quilting Fair, Inc.
6390 W. 44th Ave.
Wheatridge, CO 80033

Quilts & Other Comforts
P.O. Box 394-3
6700 W. 44th Ave.
Wheatridge, CO 80034

Quilts by Flo
5103 Rocking R. Dr.
Colorado Springs, CO 80915

Quilts in the Attic
1025 S. Gaylord
Denver, CO 80209

R & B Fabrics Inc.
304 E. 5th St.
Loveland, CO 80537

Silver Thimble, Inc.
8745 Wadsworth Bldg.
Westminster, CO 80003

Stitching Heart
821 E. 16th St.
Greeley, CO 80631-6125

Village Quilts Ltd.
P.O. Box 1601
Wheatridge, CO 80034-1601

Connecticut

Judi Boisson
89 Main St.
Westport, CT 06880

Calico Etc.
116 Elm St.
Cheshire, CT 06410

Calico Patch
P.O. Box 1304
Manchester, CT 06040-1304

Carole's Textiles
246 258 Brookfield Common
Brookfield, CT 06804

Colchester Mill Fabrics
Broadway & Clark Ln.
Colchester, CT 06415

Contemporary Quilting
173 Post Rd.
Fairfield, CT 06430

Cotton Patch Designs
440 Main St.
Ridgefield, CT 06877

Country Needle
Rt. 44 by the Wagonshed
Ashford, CT 06278

The Craft Cupboard
37 Mossa Dr.
Bristol, CT 06010

Esther's Fabric Shop
70 Liberty St.
Danbury, CT 06810

Fairfield Processing Corp.
P.O. Box 1130
Danbury, CT 06813

Patty Gagarin Antiques
Banks North Rd.
Fairfield, CT 06430

Gingham Gate
58 Greenmanville Ave.
Mystic, CT 06355

Glastonbury Quilt Shoppe
2717 Main St.
Glastonbury, CT 06033-2022

The Gray Goose
32 Cannon Rd.
Wilton, CT 06897

Phyllis Haders
158 Water St.
Stonington, CT 06378

J & N Fabrics
55 W. Main St.
Clinton, CT 06413

Jabberwocky
P.O. Box 202
Chester, CT 06412-0202

Martha Jackson Antiques
Riverside, CT 06878

Monroe Craft & Fabric
500 Monroe Tpke.
Monroe, CT 06468

New England Quilt Tradition
123 Church St.
Guilford, CT 06437

Patches & Patchwork
216 Main
Portland, CT 06480

Patches & Patterns
P.O. Box 456-T
Georgetown, CT 06829

Iris and Mel Penner
Stamford, CT 06902

Quilters Quarters
93 Faith Rd.
Newington, CT 06111

Stonington Needleworks
186 Haley Rd.
Mystic, CT 06355

Susan Bates Inc.
212 Middlesex Ave.
Chester, CT 06412

Tailend Workshop
37 Martin Rd.
E. Haven, CT 06512

Village Stitchery
Olde Mystic Village
Mystic, CT 06355

Yankee Pride
21 Morkland Ln.
Wilton, CT 06897

Delaware

Creations Plus
2612 Capitol Trail
Newark, DE 19711

Quilts & Needlecrafts
1107 Highgate Rd.
Wilmington, DE 19808

District of Columbia

American Decorative Arts
406 7th St. NW
Washington, DC 20004

Appalachian Spring
1415 Wisconsin Ave. NW
Washington, DC 20007

Marston Luce
1314 21 St. NW
Washington, DC 20036

Sheila's Hallmark
3103 M St. NW
Washington, DC 20007

Florida

Annie's Attic
2339 Wilton Dr.
Ft. Lauderdale, FL 33305

Attic Trunk
126 N. Park Ave.
Winter Park, FL 32789

Calico Bear
P.O. Box 2304
New Smyrna Beach, FL 32069

Calico Square Inc.
709 W. Alamo Dr.
Lakeland, FL 33803-9128

Cottage Country Crafts
12552 Condor Dr.
Jacksonville, FL 32223-2714

Deborah's Quilting Basket
327 W. Venice Ave.
Venice, FL 33594

Grammy's Quilt Shop
489 S. Yonge St.
Ormond Beach, FL 32074

Miami Quilting Center
208 NE 65 St.
Miami, FL 33138

Needle Arts Harbour
433 Harrison Ave.
Panama City, FL 32401

Need-L-Mania
10465 Big Tree Circle E.
Jacksonville, FL 33217

Patches & Calico
4339 Alternate A1A
Lake Park, FL 33404

Patchwork Cottage
222 E. First St.
Sanford, FL 32771

Deanna Powell
702 Endicott Rd.
Melbourne, FL 32935

Quilt Shop of Tallahassee
241 E. 6th Ave.
Tallahassee, FL 32303

Quilter's Rule, Inc.
3201 Davie Blvd.
Ft. Lauderdale, FL 33312

Quilts, Etc.
1500 S. Hwy. 301
Dade City, FL 33525

Quiltworks
P.O. Box 12051
Gainesville, FL 32604

Quiltworks, Inc.
5891 SW 73rd St.
S. Miami, FL 33143

Rainbow Quilts
143 NE Fourth Ave.
Delray Beach, FL 33444

Sandpiper Art & Needlework
385 Tequesta Dr.
Tequesta, FL 33458

School for Inquiring Mynds
241 E. Sixth Ave.
Tallahassee, FL 32303

Sewing Circle Fabrics
914 58th St. N.
St. Petersburg, FL 33710

Stitch Cottage
1690 Dundee Rd.
Winter Haven, FL 33880

Vicki's Wishing Well
7161 Pembroke Rd.
Pembroke Pines, FL 33023

Village Quiltworks
1345 US 1
Rockledge, FL 32955

Wanda's Quilting/Sewing Center
7310 Manatee Ave. W
Bradenton, FL 33529

Georgia

Clayton House Craft Shop
P.O. Box 778
Stone Mountain, GA 30086

Colonial Quilts & Crafts
832 E. De Renne Ave.
Savannah, GA 31405

Corner Sampler
6135 Peachtree Pkwy.
Norcross, GA 30092

Cotton Pickin' Shop
4842 La Vista Rd.
Rucker, GA 30084

Craft Castle
650 Ethel St. NW
Atlanta, GA 30318

Granny Taught Us How
1921 Peachtree Rd. NE
Atlanta, GA 30309

Needlecraft Corp. of America,
   Inc.
North Industrial Blvd.
Calhoun, GA 30701

Patch Works
2179 Scenic Hwy.
Snellville, GA 30278

Quilts 'n' Stuff
Rt. 1, P.O. Box 360
Cumming, GA 30130

Status Thimble
692 N. Glynn St.
Fayetteville, GA 30214

Thimbelina
517 E. Paces Ferry
Atlanta, GA 30305

Village Quilt Shop
5348 E. Mountain St.
Stone Mountain, GA 30083

Yarn Basket
16 Public Sq.
P.O. Box 2070
Dahlonega, GA 30533

Hawaii

Creative Stitches
900 Fort St. Mall, #143
Honolulu, HI 96813

EA of Hawaii
150 Hamakua Dr., Ste. 360
Kailua, HI 96734

Hawaiian Designing Collection
P.O. Box 1396
Kailua, HI 96734

Idaho

Family Heirlooms
2809 Hillway Dr.
Boise, ID 83702-0941

Hissing Goose Gallery
4th and Leadville Sts.
P.O. Box 597
Ketchum, ID 83340

Klaus B. Rau Co.
P.O. Box 1236
Coeur d'Alene, ID 83814

Patty's Patchwork
2650 Cole Rd.
Boise, ID 83705

The Quilt Barn
P.O. Box 1252
421 S. River
Hailey, ID 83333

Snip-n-Whip
1420 S. Blaine
Moscow, ID 83843

Illinois

Anna's Quilt Shop
5516 W. Belmont
Chicago, IL 60641

The Apple Basket Quilt Shop
1922 Central St.
Evanston, IL 60201

A-1 Sewing Center
1052 Stanford Ave.
Springfield, IL 62703

Betty's Quilting School
3620 Greenwood Ave.
Rockford, IL 61107

Calico Station
P.O. Box 4025, Rt. 34
Oswego, IL 60543-9445

Cardena's Quilt Shop
5319 S. Kedzie
Chicago, IL 60632

Carrow and McNerney Country
   Antiques
P.O. Box 125
Winnetka, IL 60093

Chicago Crafts & Quilts
P.O. Box 148155
Chicago, IL 60614

Cottage Quilts
625 Cottonwood Rd.
Frankfort, IL 60423

Cotton Gin
1308 South 2nd
Springfield, IL 62704

De Kalb Sewing Center
65 N. River Lane, Sta. 104
Geneva, IL 60134

Everything Nice
124 N. Randolph
Macomb, IL 61455

The Fosters
RR 2
Pittsfield, IL 62363

Frank A. Edmunds & Co., Inc.
6111 S. Sayre
Chicago, IL 60638

Grannie Annie's Shoppe
128 N. Plum
Havana, IL 62644

Granny's Quilts
4509 W. Elm St.
McHenry, IL 60050

Grist Mill Ends 'n' Things
39 E. Main St.
Carpentersville, IL 60110

Helga's
1261 Naper Blvd.
Naperville, IL 60504

Knit & Rip Shop
208 S. Grand Ave.
E. Springfield, IL 62704

Morning Call Patterns
P.O. Box 538
Wilmette, IL 60091

Needle Case
Long Grove & Old McHenry
Long Grove, IL 60047

Needlecraftsman Inc.
1607 Evanston Ave.
Evanston, IL 60201

Patchwork a' Plenty
106 W. Sixth St.
O'Fallon, IL 62269

Peddlers on the Square
8508 W. Rt. 120
Woodstock, IL 60098

Prints Charming
108 S. Third St.
Bloomingdale, IL 60108

Prints Charming Ltd.
221 Coffin Rd.
Long Grove, IL 60047

Quest 52 Quilts
166 N. Scoville Ave.
Oak Park, IL 60302

The Quilted Fox
65 N. River Ln., #104
Geneva, IL 60134

Quilter's Cupboard
1943 Grove St.
Blue Island, IL 60406-2664

Quilting Books Unlimited
156 S. Gladstone
Aurora, IL 60506

Quilting Treasures
809 N. Eddy St.
Sandwich, IL 60548-1316

I. Ronin & Co., Booksellers
1554 W. Devon Ave.
Chicago, IL 60660

Seitz Heirloom Collection
P.O. Box 1521
Barrington, IL 60011

Sew Creative
66 E. Central Park Plaza
Jacksonville, IL 62650

Simply Quilts
310 E. Leonard
Staunton, IL 62088

Stitchery Plus
3323 Vollmer Rd.
Flossmoor, IL 60422

Stitches
300 S. Main
Wheaton, IL 60187

Stitches 'n' Stuffing
790 Royal St. George Dr., Ste. 119
Naperville, IL 60540

Stitching Post
430 W. Erie St., #3
W. Chicago, IL 60610-4032

Sweet Nothings
208 N. Neil
Champaign, IL 61820

Swiss-Metrosene, Inc.
7780 Quincy St.
Willowbrook, IL 60521

Taylors Cutaways & Stuff
2802 E. Washington St.
Urbana, IL 61801

Things & Such Shoppe
217 W. St. Louis
Lebanon, IL 62254

Turn of the Century Shop
519 W. Front St.
Wheaton, IL 60187

What-Not Shop
224 Plainfield Rd.
Crest Hill, Il 60435

Winnetka Stitchery
547 Lincoln
Winnetka, IL 60093

Woodstock Wool Company
P.O. Box 284
Woodstock, IL 60098

Indiana

Alcorn's Antiques
214 W. Main St.
Centerville, IN 47330

Comforts of Home
611 E. 10th St.
Jeffersonville, IN 47130

Cotton Patch
115 S. Johnson
Bluffton, IN 46714

Country House Quilts
170 S. Main
Zionsville, IN 46077

Country Shop
1402 E. 161 St.
Westfield, IN 40674-9622

Fly by Night Arts
6416 Ferguson St.
Indianapolis, IN 46220

Folkways
Rt. 2, P.O. Box 365
Georgetown, IN 47122

Fullerton's Fabric/Yarn
6101 N. Clinton
Fort Wayne, IN 46825

Gingham Gallery
109½ N. Michigan St.
Plymouth, IN 46563

Gohn Brothers Mfg. Co., Inc.
P.O. Box 111
Middlebury, IN 46540

Rebecca Haarer
P.O. Box 52
Shipshewana, IN 46565

Hancock Fabrics
523 E. Hwy. 131
Clarksville, IN 47130

Homespun Haus
P.O. Box 1497
Columbus, IN 47202

Hoosier Patchwork
The Butternut Tree
P.O. Box 273
Vernn, IN 47282

Humble Collector
Rt. 4, P.O. Box 66
N. Manchester, IN 46962

Jenny's
Rt. 2, P.O. Box 47
Angola, IN 46703

Little School House
20033 Country Rd. 16
Bristol, IN 46507

Margie's Country Store
721 W. Main
Madison, IN 47250

Moss Patch
2597 W. Lexington
Elkhart, IN 46514

Needle in the Haystack
2307 E. 10th St.
Anderson, IN 46012

Needles in the Haystack
116 N. Illinois
Monticello, IN 47960

Quilt Parlor
RR 3, Box 105
Nashville, IN 47448

Quilters Patch
5937 E. State Rd. 45
Bloomington, IN 47401

Quilts Etc.
P.O. Box 429
Grabill, IN 46741-0429

Quilts Plus
1748 E. 86th St.
Indianapolis, IN 46240

Quilts & More Inc.
1601 S. 7th St.
Terre Haute, IN 47802

Quilt, Etc.
3550 N. Wells
Ft. Wayne, IN 46808

Sew 'n' Sew
2125 S. 4th St.
Lafayette, IN 47905

Sewing Room
1404 Wheeling Ave.
Muncie, IN 47303

Somethin Special
2524 S. Rogers
Bloomington, IN 47401

Spin a Yarn & Fabrics
109 S. Washington
Crawfordsville, IN 47933

Strings and Things
RR 1, Box 61
Oakland City, IN 47660

Value Mart
Rt. 2, P.O. Box 78A
Rising Sun, IN 47040

Village Fabrics Shop
2515 Will Crest Dr.
Indianapolis, IN 46208

Yoder Department Store
State Rd. #5, P.O. Box 245
Shipshewana, IN 46565

Yours in Stitches
207 W. College
Kouts, IN 46347

Iowa

Alexander's Fabrics
57 Jefferson
Winterset, IA 50273

Amish Quilts
P.O. Box 621
Fairfield, IA 52556

Cocking's Yarn & Craft
1404 First Ave. NE
Cedar Springs, IA 52402

Corn Patch Quilt Works
RR1
Elkhart, IA 50073

Country Quilts
N 70 W 6344 Bridge Rd.
Cedarburg, IA 53012

Cranny
2118 E. 11th
Davenport, IA 52803

Cross Patch
1514 Main
Rock Valley, IA 51247

Gingham Goose
2534 Perry Rd.
Council Bluffs, IA 51501

Hall Closet at Allie's
Main St.
Mt. Vernon, IA 52314

Heritage Quilting Designs
4111 Woodridge Dr., NE
Cedar Rapids, IA 52401

Janet's Quilt Shop
RR 1, RHCM #76
Shellsburg, IA 52332

Jensen Antiques
2017 E. 13th St.
Davenport, IA 52803

Joy Collection
1210 E. First St.
Sioux Center, IA 51250

Kalico Keepsakes
Rt. 2, P.O. Box 199
Ottumwa, IA 52501

Kalona Kountry Kreations
RR 1, Box 266
Kalona, IA 52247

Mary Ellen's—Davenport
2017 E. 13th St.
Davenport, IA 52803

Mrs. Wigg's Cabbage Patch
3600 Bel Aire
Des Moines, IA 50310-4242

The Pin Place
1508 11th Ave. N
Fort Dodge, IA 50501

The Quilting B
315 3rd Ave. SE, Ste. 207
Cedar Rapids, IA 52401

Snip & Stitch
2114 Pinetree Ct.
Clear Lake, IA 50428

Strawberry Patch Fabrics
4112 Morningside Ave.
Sioux City, IA 51106

The Yarn Hutch Inc.
2227 Jersey Ridge Rd.
Davenport, IA 52803

Kansas

Antique Quilting Shoppe
8265 Tauromee
Bethel, KS 66109

Baldwin Dry Goods
713 Eighth St.
Baldwin City, KS 66006

Calico Country Quilts
Fairview & Walton
Lucas, KS 67648

Calico Cupboard
10142 W. 86th St.
Overland Park, KS 66212

Calico Patchworks
1707 S. Murlen
Olathe, KS 66062

Cottonwood Hearth
5958 SW 24th Terr.
Topeka, KS 66614

Country Appliques
P.O. Box 7109
Shawnee Mission, KS 66209

Drapery Fashion by Debbi
RR1, Box 173
Great Bend, KS 67530

Helen M. Ericson
P.O. Box 650
Emporia, KS 66801

Golden Thimble
1415 Country Club
El Dorado, KS 67042-4302

Gramma's Calico Cupboard
1223 E. Harry
Wichita, KS 67211

Heirloom Creations
3619 21st St.
Great Bend, KS 67530

Mark's International Oriental
Rugs and Carpets
5512 Johnson Dr.
Mission, KS 66202

Minor Hobby Sewing Center
105 N. Commercial
Oswego, KS 67356-1009

Murdock Mercantile
P.O. Box 71
Murdock, KS 67111

Osage County Quilt Factory
400 Walnut, P.O. Box 490
Overbrook, KS 66524

Quilt Patch
136 S. Oliveri Rd.
Kechi, KS 67067

Quilt Patch
7715 W. 151st St.
Stanley, KS 66223

Quilter's Stitch
3714 W. 95th
Leawood, KS 66206

Quilts and Patches
815 W. 61 N.
Wichita, KS 67204

Quilts 'n Things
1851 S. Ridgeview
Olathe, KS 66062-2288

Sarah's
925 Massachusetts
Lawrence, KS 66044

Stitch On Needlework Shop, Inc.
926 Massachusetts St.
Lawrence, KS 66044

This Ol' House
½ mile E. of Janet
Nortonville, KS 66060

Village Sampler
926 Massachusetts
Lawrence, KS 66044

Kentucky

American Accents
706 Lexington Pl.
Louisville, KY 40206-2955

American Quilter's Society
P.O. Box 3290
Paducah, KY 42002-3290

Busy Bee
409 W. Broadway
Frankfort, KY 40601

Calico Cat
1359 E. Fourth St.
Owensboro, KY 42301

Cross Stitch Plus, Inc.
1110 Pollard Rd.
Ashland, KY 41101

Dee's Crafts—Home Decor
3917 Chenoweth Sq.
Louisville, KY 40207

Finishing Touch
2004 Frankfort Ave.
Louisville, KY 40206

Louisville Nimble Thimble
2521 Browns Ln.
Louisville, KY 40220

Needlecraft House
208 W. Main St.
Morganfield, KY 42437

Pauline and Donna's Quilts
4333 N. Preston Hwy.
Shepherdsville, KY 40165

Quilt Box
Hwy. 467, Walnut Springs Farm
Dry Ridge, KY 41035

Quilt Patch
1128 LaVista
Louisville, KY 40219

Quiltin' Bee
380 S. Mill
Lexington, KY 40508

Red Brick House
120 Main St.
Midway, KY 40347

Bruce and Charlotte Riddle
116 W. Broadway
Bardstown, KY 40004

Shelly Zegart's Quilts
12-Z River Hill Rd.
Louisville, KY 40207

Louisiana

Calico Patch Inc. Gallery Shop
150 W. Prian Rd.
Lake Charles, LA 70601

Cotton Patch
228 Dunleith Dr.
Destrahan, LA 70047

Country Stitches
927 Francais Dr. S.
Shreveport, LA 71118

Fiber Five
3131 Perkins Rd.
Baton Rouge, LA 70808

Friendly Needle
2240 Litchwood Ln.
Harvey, LA 70058-2219

Holdcraft Cottage
511 Dumaine
New Orleans, LA 70116

Manifestations
P.O. Box 850335
New Orleans, LA 70185

Needle Treasures
2444 Midway St.
Shreveport, LA 71108

Quilt Cottage, Inc.
801 Nashville Ave.
New Orleans, LA 70115

Quilt Shop Inc.
3131 Perkins Rd.
Baton Rouge, LA 70808

Quilt Store & More
157 Northwood Circle
West Monroe, LA 71291

Quilter's Roost
404 Ormond Dr.
Pearl River, LA 70452

Quilts & Quaints
221 N. Lee Rd.
Covington, LA 70433

The Salt Box
2310 Fagot St.
Metairie, LA 70001

Yesterday's & Today's
5223 Government St.
Baton Rouge, LA 70806

Maine

Blueberry Hill Farm
P.O. Box 740, Saddleback Rd.
Rangeley, ME 04970

Brewer Fabric Shop
Twin City Plaza
Brewer, ME 04412

Calico Basket Quilt Shop
40 Page Rd.
Windham, ME 04062

Calico Cat Quilt Shop
Rt. 202, P.O. Box 151
Alfred, ME 04002

Cuddledown
87 Pleasant
Yarmouth, ME 04096

Greenhouse Gallery
RR1, Box 6
Alfred, ME 04002

Kaleidoscope Quilting
181 Stillwater Ave.
Old Town, ME 04468

Marcia's Country Comfort
448 Woodford St.
Portland, ME 04103-2460

Needleworks
212 Center
Auburn, ME 04210

Patchwork Boutique Quilt
304 Beach St.
Saco, ME 04072

Patricia Stauble Antiques
P.O. Box 265
Pleasant and Main Sts.
Wiscasset, ME 04578

Willow Tree Designs
P.O. Box 79
Gray, ME 04039-0079

Maryland

All of Us Americans Folk Art
P.O. Box 5943
Bethesda, ME 20814

American Penny Royal
5 N. Harrison St.
Easton, MD 21601

Ann's Fabrics & Crafts
16019 Frederick Rd.
Glenwood, MD 21738

Appalachiana
10500 Old Georgetown Rd.
Bethesda, MD 20014

Ark 'n' the Dove
9736 Ocean Hwy.
Ocean City, MD 21842

Bellwether Dry Goods
137 Bayard Rd.
Lothian, MD 20820

Carol & Company
13460 New Hampshire Ave.
Silver Spring, MD 20904

Community Quilts
7710 Woodmont Ave.
Bethesda, MD 20814

Company Mouse
4935 Elm St.
Bethesda, MD 20814

Cottonseed Glory, Inc.
4 Annapolis St.
Annapolis, MD 21401

Country Antiques
RD 1, Box 35
Pry Mill
Keedysville, MD 21756

Country Quilt Shop
P.O. Box 91
Uniontown, MD 21157

Fabricworks
Maryland Ave. at State
Annapolis, MD 21401

G Street Fabrics
11854 Rockville Pike
Rockville, MD 20852

Sally Goodspeed
2318 N. Charles St.
Baltimore, MD 21218

Griffith House Antiques
21414 Laytonsville Rd.
Laytonsville, MD 20760

Heirloom Needlecrafts
2215 Defense Hwy.
Crofton, MD 21113

Jenny's Sewing Studio
311 Civic Ave.
Salisbury, MD 21801

Julie's Quilt Shop
282 N. Frederick Ave.
Gaithersburg, MD 20811

Katie's Variety Store
RR 3, Box 203
Mechanicsville, MD 20659

Moss Antiques
11510 Parkedge Dr.
Rockville, MD 29852

Nimble Thimble Quilters
58th Ave.
Berwyn Heights, MD 20740

Paper Moon
Town Hall Mall
St. Michaels, MD 21663

Patches & Pegs
7129 Deer Valley Rd.
Highland, MD 20777-9513

Patches & Pegs
9354 Gentle Way
Columbia, MD 21045-5104

Patchwork Parlor
510 National Hwy.
La Vale, MD 21502

Patchworks
5526 Hayloft Ct.
Frederick, MD 21701-6909

Pin Cushion
Hwy. 5 S., P.O. Box 27, Heritage
  Ctr.
Waldorf, MD 20601

Prince George's Quilts
6903 Ingraham St.
Riverdale, MD 20737

Quilter's Delight
804 Conowingo Rd.
Bel Air, MD 21014

Quilts Etc.
7041 Sulky Ln.
Rockville, MD 20852

Recollections
10400 Old Georgetown Rd.
Bethesda, MD 20014

Stella Rubin Antiques
12300 Glen Rd.
Potomac, MD 20854

Sandy's Fabrics Inc.
Charles Country Plaza
Waldorf, MD 20601

Seminole Sampler
P.O. Box 658
Ellicott City, MD 21043

Seminole Sampler
Savage Mill
Savage, MD 20763

Shillcraft Needle Arts
500 N. Calvert St.
Baltimore, MD 21202

Cathy Smith Antique Quilts
P.O. Box 681
Severna Park, MD 21146

Spectrum 39 Needlework
3811 Canterbury Rd.
Baltimore, MD 21218

Take One Productions, Inc.
13618 Georgia Ave.
Silver Spring, MD 20906-5213

Traditions at the White Swan
Rt. 2, Box 15AA
Hagerstown, MD 21740

Wood 'n' Quilts
Rt. 1, P.O. Box 355
Rohrersville, MD 21779-9715

Massachusetts

Art Needlecraft
P.O. Box 339
Malden, MA 02148

Art of Quilting
155 School St.
Mansfield, MA 02048

Atlas Fabrics Store Inc.
57 Green St.
Worcester, MA 01604

Sally Bates Quilt Shop
2 Grandview Ave.
Burlington, MA 01803

Bear Paw Stitchery Inc.
11 Canal St.
Lee, MA 01238

Bee Hive Studio
RD1, Box 503A
Mashpee, MA 02649-9756

Best Cottons & Calicoes
J.C. Best Co.
10 Marshfield St.
Gloucester, MA 01930

Books for Embroidery
96 Roundwood Rd.
Newton, MA 02164

Calico Stitchery Quilts
452 Main St.
W. Springfield, MA 01089

Carol's Calico Pincushion
214 Low St.
Newburyport, MA 01950

Community Industries
P.O. Box 898
Pittsfield, MA 01202

Concord River Quilts
30 Ranlett Ln.
Billerica, MA 01821

The Country Art Folks
P.O. Box 698
Centerville, MA 02632

Country House Quilts
4 Durham St., c/o S.L. Gould
Boston, MA 02115

Country Mouse House
P.O. Box 574
Agawam, MA 01001

Crafters Potpourri
366 Alden Rd.
Fairhaven, MA 02719

Cranberry Quilters
161 Bay Rd.
S. Hamilton, MA 01982

Decorative Quilting
592 E. Third St.
S. Boston, MA 02127

Fabric Nook
1087 Main St.
Holden, MA 01520

Fabric Warehouse
390 Newton St.
Waltham, MA 02154

Fabrics Warehouse Unlimited
142 Main St.
Gloucester, MA 01930

Feathered Star Antiques
27 Spruce Ln.
Holden, MA 01520-1636

Bette S. Feinstein
96 Roundwood Rd.
Newton, MA 02164

Gifted Hand
32 Church St.
Wellesley, MA 02181

Green Goose
34 South Rd.
Bedford, MA 01734

Heath Hen Quilt Shop
Beach Rd., P.O. Box 1917
Vineyard Haven, MA 02568

Heartfelt
RD 340
Vineyard Haven, MA 02568

Hobby Time Helpers
P.O. Box 128
Southwick, MA 01077

House of Patchwork
P.O. Box K56-11, Maple Rd.
S. Chelmsford, MA 01824

Ladybug Quilting Shop
612 Rt. 6A, Main St.
Dennis, MA 02638

Marks Scissors
c/o Zivi Hercules, Inc.
50 Kerry Pl.
Norwood, MA 02062

Mayflower Quilters
60 Warehouse
Rowley, MA 01969

Meadow Mouse
143 Shaker Rd.
E. Longmeadow, MA 01028

Meadows House
74 Meadowbrook Rd.
Springfield, MA 01128

Mehlco Crafts
705 Waverly
Framingham, MA 01701

Merrimack Valley Quilters
15 Kenoza Ave.
Haverhill, MA 01830

Mount Vernon Antiques
P.O. Box 66
Rockport, MA 01966

Mountain Colors
41 Elm St.
Marblehead, MA 01945

Mulberry Tree
150 Main
Northampton, MA 01060

New England Quilters
P.O. Box 73
Carlisle, MA 01741

Patches
P.O. Box 140
Dalton, MA 01226

Piecemaker Quilt Shop Society
674 Springfield St.
Feeding Hills, MA 01030

Plain People Fine Quilts
461 Main St.
Chatham, MA 02633

Quil Things
7 Jefferson Dr.
Acton, MA 01720

Quilt House
858 Main St.
Osterville, MA 02655

Quilt Patch
208 Brigham St.
Marlboro, MA 01752-3138

Quilter's Quarters
P.O. Box 534, Rt. 20
Sturbridge, MA 01566

Quilts & Things
114 Bay View Rd.
South Chatham, MA 02659-1622

Quilts by Design
311 Powder Point Ave.
Duxbury, MA 02332

Sew Crazy
78 Main St., Rt. 3A
Kingston, MA 02364

Shrewsbury Quilt Shop
48 Maple Ave.
Shrewsbury, MA 01545

Slotnick & Snow
81 East St.
Granby, MA 01033

Stitchery
204 Worcester Tpke.
Wellesley, MA 02181

Stitchery Shop
68 Central
Wellesley, MA 02181

Tumbleweed
99 Mt. Auburn St.
Cambridge, MA 02138

Tumblewood's Fantasy
170 Water St.
Plymouth, MA 02360

Wonderful Things
Stockbridge Rd.
Great Barrington, MA 01230

Worcester Craft Center
25 Sagamore Rd.
Worcester, MA 01605

Yarn Barn
317 Woburn
Lexington, MA 02173

Yarne Towne Inc.
15 Franklin St.
Leominster, MA 01453-3526

Michigan

Air Lite Synthetics Mfg., Inc.
342 Irwin St.
Pontiac, MI 48053

Amish Quilters
P.O. Box 438
Clarkston, MI 48016

Artist's Cove
6373 Belle River Rd.
Marine City, MI 48039

Barbara Bannister Needlecraft
  Books
5811 U.S. 31N
Alanson, MI 49706

Barlond Sewing Center
295 E. Columbia Ave.
Battle Creek, MI 49015

Bed 'n' Stead
6 Forest Pl.
Plymouth, MI 48170

Bishop's Sewing Center
103 E. Main St.
Niles, MI 49120

Bits 'n' Pieces
1033 Mason
Dearbon, MI 48124

Betty Boyink Publishing
818 Sheldon Rd.
Grand Haven, MI 49417

Brilliance
24865 Five Mile Rd. #2
Redford, MI 48239

Calico Cupboard
248 S. Kalamazoo Mall
Kalamazoo, MI 49007

Calico 'n' Things
P.O. Box 265
Marquette, MI 49855

Country Craftique
7810 Fifth St.
Dexter, MI 48130

Creative Quilts
15819 O'Brien Ct.
Grand Haven, MI 49417-9422

Cross Roads Fabric Quilt Shop
Saline, MI 48176

Crosspatch
1014 S. Mission
Mt. Pleasant, MI 48858

Daisy Den Stitchery
2290 44th St. SE
Grand Rapids, MI 49508

Exemplary
P.O. Box 2554
Dearborn, MI 48124

Golden Fleece
33305 Grand River
Farmington, MI 48024

Grandma's Attic
213 W. Main St.
Brighton, MI 48116

Grandville Fabrics
4045 Chicago Dr.
Grandville, MI 49418

Homestead Needle Arts
8036 Holly Rd.
Grand Blanc, MI 48439

Honey Bee Quilt Shop
7648 Riverview Dr.
Jenison, MI 49428

Kaye's Artistic Stitchery
4949 Rau Rd.
West Branch, MI 48661

Kean's Hallmark Variety
406 S. Jefferson
Mason, MI 48854

Kitchen & Fabric Center
214 E. Chicago Blvd.
Tecumseh, MI 49286

Lerouvray
90 E. Square Lake Rd.
Troy, MI 48098

Lura's Patchwork
P.O. Box 408
Plymouth, MI 48170

Margie Ann's
194 S. Beuxie Blvd.
Beulah, MI 49617

Needleart Guild
2729 Oakwood NE
Grand Rapids, MI 49505

Nimble Thimble Needlecraft
463 N. Main
Frankenmuth, MI 48734

Norwood Looms
P.O. Box 167-B
Fremont, MI 49412

The Patchwork Parlor
109 Petoskey Ave.
Charlevoix, MI 49720

Plain & Fancy Quilt Supplies
119 Church St.
Gregory, MI 48137

Quilt Basket
3359 3rd St.
Wyandotte, MI 48192

Quilt Works
13268 Dixie Hwy.
Holly, MI 48442-9723

The Quilter's Patch, Inc.
17100 Kercheval
Grosse Pointe, MI 48230

Quilts Etc.
428 Main St.
Brighton, MI 48116

Quilts & Country Crafts
406 Lakeland
Grosse Point, MI 48230

Quilts & Cover Ups
3723 Ridgefield
Lansing, MI 48906

Quilts 'n' Friends
4090 17 Mile Rd.
Sterling Heights, MI 48077

Rags to Riches
1353 Langeland Ave.
Muskegon, MI 49442-5269

Rainbow's End
125 E. Main St., P.O. Box 332
Caledonia, MI 49316

Sewing Basket
71 W. Pearl St.
Cordwater, MI 49036

Sewing Bird
7946 Emberly Dr.
Jenison, MI 49428-9104

Sue Elle's Quilt Shop
59591 Jerdean Dr.
Hartford, MI 49057

Sunny Side of the Street
6457 Main
Cass City, MI 48726

Things Americana
30 West Bridge
Rockford, MI 49341

Traurig's Quilt & Pillow
22050 Woodward Ave.
Ferndale, MI 48220

Village Connection
13201 Harper
Detroit, MI 48211

Wiffle Tree Quilt & Gift
11965 Maple Island
Fremont, MI 49412

Minnesota

Attic Workshop Quilts
4033 Linden Hills Blvd.
Minneapolis, MN 55410

A-1 Sew Craft
6894 Cavell Ave.
Champlin, MN 55316

Bakehouse Yorkshire Farm
RR3, Box 25
Owatonna, MN 55060

Blossom Shop
Main St.
Blooming Prairie, MN 55917

Calico Cat
8415 County Rd. 11
Maple Plain, MN 55359-9730

Calico Patch
309 Ave. E.
Cloquet, MN 55720

Calico Trunk Inc.
1340 Arrowhead Rd.
Duluth, MN 55811

Clausen Quilts
5412 Newton Ave. S.
Minneapolis, MN 55419

The Cotton Patch
517 Marie Ave. S.
St. Paul, MN 55075

Cotton Shoppe
2920 N. 2 St.
Minneapolis, MN 55411-1606

Country Mill
68 Plaza West Shopping Ctr.
St. Cloud, MN 56302

The Country Peddler Quilt Shop
2242 Carter Ave.
St. Paul, MN 55108

Country Quilt Shop
920 Fourth Ave.
Windom, MN 56101

Patricia Cox
6601 Normandale Rd.
Minneapolis, MN 55435

Craftsman's Touch
812 Beltrami Ave.
Bemidji, MN 56601

Dick's Calico/Hobby
5672 Cherry Hill Rd.
Hopkins, MN 55343

Down Quilt Shop
145 Southdale Ctr.
Minneapolis, MN 55435

Ellie's Sewing Center
910 Oak St.
Brainerd, MN 56401

Europa Designs
178 Peninsula Rd.
Richfield, MN 55441

Fabric House
2555 Shadywood
Navarre, MN 55392

Gingham Patch
RR2, Box 59
Blue Earth, MN 56013

Glad Creations Quilts
3400 Bloomington Ave. S.
Minneapolis, MN 55407

Hand-You-Downs
1562 Goodrich Ave.
St. Paul, MN 55105

Heirloom Needle Arts
12 Bridge Sq.
Anoka, MN 55303

Herberger's
110 N. Minnesota St.
New Ulm, MN 56073

Jeanie's Needleart
5820 Aldrich Ave. N.
Minneapolis, MN 55430

Kathy's Quilts
Rt. 1
Isle, MN 56342

Ker Spinning Wheel Loom
RR 2
Mora, MN 55051-9802

Li'l Prints Shop
204 NW First Ave.
Grand Rapids, MN 55744

Lou's Country Fabric
909 S. 6th
Brainerd, MN 56401

Millbridge Country Store
1675 S. Plymouth Rd.
Minnetonka, MN 55343

Monestead
113 E. Lincoln Ave.
Fergus Falls, MN 56537

Needle Point of View
825 Washington Ave. SE
Minneapolis, MN 55414

Northwoods Pioneer Craft
Hwy. 61 E.
Two Harbors, MN 55616

Patchwork Alley
3972 Cedarvale Shopping Ctr.
Eagan, MN 55111

Patchwork Shop
116 Minnesota Ave. N.
Aitkin, MN 56431

Potpourri
20 SW Third St.
Rochester, MN 55902

Quilt Shop
16240 Hillcrest Ln.
Eden Prairie, MN 55343

Quilters Closet Ltd.
3972 Hwy. 13
Eagen, MN 55122

Quilters' Retreat
6601 Normandale Rd.
Richfield, MN 55435

Ram Wools
400 First Ave.
Minneapolis, MN 55401

The Sampler
314 Water St.
Excelsior, MN 55331

Ship 'n' Stitch
106 St. Olaf
Canby, MN 56220

Shoe String
11 N. Main
Mabel, MN 55954

Spinning Wheel
248 E. Second St.
Redwood Falls, MN 56283

Stitchin Time
57 S. Lake St.
Big Lake, MN 55309

Wayzata Quilt Emporium
856 E. Lake St.
Wayzata, MN 55391

Mississippi

Gray Squirrel
9116 Dixie St.
Ocean Springs, MS 39564

Helene's Quilt Korner
P.O. Box 896
Riegeland, MS 39157

Linen & Calico Shoppe
Clinton Plaza
Clinton, MS 39056

Marge Murphy
P.O. Box 6306
6624 April Bayou
Biloxi, MS 39532

Pitty Patts Calicos
717 Fort Hill Dr.
Vicksburg, MS 39180-2135

Quilt Gallery
Rt. 5, P.O. Box 250
Booneville, MS 38829

Missouri

Art Mart Inc.
2355 S. Hanley
St. Louis, MO 63144-1502

Brewer Quilting Shop
418 Manchester
Manchester, MO 63011

Calico Corner Quilt Shop
928 W. Daugherty
Webb City, MO 64870

Calico Crafts
8848 E. 18th St.
Independence, MO 64052

Calico House
RR 2, Box 16E
Washington, MO 63090-9602

Susan Davidson Antiques
102 S. Elm
St. Louis, MO 63119-3018

Economy Quilting
9324 St. Charles Rock Rd.
St. Louis, MO 63114

Feather Circle Quilts
410 E. Promenade
Mexico, MO 65265

Hapco Products Inc.
46 Mapleview Dr.
Columbia, MO 65201

Huning's Department Store
201 N. Main
St. Charles, MO 63301

Kenley's Quilt & Fabrics
420 S. Main
Independence, MO 64050

Patches Quilt Shop
337 S. Main
St. Charles, MO 63301

Patchwork
25 N. Gore
Webster Groves, MO 63119

Patchwork Sampler
168 Parsons
St. Louis, MO 63119

Quilt Cottage
1108 Sunset Ln.
Columbia, MO 65203-2253

Quilt Shoppe
2762 S. Campbell
Springfield, MO 65807

Quilt Square
13426 Clayton Rd.
St. Louis, MO 63131

Quilting Frame
920 Church
St. Joseph, MO 64501

Sign of the Turtle
5223 Gravois Blvd.
St. Louis, MO 63116-2309

Stitchery
115 E. Third
Cameron, MO 64429

Taylor's Fabric House
204 Main
Festus, MO 63028

Village Sampler
11420 Gravois Ave.
St. Louis, MO 63126

Montana

Lost Arts & Stitchery
33 N. Main
Butte, MT 59701

Patchwork Parlour
2609 Selvig Ln.
Billings, MT 59101

Patchworks
271 S. Wilson
Bozeman, MT 59715

Quilt Gallery
721 Central Ave. #2
Great Falls, MT 59401

Quilt Gallery
1325 Hwy. 2 W.
Kalispell, MT 59901

Quilt Teachers Co-op
5100 S. 19th Rd.
Bozeman, MT 59715

Stitching Post
3965 Hwy. 93
Stevensville, MT 59870

Stitchin' Time
P.O. Box 1314
Dillon, MT 59725

Nebraska

Aunt Faith's Cupboard
1715 Vinton St.
Omaha, NE 68108

Calico House
5221 S. 48th St.
Lincoln, NE 68516

Heart's Content
Piedmont Shopping Center
Lincoln, NE 68510

Log Cabin Quilt Shop
1123 S. 119th St.
Omaha, NE 68144

Nancy's Quilting Shop
3702 N. 16th
Omaha, NE 68110

Patch Works
1216 W. Second St.
Grand Island, NE 68801

Rag Bag, Inc.
P.O. Box 1124
Scottsbluff, NE 69361-1124

Nevada

Log Cabin Calicoes
184 E. Plumb Ln.
Reno, NV 89502

Quilter's Corner
2470 E. Tropicana
Las Vegas, NV 89121

Sew Special Inc.
4012 Rainbow Blvd., #K
Las Vegas, NV 89103

New Hampshire

Blueberry Cottage
159 Water
Exeter, NH 03833

Cabin Fever Calicos
54 Range Rd.
Center Sandwich, NH 03227

Calico Cupboard
Main St.
Lincoln, NH 03251

Covered Bridge Quilting Shop
449 Amherst St.
Nashua, NH 03063

Dorr Mill Store
P.O. Box 88, Hale St.
Guild, NH 03754

Fabric Patch Inc.
RD 6, Box 461
Guilford, NH 03246

G & G Fabrics
16 Pleasant St.
Laconia, NH 03246

Joseph's Coat
26 Main St.
Peterborough, NH 03458

Mountain Patchworks
P.O. Box 24, Main St.
Center Conway, NH 03813

Patchwork Schoolhouse
RD 1, Box 206
Laconia, NH 03246

Patchworks
133 Bedford Center Rd.
Bedford, NH 03102

Patience Corner Quilt Shop
The Hill
Portsmouth, NH 03801

Quilting Barn
P.O. Box 2217
Seabrook, NH 03874

Rumney Furniture & Calico
Main St., P.O. Box 245
Rumney, NH 03266

Sandwich Quilts
P.O. Box 107
Center Sandwich, NH 03227

The Silver Thimble Quilt Shop
Rt. 1, Lafayette Rd.
Hampton Falls, NH 03827

Stencil Ease
P.O. Box 209
New Ipswich, NH 03071

Village Fabrics
Main St.
Meredith, NH 03253

White Mountain Mill & Craft
Seavey St.
N. Conway, NH 03860

Wooly Mouse
8 Foundry
Amherst, NH 03031

New Jersey

Amanda's Antiques
RD 1, Box 243
Pittstown, NJ 08867

Aunt Pittypat's Parlour
57 Main St.
Chester, NJ 07930

Bear's Paw Quilt Shop
RD 8, Box 214
Newton, NJ 07860-8905

Cerberus Quilts
Box 470
Frenchtown, NJ 08825

W.H. Collins
21 Leslie Ct.
Whippany, NJ 07981

Contemporary Needlepoint
180 White Oak Ridge Rd.
Short Hills, NJ 07078

Contented Heart
39A S. Finley Ave.
Basking Ridge, NJ 07920

Continental Quilt
P.O. Box M518
Landing, NJ 07850-0518

Creative Quilting Shop
16 Emerson St.
E. Brunswick, NJ 08816

Dot's Quilting Spot
50 Dogwood Dr.
Jackson, NJ 08527

The Emporium
71 Main St.
Chester, NJ 07930

Eric Kahn Fine Quilts
32 Main St.
Kingston, NJ 08528

Karolee's Quilts
155 Stephens Park Rd.
Hackettstown, NJ 07840

Hand Maids
37 Maple St.
Summit, NJ 07901

Hands all Around
P.O. Box 205
Peapack, NJ 07977

Krafts & Kalico Korner
Trench Rd.
Bridgeton, NJ 08302

Little Shop
143 E. Kings Hwy.
Haddonfield, NJ 08033

Madison Yarn Shop
20 Main
Madison, NJ 07940

The Main Street Press
William Case House
Pittstown, NJ 08867

Morning Star Quilts
70 Bridge Ave.
Bay Head, NJ 08742

Needle & Frameworks
Ironstone Village
Medford, NJ 08055

Needlework House Inc.
130 County Rd.
Tenafly, NJ 07670

Old Times Spinning Wheel
P.O. Box 122
Princeton, NJ 08540

Penny's Corner
1833 Front St.
Scotch Plains, NJ 07076

Robert Peterson
Box 425
Quakertown, NJ 08868

Quilt Country USA
13 Union
Rockaway, NJ 07866

Quilt Gallery
62 Main St.
Lebanon, NJ 08833

Quilted Creations
2406 Rt. 71, #6C
Spring Lake Heights, NJ 07762

Quilters Corner
308 Karr Ave., RD4
Berlin, NJ 08009

Quilter's Corner
512 Gorham Ave.
Woodbridge, NJ 07095

Quilts 'n' Things
835 Bogert Rd.
River Edge, NJ 07661

Simply Elegant Needle Arts
501 New Rd.
Somers Point, NJ 08244

Tewksbury Antiques
The Crossroads
Oldwick, NJ 08858

Viking Needlecraft
Pheasant Run Plaza
Warren, NJ 07060

Washington One Stop
348 Rt. 31
Washington, NJ 07882

West End Fabrics
588 River Rd.
Fair Haven, NJ 07701

New Mexico

Jo Bryant Books
630 Graceland SE
Albuquerque, NM 87108

Quilt Shop of Clovis
Star Rt., Box 30
Clovis, NM 88101

Quiltworks
11117 Menaul NE
Albuquerque, NM 87112

New York

Addie's Corner Shop
1484 Montauk Hwy.
Mastic, NY 11950

America Hurrah
766 Madison Ave.
New York, NY 10021

American Country Antiques
315 E. 68th St.
New York, NY 10021

American Folk Art Gallery
180 Rock Creek Ln.
Scarsdale, NY 10583

Amish Classics
250 Crows Nest Rd.
Tuxedo Park, NY 10987

Antique Buyer's International
Inc.
790 Madison Ave.
New York, NY 10021

Antiques & Country Things
44 Montauk Hwy.
Amityville, NY 11701

ARDCO Templates
Victory Tool & Die Co., Inc.
131 Colvin St.
Rochester, NY 14611

Barnyard Calicos
14029 Ridge Rd.
West Albion, NY 14411

Beehive Patchworks
208 E. Main St.
Port Jefferson, NY 11777

Ben Franklin
42 Indian Head Rd.
Kings Park, NY 11754

Judi Boisson
Studio 3F
4 E. 82nd St.
New York, NY 10028
or
28C Job's Lane
Southampton, NY 11968

Bonner's Barn
25 Washington St.
Malone, NY 12953

Boro Quilt Shop
2065 86th St.
Brooklyn, NY 11214

Bridgehampton Quilt Gallery
Main St.
Bridgehampton, NY 11932

C.J. Brown
P.O. Box 226
Staten Island, NY 10308

Buffalo Batt & Felt
3307 Walden Ave.
Depew, NY 14043

Calico Basket
10 Leach St.
Massena, NY 13662

Calico Country
803 W. State St.
Olean, NY 14760

Carl's
430 State St.
Schenectady, NY 12305

Cave to Castle
Rt. 9
Wappingers Falls, NY 12590

China Thimble
1363 Union Rd.
West Seneca, NY 14224

Chipman Stitchery
Brandy Brook Rd.
Madrid, NY 13660

Anthony Cibelli
50 Hamden Ave.
Staten Island, NY 10306

Clarence Center Emporium
P.O. Box 218
Clarence Center, NY 14032

Colden Valley Quilts
P.O. Box 25
Colden, NY 14033

Come Quilt with Me
P.O. Box 1063
Brooklyn, NY 11202

The Cotton Patch
5417 Main St.
Williamsville, NY 14221

Country Curtain
159 N. Country Rd.
Mt. Sinai, NY 11766

The Country Quilter
Bonny Dr.
Somers, NY 10589

A Country Store
1262 Madison Ave.
New York, NY 10128

Cozy Calicos
153 Greene St.
Hudson, NY 12435

Craft Barn
North Country Rd.
Wading River, NY 11792

Creative Craft Boutique
8 Parkway Plaza
Canandaigua, NY 14424

Cross Patch Quilting Center
Rt. 9 and Snake Hill Rd.
Garrison, NY 10524

Custom Patchworks
202 Aviation Rd.
Glens Falls, NY 12801

Dalva Brothers, Inc.
44 E. 57th St.
New York, NY 10022

Diane's Fabric Shoppe
42 3rd
Troy, NY 12180

Domino Patchworks
100 Sixth Ave.
New York, NY 10003

E.P. Dutton, Inc.
2 Park Ave.
New York, NY 10016

Fabric Barn
105 Brooklea Dr.
Fayetteville, NY 13066

Fabric Shoppe
P.O. Box 500
Baldwin Place, NY 10505

Fabric Unique
Rt. 14
Montour Falls, NY 14865

Fabrics and Crafts
41 Broadway
Saranac Lake, NY 12983

Fabrics East
Colonial Corners
Southold, NY 11971

Fabrics & Findings
50 Anderson Ave.
Rochester, NY 14607

Laura Fisher
Antique Quilts & Americana
Gallery 57, 1050 Second Ave.
New York, NY 10022

Folk Heritage Gallery
1044 Madison Ave.
New York, NY 10021

Four Wives
130 Main
Cold Spring Harbor, NY 11724

Gallery 57
1050 Second Ave.
New York, NY 10022

The Gazebo of New York
660 Madison Ave.
New York, NY 10021

Gingerbread House
296 Main St.
Farmingdale, NY 11757

Gramma's Graphics, Inc.
20 Birling Gap, Dept. TQC
Fairport, NY 14450

Grandma Taught Us
15 Marirod Ct.
Northport, NY 11768-3354

Great American Quilt
25 Gemini Ln.
Nesconset, NY 11767-1707

Gutcheon Patchworks, Inc.
P.O. Box 57, Prince St. Sta.
New York, NY 10012

Hands All Around, Inc.
971 Lexington Ave., 1B
New York, NY 10021

Harvey's Quilt Barn
505 W. Thomas
Rome, NY 13440

Haybarn
Rt. 10
Summit, NY 12175

Heart of the Country
120 E. Main St.
Port Jefferson, NY 11777

Highland Needlecrafts
Rt. 9
Garrison, NY 10524

Hired Hand
1342 Lexington Ave.
New York, NY 10028

Inverness Fabrics
1142 Quarry Rd.
Caledonia, NY 14423

Janos and Ross
110 East End Ave.
New York, NY 10028

Kelter-Malce
361 Bleeker St.
New York, NY 10014

Madison Quilt Shop
2307 Grand Concourse
Bronx, NY 10468

William Morrow & Co., Inc.
105 Madison Ave.
New York, NY 10016

Mountain View Calico Workshop
986 Mountain View Dr.
Pine City, NY 14871

Once Upon a House
3832 Sunrise Hwy.
Seaford, NY 11783

Susan Parrish at
Spirit of America
269 W. 4th St.
New York, NY 10014

Pillow Finery
979 3rd Ave., 709M
New York, NY 10022

Patch Basket
Rt. 94
Blooming Grove, NY 10914

Patchworks
119 Main St.
Stony Brook, NY 11790

Pine Grove Workshop
5410 Stone Rd.
Lockport, NY 14094

G.P. Putnam's Sons
200 Madison Avenue
New York, NY 10016

Quilt Basket
5832 Federal Rd.
Conesus, NY 14435

Quilt Corner
Elm Hill Plaza
Camillus, NY 13031

Quilt Gallery
Main St.
Bridgehampton, NY 11932

Quilt Patch
P.O. Box 307
Sea Cliff, NY 11579

Quilt Shop of Webster
100 E. Main St.
Webster, NY 14580

Quilter's Corner
83 Main St.
Tappan, NY 10983

Quilter's Peace, Inc.
P.O. Box 349, Albany Post Rd.
Garrison, NY 10524

Quilting on a Country Lane
4594 Harvey Rd.
Rushville, NY 14544

Quilts and Americana
712 Lafayette Ave.
Buffalo, NY 14222

Quilts 'n' Stuff
Cosmos Heights
Cortland, NY 13045

Random Patches
11 Singer Ln.
Smithtown, NY 11787

Sayville Patchworks
89 Main St.
Sayville, NY 11782

Screen Process Printers
RD 1, Box 2341
Schuylerville, NY 12871

Judith Selkowitz Fine Arts, Inc.
c/o Levy and Cantor
745 Fifth Ave.
New York, NY 10151-0001

Sentimental Stitches Inc.
181 Main St.
Cold Spring Harbor, NY 11724

Judy S. Short Antiques
RD 1, Dunbar Rd.
Cambridge, NY 12816

Show & Sew Fabrics
6153 Park Ave.
Hamburg, NY 14075

Something Special
83 Main
Brockport, NY 14420

Spinning Wheel Needleart
32 Church St.
Canajoharie, NY 13317

Spirit of America
269 W. 4th St.
New York, NY 10014

Stitch in Time
15 E. Webster
Merrick, NY 11566

A Stitch in Time
3410 Miller Rd.
Niagara Falls, NY 14304

Stitch Witchery
1873 Beech St.
Wantaugh, NY 11793-3431

Stitchery Shop
23 E. Main
Victor, NY 14564

Strawberry Heart
1128 Troy Schenectady Rd.
Latham, NY 12110

Studio Bee
P.O. Box 16
Bart, NY 14028

Sweet Nellie
1262 Madison Ave.
New York, NY 10128

Thimble
57 Main
Geneseo, NY 14454

Tonowanda Quilt Shop
110 Elmwood Park
E. Tonowanda, NY 14150

Village Quilt
32 W. Main St.
Washingtonville, NY 10992

Village Variety Store
191 Dellwood Rd.
Eggertsville, NY 14226

Van Vryling
Rt. 22
Essex, NY 12936

Thos. K. Woodard, American Antiques and Quilts
835 Madison Ave.
New York, NY 10021

Wooden Goose
308 D. Main St.
Greenport, NY 11944

Bonnie Lynn Young
314 S. Clinton Ave.
Lindenhurst, NY 11757

North Carolina

Boone's Antiques, Inc.
Hwy. 301 S.
P.O. Box 3796
Wilson, NC 27893

Calico Quilts & Crafts
2162 Wrightsville Ave.
Wilmington, NC 28402

Calico Square Quilts & Gifts
805 Evans St.
Greenville, NC 27834

Counterpane Quilt Shoppe, Inc.
P.O. Box 1484
Highlands, NC 28741

Country Attic Quilt
Rt. 1, P.O. Box 758
Wingate, NC 28174-9761

Crafty Owl Crafts
175 Pinehurst Ave.
Southern Pines, NC 28387

Creative Beginnings
102 Homewood Ave.
Greensboro, NC 27403

Creative Pastimes
201 S. Estes Dr.
Chapel City, NC 27514

Designs by RD
260 Crestwood Circle
High Point, NC 27260

Downie Enterprises, Inc.
1208 Gordon St., P.O. Box 9526
Charlotte, NC 28299

Fabrics 'n' Such
1706 Weldon Rd.
Roanoke Rapids, NC 27870

Fran's Quilt Shop
521-A State St.
Greensboro, NC 27405

Gingher, Inc.
P.O. Box 8865
Greensboro, NC 27419

Grandma's Quilt Shop
Poplar Tent Exit
Concord, NC 28025

Haberhouse
1301 Brookwood Rd.
Shelby, NC 28150

House of Quilting
Rt. 3, P.O. Box 433
Fayetteville, NC 28306

Sandy Hunter, Inc.
P.O. Box 945
422 Fifth Ave. W
Hendersonville, NC 28793

Juan's Quilt Cabin
P.O. Box 1247
Waynesville, NC 28786

Leisure Time
P.O. Box 8108
Wrightsville Beach, NC 28480

Phipps Quilters Haven
119 Salisburg St.
Mocksville, NC 27028

Quilt House
P.O. Box 67
Fletcher, NC 28732

Quilters' Comfort
520 Dana Rd.
Hendersonville, NC 28739-3834

The Quilter's Gallery, Inc.
1329 East Blvd.
Charlotte, NC 28203

Quilts and Collectibles
P.O. Box 752
Banner Elk, NC 28604

Quilts Galore
704 Brookstown Ave.
Winston-Salem, NC 27201

Rainbow Roost
5 Bellows Ct.
Greensboro, NC 27407-6755

Soft Creations
P.O. Box 2383
New Bern, NC 28560

Thimbles 'n' Roses
4731 Mitchell Ave.
Greensboro, NC 27410

North Dakota

Country Arts Collective
Block 6, 620 Main
Fargo, ND 58103

Ohio

Amish Home Quilt Shop
16858 Kinsman Rd.
Middlefield, OH 44062

Antiques Country Manner
18900 Van Aken Blvd.
Shaker Heights, OH 44122

Darwin Bearley
98 Beck Ave.
Akron, OH 44302

Because You Count
6012 Market St.
Youngstown, OH 44512-2918

Calico Basket
11 E. High St.
London, OH 43140

Calico Cottage
1536 Murial Dr.
Streetsboro, OH 44240

Calico Loft
999½ Sweitzer St.
Greenville, OH 45331

Calico, Wicker & Thyme
4205 State Rt. 43
Brimfield, OH 44240

Central Press Publications
P.O. Box 172-Q
Canal Winchester, OH 43110

Bruce and Margie Clawson
Blue Creek, OH 45616

Cloth Tree
2716 Cleveland NW
Canton, OH 44709

Comforts of Home
9441 Main St.
Cincinnati, OH 45242

Corner Cupboard of Zoar
P.O. Box 627
Zoar, OH 44697

Cotton Candy
980 W. Duff-Wasah
Oak Harbor, OH 43449

Michael Council
583 S. Fifth St.
Columbus, OH 43208

Country Charm Fabrics
1422 Township Rd.
Ashland, OH 44805

Country Pickins
431 Merriman Rd.
Akron, OH 44303-1540

Country Post
P.O. Box 1821
Kettering, OH 45429

Country Quilts
6 Lintner Ct.
Navarre, OH 44662

Country Store
Front
Grand Rapids, OH 43522

The Crazy Quilters
87 N. Paint St.
Chillicothe, OH 45601

Creative Cloth
13 E. Main St.
New London, OH 44851

Nancy Crow
P.O. Box 37
Baltimore, OH 43105

Dresden Plate
7976 Mayfield Rd.
Chesterland, OH 44026

Fashion Stitch Quilts
827 A. Scioto St.
Urbana, OH 43078

Federation Antiques, Inc.
2030 Madison Rd.
Cincinnati, OH 45208

Friend
Box 1101
Mt. Vernon, OH 43050

Donna Gallagher, Creative
Needlearts, Inc.
6060 Chickadee Pl.
Westerville, OH 43081

The Gibbs Manufacturing Co.
606 6th St. NE
Canton, OH 44702

Glass Thimble
3434 N. High St.
Columbus, OH 43214

Goose Tracks
P.O. Box 269
Cuyahoga Falls, OH 44222

Hand Maiden
1521 Ridgeway Rd.
Dayton, OH 45419

Hearts Content Inc.
5045 Johnnycake Rd., NE
Canton, OH 44705-3029

Hoops 'n' Hollers Quilt Shoppe
24888 Lorain Rd. N.
Olmsted, OH 44070

Jan Dell Inc.
19350 Detroit Rd.
Rocky River, OH 44116

Jo Da Knits & Sew On
606 S. Broadway
Greenville, OH 45331

Knitting Etc. Corners
4254 Boardman
Canfield, OH 44406

Midwest Quilt Exchange
495 S. 3rd St.
Columbus, OH 43215

Miller's Dry Goods Center
RR 4, Box 103A
Millersburg, OH 44654

Sandra Mitchell
739 Mohawk
Columbus, OH 43206

Mountain Mist
The Stearns Technical Textiles
Co.
100 Williams St.
Cincinnati, OH 45215

Needle Craft Shoppe
1555 Allentown Rd.
Lima, OH 45805

Oh Suzanna
6 S. Broadway
Lebanon, OH 45036

Old Log Cabin Gift Shop
7771 Miller Rd.
Greenville, OH 45331

Olde House Antiques and Quilts
5069 Township Rd. 56
Huntsville, OH 43324

Patch Place
4111 Cleve Massillon Rd.
Norton, OH 44203-5604

Patch Works
2328 Denzer Rd.
Bucyrus, OH 44820-9418

Patchwork Factory
671 Sawburg Ave.
Alliance, OH 44601

Pumpkin Vine Line
5110 Pleasant Ave.
Fairfield, OH 45014

The Quilt Basket
38123 W. Spaulding St.
Willoughby, OH 44094

Quilt Foundry
234 W. Wayne St. Dr.
Maumee, OH 43537

Quilt Frame
7029 State Rt. 164
Lisbon, OH 44432

Quilt 'n' Center Studio
811 Wilcox Rd.
Youngstown, OH 44509

Quilt 'n' Patch
2965 W. Sylvania
Toledo, OH 43613

The Quiltery
2905 North High St.
Columbus, OH 43202

Quilting by Carole Serio
P.O. Box 3257
Columbus, OH 43210

Quilting Room
229 King Ave.
Columbus, OH 43201

Quilts
583 S. 5th St.
Columbus, OH 43206

Quilts 'n' Stuff
911 City Park
Columbus, OH 43206

Red Duck Antiques
P.O. Box 307
Howard, OH 43028

Sally's Shop
139 College St.
Wadsworth, OH 44281

Sampler
36976 Detroit Rd.
Avon, OH 44011

Schoolhouse Collection Ltd.
Schoolhouse Quilt Shop
4315 Hills & Dales Rd.
Canton, OH 44708

Shaker Simplicity
4666 Quaker Trace Rd., Dept.
MS87
Eaton, OH 45320

Stencils and Stuff
72 12th St., NW
Strasburg, OH 44680

Stitch 'n' Post
3 Georgetown Rd.
Lakewood, OH 44107

A Stitch in Time
1655 Shady Lane Rd.
Columbus, OH 43227

A Stitch 'n Time Quilts
6th & High St.
Lancaster, OH 43130

Stitchery Plus
32 S. High St.
Dublin, OH 43017

Stitches 'n' Such
702 Niles Rd.
Fairfield, OH 45014

Stitchin Post-Yarn Boutique
14227 Old State Rd.
Middlefield, OH 44062

Stow Needlecraft
3310 Kent Rd.
Stow, OH 44224

Susan's Stitching Supplies
32 S. High St.
Dublin, OH 43017

Thread 'n' Thimble Shoppe
8979 Brecksville Rd.
Brecksville, OH 44141

John Townsend
4215 Utica Rd.
Lebanon, OH 45036

Travelling Needle
60 Bellbrook Plaza
Bellbrook, OH 45305-1956

Valley Quilt Cross
5300 Bennett Ct.
Dublin, OH 43017-9707

Village Shop Antiques
455 N. Main St.
North Canton, OH 44720

Western Reserve Needlework
5000 E. Market St.
Warren, OH 44484

White Sewing Products Co.
11750 Berea Rd.
Cleveland, OH 44111

Yarn Barn
141 E. Winter St.
Delaware, OH 43015

Yarn Dome
1113 E. Main St.
Greenville, OH 45331

Oklahoma

Arts of Tulsa
2626 E. 15th
Tulsa, OK 74104

June Blackburn
4148 S. Norfolk
Tulsa, OK 74105

Buckboard Antiques and Quilts
1411 N. May
Oklahoma City, OK 73107

Calico Patchworks
P.O. Box 1646
Bartlesville, OK 74005-1646

Cotton Patch
8250 E. 71st
Tulsa, OK 74133

A Crazy Quilt
3223 N. College
Bethany, OK 73008

Fran's Fabrics
10924 N. May
Oaklahoma City, OK 73120

Grandma's Scrapbook
5617 S. Penn
Okalhoma City, OK 73119

In Stitches
1116 Ferris
Lawton, OK 73501

Quality Quilting Co.
611 W. Third
Edmond, OK 73034

Quilt Basket
501 6th NW
Ardmore, OK 73401

Quilt Corner
715 E. Main
Ada, OK 74820

Quilter's Stitch
2704 Old Farm Lane
Edmond, OK 73034

Quilting Bee
4200 Windchime Dr.
Oklahoma City, OK 73120

Quilting Parlor
2123 W. Garriott
Enid, OK 73701

Sew Pretty Ltd.
3336 E. 32nd St. #2
Tulsa, OK 74135

SJS Designs
555 S. 99th E Ave.
Tulsa, OK 74128

Will Rogers Store
5970 E. 31st
Tulsa, OK 74135

Oregon

Amity Publications
78688 Sears Rd.
Cottage Grove, OR 97424

Amish Quilt Shop
5331 SW Macadam Ave.
Portland, OR 97201

Cinnabar Centre
P.O. Box 751
Lincoln City, OR 97367

Cloth & Sew On
Rt. 2, Box 2892
Vale, OR 97918

Country Cloth
416 Oak St.
Hood River, OR 97031

Dianna's Quilting Supplies
1294 32nd Ave. NW
Salem, OR 97304

Grandma's Attic
316 W. Clark St.
Medford, OR 97501-2321

Jane's Fabric Patch
903 Pacific
Tillamook, OR 97141

Oregon Rule Co.
P.O. Box 5072
Oregon City, OR 97045

Oregon Treasures
Rt. 2, P.O. Box 2892
Vale, OR 97918

Patches Quilt & Fabrics
4340 SW 110th Ave.
Beaverton, OR 97005

Patches Quilt/Fabrics
7400 SW Newton Pl.
Portland, OR 97225-2053

Patchwork Peddlers Quilt Shop
2106 NE 40th Ave.
Portland, OR 97212

Patchwork Quilt Shop
7103 SE 92nd
Milwaukie, OR 97266

Quilt Basket
259 Santiam Hwy.
Mill City, OR 97360

Quilt Patch
1437 Oak St.
Eugene, OR 97401

Quilt & Sew Shop
11123 SE 30th Ave.
Milwaukie, OR 97222

Quiltwork Patches
430 NW 6th St.
Corvallis, OR 97339

Scrap Drawer
425 Oxford St. SE
Salem, OR 97302

Scrap Happy
65 Division Ave., B-21
Eugene, OR 97404-2485

Stitchin Post
161 Elm
Sisters, OR 97759

Thread Bear Studio
1313 Mill SE
Salem, OR 97301

Treasures Unlimited
5955 SW 179th Ave., Dept. QC
Beaverton, OR 97007

Pennsylvania

Amazing Acres
RD 1329
Womelsdorf, PA 19567

Art 'n' Things
Donaldson Crossroads
McMurray, PA 15317

Ashley Quilting Co.
46 E. Liberty
Ashley, PA 18706

Aunt Ruth's Quilt Shop
4618 Liberty Ave.
Pittsburgh, PA 15224-1930

Benjamin Halpern Dry Goods
804 Penn Ave.
Pittsburgh, PA 15222

Boalsburg Needleworks
P.O. Box 55
Boalsburg, PA 16827

Calico Patch Quilt Shoppe
5158 Peach St.
Erie, PA 16509

Carol's Cloth Shoppe
P.O. Box 761
Latrobe, PA 15650

City Quilt Shop
411 S. Craig St.
Pittsburgh, PA 15213

Country Patchwork
1603 Carlisle Rd.
Camp Hill, PA 17011

Creative Quilting
415 High St.
Bethlehem, PA 18018

Dymond's Craft & Quilt
RD 2, Box 353
Harvey's Lake, PA 18618

Fabric & Things
Rt. 272
Akron, PA 17501

M. Finkel and Daughter
936 Pine St.
Philadelphia, PA 19107

James and Nancy Glazer
Antiques
2209 Delancey Pl.
Philadelphia, PA 19103

Good Books
Main St.
Intercourse, PA 17534

Grandmother's Patches
Rt. 100, Box 398
Uwchland, PA 19480

Grant Street
126 E. Grant St.
Lancaster, PA 17602

Hand Made Quilts
P.O. Box 215
Lampeter, PA 17537

William P. Hayes Antiques
RD 1, Box 134
Belleville, PA 17004

Jolies Art Quilt Works
520 South St.
Philadelphia, PA 19147

Kathy's Kreations
141 E. Main St.
Logonier, PA 15658

Kay's Kraft Korner
1107 Scott Dr.
Coatesville, PA 19320

Key and Quill Shop
129 S. Second St.
Philadelphia, PA 19106

Kountry Kourtyard
1195 W. Main St.
Mount Hoy, PA 17552

Joe and Mary Koval Antiques
550 Lutz School Rd.
Indiana, PA 15701

Leola Needlework
337 Sun Valley Dr.
Leola, PA 17540-1236

Ligonier Quilt Shop
305 E. Main St.
Ligonier, PA 15658

Lovely Lady Comfort Co.
4920 N. 20th
Philadelphia, PA 19144

Needlepoint Place
1207 Penn Ave.
Wyomissing, PA 19601

Needles and Hoops
P.O. Box 165
Abington, PA 19001

Nimble Needle
140 W. High St.
Bellefonte, PA 16823-1625

Nimble Thimble
45 N. Market St.
Lancaster, PA 17603

Old Country Store
Main St.
Intercourse, PA 17534

A Patch of Country Inc.
34 Olde Ridge Village
Chadds Ford, PA 19317

Penn Dutch Cottage Crafts
2323 Lincoln Hwy. E
Lancaster, PA 17602

Pied Piper Gallery
537 E. Girard Ave.
Philadelphia, PA 19125

The Pink House
Rt. 179
New Hope, PA 18938

J.D. Query Antiques
RD 2
Martinburg, PA 16662

The Quilt Patch
1897 Hanover Pike
Littlestown, PA 17340

The Quilt Square
752 N. Main St.
Meadville, PA 16335

Quilters Needs
4014 Concord St.
Harrisburg, PA 17249

Quilters' Needs
P.O. Box 56, Meadon St.
Rockhill Furnace, PA 17109

Quiltery
1 Hall Sq.
Nazareth, PA 18064

Quilter's Barn
P.O. Box 294
Allentown, PA 18501

The Quilting Bee
126 S. Market St.
New Wilmington, PA 16142

Quilting Cottage
1910 Darby Rd.
Hagertown, PA 19083

Quilts Incredible
Street Rd. and Rt. 22
P.O. Box 11
Lahaska, PA 18931

Ruff Creek Woodworks
Rt. 19, P.O. Box 934
Waynesburg, PA 15370

Sew Smart Fabrics
53 W. State St.
Doylestown, PA 18901

Souder Store
Main & Summit Sts.
Souderton, PA 18964

Stitch in Time
3101 Limestone Rd.
Oxford, PA 19363

Stitchcraft
5223 N. 5th
Philadelphia, PA 19120

Strawberry Sampler
Rt. 202 & Ridge Rd.
Chadds Ford, PA 19317

Tina's Quilts
1308 E. Columbia Ave.
Philadelphia, PA 19125

Williamsport Dry Goods
130 W. 4th St.
Williamsport, PA 17701

Wilson's Calico Corner
RD 3, Box 629
Hamburg, PA 19526

Rhode Island

Bear Threads Inc.
250 Main St.
Pawtucket, RI 02860

Catherine's Home Decor
2 School
Johnston, RI 02919

Patch Works
209 Buttonwood Ave.
Warwick, RI 02886

Quilt Artesan
39 Memorial Blvd.
Newport, RI 02840

Quilt Workings
21 W. Main, P.O. Box 475
Wickford, RI 02852

Rainbow's End
78 State
Bristol, RI 02809

South Carolina

Back Door
P.O. Box 1467
Sumter, SC 29150

Dritz Corporation
P.O. Box 5028
Spartanburg, SC 29304

Huckleberry Stitches
1756 Huckleberry
Aiken, SC 29801

James Island Sewing Center
Cross Creek Shopping Center
Charleston, SC 29412

A Tisket A Tasket
1185 Dorchester Rd.
Summerville, SC 29483

South Dakota

Cottage Quilts
2715 W. Rapid St.
Rapid City, SD 57702

Dakota Factory Outlet
P.O. Box 120
Webster, SD 57274

Tennessee

American Country Furniture and
 Accessories
433 Scenic Dr.
Knoxville, TN 37919

Cloth Connections
3764 Summer Ave.
Memphis, TN 38122

Contemporary Quilts
5305 Denwood Ave.
Memphis, TN 38119

Crafter's Nook
4125 Eastridge Dr.
Chattanooga, TN 37412-2307

Enchanted Needle & Frame
2330 S. Germantown Rd.
Memphis, TN 38138-5931

Fabric Addict
P.O. Box 620
Nashville, TN 47448

Heirloom Stitchery/Frame
5788 Stage Rd.
Memphis, TN 38128

J & S Sales
7202 Levi Rd.
Hixson, TN 37343-1641

John's Country Shop
716 Mendenhall Rd. S.
Memphis, TN 38117

Lone Oak General Merchandise
Rt. 2, Hwy. 73
Cosby, TN 37722

Mud Island Retail Stores
125 N. Main St.
Memphis, TN 38103

Needlecrafter of Memphis
1531 Cherry Rd.
Memphis, TN 38117

Once Upon a Quilt
2108 Crestline Dr.
Donelson, TN 37214

Quilters Haven
P.O. Box 151
Wartrace Rd.
Bell Buckle, TN 37020

Quilters Workshop
Rt. 4, Box 399B
Paris, TN 38242

Quilting Corner
109 Towne Rd.
Oak Ridge, TN 37830

Stitch 'n' String
P.O. Box 140876
Nashville, TN 37214

Toll House Quilts
3900 Taft Hwy.
Signal Mountain, TN 37377

Texas

Berry Patch Fabrics
5220 Camp Bowie Blvd.
Fort Worth, TX 76107

Betsy's Needle Work
777 S. Central, #6D
Richardson, TX 75080-7412

Blanche's Bernina Center
1910 26th St.
Snyder, TX 79549

Calico Heart
1003 Dallas Dr.
Denton, TX 76201

Chantilly Boutique
11505 Princewood Dr.
Austin, TX 78750

Country Quilt Shop
Rt. 14, Box 116A, FM 989
Texarkana, TX 75501

Country Fair Quilt Patch
1401 Lake Air Dr.
Waco, TX 76710

Cutting Corner
1815 Freeland
San Angelo, TX 76901

Fabric Collection
101 N. Swenson
Stamford, TX 79553

Gingerbread House Quilts
601 First St.
Humble, TX 77338

Gloria Lang Interiors
5014 W. Grove Dr.
Dallas, TX 75248

Good Old Days
404 N. Third St.
Conroe, TX 77301

Great Expectations Quilts, Inc.
14520 Memorial, Ste. 54
Houston, TX 77079

HB Enterprises
P.O. Box 161
Stockdale, TX 78160

Helen's Place
505 Roberts
Cedar Hill, TX 75104-1935

Hidden Treasures
5116 Lawndale Ave.
Houston, TX 77023

Hill Country Quilts
P.O. Box 680132
San Antonio, TX 78268-0132

Hobbs Bonded Fibers
Craft Products Division
P.O. Box 151
Groesbeck, TX 76642

House of Harriette & John
13719 Hwy. 71 N.
Austin, TX 78734

House of Joseph
Rt. 2, Box 162AB
Smithville, TX 78957

Jan's Quilt Shop
2433 I-40 W.
Amarillo, TX 79109

Jenny Lynn Fabrics
9723 N. Central Expy.
Dallas, TX 75231

Judy Beans Fabrics & Fun Shop
P.O. Box 281
Kirbyville, TX 75956

Just Folks
2703 Greenwood
Texarkana, TX 75501-2767

Las Colchas
129 W. Mistletoe
San Antonio, TX 78212

Memories Made Inc.
10904 Scarsdale Blvd.
Houston, TX 77089-6034

Miscellaneous Inc.
631 N. Davis St.
Sulphur Springs, TX 75482

Larry A. Mulkey & Assoc.
World Trade Center 9074
P.O. Box 58547
Dallas, TX 75258

Needle Nook
2207 N. Big Spring
Midland, TX 79705

Needle's Eye
1317 W. Wilson
Borger, TX 79007

O'Krent Fabrics Inc.
306 San Pedro
San Antonio, TX 78212

Patchwork Girl
733 W. Mill
New Braunfels, TX 78130-5540

Pat's Patchings
Kerr Rt., Box 145
Junction, TX 76849

Perfect Quilt Company
5800 Corporate
Houston, TX 77036

Prairie Star Quilt Shop
1395 Albany
Abilene, TX 79605

Quilt Box
6033 Wimbleton Way
Ft. Worth, TX 76133-3609

Quilt Collector
2034 West Gray
Houston, TX 77019

Quilt Market
155 Town & Country Village
Houston, TX 77024

Quilt Patch
2201 Colcord Ave.
Waco, TX 77607

Quilt Patch
1651 S. Voss
Houston, TX 77057

Quilt Shop
4525 50th St.
Lubbock, TX 79414

Quilted Hearts and Co.
2417 W. Park Row, #A
Arlington, TX 76013-3305

Quilter's Cupboard
615 Pecan
McAllen, TX 78501

Quilters' Tradition
6020 Redcoat Ln.
Tyler, TX 75703-4537

Quilts 'n' Such
5815 Highway Blvd.
Katy, TX 77450

Quilt-Maker
617 Fredericksburg
New Braunfels, TX 78103

Sewing Shack
3100 Independence
Plano, TX 75075

Stitchin Inn
122 Tyne Bay Dr.
Hendersonville, TX 37075

Taylor Bedding Mfg. Co.
P.O. Box 979
Taylor, TX 76574

Texas Quilt Company
6940 Robin Willow
Dallas, TX 75248

TJ's Quick Quilter
218 Quinlan, Ste. 372
Kerrville, TX 78028

Yarn Barn
303 Elm St.
Keller, TX 76248

Yarn Shop
806 Brook St.
Wichita Falls, TX 76301

Utah

Fabric Shop
55 S. State St.
Orem, UT 84058

Gardiner's Sew & Quilt
1508 Washington Blvd.
Ogden, UT 84404

Gentler Times
5880 Highland Cir.
Salt Lake City, UT 84117

Grandma's Quilts
395 S. Main
Logan, UT 84321

Ladybug Quilt Cottage
111 W. 7th St.
Salt Lake City, UT 84101

Misty Isles Designs
811 N. University Ave.
Provo, UT 84601

Old & Nue Shoppe
69 E. Center
Moab, UT 84532

Patterns by Jeaneau
P.O. Box 17407
Salt Lake City, UT 84117

Quality Line Products
320 N. 3rd W.
Hyrum, UT 84319

Quilting Boutique
30 W. Center St.
Panguitch, UT 84750

Quilting Supply House
290 N. 300 W.
Logan, UT 84321

Sara's Quilting
8872 Piper Ln.
Sandy, UT 84070

The Vanessa-Ann Collection
P.O. Box 9113
Ogden, UT 84409

Vermont

Butternut Tree
RD
Hartland, VT 05048

Delectable Mountain Quilts
20 Elliot St.
Brattleboro, VT 05301

Hearthside Quilts
Church Hill Rd.
Charlotte, VT 05445

Hearthside Quilts
P.O. Box 429M
Shelburne, VT 05482

Island Country Quilts
221 South St.
S. Hero, VT 05486

L.T. Hall Quilts
26 Central St.
Woodstock, VT 05091

Needlework
P.O. Box 458
Stowe, VT 05672-0458

Norton House
1836 Country Store Village
Wilmington, VT 05363

Otter Creek Quilt Works
Quarry Rd.
New Haven, VT 05472

Prints and Patches
Mountain Rd.
Stowe, VT 05672

Mary K. Ryan Design
Grandview Terr.
Rutland, VT 05701

The Vermont Patchworks
229 Old Plymouth Rd.
Shrewsbury, VT 05738

Yankee Notions
215 Grandview St.
Bennington, VT 05201

Yankee Pride
Champlain Mill
Winooski, VT 05404

Virginia

American Sampler
P.O. Box 27
Middleburg, VA 22117-0027

Apple Pie Country Design
1382 Chain Bridge Rd.
McLean, VA 22101

Barbie Beck
113 Caroline St.
Fredericksburg, VA 22401

The Brass Goose
328 S. Royal Ave.
Front Royal, VA 22630

Busy Bee
11934 Centre St.
Chester, VA 23831

Calico House
Rt. 4, Box 16
Scottsville, VA 24590

Iva Capps
3 Sylvan Ct.
Fredericksburg, VA 22405

Charlottesville Quilts
Castle Hill
Cobham, VA 22929

Country Corner
410 W. Market St.
Petersburg, VA 23803

Country Sampler
13212 Poplar Tree Rd.
Fairfax, VA 22033

Country Shop
302 Mill St.
Occoquan, VA 22125

Countryside Shops
1985 Landstown Rd.
Virginia Beach, VA 23456

Crafts 'n' Stitchery
2020 Plank Rd.
Fredericksburg, VA 22401

Folk Art Emporium
3591 Forest Haven Ln.
Chesapeake, VA 23321

Geary Associates
5209 Portsmouth Rd.
Fairfax, VA 22032

Glass and Calico II, Inc.
6030 K Burke Commons Rd.
Burke, VA 22015

Gresham's Country Store
6735 Midlothian Pike
Richmond, VA 23225

Holland Corner
2042 Esquire Rd.
Richmond, VA 23235

Jane Whitmire's Needlework
2353 S. Meade
Arlington, VA 22202

Little Shop
Main St.
Madison, VA 22727

Mary Penders Quilt Class
2600 Oak Valley Rd.
Vienna, VA 22180

Patchworks
1516 Harmon St.
Norfolk, VA 23518

Paula Lewis Court Square
213 Fourth St., NE
Charlottesville, VA 22901

Quilt Haven
101 Dangerfield Rd.
Williamsburg, VA 23185

Quilt Patch
3932 Old Lee Hwy.
Fairfax, VA 22030

Quilt Shop
8800 Timberlake Rd.
Lynchburg, VA 24502

Quilt Works
3590 Holland Rd., #106
Virginia Beach, VA 23452

Quilting Niche
105 W. Main St.
Purcellville, VA 22132

Quilt-n-Stuff, Inc.
687 S. Washington St.
Alexandria, VA 22314

Quilts Unlimited
The Homestead Resort
Hot Springs, VA 24445
or
431 Prince George St.
Williamsburg, VA 23185

Rocky Road to Kansas
215 S. Union St.
Alexandria, VA 22314

Running Stitch
105 Woodberry Ln.
Lynchburg, VA 24502

Scotland House
11 E. Washington St.
Middleburg, VA 22117

Sew Special, Inc.
9215 Midlothian
Richmond, VA 23236-4946

Stitches Country Store
414 E. Main St.
Charlottesville, VA 22901

Talio Antiques
Rt. 3, Box 5035
Berryville, VA 22611

Tapestry Room Quilt Patch
3936 Old Lee Hwy.
Fairfax, VA 22030

Village Quilt Shop Inc.
3128 Grandin Rd. SW
Roanoke, VA 24015

White Parlour
5 W. Loudoun St.
Leesburg, VA 22075

Washington

American Gallery
345 Vernhardson St. NW
Gig Harbor, WA 98335

Ann Louise Fabrics & Art
106½ N. Fifth Ave.
Yakima, WA 98902

Cabin in the Foothills
18009 SE 372nd
Auburn, WA 98002

Calico Basket
412 Main St.
Edmonds, WA 98020-3138

Country Quilt Shop
28 N. Wenatchee
Wenatchee, WA 98801

Especially For You
4723 82nd Pl. NE
Marsville, WA 98270

Fabric Gallery
28 N. Wenatchee
Wenatchee, WA 98801

Fiddlesticks
1601 Summit View
Yakima, WA 98902

Gingham Goose
420 S. Steele
Olympia, WA 98501

Marsha McCoskey
2151 7th Ave. W.
Seattle, WA 98119

Nancy's Sewing Basket
2205 Queen Anne N.
Seattle, WA 98109

Patchworks
1243 Alki St. NE
Olympia, WA 98506

The Pattern Factory
8724 104 St. E
Puyallup, WA 98373

Purple Pocket
W. 814 Main
Spokane, WA 99201

Quilt Barn
1206 E. Main
Puyallup, WA 98372

Quilting Bee
8405 Dishman Mica Rd.
Spokane, WA 99206

Quilting Patch
P.O. Box 595
Vashon, WA 98070

Running Stitch Studio
5251 University Way NE
Seattle, WA 98105

Sampler
N 5521 Alberta
Spokane, WA 99205

Stitchin' & Stuff Inc.
W 510 First Ave.
Spokane, WA 99204

The Sewcase
SE 730 Derby
Pullman, WA 99163

37 Fabric Land
25420 104 SE
Kent, WA 98031

Yardage 'n More
1229 Commerce
Longview, WA 98632

West Virginia

Cabin Creek Quilts
200 Broad St.
Charlestown, WV 25301

Carriage Trade Needlecraft
218 D Street S.
Charleston, WV 25303

Centenary House
Rt. 4, Box 349
Cameron, WV 26033

Fern's Handcraft Shoppe
Rt. 34, Box 6130
Winfield, WV 25213

General Store
450 E. Main St.
W. Union, WV 26456

O'Carroll Productions, Ltd.
292 S. Green St.
Berkeley Springs, WV 25411

Patches Inc.
P.O. Box 39
Harpers Ferry, WV 25424-0039

Quilts Unlimited
P.O. Box 1210
203 E. Washington St.
Lewisburg, WV 24901

Ram's Horn
71 Main St.
St. Albans, WV 25177

Zepora's Quilt Shop
203½ Second
St. Mary, WV 26170

Wisconsin

Alpine Gardens & Calico
1817 10th St.
Monroe, WI 53566-1830

Calico Canvas & Colors
712 Grove Ave.
Racine, WI 53405

Calico Cupboard
124 W. Ash St.
Mason, WI 48854

Calico Peddler
P.O. Box 326
Cheteck, WI 54728

Country Crafter
13926 Meggers Rd.
Kiel, WI 53042

Country Creations
P.O. Box 651
Meno Falls, WI 53051-0651

Countryside Patchworks
2162 Country Sq.
Richfield, WI 53076

Craft Corner
Rt. 2, Box 119
River Falls, WI 54022-8218

Creative Shop
909 E. 1st
Kimberly, WI 54136-1601

Creative Showcase
5033 Deerwood Dr.
Racine, WI 53406

Farmhouse Fabrics
708 Lisbon Rd.
Oconomowoc, WI 53066

Fiberspace
1179 Emilie St.
Green Bay, WI 54301-3107

Fibre Arts
6606 W. North Ave.
Milwaukee, WI 53213

Fiskars Mfg. Corp.
7811 W. Stewart Ave.
Wausau, WI 54401

Geri's Fabric Patch
25 Brown St.
S. Rhinelander, WI 54501

Ginny Greer Ltd.
2419 W. Washington
West Bend, WI 53095

Hearthside Quilters Nook
10731 W. Forest Home Ave.
Hales Corner, WI 53130

Hiles Patchwork Place
501 W. Bent
Oshkosh, WI 54901

Hinterberg Design
467 N. Main St.
West Bend, WI 53095

Julie Ann Fabrics
1719 S. Main
West Bend, WI 53095

J. J. Stitches & Co.
221 E. Main St.
Sun Prairie, WI 53590

Kay's Fabrics
24920 73rd St.
Salem, WI 53168

Maple Springs Farm
1828 Hwy. PB, Dept. QC
Verona, WI 53593

Needle & I, Ltd.
2510 Michel Rd.
La Crosse, WI 54601

Needles 'n' Things
923 Washington St.
Manitowoc, WI 54220

Nelson's Quilting Shop
104 E. Mason
Milwaukee, WI 53202

Northwest Fabrics
Thunderbird Mall #1511
Menomonie, WI 54751

Old Tyme Quilt Shoppe
RR 1, Box 254
Rush Creek Rd.
Ferryville, WI 54628

Patched Works, Inc.
890 Elm Grove Rd.
Elm Grove, WI 53122

Pine Needle
1620 Garfield Ave.
Waukesha, WI 53186

Plumhill Farm
W9418 Woodside Rd.
Cambridge, WI 53523

Putnam Company, Inc.
P.O. Box 310
Walworth, WI 53185

Quilt Design Studio
516 Second St. N.
Stevens Point, WI 54481

Sawmill Crafts
1729 Wolf Rd.
Richfield, WI 53076

Scarlett Letter
20215 W. Coffe Rd.
New Berlin, WI 53151

Sew 'n' Sew Fabrics
224 N. Main St.
Oconto Falls, WI 54154

Stitch 'n' Time
820 Water St.
Sauk City, WI 53583

Stitchery
Rt. 4, Box 232
Delevan, WI 53115

Stitcher's Crossing
6816 Odana Rd.
Madison, WI 53719

Stitching Post
RR 1, Box 321
Prairie Du Chien, WI 53821-9703

Village Quilters
5589 N. Diversey Blvd.
Whitefish Bay, WI 53217

Wyoming

Country Quilt Needlework
48 E. Brundage
Sheridan, WY 82801

Heritage Quilt Shop
2622 Pioneer Ave.
Cheyenne, WY 82001

Jean's Fabrics
3060 Allendale
Casper, WY 82601

Sewing Room
129 W. Main St.
New Castle, WY 82701

Index